Undercover

Undercover

Police Surveillance in America

Gary T. Marx

A TWENTIETH CENTURY FUND BOOK

University of California Press
Berkeley · Los Angeles · London

University of California Press
Berkeley and Los Angeles, California

University of California Press, Ltd.
London, England

© 1988 by
The Twentieth Century Fund

Library of Congress Cataloging-in-Publication Data

Marx, Gary T.
   Undercover: police surveillance in America.

   "A Twentieth Century Fund book."
   Bibliography: p.
   Includes index.
   1. Undercover operations—United States.
2. Criminal investigation—United States. 3. Police
patrol—Surveillance operations. I. Title.
HV8080.U5M37   1988   363.2'32   88-1254
ISBN 0-520-06286-8 (alk. paper)

Printed in the United States of America

1 2 3 4 5 6 7 8 9

I'll be very honest with you. I'm troubled by it. Most of our investigations involve surveillance, paid-for information and search warrants, and I think that's the best way to go. However you can't get by without undercover officers. They are a necessary evil.

—*A police supervisor*

Contents

List of Tables   ix

Foreword   xi

Acknowledgments   xiii

Preface   xvii

1. The Changing Nature of Undercover Work   1
2. A Selective History of Undercover Practices   17
3. The Current Context   36
4. Types and Dimensions   60
5. The Complexity of Virtue   89
6. Intended Consequences of Undercover Work   108
7. Unintended Consequences: Targets, Third
   Parties, and Informers   129
8. Unintended Consequences: Police   159
9. Controlling Undercover Operations   180
10. The New Surveillance   206

Notes to Chapters 1–10   235

Index   273

Tables

1. Types of Police Work   12
2. Prior Intelligence and Specificity in Target Selection   69
3. Results of the LEAA Property Crime Program
    in Selected Cities   113
4. Results of Two Anticrime Decoy Programs   117

Foreword

The Abscam scandals drew public attention to the use of undercover agents. There is of course nothing new about this practice. It has in fact been around long enough to become a staple of fact and fiction. G. K. Chesterton had an undercover agent in his *The Man Who Was Thursday*. The New York Police Department had an undercover man on its force who infiltrated the so-called Black Hand Society around the turn of the century and was later assassinated. And the Federal Bureau of Investigation has at times been extremely well-represented in the Communist party.

Nowadays covert action by law enforcement agencies on the local level has become so commonplace that few of the many operations each year are even given much coverage by the media. This increase in the use of covert action is partly due to the changes that have taken place in the nature of crime. It is doubtful that much could be done about apprehending drug dealers or uncovering the high-stakes skulduggery in business dealings without using covert action. To be sure, there are risks involved in such activity: sometimes undercover agents are found out; and sometimes they are corrupted and "turned," themselves becoming criminals instead of trapping them.

The Twentieth Century Fund, in pursuing its interest in urban social problems, found that the issue of urban crime loomed large. We sought an author who would examine the broader problems posed by crime and the measures taken by the police to combat it. In Gary T. Marx, professor of sociology at the Massachusetts Institute of Technology, we found a scholar who, after twenty years of studying criminal justice, understood the broader issues. He was prepared to look at the moral and social questions raised by the use of deceptive tactics on the part of official agencies.

His study provides a thoughtful analysis of why our nation is making such extensive use of covert operations and their effects on law enforcement. He also carefully investigates their effects on the rest of us. The Fund is grateful to him for carrying out so useful an investigation, and so I think should be his readers.

M. J. Rossant, Director
The Twentieth Century Fund
March 1988

Acknowledgments

I am grateful to the National Institute of Justice for rejecting a proposal to fund this project. Had they done otherwise, I would never have had the good fortune to work with Gary Nickerson and the other people at the Twentieth Century Fund. Gary was an able guide and critic who helped me always keep larger audiences and issues in mind. Carol Kahn was a superb and caring editor.

I was fortunate to have two of my former students—Professor Nancy Reichman (now with the University of Denver) and Dr. Jay Wachtel (now with the United States Treasury Department)—as research associates. Their intelligence, dedication, and friendship greatly enhanced the book. Nancy helped write chapters 6 and 9. Other work we have done on computer matching and profiling helped me in thinking about new directions in social control. Jay carried out a majority of the police interviews at the local level. His extensive law enforcement experience, moral concerns, and intellectual honesty provided significant insights otherwise unavailable to the outsider.

Much of the literature on controversial police topics breaks down into two categories—uncritical work by well-informed insiders and critical work by uninformed outsiders. Whether this book is seen as sufficiently critical or uncritical depends on the values of the reader. What I hope is not at issue is the informed nature of the analysis. In that regard, I am particularly grateful to Floyd I. Clarke, Assistant Director of the Criminal Investigative Division of the FBI, and to Bob Lill, Chief of the FBI's Undercover and Sensitive Operations Unit, for the access and insight they helped me obtain. I am indebted to the many persons who participated in the study. In the hope of encouraging candor, they were promised anonymity, so this acknowledgment must be general.

I am grateful to those who so carefully went over the entire manuscript: Nancy Blumenstock, Tony Bouza, Elspeth and John Cairns, Stan Cohen, Ron Corbett, Jr., Murray Davis, Bob Fogelson, Rosabeth Moss Kanter, Martin Levin, J. Robert Lilly, John Lofland, Craig McEwen, Peter Manning, Al Reiss, Betsey Scheiner, John Shattuck, Jim Thomas, Mike Useem, Diane Vaughan, Chuck Wexler, and Jim Wood.

Others who critically commented on part of the manuscript or provided materials, ideas, information, or support include: Roger Adelman, Judith Auerbach, Hugo Bedau, Keith Bergstrom, Egon Bittner, Donald Black, Sissela Bok, Bob Bowers, Jeffrey Broberg, Bill Brown, Leonard Buckle, Suzanne Buckle, Gerald Caplan, Paul Chevigny, John Conklin, Scott Cook, Janice Cooper, Bill Darrough, Father Robert Drinan, Bob Duff, Susan Eckstein, Congressman Don Edwards, Fred Elliston, Stanley Fisher, Bernard Frieden, Ross Gelbspan, Michael Giordo, Sal Giorlandino, Glenn Goodwin, Paul Hans, Phil Heymann, Travis Hirschi, David Johnson, Jack Katz, Wayne Kerstetter, Tom Kiely, Carl Klockars, Bill Kolender, Ken Laudon, Catherine Le Roy, Tom Legget, Charles Lemert, Felice Levine, S. M. Lipset, Bob Luskin, John McCarthy, Susan Martin, Nicki D. Marx, Vanessa Merton, George Miller, W. R. Miller, Dominique Monjardet, Ethan Nadelman, Chris Nelson, Russ Neuman, Ed Powell, Tom Puccio, Norma Rollins, Zick Rubin, Jim Rule, the late Ed Sagarin, Leonard Saxe, Manny Schegloff, Kim Scheppele, Frank Schubert, Herman Schwartz, Louis Seidman, Sanford Sherizen, Lawrence Sherman, Jim Short, Susan Silbey, Louise Simmons, Neil Smelser, Steve Smith, Steve Spitzer, Barry Stein, Geoffrey Stone, Ezra Stotland, Richard Uviller, John Van Mannen, Lod Von Outrive, Sam Walker, Marilyn Walsh, Dan Ward, Lloyd Weinreb, Alan Westin, Ron Westrum, Jay Williams, Mary Ann Wycoff, and Franklin Zimring.

Over the years, Rolf Engler and the Department of Urban Studies and Planning at the Massachusetts Institute of Technology have offered an environment rich in Xeroxing, secretarial support, and time to work. Meg Gross was particularly helpful in typing, transcribing, and deciphering. The M.I.T. Humanities, Arts and Social Sciences Committee kindly provided several small grants. I am also grateful to Lloyd Ohlin and Jim Vorenberg for several years spent at the Criminal Justice Center at the Harvard Law School. My contact with the criminal justice practitioners in residence there was instructive in many ways. The Center for Advanced Study in the Behavioral Sciences at Stanford, with the support of NSF grant no. BNS 8700864, provided an ideal setting for the completion of the book.

Additional support and audiences came from the Hastings Institute of Society, Ethics, and the Life Sciences for a conference in Cambridge where a version of chapter 4 was presented; from John Jay College of Criminal Justice for a New York conference where some of chapter 5 was presented; from The Massachusetts Foundation for the Humanities and Public Policy for a conference at Boston University where an overview of the project was presented; from the Rockefeller Foundation for a conference at Bellagio where some material from chapters 6 and 8 was presented; from the Council of Europe for a conference in Strasbourg on George Orwell where some of chapter 10 was presented; and from Boston University, Bowdoin College, the University of Louvain, the University of Texas at Austin, Stanford, the University of Delaware, the University of California at Irvine, Los Angeles, San Diego, and Santa Cruz, Pitzer College, Harvard, Arizona State University, the University of Arizona, the University of Lowell, Northeastern University, SUNY Albany and Stony Brook, and the University of Montreal, where colloquiums were given. Papers based on this work were also presented at the meetings of the American Sociological Association in 1980 and 1984, at the Society for the Study of Social Problems in 1982 and 1986, at the American Society of Criminology in 1982 and 1987, and at the Law and Society Association in 1984 and 1985. An early version of chapter 5 appears in a book edited by William Heffernan and Timothy Stroup,[1] and some of the material in chapter 10 appears in a book edited by Jim Short.[2]

Finally, there are some broad debts that I am glad to have the chance to acknowledge: to my parents, Ruth and Don Marx, for providing me with a loving upbringing in which honesty with oneself and others was a central value. My sons, Joshua and Benjamin, were respectful of my need to work, even though the door to my study was always open and they knew they came first. With respect to privacy and liberty, I hope their world and that of their children will remain the one we are familiar with, in spite of the harrowing potentials noted in the last chapter. I am

1. W. Heffernan and T. Stroup, *Police Ethics: Hard Choices in Law Enforcement* (New York: The John Jay Press, 1985).
2. J. Short, *The Social Fabric* (Beverly Hills, Calif.: Sage, 1986).

grateful to my wife Phyllis for being all that I could ask for in an emotional and intellectual companion. Although she is a thoroughly modern woman with her own career, she also managed to provide a home environment rich in the support, protection, and tolerance said to have been enjoyed by Talmudic scholars of old.

Preface

The French poet Paul Valéry observed that "in truth there is no theory which is not a fragment . . . of an autobiography."[1] My initial interest in covert police tactics grew out of an incident in Berkeley, California, in 1963 when I was a student. I was active in CORE (the Congress of Racial Equality), an organization dedicated at that time to integration through nonviolence. After a major fund-raising effort, an event occurred that severely damaged the group—our treasurer disappeared with the money. It turned out she was a police agent, as were several other disruptive members.

I felt betrayed by the treasurer, a person I had respected and trusted. I was shocked and angered that a peaceful democratic organization dedicated to ending racial discrimination could be a target of such police action. The youthful image I held of police as archetypical boy scouts, derived from participation in a scout troop sponsored by the Los Angeles Police Department, was challenged.

At the same time, my graduate studies were posing questions and presenting perspectives that made these kinds of actions of more than personal interest. In studying the creation and presentation of social reality, it was clear that things are often not as they appear, that rule breaking and rule enforcement could be intricately intertwined. Were police best seen as paragons of virtue beyond reproach or as morally pragmatic figures enmeshed with the forces of evil? Social reality,

1. P. Valéry, *Oeuvres* (Paris: Editions Gallimard, 1965).

particularly when secrecy is involved, could have paradoxical elements that complicated efforts at understanding and action. Democratic social orders are fragile. They might be threatened by extremist political groups, as well as by the state.

My personal and professional interests came together in 1967 when I studied police behavior in riots as a staff member of the National Advisory Commission on Civil Disorders. One of the commission's findings was that, in responding to disorders, police may contribute (whether intentionally or unintentionally) to the very conditions they seek to control.[2]

Not long after this, police accountability and the duality of social control received widespread public attention through revelations regarding the "dirty tricks" campaigns directed at the civil rights, antiwar, and other movements, and through Watergate and its aftermath. These events made clear the dangers of a secret political police and the ease with which the state could engage in practices abhorrent to a free society.

The issues were relatively straightforward. The excesses noted by the Senate's Church Committee and the Presidential Rockefeller Commission have no place in a democratic society.[3] The question posed by William Butler Yeats: "What if the Church and the State are the mob that howls at the door?" suggested a research agenda. My initial research on covert police sought to document and explain such behavior.[4]

This book, then, grew out of that interest in political policing. As the social movements of the 1960s subsided and police reforms appeared, the use of undercover tactics against legal political groups greatly declined. But undercover tactics took on new life elsewhere. I took the same values and concerns to the study of secret police tactics directed at conventional criminal activities as I had to those directed at legal political activities. As this study progressed, my feelings changed. Social con-

2. President's National Advisory Commission on Civil Disorders, *Report of the National Advisory Commission on Civil Disorders* (Washington, D.C.: GPO, 1968); G. T. Marx, "Civil Disorder and the Agents of Social Control," *Journal of Social Issues* 26, no. 1 (1969): 19–57.

3. U.S. Congress, Senate. 94th Cong., 2d sess. Church Committee (Select Committee to Study Governmental Operations with Respect to Intelligence Activities), *Supplementary Detailed Staff Report on Intelligence Activities and the Rights of Americans*, Book III, Final Report (Washington, D.C.: GPO, 1976); Rockefeller Commission Report, *Report to the President by the Commission on CIA Activities Within the U.S.* (Washington, D.C.: GPO, 1975).

4. G. T. Marx, "Thoughts on a Neglected Category of Social Movement Participant: Agents Provocateurs and Informants," *American Journal of Sociology* 80, no. 2 (1974): 402–42, "External Efforts to Damage or Facilitate Social Movements: Some Patterns, Explanations, Outcomes, and Complications," in *The Dynamics of Social Movements,* ed. M. Zald and J. McCarthy (Cambridge, Mass.: Winthrop, 1979), pp. 94–125.

trol directed at serious violations (robbery, consumer fraud, or corruption) for purposes of prosecution is very different from that directed at the expression of unpopular political beliefs for purposes of disruption.

To some extent, the good guys and the bad guys changed places. The sympathy I felt for civil rights and peace activists confronted by the likes of Bull Connor and agents provocateurs did not translate into sympathy for rapists and corrupt politicians. The indignation that could so easily be directed at the misuse of secret police during early labor struggles and against later civil rights and peace activists could not be automatically transferred to the new infiltrators of the 1980s.

Of course, a key civil liberties principle is that official behavior ought to be judged according to law and policy, not according to whether or not one is sympathetic to the group that is the subject of police actions. Personal feelings aside, the problem of much of the political policing of the 1960s and early 1970s was that its targets were engaged in dissent, not crime. This helps explain why disruption was a much more important goal than prosecution.

In starting this book, I viewed undercover tactics as an *unnecessary evil*. But, in the course of the research I have concluded, however reluctantly, that in the United States they are a *necessary evil*. To be sure, the analysis goes much further in documenting problems and pitfalls of covert tactics than it does in singing their praises. This is partly because good news has a way of taking care of itself, while secrecy makes it all too easy to cover up the bad news. It is also because the tactic is inherently risky and involves costs not present with more conventional tactics.

However, it is still sometimes difficult to separate the heroes from the villains. The issue is complicated by the striking paradoxes, ironies, and trade-offs that are, or might be, present: to do good by doing bad—preventing crime or apprehending criminals by resorting to lies, deceit, trickery; preventing crime by facilitating it; seeking to reduce crime by unintentionally increasing it; preventing harm at a cost of uncertainty about whether it would in fact have occurred; seeing police who pose as criminals become criminals; seeing criminal informers act as police; seeing restrictions on police use of coercion lead to an increase in the use of deception; seeking rational control over emerging and unpredictable events through secret intervention into settings where information is limited; and witnessing the double-edged nature of a tactic ever ready to backfire.

I have sought to describe and explain some fascinating changes that have occurred in American policing. Even if these changes had not occurred, the topic of covert investigations is important because it involves fundamental social processes of trust, lying, deception, and the interdependence of rule enforcers and rule breakers. Secrets and covert intelligence gathering and testing are found in all organizations from the corporation to the family. The offering of quiet little temptations is inherent in child rearing. It is also an element in building up the trust found among friends. Studying deception and temptation in face-to-face encounters and organizations can yield insight into basic elements of social life. To set up a fake organization or to present a fake identity, one must understand how real organizations and identities are constructed. This is the heart of the sociological enterprise. Police are, in a sense, lay sociologists and psychologists. Investigating how they create reality can contribute to our understanding of society and the individual.

I have approached the topic of covert practices as a sociologist interested in the criminal justice system and in the nature of social control. My interest is in the nature of the work and the persons involved in it and in the organizational and societal contexts in which it is carried out. This inquiry casts a broad net: social, historical, legal, technical, ethical, and policy aspects are considered. My analysis is not restricted to one level of government, to a given enforcement agency, to a crime problem where undercover means are central, or to a particularly celebrated investigation. I have looked for themes that are applicable to all of these, assuming that the fundamental techniques used and issues raised are similar. Although each United States law enforcement agency is unique, they have much in common as they operate within the same broad sociocultural framework. There is a greater interchange of ideas, resources, procedures, and personnel among and between federal and local agencies than at any previous time in American history. Undercover practices are one factor in this.

My emphasis is more on the new forms of covert operation, such as the property sting and corruption investigation, than on the traditional, better-understood forms involving political groups or narcotics. The book deals with domestic law enforcement (both federal and local), rather than foreign intelligence and counterintelligence activities. While there is some overlap, the latter raise significantly different issues and are subject to different laws and policies. The book focuses on public rather than private police. This restriction is a function of resource limitations rather than a belief that the undercover activities of private police are unimportant or uninteresting. As the historical record of the Pinkerton and Burns detective agencies or the contemporary record of private police agencies in response to the antinuclear and environmental movements suggest, this is not the case. The undercover activities of private police and public police may also be connected.[5]

The study is based on interviews and the analysis of documents. I have generated new empirical data, and I have sought to summarize, assess, and integrate existing materials. One hundred and fifty-one persons were interviewed. At the federal level most of the interviews were carried out with the FBI. Among those interviewed there were senior officials who set policy and sit on the committee that must approve all proposals for major covert operations; those responsible for selection, training and logistical support; those responsible for headquarters' programs concerned with informers, organized crime, narcotics and public corruption, field supervisors, case and contact agents and the undercover agents who actually do the work.

Interviews also were carried out with agents from the Internal Revenue Service, Bureau of Alcohol, Tobacco and Firearms, and six other federal agencies. Interviews were conducted with prosecutors and other Justice Department officials, and those involved in Congressional oversight. At the local level, interviews were carried out in nine police departments and with one regional task force. A scientific sample was not drawn, but the departments were chosen to be broadly representative, by size and geographic region, of urban areas. Additional interviews were carried out with local prosecutors, defense attorneys, informers, and targets of investigations. I also participated in a week-long training program for federal undercover agents.

Among the primary documents analyzed were court records, videotapes, congressional hearings, training materials, policy guidelines, and agency reports and memos including records released under the Freedom of Information Act. Written materials were obtained from an additional fifteen departments (beyond those in which interviews were carried out). Data were also analyzed from a variety of secondary sources, including evaluation studies, academic and popular literature, and media accounts.

Popular literature and media accounts are too often ignored by academic analysts. I have found them an invaluable source of cases, ideas, and questions. In the case of news stories, for example, more detailed information was often easily obtained from a phone call or written re-

5. G. T. Marx, "The Interweaving of Public and Private Police in Undercover Work," *Criminal Justice Systems Annals* 21 (1987).

quest to the reporter or attorney involved in a case. Such sources vastly extend the researcher's range at minimal cost.

All examples presented are from actual cases. These are usually referenced only when they involve a particularly important court case or where they are treated in readily available books and articles. My major concern is with the case as an illustration of a broad phenomenon or type, rather than with the details of a case in and of itself. Wherever possible, I have sought to cross-check sources, but the book's arguments do not stand or fall on the correctness of any given empirical source.

In spite of the book's empirical grounding, the data in general are not presented quantitatively. The terrain is vast, varied and complicated. The prior systematic empirical literature on undercover means is minimal. In the interviews, case studies, and documents analyzed here, I have sought to broaden our knowledge base. Yet the empirical generalizations offered are fewer and more tentative than I would like. In addition, given the broad concerns of the study, many of the questions raised do not lend themselves to the seeming certainty offered by even the best statistical analysis and sampling. Yet if we are to move toward better understanding and practice, systematic empirical data on the distribution and correlates of the many facets of covert investigations are certainly needed. I hope that future research, drawing on the ideas and information presented in this initial exploratory inquiry, can provide us with such data.

One might assume that access to data on covert practices would be difficult to obtain, and that even if it were obtained, getting straight answers might be "like trying to nail Jell-O to the wall" (a phrase used by Senator Mondale in describing the CIA's response to Congressional questions regarding assassination attempts). Yet this turned out not to be the case. In fact, the research challenge came from having too much information rather than too little.

Of the many agencies approached about participating in this study, only one refused, and some volunteered to participate without being asked. Cooperation may have been forthcoming because (beyond the promise of anonymity) the focus was on the tactic as such, rather than on a particular agency or investigation.

Those interviewed were generally eager to share their experience and concerns and were often more candid than I expected. Interviewing those who are professional at dissimulation requires some skepticism, but this was balanced by the opportunity such interview situations offered to create a bond in the sharing of secret information.[6] The dramatic elements of the sting, with its surprises and parallels to theater, also make for great storytelling and conversation. Each investigation is a morality play and a potential tragedy where a fall from grace is possible—for all characters. When elements of irony or poetic justice occur, the story is even better.[7]

The tactic generates strong emotions and is conducive to self-reflection. Some of those questioned felt misunderstood and insufficiently appreciated by the public. Participation in this analysis, they believed, was one way to tell their story and set the record straight. Others were interested in policy guidance and pragmatic results.

Of course, there were limits. No ongoing operations were observed; nor were current investigations discussed. Given the sensitive nature of the topic, some self-restraint in questioning may have crept in. It was rare, however, for an interviewee to duck a question, and interviews frequently went beyond the allotted time. At the local level, most were conducted by a former law enforcement official with extensive undercover experience. This helped establish a rapport.

As an academic social scientist, I have tried to be systematic, empirical, and objective, and to put what I have learned in the context of the research literature.

For the scholar, the book offers documentation and explanation of recent changes in undercover means (chapters 1, 3); a conceptual framework for classifying the major types and dimensions (chapter 4); empirical data on social and psychological dynamics (chapters 7, 8); hypotheses for future testing (chapters 6, 9); and some reflections on broad trends in social control (chapter 10).

In addition to writing for colleagues and seeking knowledge for its own sake, I have sought to reach a more general audience of those concerned with policy. The latter includes both executives who determine undercover policy and those directly engaged in operations, whether as managers or agents. For them the key issue is not what is original in the work, but what is useful. I hope that chapter 5, which suggests a means

6. Georg Simmel discusses the sense of power and importance that attends the holding and sharing of secrets (*The Sociology of Georg Simmel*, ed. K. Wolff [New York: Free Press, 1950]).

7. The classic cases are "Elmer Gantry" moralizers impaled on the vice they rally against, e.g., the head of a religious university in Iowa, who was arrested for soliciting a decoy prostitute, had earlier cancelled a play on his campus that involved nudity and sexuality.

for assessing ethics; chapter 6, which summarizes research on the impact of fencing stings and anti-crime decoys; chapters 7 and 8, which document the myriad problems that may occur; and chapter 9, which deals with the control of undercover investigations, will meet the test of usefulness.

Writing for both traditional academic and policy audiences may pull the author in opposing directions. Academic audiences seek empirically rather than normatively based statements (and fresh ones at that) and have little interest in hearing what is in secondary sources. Social scientists seek to build a body of cumulative knowledge and theoretical explanations; those in applied settings want advice and are likely to be uninterested in theories, classification schemes, and systematic data for their own sake. Both audiences seek to learn something they didn't know before, but, given different starting points, what pleases one may well displease the other.

Yet writing for both audiences can also be beneficial. Some attention to policy concerns can prevent the work of scholarship from descent into arcane and lifeless pedantry, while attention to scholarly concerns can mean guidance that is more logical, more empirically grounded, and more informed by awareness of the broad picture. To give sound advice, one must first understand the phenomena. And, to have some understanding of an issue as significant as this one and not to consider the policy aspects is probably irresponsible. J. R. R. Tolkien has advised: "Go not to the Elves for counsel, for they will say both yes and no." The same might be said of much academic analysis. I have generally not offered specific recommendations; I have tried to clarify what is at stake, what the choices are, and what kinds of factors ought to be considered in making policy decisions.

On balance, the book neither argues for the expanded use of covert tactics nor for their abolition. There are some areas where, if the suggested criteria and procedures for controlling undercover activities were applied, use of the tactic would decrease. There are other areas (white-collar violations) where it might increase. But it should be a tool of last resort, used with the utmost caution and only by agencies with the requisite skills, resources, and controls. Even then, there are times when it is better to do nothing.

A fundamental and distinguishing feature of our society is that means, as well as ends, have a moral component. Covert practices entail short-

and long-run risks that are not found with more conventional tactics and that must give us pause. Their significance goes far beyond their use in any given case. Secret police behavior and surveillance go to the heart of the kind of society we are or might become. By studying the changes in covert tactics, a window on something much broader can be gained.

The Changing Nature of Undercover Work

I hope we won't go back to the days, Mr. Chairman, when our
agents walked into bars and ordered glasses of milk.

—*FBI Director Webster*

Undercover work has changed significantly in the United States in the
past decade, expanding in scale and appearing in new forms. Covert
tactics have been adopted by new users and directed at new targets and
new offenses. Applying ingenuity previously associated only with fictional accounts, law enforcement agents have penetrated criminal and
sometimes noncriminal milieus to an extraordinary degree. Even organized crime, long thought to be immune, has been infiltrated. (In a
stellar performance, FBI agent Joe Pistone spent five years as a close associate of members of the Bonanno family.) The lone undercover worker
making an isolated arrest has been supplemented by highly coordinated
team activities involving complex technology, organizational fronts,
and multiple arrests. What was traditionally viewed as a relatively marginal and insignificant weapon used only by vice and "red squads" has
become a cutting-edge tactic.

This book speaks to our understanding of contemporary social control and to what undercover tactics say about our society. It also speaks
to those in law enforcement.

Those with the practical task of enforcing the law rarely have the lux-
ury of thinking about the broad questions. Their concerns are immediate, short-range, and pragmatic. Crime and the fear of it are major social issues, and there is enormous public pressure for action. Viewed
from this perspective, undercover means are simply one more tool for
law enforcers. For them, the key questions concern the selection, training, and supervision of agents, and the tactical choices that determine
the nature of an operation.

However, the issues around undercover work go far beyond tactical and strategic questions and even beyond whether, in any given investigation, justice was done. Specifically, they include consideration of what may be a subtle and deep-lying shift in the nature of American social control. Social control has become more specialized and technical, and, in many ways, more penetrating and intrusive. In some ways, we are moving toward a Napoleonic view of the relationship between the individual and the state, where the individual is assumed to be guilty and must prove his or her innocence. The state's power to seek out violations, even without specific grounds for suspicion, has been enhanced. With this comes a cult and a culture of surveillance that goes beyond government to the private sector and the interaction of individuals.

As powerful new surveillance tactics are developed, the range of their legitimate and illegitimate use is likely to spread. Where there is a way, there is often a will. There is the danger of an almost imperceptible surveillance creep. It was roughly half a century ago that Secretary of War Henry Stimson indignantly observed, in response to proposed changes in national security behavior: "Gentlemen do not read each other's mail." His observation seems touchingly quaint in light of the invasions of privacy that subsequent decades have witnessed. The question is whether 50 years from now observers will find our concerns over current surveillance and undercover operations equally quaint. Will the occasional incidents seen in the past decade of police posing as priests, newspaper reporters, lawyers, psychologists, lovers, or students; of their selling drugs, distributing pornography, running casinos and houses of prostitution, filing false affidavits, lying under oath and bugging a judge's chambers; and of covert operations carried out in our most hallowed institutions—churches, elections, courts, and legislatures—have become commonplace? Are we taking slow but steady steps toward making the informer a national hero? Is the moral distinction between crime and criminal justice weakening? Are we moving toward a society where suspiciousness and mistrust will become the norm?

Some recent changes may be attributed to a temporary perception of a crisis in law and order and to the new availability of federal funds to conduct covert operations. As that perception recedes and as funds are reduced, so too will the use of covert tactics. They may also lessen as criminals become "wise" and learn to take defensive actions.

There will always be ebbs and flows in the power of social control, but I think it is wrong to view recent changes only in this context. More sophisticated covert practices are one part of an extension and redefinition of social control, which, together with other practices, constitute what can be called the "new surveillance."

The popular song "Every Breath You Take," sung by a celebrated rock group known as the Police, is a love song, rather than one of protest, but it calls attention to an important social issue and offers examples of the new surveillance. It contains these lines:

Every breath you take	[breath analyzer]
Every move you make	[motion detector]
Every bond you break	[polygraph]
Every step you take	[electronic anklet]
Every single day	[continuous monitoring]
Every word you say	[bugs, wiretaps, mikes]
Every night you stay	[light amplifier]
Every vow you break	[voice stress analysis]
Every smile you fake	[brain wave analysis]
Every claim you stake	[computer matching]
I'll be watching you	[video surveillance].

The new forms of social control tend to be subtle, invisible, scattered, and involuntary. They are often not defined as surveillance, and many people, especially those born after 1960, are barely conscious of them. They have, after all, been brought up in an age of police stings, computerized dossiers, X-rayed luggage at airports, video cameras in banks, lie detector tests for employment, urinalysis tests for drugs, tollfree hotlines for reporting misdeeds and suspicions, and electronic markers on consumer goods, library books, and even people. To them, these conditions represent the normal order of things. Their elders too are often unaware of the extent to which surveillance has become embedded in everyday relationships.

My focus is only on the undercover component of surveillance, but all the tactics are spawned in the same environment and often reinforce each other.

The new surveillance is related to broad changes in both technology and social organization. The rationalization of crime control that began in the nineteenth century has crossed a critical threshold as a result of these changes. Technology has enhanced the power of social control. The information-gathering powers of the state and of private organizations have torn asunder many of our conventional notions of privacy. Traditional lines between private and public and between the rights of the individual and the power of the state are being redrawn. By studying one form of this phenomenon in detail, we may obtain insight into the general phenomenon.

NEW AND TRADITIONAL USERS

THE FBI

The agency with the greatest change in its application of undercover operations is the Federal Bureau of Investigation (FBI). It has moved from viewing them as too risky and costly for routine use to viewing them as important tools. The FBI has come a long way from the description offered by leading agent Melvin Purvis in 1936: "No government operative may enter into illegal compacts or pursue illegal courses of action; it does not matter what desirable ends might be served."[1] Four decades later, an FBI agent wrote: "Undercover operations have become the cutting edge of the FBI's effort to ferret out concealed criminal activity."[2]

The FBI began using undercover agents in criminal investigations in 1972, following J. Edgar Hoover's death. Internal agency rules regarding things such as dress, hair style, the prohibition of alcohol consumption on duty and the need to frequently report in when in the field, which worked against complex covert operations, were loosened. In 1973 and 1974, undercover agents were used in approximately 30 "investigative matters," apart from the collection of domestic intelligence. From 1977 to 1985, the numbers were as follows:

1977	53
1978	176
1979	239
1980	314
1981	463
1982	384
1983	387
1984	391
1985	350

The FBI's first appropriation request for undercover activities appeared in 1977.[3] From 1977 to 1984 the requests were as follows:

1977	$ 1,000,000
1978	3,000,000
1979	2,910,000
1980	2,910,000
1981	4,500,000
1982	7,500,000
1983	9,008,000
1984	12,518,000

Hoover fought against a proposal to merge the FBI with the Prohibition Bureau and kept his agents away from narcotics enforcement. But in 1982 President Reagan authorized the FBI to play a more active role. The FBI was given supervision over the Drug Enforcement Agency and in 1985 there were over 800 joint investigations (no pun intended). By mid-1985 one in eight agents was working full time on drugs. In 1981 the FBI expended $8.3 million on narcotic-related matters and in 1984 $97.2 million. The FBI has emphasized drug enforcement as it relates to its high-priority areas—organized crime, financial crime and public corruption.

OTHER ENFORCEMENT AGENCIES

The Bureau of Alcohol, Tobacco and Firearms (BATF) foreshadowed this expansion by significantly increasing its use of undercover methods after the passage of the 1968 Gun Control Act. An executive of the Immigration and Naturalization Service (INS) reports that his agency is "increasing the undercover capacity and the undercover techniques that we use."

In 1982 the Internal Revenue Service (IRS), as part of a "new and wide-ranging investigative toughness," vastly expanded its intelligence and undercover activities. A special unit was created with unprecedented powers to collect and analyze data on taxpayers, including the increased use of undercover agents and sting operations.[4]

United States marshalls have made extensive use of covert tactics to facilitate the location and apprehension of fugitives through Operation FIST (Fugitive Investigative Strike Team). In what was heralded as the "largest and most successful manhunt in U.S. history," thousands of wanted persons were tricked into turning themselves in. In Florida, more than three thousand persons were lured out of hiding by promises of free trips and prizes; many of them showed up at a fake airline counter after receiving a letter that began, "Congratulations! You are the winner of a weekend retreat in the Bahamas. Enclosed please find your champagne flight boarding pass." In California, several thousand fugitives were arrested when notice was sent to their last-known addresses that they could claim a nonexistent "valuable package" from the fictitious "Fist Bonded Delivery Service." In Denver the lure was free Super Bowl tickets, and in New York persons wanted on drunk-driving charges were arrested after responding to an invitation to a "cocktail party and banquet" to "test" a new alcoholic beverage.

Following the recommendations of several national commissions, covert means have also become more sophisticated and significant at the local level since the late 1960s. The Commission on Law Enforcement and Administration of Justice (1967) urged every major city to establish "a special intelligence unit solely to ferret out organized crime," and the Kerner Commission (1968) called on cities to develop intelligence units that would use undercover police personnel and informants to learn about actual or potential civil disorders.[5]

In many local law enforcement departments, undercover work has come to be seen as an important and innovative tactic, carried out by carefully chosen, elite units. Increased prestige and professional recognition result from assignment to tactical or special squads that use undercover methods in new ways. Competition for assignments to these units, for example, anticrime decoy or intelligence squads, is often intense.

The past decade has also seen state attorneys general, county district attorneys, and special prosecutors taking greater independent initiatives against crime, often using their own investigators and conducting their own undercover operations. In addition, undercover operations have brought what were often relatively uncooperative federal, local, or regional police agencies together in joint ventures via the task force approach. Joint public-private undercover investigations have also appeared, as with an FBI-IBM (International Business Machines) operation against Japanese companies in Silicon Valley involving the sale of supposedly stolen IBM secrets.

NONENFORCEMENT AGENCIES

Federal agencies whose primary goal is not criminal law enforcement, such as the departments of Agriculture, Interior, and Housing and Urban Development; the Customs Service; the Government Services Administration; the Nuclear Regulatory Commission; the Commodity Futures Trading Commission and the Securities and Exchange Commission; and congressional committees have also made increased use of undercover tactics, as have consumer, health, environmental protection, and motor vehicle agencies, and departments of investigation at the state and local levels. Even Smokey the Bear may be going undercover. In 1985 the U.S. Forest Service revealed a plan to crack down on marijuana growing in national forests involving the use of 500 special agents and the expenditure of up to $20 million a year. Under former Director William Casey, the Central Intelligence Agency (CIA) was given new authority to conduct domestic undercover operations.[6] The tactic is being used for civil and administrative, as well as for criminal, violations.[7]

NEW TARGETS

Not only has the number of covert operations increased, so has the variety of targets. Traditionally, undercover operations were targeted against consensual crimes (a crime between consenting individuals, such as a buyer and a seller of drugs), and they tended to focus on petty operators, street criminals, and other so-called lower-status persons. This has changed.

Anticrime decoys, fencing stings (police posing as purchasers of stolen goods), and infiltration have brought the tactic to relatively unorganized street crime and burglary, thus including crimes where there is a clearly identifiable victim. Undercover agents have adopted a new role—that of victim rather than co-conspirator. For example, a police officer may now pose as a derelict with an exposed wallet in order to foster a crime.

New targets also have emerged within traditional vice operations. In what is termed the "sell-bust" strategy, customers (whether consumers or distributors) have joined "suppliers" as targets. For example, policewomen may pose as prostitutes and arrest men who proposition them.[8] This contrasts with the more traditional undercover role where a male agent pretends to be a customer. Undercover officers may offer to sell drugs and other contraband instead of just buying it.

The sell-bust technique may also be seen in some antifencing operations. In spite of their name, most antifencing police storefronts target thieves rather than fences. This is not the case with "bait sales," where the undercover agent pretends to be a thief and offers to sell "stolen" property to a person thought to be a fence.

The expansion of covert operations into white-collar crime means that corporate executives, bankers, persons in retail and service businesses, labor leaders, and elected and other government officials (including judges, police, and prosecutors) have all become targets. This represents a shift in emphasis to crimes involving corruption, labor racketeering, industrial espionage, and export trade law violations.

This expansion may also help explain the increased public controversy around the tactic. When lower-status drug dealers and users or prostitutes were the main targets, the tactic tended to be ignored, but, when congressmen and business executives who can afford the best legal counsel became targets, congressional inquiries and editorials urging caution appeared.

In the late 1970s, the Drug Enforcement Agency (DEA) began to favor quality, high-level cases over quantity arrests. This meant increased attention to large-scale operations instead of street sales. Similarly, the IRS, which previously went after "Mom and Pop" operations, flea markets, or garage sales to monitor cash exchanges, has started putting agents "in banks and businesses instead."

Other new targets include foreign businesses suspected of trade violations, exporters of high technology and military equipment, dumpers of hazardous wastes, promoters of tax shelters, landlords, building inspectors, automobile salesmen and mechanics, fixers of horse races, poachers of cacti, elk, bighorn sheep, and bear, and traffickers in endangered or protected plants and wildlife, such as Jamaican boa constrictors and great horned owls.[9] Even baseball fans are facing increased covert surveillance. Thus, in 1982 the New York Yankees began an ambitious program of placing plainclothes police in the stands pretending to be fans. Hip, young, and wearing running shoes and rock star T-shirts, they were barely distinguishable from the potential troublemakers they sought to eject.

NEW GOALS

Rather than being directed at specific crime categories, investigations may start with suspect groups or individuals to find out what offenses they might be committing. In other words, authorities now actively seek out violators. With this focus on potential offenders and offenses, targeting has become more fluid and based more on probabilities. Investigations, for example, may be directed at various white-collar groups (business people, labor leaders, government officials) where a variety of offenses may be occurring.

The scope of most traditional undercover investigations (excluding those against political groups) has been relatively limited. Their goal has been to apprehend either a specific person or persons believed likely to commit a limited range of previously identified offenses. The investigations are reactive in that they occur in response to a particular crime, a crime pattern, or to specific factors that arouse police suspicion. This investigative model has been supplemented by one that is more proactive, diffuse, and open-ended. The new model involves a radar-like discovery sweep. Many investigations have become uncoupled from specific complaints, suspects, or offenses and (at least initially) less focused. Deterrence and intelligence gathering have become important objectives, along with the traditional goal of apprehending those responsible for specific offenses.[10]

The above changes are illustrated by the FBI's Silicon Valley and Abscam investigations. Neither began with the specific targets and offenses with which it ended. The Silicon Valley operation, one of the largest industrial espionage cases in U.S. history, was set up "to get a little better handle on problems in Silicon Valley, like the gray market [trading in stolen chips] and the sale of defective parts to the military." The "operation got off on a tangent with the Japanese thing" when the "unexpected opportunity" to investigate trade law violations was presented.

Abscam (short for Abdul scam) involved an FBI agent posing as a sheik. It began as an inquiry into stolen art and securities, but it ended as an investigation of political corruption. When a subject spoke of his ability to influence politicians, the focus of the investigation changed. As a Senate committee of inquiry observed: "Abscam was virtually unlimited in geographic scope, persons to be investigated and criminal activity to be investigated . . . [it] was in practical effect, a license for several special agents to assume false identities, to create a false business front, and to see what criminal activities could be detected or developed throughout the country."[11]

There is a parallel to fishing in rich waters with a big net and attractive bait. One can never be sure what kind of fish will be caught. To quote a prosecutor who played a key role in an unfocused corruption investigation, "you leave your bait out long enough, you gotta catch something. One way or the other, we got ourselves a fish fry."[12] The contrast with more defined conventional investigations that occur in re-sponse to a crime, or more focused undercover operations, is clear.

Abscam departed from many other undercover operations that lack prior suspects but that are at least organized to yield a strong presumption of guilt. For example, in police-run fencing fronts, there are reasonable grounds for suspecting anyone who comes to the fence with property to sell at a fraction of its value. But in Abscam, showing up at a meeting to discuss campaign contributions did not offer equivalent grounds for suspicion. For a crime to occur, the government agent had to make a bribe offer. Nor was Abscam a passive operation in the sense of being dependent on suspects who voluntarily came forward; those to be tempted were brought in by unwitting informers.

UNWITTING INFORMERS

The increased use of informers who do not know they are part of a law enforcement operation is an important factor in the new undercover model. In Abscam, unwitting informers were delegated the initial role in choosing the politicians to be tempted. This is in sharp contrast to traditional corruption investigations that are likely to involve either a person from whom a bribe is demanded, playing along under police supervision, or a "turned" suspect who agrees to cooperate with authorities in return for leniency.[13]

The case of businessman John DeLorean offers an example of an offense that is an artifact of the investigation. The government went to great lengths to involve him in a cocaine caper, having no reason to believe that he was a drug dealer. DeLorean was eager to raise money to save his car company. A neighbor who was a con man and an FBI informer put DeLorean in touch with a drug dealer. The idea for the drug buy appears to have come from the informer who told DeLorean he could earn $60 million by financing a major cocaine deal. The informer introduced DeLorean to an FBI agent posing as a banker, and the "banker" loaned DeLorean the money. The agent testified that, if he had not offered DeLorean a method of financing the deal, the caper would not have occurred. The government thus provided a person not previously involved in drug trafficking with both a drug dealer and the money to finance a drug deal. DeLorean was vulnerable. Whether he was entrapped is a legal question that is separate from the criteria that ought to be used in selecting those whose honesty will be tested.

Secret testing on a random basis is a well-established aspect of private policing, for example, the testing of cashiers, and it has become more common in the public sector as well. Some investigations have taken as their implicit goal the determination of whether or not a person can be induced to break the law, rather than whether the person is in fact breaking the law.

The question "Is he corrupt?" may be replaced by the question "Is he corruptible?" Some operations amount to random integrity testing. Rather than intervention into ongoing criminal activities, there is an effort to create them apart from specific grounds for suspicion. Using the tactic for general intelligence purposes or to test at random represents a significant extension of law enforcement discretion.

DEFINING TYPES OF POLICE WORK

The difference between undercover and conventional police tactics is highlighted when we consider two dimensions: whether the law enforcement nature of the operation is overt or covert and whether the police work is nondeceptive or deceptive. Although covert and deceptive practices are often linked, just as overt and nondeceptive practices are, in principle they are independent.[14] When these aspects are combined, we identify four types of police activity (table 1).

Most police work is *overt and nondeceptive* (cell A). In conventional criminal investigations, victims, witnesses, or others notify police that a crime has occurred; less frequently, uniformed patrols discover an offense. Persons whose police identity is clear then make inquiries and gather evidence. Such police-citizen encounters are reasonably straightforward and involve questioning; giving aid, orders, or information; making arrests; or issuing citations.

But police work may also be *overt and deceptive* (cell B). The television detective Columbo illustrates this. In weekly episodes, he tricked interrogated suspects into confessing by telling them they faced a long prison sentence, that a companion had confessed, or that police had incriminating witnesses or evidence—none of which was true. This has its real-life counterpart when police issue threats that they have no intention of carrying out. They may also use deception to get around various legal restrictions, e.g., creating a false arrest, or by falsely claiming that contraband was dropped or a weapon was in plain view in order to justify a search.[15]

Overt deception is also used to create the impression of police omnipresence. This so-called "scarecrow" (misinformation) phenomenon includes visible surveillance cameras with blinking lights but no film or monitor; signs warning of monitoring through one-way mirrors or elec-

TABLE I   TYPES OF POLICE WORK

		Are police actions	
		overt?	covert?
Does police action involve	nondeception?	A. uniformed patrol	C. passive surveillance
	deception?	B. trickery by persons whose police identity is known	D. undercover

tronic devices, and notices that "violators will be towed" or signs stating that traffic laws are strictly enforced when that isn't the case; or highway patrol cars strategically placed along busy roads with a visible radar device and mannequins seated inside.

Covert techniques need not involve active efforts to deceive. Much secret electronic or direct visual surveillance is *covert and nondeceptive* (cell C). A camera, transmitter, interceptor, or tape recorder may simply be hidden (though rarely in anything so exotic as a martini olive!). An agent who watches a suspicious corner from a rooftop, follows a likely victim at a discreet distance, listens to speeches at a demonstration, or monitors a suspect's mail is not actually deceiving anyone in face-to-face interaction. Unobtrusive surveillance does not directly intervene to shape the suspect's environment, perceptions, or behavior.

Undercover work is both *covert and deceptive* (cell D). Unlike conventional police work, which, in a protracted process, tends to move from discovery of the offense to discovery of the identity of the perpetrator, then to arrest, the investigation may go on *before and during* the commission of the offense. It may start with the offender and only later document the offense. Discovery of the offender, the offense, and the arrest may occur almost simultaneously.

Covert and deceptive (undercover) techniques seek to overcome the limitations of conventional means. The latter tend to be irrelevant when police do not know that a crime has taken place and ineffective when no one will cooperate or adequate evidence cannot be gathered. They permit the state to observe directly actual or planned criminal activity.

Covert or deceptive tactics often resemble undercover practices. They also offer a means of discovering otherwise unavailable information, and they may constitute an invasion of privacy or a violation of trust.

But it is the deliberate convergence of covertness and deception that makes undercover practices so powerful and sometimes problematic.

THE INCREASE IN UNDERCOVER WORK

Unlike a singular tactic, such as legal wiretapping, for which agencies must file annual reports with the Justice Department, there are no standard means of measuring undercover practices, nor is there a central agency to receive reports. The topic must be dealt with obliquely and through rough estimates. Little information is routinely collected, and even less is made public. The quality and nature of the data that are available are not usually in a form that is useful for explanatory or comparative purposes (whether across agencies, over time, or among types of operation). Nonetheless, some generalizations can be made.

Undercover practices are more characteristic of federal police than of local; of detective units than of patrol; and of private police than of public. They are most likely to be used for offenses that are consensual (e.g., vice); that involve a recurring organized set of exchanges; where victims or witnesses are lacking because they are unaware of the crime (e.g., consumer fraud) or fail to come forward because they are intimidated, fearful, rewarded, indifferent, or apathetic.

The most direct measure of the increase in undercover work is simply to make yearly comparisons. Such data, as I have noted, exist only for the FBI, but other indirect measures are available. One indication is the size of federal police compared to local police. Because federal police are primarily detective agencies, and local police are primarily uniformed patrol agencies, a relative expansion of the former would be consistent with an increase in undercover work. Between 1970 and 1981, federal expenditures for police protection increased from 9 to 13 percent of total national police expenditures.

Within local police departments, the expansion of investigative work relative to other police work is also consistent with the increased use of undercover tactics. Data gathered from seven large cities showed that the number of police assigned to investigative jobs increased by almost one-third from 13 percent in 1971 to 17 percent in 1981 of total police positions.[16] The number of officers assigned to intelligence work, perhaps the category most closely linked to undercover means and informers, almost doubled; those assigned to criminal investigations increased by almost one-third; and vice assignments increased by 9 percent. When disaggregated by city and personnel category, the increases held for 18 of 21 possible comparisons.

As we note in more detail in chapter 3, programs and resources associated directly or indirectly with covert work have also increased (e.g., witnesses in the Federal Witness Protection Program or interagency strike forces). It is likely that the number of unmarked police vehicles, body recorders, transmitters, and related surveillance equipment has increased. Confidential funds (for the purchase of contraband or to pay informers) have probably increased, both absolutely and relatively, as a share of police budgets.

Finally, indirect evidence of the expansion of undercover means can be seen in changing local arrest patterns. Between 1960 and 1980, arrests for offenses where undercover tactics are often used rose from 5.8 to 10.8 percent of the total. There was a significant increase in arrests for narcotics, prostitution and commercial vice, fraud, and possessing and receiving stolen property; only gambling arrests declined.

The expansion and change in the nature of undercover work has been neither uniform across agencies and types of offenses nor perfectly linear over time. If the overall profile is upward, its contours are jagged. Thus, the increased attention to narcotics and property crime has been at least partly offset by a deemphasis on political and gambling cases.

Even with the extended application of undercover tactics, we are not in the midst of a massive conversion from overt to covert policing. George Orwell is not yet around the corner. At the local level, the uniformed patrol is and will remain the predominant means of carrying out police work. Even at the federal level, undercover means are only one of several prominent investigative means. The fraction of resources going into deceptive investigations is still small. Judged quantitatively, the increases in undercover means are insignificant in the broad enforcement picture, but, compared with other democratic industrial nations or with the United States in 1960 (or 1860 or 1760), they are worthy of note.[17]

However, even if this were not the case, important qualitative changes have occurred. Their subtlety would not necessarily be captured by quantitative data, even if better data were available. The fact that the FBI, the most prestigious and powerful American law enforcement agency, now routinely uses undercover tactics—often in highly publicized ways—is significant.

Undercover means have become a prominent and sophisticated part of the arsenal of American law enforcement. This represents a marked departure from the police activities envisioned by the founders of the country and from the Anglo-American police ideal that eventually evolved.

The extension of covert means in the United States has had an international impact. Via cooperative investigations and the provision of models, resources, and instruction, the United States is helping to spread criminal undercover investigations worldwide. Ironically, practices that came to the U.S. from Europe are being reintroduced there in new American forms.[18]

MAJOR QUESTIONS

These changes in undercover activity raise important questions for social understanding and public policy. Given the protective secrecy surrounding the tactic and its potential conflict with the lofty ideals of American democracy, police accountability, civil liberties, and fair play, our lack of knowledge is not surprising. However, the importance of the issues involved and the risks to cherished liberties make our ignorance disquieting.

There has been almost no comprehensive analysis of undercover practices. Criminologists, public policy analysts, and other social scientists have rarely approached the topic, except as an adjunct to a consideration of narcotics enforcement, political surveillance, an enforcement agency, or a particularly celebrated investigation. There is a body of legal literature, although it is largely restricted to issues around entrapment. There is a small philosophy literature. There is a practitioner's literature that takes as "given" the desirability of the tactic. There is an interesting, although in general nonprobing, descriptive literature involving first-person and journalistic accounts and novels.[19]

In the absence of carefully specified criteria, adequate data, and systematic analysis, many observers have "knee-jerk" responses to undercover police tactics. The operations are considered either all good and beyond reproach or all bad and beyond justification. Proponents stress their unique effectiveness and argue for increased use; problems are minimized or seen as worth the risk. Opponents stress their unique problems and argue for decreased use; policy solutions are dismissed as unworkable, and potential risks are treated as matters of fact rather than as questions to be researched.

Such sweeping generalizations and a priori assumptions about whether undercover tactics are the problem or the solution fail to make distinctions among the types of undercover operations or to note the extensive variation within them. They do not define the broad array of criteria by which the tactic can be judged. Nor do they consider empirical data for assessing the frequency with which a given problem or advantage occurs. They fail to specify the policy measures that are likely to minimize or maximize desirable or undesirable outcomes.

Given societal changes and a high degree of public concern over crime, shifts in law enforcement activity may well be appropriate. However, changes in such a sensitive area as covert operations should be preceded by a careful assessment of how the tactic works, the possible risks, the hidden costs, and the unintended consequences.

To begin to grasp the complexity of the topic and to make informed decisions, answers to nine broad questions are needed:

1. What is the history of undercover practices?

2. What accounts for recent changes?

3. What are the main types of undercover operation, and what are the major sources of variation within them?

4. What competing values are at stake, and what questions should be asked in deciding whether or not undercover means are desirable as a broad strategy and as tactically implemented?

5. What does the available research reveal about their intended impact and effectiveness?

6. What unintended consequences can the tactic have for targets, third parties, and informers?

7. What unintended consequences can the tactic have for police?

8. What means are available to control undercover activities?

9. How do covert practices relate to other trends in surveillance and social control, and what are the broad implications of undercover practices for society in the future?

Each of these questions forms the basis for the chapters that follow.

A Selective History of Undercover Practices

The serpent beguiled me, and I did eat.
—*Genesis* 3:13

The system of espionage being thus established, the country will swarm with informers, spies, delators, and all the odious reptile tribe that breed in . . . despotic power. The hours of most unsuspected confidence, the intimacies of friendship or the recesses of domestic retirement, will afford no security.
—*Congressman Edward Livingston, 1798*

Contemporary undercover practices can be better understood by looking at them in a historical context and noting what social, legal, and technical factors affect them. I will describe some salient themes in the development of undercover practices focusing on the middle of the nineteenth century through the mid-twentieth century.

Deception, temptation, and informers are ancient and virtually universal forms of social control. The Bible is filled with examples—Eve and the serpent, God testing Abraham and Job, and Judas informing on Jesus. The devil has often been depicted as wearing angel's clothes and talking sweetly. Plato wanted his guardians to undergo periodic secret testing. From Ulysses to Hamlet, folklore and literature are rich in tales of rulers or deities who have secretly gone among their people to administer tests and discover the truth. Whatever the literary appeal of such tactics, Western societies lacked the means for broad systematic undercover policing until the last two centuries. With the rise of the modern state, however, the routinization of covert, as well as overt, means of policing became possible. The traditional system of policing a feudal society was inadequate in the face of the greatly increased (and new forms of) crime and disorder that accompanied urbanization and industrialization.

FRANCE

French and English innovations of the eighteenth and early nineteenth centuries underlie American undercover practices. In both Eu-

17

rope and the United States, the systematic and formal use of covert means for conventional (as opposed to political) crime owes much to François Vidocq (1775–1857).[1]

As a young man, Vidocq was imprisoned for a minor crime. He escaped from prison and sought police protection from blackmailers. As part of an effort to clear his name, he voluntarily reentered prison as a police spy. He remained there for 21 months and provided authorities with a wealth of information. Vidocq subsequently became a police agent and established a unit for criminal investigation within the Paris police, modeled after the secret political police that had been created for Napoleon in the preceding decade.[2] Vidocq headed the criminal investigation division from 1810 until 1827. *La Police criminale*—the criminal police (some in both senses)—emerged from this.

Vidocq's great innovation was to have police agents become directly, if surreptitiously, involved in the criminal world. He believed that "crime can only be fought by criminals" and that "it takes a thief to catch a thief." His first detectives were former criminals. They were paid from secret funds not shown on the official budget (a practice that unfortunately continues to the present day in some jurisdictions).

In his first years, Vidocq made spectacular arrests. His innovative tactics led him to the heart of the burgeoning Paris underworld, a netherworld previous police inspectors had not dared to enter. He was a master of disguise and an effective and dramatic publicist who sought to create fear in the underworld that at any moment he might suddenly appear. He made extensive use of infiltration and deception, staged arrests and escapes, and contrived crimes. "Informing" became more systematized.

Vidocq clearly saw that the traditional system of policing (which had been based on the military or the use of irregular generalists restricted to one neighborhood) was inadequate in an expanding urban setting, such as Paris. In his memoirs Vidocq tells us that "never had any period been marked with more important discoveries than that which ushered in my debut in the service of the police." To deal with crime more effectively, police needed a greater degree of central control and geographical mobility. He recognized that crime could be dealt with in an anticipatory, preventive and/or damage-containing mode, as well as after the fact. Police would sometimes have to pretend to be criminals and sometimes have to use criminals as their agents. Police and criminals would sometimes become indistinguishable—or such were the accusations that the police faced.

The potential for corruption or its appearance made Vidocq's system vulnerable and suspect, despite its successes. Regular police officers resented his accomplishments and felt stigmatized by a police unit headed by an escaped convict who chose his detectives from the criminal class.[3] He eventually resigned under suspicion and pressure, but his idea of a central criminal investigative division was well established.[4] Later heads of the Paris detectives did not follow Vidocq's hiring principle and sought instead to create a detective branch above suspicion. But they continued to make extensive use of criminals as their delegated agents. Indeed, *moutons* (informers) remain a crucial part of the French criminal justice system.

GREAT BRITAIN

Rather than establishing a permanent state police system, creating a special detective force, or formally incorporating criminals into the police as the French had done, Great Britain in the early eighteenth century institutionalized a do-it-yourself system of "common informers" and "thief takers." The goal was to involve citizens, rather than the state, in crime control. Any citizen could become a thief taker, catching criminals and recovering stolen property. In return, he or she could expect a share of the property or a reward. This gave rise to the derogatory term "blood money." Pardons were offered to persons who had committed crimes (but were not in prison) if they would become informers.

The contemporary property sting has its roots partly in this system.[5] Jonathan Wild (1682–1725) was the most famous practitioner of the British system.[6] He was a thief, a fence, and a control agent. Wild was known as the "Thief Taker General of Great Britain and Ireland." He was the silent partner of Charles Hitchen, a notorious London marshall and a receiver of stolen property. Wild organized the London underworld and became wealthy; he collected fees for the return of property that he had secretly arranged to have stolen. Thieves who would not cooperate were turned in. He was responsible for numerous arrests and sent more than 100 thieves to the gallows.

Wild was a person of monumental *chutzpah*, great daring, cunning, and physical courage. When he himself was finally led to the gallows, he had syphilis (and was suffering from an even worse cure for it), 17 sword and pistol wounds, and a skull covered with silver plates.

Wild's "career" exemplifies the problems of delegating authority to criminals. It is an easy and tempting move from crime control to deceptive collusion in committing crime. Thief-taking easily becomes thief-making. In England this system created an army of inventive and deceitful professional informers eager to commit perjury for gain.[7] It contributed to the crime and disorder that engulfed a changing English society as it entered the nineteenth century. The laws in eighteenth-century England were severe, with capital punishment prescribed for even minor offenses, yet there was minimum provision for actually enforcing the law. Nevertheless, the English were hesitant to follow the lead of France and establish a permanent police and detective force. They preferred their relatively ineffective, corrupt and inexpensive system of part-time constables and inept watchmen, with occasional recourse to the military. They were fearful of centralized authority, even though England had had a secret intelligence service, the King's Messengers, since Elizabethan times. Although the primary concern of the Messengers was foreign espionage, they also directed attention to domestic dissidents and infiltrated antigovernment organizations. Domestic spying came under severe Parliamentary criticism in 1817, when an agent named Oliver was discovered to be a provocateur.[8] His actions drew others into subversive acts for which they were hung. The idea of creating a new police force did not find favor in this climate.

Many influential persons resisted the proposal to create a permanent police force. They feared this would lead to a despotic regime and the extension of the powers of the Crown. It was seen as a foreign idea alien to English ways. Avoiding infringements on liberty was a higher priority than a more effective response to crime and disorder, but it was not possible for an urbanizing and industrializing England to remain an unpoliced society.

The sentiments of Police Magistrate Patrick Colqhoun, who argued in 1795 that increasing levels of crime and disorder rendered "it more than ever necessary to establish a system of unremitting vigilance," gained prominence. Colqhoun admired the French system and argued for adopting some of its elements. The traditional British thief-taker system could mean prolonged public victimization as "criminals were permitted to ripen from the first stage of depravity until they were worth forty pounds."[9]

After intense debate, a permanent municipal public police force was created in London in 1829 under the leadership of Sir Robert Peel (the "bobbies"). Drawing on ideas of the utilitarian philosophers and police theorists, such as Henry Fielding and Colqhoun, the British police were to be unarmed, uniformed, and on duty 24 hours a day throughout the city. It was anticipated that this pervasive, visible force would offer protection via deterrence; hence, the police were labeled preventive. The likelihood of apprehension would cause the criminally inclined to alter their ways.

Advocates of this system argued that it was more consistent with British traditions of liberty, and more humane and effective, to prevent crime from ever occurring. The alternative was to rely on draconian punishment after the fact, which required a secret detective force enmeshed with criminals. It was believed that liberty could be maintained best by having all police readily identified by a nonmilitary uniform, though in an organization and with supervision of a quasi-military nature.[10] The fear of spying was thus lessened, though at considerable unintended benefit to criminals.

With a uniformed police force, there was a moral separation of police from criminals and a visual separation of police from everyone else. It was thought that citizens would be more likely to come to the aid of an officer in uniform if requested. The uniform might also compel police "to intervene and restore order instead of vanishing into the crowd for fear of being noticed" and prevent their "habitual frequenting of taverns and persistence in bad habits, such as intemperance and gambling."[11]

In its first decade, the London police, in contrast to the police in Paris, had minimal public organizational provision for detecting and investigating crime. The highest priority was placed on gaining the approval of a skeptical public. The secret police tactics associated with France and Russia were not publicly sanctioned.[12]

London's experiment in visible preventive policing was innovative in its permanence, its use of daytime patrols, and its centrally controlled neighborhood beats. The system was relatively effective in maintaining order in the streets. However, it was incapable of dealing with the increasingly sophisticated and cross-jurisdictional urban crime.

The 1829 decision to have an all-uniformed force illustrates a tradeoff between crime prevention and apprehension that is still with us. A uniformed police officer is likely to prevent crime from occurring in his presence, but his very uniform is also a warning signal to criminals and hence can work against their apprehension. Because police cannot be everywhere, the calculating criminal is thus offered an advantage by an all-uniformed force; the accountability and protection of liberty thought to be associated with the uniform in a democratic society comes at a cost.

Although preventive policing as then defined could be carried on by uniformed officers simply making their rounds, the systematic detection of offenders required sustained contact and varying degrees of collaboration with criminals. In spite of opposition, a relatively autonomous nonuniformed Criminal Investigation Division (CID) was started in 1842 in New Scotland Yard. It consisted of two inspectors and six sergeants who were directed to mingle with thieves. An observer at the time found "the sort of odd intimacy that commonly exists between the thief and his natural enemy, the detective policeman, is very remarkable; the latter is as well acquainted with the haunts of the former as he is with the abodes of his own friends and relatives." [13]

Following a scandal in 1877, the detective force was reorganized and headed by Howard Vincent, a controversial former army officer. Vincent had studied French clandestine detective practices and sought to introduce them to England, but his efforts were criticized. In an early version of the buy-bust, several of his detectives and a police matron were indicted by a grand jury in 1880 for inducing a druggist to sell abortion fluids.

The then police commissioner Sir Edward Henderson acknowledged that, "There are many and great difficulties in the way of a detective system; it is viewed with the greatest suspicion and jealousy by the majority of Englishmen and is, in fact, entirely foreign to the habits and feelings of the Nation." [14] The literal and symbolic separation of the bobbies from criminals and the public could not last. However reluctantly, the English police developed a detective system and extended secret police tactics to more conventional crimes. By the early 1880s, the CID had grown to more than 800 persons.

From its inception, the London police quietly spied on dissident groups, but in 1883 a "Special Irish Branch" was formally established within the CID to focus on Irish revolutionaries. Later known as the "Special Branch," its concerns were broadened to other foreigners and political dissidents.

THE UNITED STATES

THE MUNICIPAL POLICE

The United States once shared with England the fear of a centralized, permanently organized police force and the associated "informers, spies, and delators" that accompanied despotisms. These concerns were even more pronounced in the United States because of the American struggle for independence.

The first municipal police force in the new nation consisted of non-uniformed and unarmed men, reflecting the country's antimilitary attitudes. Fears of a strong central government with a well-developed standing army, along with budgetary concerns, account for this. However, there were counterarguments. In response to increased crime and disorder, a Philadelphia reformer in 1830 argued for an anticipatory "system constantly in motion," which would provide "accurate and detailed information as to all persons, places and things which are, or probably may become, the subject of criminal prosecution." [15] As the United States became more urban and ethnically diverse, it was no more able to resist the need for a formal, specialized police system than was Great Britain.

Imitating London, many large American cities had created uniformed municipal police departments by the 1850s. These departments were local, civilian controlled, and highly decentralized. They were subject to popular political control through ward leaders, political bosses, and elected officials, rather than to control by the national government or law, as was the case in England.

As in England, the emphasis was on a visible police presence that would (hopefully) deter criminals and the disorderly. Police were to come to the aid of citizens in need but were generally not expected to take the initiative in discovering violations. Indeed, much of the assistance they rendered had nothing to do with crime. In the words of a Boston city councilman: "The police should enforce the law, but they should not employ spies, resort to entrapment, or otherwise let their determination to stamp out crime carry them beyond the point at which decent and honorable men must stop." [16]

Most of the municipal departments initially had limited or no formal provisions for crime detection. They were at a disadvantage in dealing with consensual crimes and those carried out by skilled conspirators (counterfeiters, con artists, and professional thieves). As the editor of the *Chicago Tribune* put it in 1857, "the present [uniformed] police force is no doubt as good and efficient a body of men as is needed for the preservation of order . . . but for the purposes of catching adroit and experienced rogues, they are useless, and it is unreasonable to expect them to be otherwise." [17]

Some of the new municipal departments initially resisted pressures to add a detective bureau. There was fear that detective scandals might throw the fragile legitimacy of the uniformed branch into question. Increasing the size of the uniformed force was seen as the preferred solution to obvious crime problems, but this was costly and did not lead to greater effectiveness.

Small detective branches thus developed in most cities by the later nineteenth century, though there was considerable ambivalence toward them because their specialized function carried with it the imperative to become involved with criminals.[18] The first detectives came from civilian life—not infrequently its criminal fringe or even its criminal core. Some had previous experience as constables or private detectives who recovered stolen property for a fee. The scandals engendered by this form of recruitment led to a new policy of selecting detectives from the uniformed patrol.

Nonetheless, the detective's skill was based largely on his knowledge of, and contact with, lawbreakers. Among the most common forms of this were licensing of vice providers, infiltration, and a system for the recovery of stolen property known as "compromises." Echoing Vidocq, it was widely believed that "you cannot expect a detective to be an angel of light . . . if our detectives only associated with merchants . . . they would not be in a position to detect lawbreakers and bring them to justice."[19]

But nineteenth-century detectives were rather passive, unless offered a reward. Through the system of compromises, they negotiated with thieves and offered immunity for the return of property. The victim would then pay the detective a "reward," which the detective would share with the thief. The primary goal of the detective was to recover the property and to share in the reward, not to arrest the thief. In contrast with the contemporary property sting, the detective's true identity was known to the thief. As a nineteenth-century account put it, this system amounted to "keeping a set of rogues in pay, for the benefit of police officers."[20]

This meshing of detectives and criminals led to frequent charges of corruption and calls for reform. The first of the ubiquitous American inquiries into corruption took place in 1840 in New York and Philadelphia. By the turn of the century, the system of compromises was generally abolished; police were prohibited from taking payment from citizens for services; and in many cities detective units were reorganized.

Even with the creation of detective units, the main emphasis of municipal departments continued to be on prevention via uniformed patrol. In a crisis, such as an outbreak of pickpocketing, uniformed patrolmen might be assigned to plainclothes and criminal investigation, but this was temporary. In fact, the police commissioner of New York complained bitterly at the turn of the century that, although New York was overrun with "criminals of all nations," its police department was at a disadvantage because it "is unable to employ a secret service. All of the members of the detective bureau as it is at present constituted are easily known to the criminals." The commissioner believed that, with a secret detective service whose identity would be known only to top officials, "wonderful results could be accomplished in the breaking up of criminals' organizations."[21]

In 1906 New York established its "Italian" squad. Foreign radicals, anarchists, socialists, Wobblies, labor organizers, and secret societies, such as the Italian Black Hand and Chinese tongs, were perceived as dangerous new threats by the established order. When cities were smaller and more homogeneous, ethnic diversity did not pose significant problems, but, increasingly, urban departments began to create special squads for ethnic, political, and labor policing. These relied heavily on infiltration and sometimes on provocation. Ironically, they introduced a degree of equal opportunity into local departments because, in order to infiltrate Italian, Black, Jewish, or Chinese groups, one had to use an undercover agent from that group.[22]

Under the impact of early twentieth-century progressive reformers, local police departments became organizationally more complex. In addition to the ethnic squads, there were units concerned exclusively with vice, alcohol, narcotics, gambling, labor, and radicals. All made extensive use of covert means.[23] In addition, departments shifted their focus away from being all-purpose service agencies to giving increased priority to crime. Arrests became increasingly important as both a means and an end.[24] Some of the nonlaw enforcement tasks carried out in many jurisdictions (cleaning streets, driving ambulances, supervising elections, and health, market, and housing inspections) were given up. This meant greater resources for the new specialized units concerned with crime fighting.

With respect to property crime, detectives appeared to become more conscientious and less corrupt, more oriented to organizational goals. They could not avoid involvement with criminals, but the nature of this involvement changed. Detectives shifted from the profitable role of being the direct partner or supervisor of the thief, pickpocket, or con man to playing a greater role in the prevention or limiting of harm.

As the system of compromises broke down, new currencies appeared. Paid informers or "stool pigeons"—those who cooperate with detectives by divulging information or gathering evidence against other criminals— became more important.[25] Police either paid them to "squeal" or else offered leniency for their infractions. The informer's fee became the functional equivalent of the reward previously offered by the victimized person. In most cases, the fee was not paid to the criminal responsible for the crime; instead, an intermediary group emerged that thrived on reporting the wrongdoing of others. Their appearance was part of the development of a more adversarial relationship between police and criminals.

Informers helped make possible undercover operations on a broader and deeper scale. They permitted the police to take a more active interventionist attitude toward crime. This activist stance was aided by efforts to shift control over police from neighborhood (and sometimes corrupt) political leaders to central (and more impersonal) police authority. It was believed that a central authority would be freer to pursue an active fight against crime, vice, and corruption.

By the 1920s the first modern "war on crime" appeared. Many tasks had been taken away from neighborhood patrolmen and precincts and given to specialized units in central headquarters. There were even efforts to "stamp out" vice, rather than simply to license it. Reformers argued that vice could not be eliminated if police were restricted to responding to citizen complaints; they must also be able to act independently. Ironically, the reformers' crusade against corruption came at the cost of breaking with established American traditions that abhorred secret police practices.

THE WESTERN FRONTIER

The Western migration and the technical changes that followed the Civil War created new opportunities for crime and for covert practices in the absence of established law enforcement mechanisms. Robberies of trains, stagecoaches, banks, and the mails, and the theft of cattle and horses were common, as were disputes between various interests, such as cattlemen and homesteaders. The mobility and independence characteristic of the West was conducive to the violation of trust, whether by criminals or police in pursuit of them. Criminals easily switched over to law enforcement or worked both sides of the street simultaneously.[26] Among the well-known Western lawmen who rose from the ranks of gunmen and desperados were Ben Thompson in Texas and Tom Horn in Colorado.

A tactic sometimes used by agents on the frontier and popularized in dime novels was the infiltration of outlaw gangs. A famous Texas Pinkerton agent, Charles Siringo, successfully infiltrated Butch Cassidy's Wild Bunch and captured some of its members. Less successful was the Pinkerton agent who was killed as he tried to infiltrate the Jesse James gang. Arrested criminals, such as the famous Charles (Black Bart) Bolton captured by Wells Fargo detectives, were recruited as undercover operatives.

The reward and fee system was an important feature of early Western law enforcement, and it led to abuses. Sheriffs, marshalls, and private police could supplement their limited income through rewards for capturing wanted men. Wells Fargo, for example, offered a standing reward for each offender arrested for robbing its facilities. As with earlier thief takers, the system sometimes served to increase rather than decrease theft. Aggressive control agents might "gain considerable extra remuneration" by "suggesting or encouraging criminal activity and subsequently making arrests."[27] These kinds of problems led to such reforms as fixed salaries.

PRIVATE AND FEDERAL POLICE

In spite of the romanticized tales of bravado and outlaw gangs and the inherently unstable system of compromises, nineteenth-century undercover practices at the local level were simple, occasional, and organizationally marginal. The private and federal police agencies that began to appear in the later part of the nineteenth century, however, gave American undercover practices a significant boost.

The Anglo-American tradition in the United States and the paucity of federal criminal statutes worked against the establishment of a national police force of any significance until the twentieth century. In Europe, with stronger, more centralized states, national police systems were well developed by the nineteenth century, but in the United States this was not the case. In the absence, then, of anything but the most minimal federal-level police, private agencies filled the void. Burns, Pinkerton, and other agencies were established primarily on behalf of private industrial interests, such as railroads, banks, mines, and factories. Undercover means were central to their operations.

Allan Pinkerton (1819–1884) helped bring covert police practices to the United States. He was an avid abolitionist and experienced in deception through his work on behalf of the Underground Railroad, which helped slaves escape to Canada. He was also a fugitive, having fled his native Scotland in 1842 when he faced arrest for his political activities in support of the Chartist movement.

The symbol of Pinkerton's agency—an observant eye, and its motto, "We Never Sleep"—gave rise to the term "private eye." This appears to have had an unintended second meaning. Not only did the prying eye work for private interests, but it was an eye that was able to peer into normally private places and relationships. It was standard procedure for Pinkerton's agents to gain access by any available means. As Tom Reppetto observes, "the porter who cleaned the suspect's room, the man who shared his cell, or the lady he made love to might be an agent." [28]

Private agencies were also used by the United States government. Until the end of the Civil War, the Treasury Department, as well as the U.S. Post Office, lacked their own detective force and relied on agents, such as Pinkerton's. But in 1865, in response to serious problems of counterfeiting and the filing of fraudulent war bounty claims, the U.S. Treasury created the Secret Service, the first national police force of any significance. The new department drew heavily on the methods and personnel of private detectives. Indeed, during the early years the line between the public and private sectors was blurred as detectives went back and forth, sometimes working for both simultaneously.

The U.S. Post Office established an Office of Inspection in 1836 but made use of private agents for much of its detective work. (Pinkerton worked as an agent for the Chicago post office in the early 1850s.) A major problem for the post office, before the registered mail system was developed, was the theft of mail containing valuables. In a case that a newspaper called the "most important arrest in the annals of Post Office depredations ever brought to light," Pinkerton arrested two postal employees (relatives of the Chicago postmaster at that) for mail theft. [29] Pinkerton's tactic consisted of mailing and then secretly monitoring the passage of decoy letters and packages of the kind reported stolen.

Pinkerton also tested employee honesty and conformity to work rules on the rapidly expanding rail lines. He introduced a more modern rationalized form of undercover work where the investigation was not dependent on a specific complaint. New goals involving general intelligence and prevention emerged alongside the more traditional goals of containment and apprehension of specific offenders.

By the late 1850s, much of Pinkerton's railroad business depended on covertly watching and testing employees. Railroad conductors who collected fares had unique opportunities for corruption and were therefore special targets. The famous 1855 case of conductor Oscar Caldwell is illustrative: through Pinkerton's surreptitious surveillance, Caldwell was arrested for pocketing ticket fees and subsequently sentenced to a year in jail. Workers flocked to his defense and protested Pinkerton's tactics. Management welcomed the tactic as a means by which the railroads could gain greater control over their agents.

In another controversial case, Pinkerton agent James McParland, an Irish immigrant, infiltrated the Molly Maguires. The "mollies" were a group of Irish miners in Pennsylvania believed to be responsible for attacks on mine owners. McParland testified in a series of sensational trials about the inner workings of the group. As a result of his testimony, 12 men were hanged and others imprisoned, even though there were allegations that McParland had lied under oath and acted as a provocateur.[30]

In another case involving immigrants in 1890, the chief of police of New Orleans was gunned down by a group of Italians thought to be responsible for a wave of murders and shakedowns. There was a great public outcry, and 19 Italians were jailed, but the case against them was weak. There were no eyewitnesses and no confessions. If they were to stand trial, better evidence was needed. An Italian-speaking Pinkerton agent, Frank DiMaio, became a "prison spy" and spent four months in jail alongside the suspects, posing as an arrested counterfeiter. The evidence he gathered was presented at their trial, although they were acquitted. As did some other renowned detectives of the time, DiMaio built a career around his knowledge of, and ability to infiltrate, his ethnic group. He went on to become head of Pinkerton's special "Italian squad."

In the 1890s and later, private detective agencies, such as Pinkerton and Burns, came under heavy criticism for their antilabor activities. Although much of this involved the use of guards, goon squads, and strikebreakers, covert strikebreaking efforts and labor spying were also common.

FEDERAL POLICE

The post–Civil War reconstruction era spurred the growth of federal law enforcement to police the vanquished South. Undercover means were used to ensure compliance with measures that met with popular resistance, such as enforcing civil rights for blacks and chasing moonshiners. The new Secret Service and Internal Revenue Service detectives and their informers worked under United States district attorneys.[31]

Postal authorities were among the first federal agents to use undercover tactics. Persons using the mail to distribute pornographic materials were early targets. In the first Supreme Court case involving undercover means, postal inspectors posed as customers and ordered contraband literature through the mail. The material they obtained was admitted into evidence and led to convictions upheld by the Supreme Court.[32]

The Harrison Act of 1914 (making the distribution of nonmedicinal drugs a federal crime) and the Eighteenth Amendment of 1920 (mandating Prohibition) resulted in the creation of narcotics and alcohol enforcement units within the Treasury Department. A tax enforcement intelligence unit was created in 1919. In the 1920s the FBI had only about 300 agents. Within a few years, the number of federal prohibition agents reached 4,000, a figure that dwarfed all previous federal detective forces. The ban on narcotics and alcohol was accompanied by inventive and sometimes questionable covert police practices. Consequently, a body of judicial doctrine emerged that established certain protections for citizens under the Fourth and Fifth amendments, including the landmark Sorrells entrapment case.[33]

In the Sorrells case, the court held that an undercover federal agent had gone too far in the illegal purchase of a half-gallon of liquor. The agent, posing as a tourist, engaged the defendant in conversation over their common war experiences. Having gained the defendant's confidence, the agent asked for liquor. He was twice refused but was provided with liquor on the third try. The agent promptly arrested the defendant, who was then prosecuted for violating the National Prohibition Act. The court found that an otherwise innocent person, with no previous disposition to commit an offense, was lured into it by repeated and persistent solicitation, enhanced by the exploitative and questionable use of friendship. (This case involves a recurring dilemma of covert practices—the distinction between being corrupt and being corruptible.)

Early efforts to enforce alcohol and narcotics prohibitions foreshadowed problems that were to emerge on a larger scale in the 1960s. For example, by 1928 when Prohibition enforcement was shifted to the Department of Justice from the Treasury, 706 agents had been fired for theft, and one-third of them were prosecuted.

The Bureau of Investigation (later called the FBI) was established by Theodore Roosevelt in 1908 against the wish of Congress.[34] Prior to that time, the Department of Justice had no permanent detective force and was reduced to borrowing Treasury agents. Attorney General Charles Bonaparte, a relative of Napoleon, was instrumental in founding the new force. With a small number of agents, few laws to enforce, and limited power, it did not become a significant national police force until the 1930s. It initially dealt primarily with auto theft and offenses against banks.

The FBI made extensive use of informants and passive surveillance in its search for fugitives and in its quest for information. For example, after the 1934 escape of John Dillinger, the FBI

> began as organized a search as was possible, making new contacts, utilizing new underworld informers. Every spot where he had ever been was covered or planted. A plant is the covering of a spot from another point, usually by the renting of a room or an apartment across the street from the place under observation. Many addresses where Dillinger had previously been seen or where any member of his gang was known to have been seen were covered night and day, week after week. His relatives at Mooresville were placed under surveillance.[35]

FBI agents sometimes might play a modest undercover role in crime, for example, posing as a cab driver to deliver ransom in a kidnapping, infiltrating a workplace to observe a suspected extortionist or saboteur, or infiltrating a mental hospital as a patient to gather evidence on a suspect feigning insanity to avoid standing trial. But the FBI, unlike the Department of the Treasury or the Bureau of Narcotics, made little use of complex undercover activities for investigating conventional crime. Covert means were used, however, in political cases, and the FBI faced early criticism because of the "Palmer Raids" (an illegal roundup and deportation of suspected radicals). Until the "Red scare" period that followed World War I, most of the policing of politics in the United States was done by local or private agents.[36]

J. Edgar Hoover is particularly interesting because he was brought in as director of the FBI in 1924 as a reform administrator appointed by Attorney General H. F. Stone. Stone and other leading jurists were concerned that secret police would become a menace to free government and institutions.[37] Hoover's initial public statements were consistent with this emphasis. Thus, in 1932 he recommended that the attorney general *not* give the bureau authority to investigate U.S. Communist activities because "the Bureau would undoubtedly be subject to charges in the matters of alleged secret and undesirable methods . . . as well as to allegations involving the use of 'Agents Provocateur.'"[38]

Covert practices took on new life for the FBI in 1936. President

Franklin Roosevelt charged it with the investigation of Communist and Fascist groups operating in the United States. As part of its domestic intelligence goals, the FBI became responsible for combatting espionage, sabotage, and subversion.

In the postwar period, the FBI's attention was focused primarily on the heavily infiltrated Communist party. As political unrest, social movements, and civil disorders increased during the 1960s, it broadened its domestic intelligence concerns to include New Left, Black, antiwar, and Ku Klux Klan groups. Its activities went beyond gathering intelligence to counterintelligence actions. These activities drew on traditional techniques for dealing with vice and were aided by the Cold War ethos and the presence of former military intelligence agents in police departments.

A more analytic view and more planning came to agencies that traditionally had responded to, rather than seeking to shape, their work environment. A military preparedness view stressed the need for information and taking the offensive. Enhanced intelligence and undercover activities were believed necessary to prevent or limit violations and to position authorities for arrest should incidents occur.

Congressional hearings on the FBI's COINTEL program revealed an extensive program of surveillance, infiltration, disruption, and provocation, much of which was ethically questionable and some of which was clearly illegal.[39] Revelation of such abuses in a context of post-Watergate morality led to reforms and a significant reduction in the secret policing of politics by the mid-1970s.

As protest movements subsided, some of the covert resources that were developed or strengthened in the 1960s were redirected into conventional crime. The 1970s thus saw a greatly expanded federal crime control effort, including the pursuit of nonpolitical undercover activities on an unprecedented scale.

SOME IMPLICATIONS

This chapter has highlighted some major undercover trends and noted some general features in the development of social control.[40] Two conclusions can be drawn: (1) whenever undercover means have been used, certain problems appear; and (2) formal means of control have become more extensive and intensive as the state has grown.

Any treatment of the history of undercover practices in a democratic society is likely to find recurrent problems in their use. They are not simply another investigative tool. Many of the value and policy questions regarding secret detective practices heard in the debates of the 1840s and in the many controversies since then have a contemporary ring. Concern over the invasion of privacy, restrictions on liberty, entrapment, corruption, and stigmatizing of the justice system as a result of its alliances with criminals have been constant features accompanying the use of covert practices. These problems require practitioners and advocates to ask what can and is being done to avoid them and to specify how the competing values ought to be weighed.

The United States has moved far in a short period of time with respect to the acceptance of secret police practices. What once occurred infrequently and was viewed with disdain as a characteristic of continental despotism is now routine administrative practice. This is related to broad changes in social organization, the nature of crime, and the relation of police to the law. In its gradual embrace of covert practices over the past century, the U.S. has broken sharply with its earlier attitudes. There has been a move away from the early British notion of a clearly identifiable citizen- or community-based police, where control agents do not have significant power beyond that of the ordinary citizen, toward the idea that police agents have much greater power than citizens and that policing is a function of the state, not of the citizen.

Elements of a European model of a "high" or "absorbent" political policing involving comprehensive surveillance have been adopted and extended into nonpolitical spheres.[41]

Police figures, such as Allan Pinkerton and J. Edgar Hoover (in an ironic shift from his early days as a reformer), helped convince the American public of the need for, and acceptability of, these tactics. As Pinkerton noted in the popular usage of the 1860s, when he began his career, "the word detective was synonymous with rogue."[42] The sixteen popular books he wrote sought to change this image. He described terrible criminal conditions and exemplary behavior on the part of principled secret agents in response. Several generations later, Hoover, after initially keeping a low public profile, made extensive use of the media to glorify the G men. His adroit manipulation of Cold War and domestic conspiracy fears helped extend and redefine American surveillance attitudes and practices.

Cultural images of social control have changed. Fear of crime has largely replaced fear of a militaristic police. A national poll in 1971 found that only 14 percent of the people felt that the FBI "had gone too far" in "having agents or informers pose as members of militant protest groups," while 29 percent felt they had "not done enough." The secret agent, whether enshrined in film and television, literature, or song, has become something of a cultural hero. Undercover activities work especially well when presented dramatically because the audience knows the double identity of the agents, whereas the other characters don't. Police television programs such as "Hill Street Blues" often involve undercover episodes; earlier programs, such as Jack Webb's "Dragnet," almost never did. Given the role of television in American life, the spread of undercover practices may represent the turning of a dramatic convention into fact, as well as the reverse.

Broad processes of social transformation involving urbanization and industrialization created a context in which both crimes of deception and undercover means would increase. As the informal social controls associated with the small community and traditional family weakened and changed, formal control institutions grew in power. Large urban areas, rapid transportation, geographical and social mobility, and increased interaction with strangers, or interaction carried out electronically (by telegraph and later by telephone, teletypes, and computers) make deception easier. The impersonal relationships and anonymity associated with these conditions provide fertile ground for the projection of false selves, whether against or on behalf of the law.

The local bumbling gangs, street criminals, drunks, and relatively unorganized rioters who shocked upright citizens in the first half of the nineteenth century were supplemented in the last half of that century by skilled and inventive professionals using the latest technology and knowing how to manipulate the enforcement system. Deceit and trickery were seen as necessary to respond to the con artists, pickpockets, counterfeiters, safecrackers, and ideologically or ethnically based conspirators who were appearing in increasing numbers. New forms of criminality appeared, and greater enforcement priority was given to types of crime for which evidence is not easily gathered by overt means, for example, counterfeiting and other monetary violations, fraud, and narcotics. The planned and conspiratorial nature of these lend themselves to secret means of discovery.

There is symmetry in the fact that concrete property rights and visible offenses seemed to call forth uniformed patrols and coercion for protection, while more abstract property rights and invisible offenses called forth invisible police and deception.

There has been a vast expansion of laws and of licensing and regulatory requirements, resulting in a quantum increase in the state's need for information. Federal law enforcement jurisdiction in particular has grown dramatically over the last century. Covert means are sometimes the best or the only way of gathering the relevant information.

Changes in the relation of police to the law also contributed to the expansion of covert practices. At the turn of the century, police, while formally engaged in law enforcement, were not much oriented toward legal norms.[43] As the twentieth century developed, law became increasingly important to the functioning of the criminal justice system, and legal norms have come to play a more prominent role in structuring and limiting police behavior. In the face of restrictions on traditional practices, undercover techniques have become more important as a means of gaining admissible evidence.

The broad increase in covert means over the past century is part of a gradual shift in the United States from a largely rural, unpoliced society to an industrial, policed society. It is rooted in the rise of national and local police institutions. The significant increase in the number and power of the police is part of a broad trend involving the growth of the modern bureaucratic state.

THREE

The Current Context

All my years on the job, it's been the same thing—"catch them
redhanded" or forego prosecution. The number one impetus behind
undercover work is evidence.

—*A Treasury agent, 1984*

The traditional love of liberty, which in this country has always
opposed espionage with so much resolution, is all together
admirable; but like everything else that is precious, it has to be
purchased at a price, and in this case the price is the dangerous
latitude conceded to "the powers that prey."

—*Captain Melville-Lee, 1901*

Recent changes must be seen against a historical background, but a
focus on contemporary events is also needed to understand the expansion of undercover investigations. The diversity of undercover activity
and the absence of standard measures mean that my analysis must be
rather general. Yet it is possible to describe the major causal factors involved in this shift.

Changes in crime patterns, public attitudes and law enforcement priorities, in conjunction with organizational, legislative, judicial, and
technical changes, help account for the shifts in undercover investigations. Several causal sequences can be identified. In perhaps the most
important, changes in crime patterns and priorities encouraged the
search for more effective means. But apart from any changes in crime,
undercover means have spread as a result of:

1.   Moral entrepreneurs, who believed in the potential worth of
undercover means and lobbied for new resources and laws that legitimated and called for use of the tactic[1]

2.   Legal developments associated with the Warren Court that were
perceived to make traditional means less effective and that led to a
search for better means

3.   Technical developments (e.g., improved means of video and
audio surveillance) that made it easier to respond to crimes that once
tended to be ignored.

CHANGING CRIME PATTERNS AND PRIORITIES

Crime patterns and enforcement priorities in recent years have been conducive to increased undercover work. This is true for traditional street crime (which increased significantly from the early 1960s to the early 1970s) as well as for more sophisticated white-collar crime. Political assassinations, civil disorders, and an increase in crimes involving weapons made violence a national issue. Organized crime seemed well entrenched and appeared to be spreading to new areas. Heroin and other serious drug use increased; sophisticated international distribution networks appeared.

The increase in crime was accompanied by a reluctance on the part of citizens to come forward and provide police with information, either as victims, complainants, or witnesses. Whether because of intimidation, increased police-community conflict, or cynicism about whether the police could or would actually do anything, it became more difficult for police to get information at the very time that their need for it increased.[2] This meant greater efforts to develop other sources of information through informants, undercover agents, and electronic surveillance.

The criminal justice system was widely perceived to be overburdened and inadequate.[3] Relative to prior decades, it appeared that a decreasing proportion of offenders were arrested, charged, found guilty, and sentenced. The perception was widespread that the system was in crisis and that new approaches were needed. A "war on crime" was one response. The systematic and imaginative use of traditional undercover means (anticrime decoys, antifencing stings, narcotics sales and purchases) was a part of this new emphasis. The 1970s also saw covert tactics applied to new areas. This reflected changes in priorities, as well as the emergence of white-collar offenses that were virtually nonexistent in earlier time periods.

The increase in white-collar crime has been an important stimulant to the use of covert means. White-collar crimes constitute an increasing proportion of all offenses, and there is considerable public support for enforcement efforts in this area.[4] The proportion of the population working in bureaucratic settings has risen steadily. More and more transactions occur within organizations removed from public observation and control. Organizations have thus emerged as important criminal actors and settings for crime, with offenses carried out either within or on behalf of these institutions.[5]

The nature of property and property transactions has also changed. Forms of property, such as insurance policies, stock options, pensions, and royalties, have become more prevalent, and entitlement programs have expanded.[6] For example, in 1959 entitlement programs were 15 percent of the federal budget; by 1981 they were almost half the budget ($300 billion). This has given rise to new deceptive forms of violation.[7] The evaluation of claims often requires retroactive reviews that rely on third parties.[8] These are subject to falsification and distortion. Protecting this kind of property through simple nineteenth-century uniformed patrols is clearly inadequate.

Unlike traditional crimes, white-collar offenses are often consensual, for example, price fixing and arson, and do not involve victims who are aware of their victimization. Victimization is mediated and diffused across a broad population, for example, the higher prices paid by consumers as a result of price fixing or kickbacks, the higher taxes or poorer services that may result from corruption in government or tax evasion, and the debasement of the grading system that results from the sale of term papers to college students. As with consensual vice offenses, it may be difficult to identify a specific class of victims that has an interest in reporting the offense.

In other cases, as with some environmental and occupational safety violations, for example, toxic dumps and exposure to hazardous substances, victimization may surface only years later. With job changes and geographical mobility, the link between the symptom and cause may never be made. The dispersal or disaggregation of victims prevents the situation from being identified as criminal or being seen as harmful.

White-collar crime is inherently difficult to prosecute because it is often consensual, organized, hidden, insulated, and technical. A ready complainant is often not available, particularly for highly technical violations. Organizational privacy and segmentation lessen visibility.[9] There is no "smoking gun." The offense may occur over time, and information about it may be widely dispersed across institutional settings. Responsibility and intent can be difficult to prove; they may be hidden or diffused throughout an organization. Violators often claim they were merely following orders. The high status of the offender and the resources of the organization can work against conviction, without compelling evidence. Undercover means offer one way of overcoming these difficulties.

It used to "take a thief to catch a thief," but now it may take an organization to catch an organization. As crime becomes more organized, devious, specialized, and complex, so too does law enforcement. A person or organization sharing attributes of the suspects or appearing as a likely victim may be required to gain access and to make sense of highly complex phenomena. Offenses that may not become manifest until years later require a preventive and anticipatory enforcement ethos. For certain white-collar offenses, undercover tactics may not just be the most effective, but the only, means of enforcement.

There is decreasing public tolerance for white-collar offenses. One factor is society's increasing interdependence: many white-collar offenses, such as those involving the environment, pollution, or occupational and product safety, that once might have been regarded as private or insignificant are now seen as vitally affecting the public at large.

Most white-collar violations were treated as civil rather than criminal matters. Large organizations found it relatively easy to resist sanctioning for civil offenses. Even when applied, penalties were often trivial and seemed to have limited deterrent effect. The perception of white-collar offenses as serious and inappropriately sanctioned led to pressure to treat them as criminal rather than civil matters. As the literature suggests, there are also theoretical reasons for expecting that responding to corporate violations via criminal sanctions will have greater impact than is the case with traditional crime.

The civil rights movement helped call attention to the inequity in focusing on the crimes of the powerless, while giving less attention to those of the powerful, or treating their violations as civil rather than criminal matters. Public concern over white-collar crime is related to the diminished faith in institutions revealed by surveys during the 1970s.[10] There is the belief that crime can be found everywhere—even among vice presidents and presidents of the United States, the members of Congress, and the heads of corporations. It thus becomes fair and appropriate to look everywhere and prosecute everyone. Watergate both reflected and contributed to this. Public servants are held to increasingly higher standards.

In the mid-1970s, concerns over white-collar crime were expressed by three high-level government committees. The Attorney General's Committee on White Collar Crime urged aggressive and expanded enforcement efforts. In response to criticism of the FBI after Watergate, a Justice Department committee headed by Harold R. Tyler examined the FBI's priorities and operational guidelines.[11] Its report recommended a shift in emphasis from auto theft and bank robbery to organized crime, white-collar crime, and political corruption. A report by Congressman Don Edwards's House subcommittee charged with FBI oversight made similar recommendations. The report was critical of the FBI for not undertaking more complex investigations and for not making more extensive use of undercover means.

Other pressures came from international sources. In the past decade, Soviet bloc countries appear to have significantly increased their efforts to obtain classified American information and restricted technologies. This and attendant spy scandals, along with threats to bring terrorism to the United States, generated new security concerns.

Heightened concern over both traditional and white-collar crime, as well as national security, led to new enforcement priorities (particularly at the federal level), increased resources for law enforcement, judicial and legislative actions, and the application of new technologies that favor undercover tactics.

ORGANIZATIONAL AND RESOURCE SUPPORTS

These changes in crime patterns and priorities contributed to a significant expansion in the resources available for law enforcement in general and undercover means in particular. They resulted in greater federal funding for local law enforcement, the creation of new units and federal programs, increased support from state and local prosecutors, and more contributions from the private sector. New bureaucratic actors and entrepreneurs appeared.

The importance of the federal government to the spread of undercover police work, whether through the actions of its own agents or through resources provided to local areas, is part of a broader change in the relations between national and local government. In the 1960s a great many local problems—poverty, social welfare, pollution, transportation, housing, and crime—were in a sense nationalized. Federal intervention was generally expected and valued.

The 1968 Omnibus Crime and Safe Streets Act created the Office of Law Enforcement Assistance and changed federal-local law enforcement relations.[12] For the first time, vast federal resources and guidance were made available to local agencies. By the time the Law Enforcement Assistance Administration (LEAA) was phased out in 1982, it had given away over $8 billion.

LEAA was a new interest group whose main organizational goal was to change local law enforcement. It went beyond merely making funds available to selling its programs and ideas. For example, with what seemed to some observers to be missionary zeal, LEAA representatives from the Property Crime Program toured the country introducing local agencies to the idea of fencing stings and offering financial aid and help in setting them up. It sponsored courses on anticrime decoy tactics for local departments. Descriptive material and operations manuals were widely circulated.

A nice example of this can be seen in the origins of the Multnomah County, Oregon, Sheriff's Department stings. The department ran three highly successful stings over a four-year period. The department approached LEAA in 1978 about funds for a white-collar crime project. It was told that an LEAA grant to run a sting operation was available. The police official in charge said, "Fine, but what's a sting grant?" The answer was $450,000 for expenses associated with the investigation, for surveillance equipment, cameras, cars, "buy" money for the purchase of stolen goods, and so on. According to the head of the project, "it was mind-boggling. One of the biggest problems was getting the officers thinking in terms of spending money. They were used to having to get permission to spend three dollars."

This entrepreneurial activity by LEAA was a major factor in the establishment of property stings and anticrime decoys. Once established in large departments that were integrated with national policing networks, the tactic spread rapidly to small, more isolated departments. The tactic generated significant positive publicity. The closing down of a year-long fencing sting was likely to involve many arrests and the recovery (if not necessarily the return) of vast amounts of stolen property. The cases were dramatic and seemed to be a clear moral victory for the good guys, as the deceivers were deceived.

At a time when law enforcement was widely criticized for lack of success and abundance of excess, these tactics had obvious public relations benefits. Here was something that finally seemed to work. A new appreciation for undercover operations developed among many law enforcement officials. Investigators experienced in the use of traditional means were often surprised at how easy it was to penetrate and learn about the urban criminal milieu. As one agent put it, "That shit really works." Imaginative investigators sought new ways to use it. Its success in one context was conducive to its application in others.

The FBI moved from buying stolen property in storefronts to selling truckloads of supposedly stolen goods to fences. Agents realized that "buying stolen car radios and typewriters" did not help them in arresting fences. Secret police simply became rivals to established fences who had their own suppliers of stolen goods. Even the more direct targeting of fences did little for the new federal law enforcement priorities. Property stings rapidly became "ancient history," to be replaced by more sophisticated investigations directed against organized and white-collar crime and corruption.

The FBI created national and local sections concerned with organized crime and public corruption. In 1977 it began requesting appropriations for covert operations and created a national undercover and sensitive operations unit to support local field offices. The FBI's new priorities coincided with the retirement of hundreds of Hoover-era agents. In their place came a new, more diverse, aggressive, and innovative cohort of younger agents, including more women and minority group members.

In January 1976 the Department of Justice created a public integrity section within its criminal division. This was staffed by 7 attorneys the first year; by 1981, 25 attorneys were involved. The section took pride in its "considerable expertise in the supervision and oversight of the use of undercover operations in serious corruption cases." This expertise included offering training seminars, lectures, and consultations to prosecutors and investigators "in substantive and procedural matters necessary for the successful prosecution of corruption cases." Over the next decade, the number of federal indictments involving corruption charges increased almost fourfold to 1,182 in 1985.[13]

Other new federal resources supportive of undercover activities came from the Federal Witness Protection Program, the organized crime strike forces, the Federal Law Enforcement Training Center in Georgia, offices of Inspectors General, and the Central Intelligence Agency.

The Organized Crime Control Act of 1970 sought to enhance witness cooperation by providing better protection. What began as "safe houses" run by the U.S. Marshall's Service expanded by the end of the decade to a program that provided new identities. By the end of 1987, almost 12,000 witnesses and family members had been relocated.[14] Many of these people only gave testimony, but some became involved in undercover operations. The ability to offer an informer a new identity is an important inducement to cooperate, particularly when it is combined with a promise of avoiding prosecution.

Through the Fugitive Investigative Strike Team (FIST), which appeared in 1981, the Marshall's Service has also sponsored joint federal-local covert efforts to trap fugitives. This matches the organizational resources and expertise of the federal marshalls with the knowledge of local police. Local police are deputized as U.S. marshalls and thus become empowered to arrest fugitives throughout a state.

The strike force approach to organized crime is typically led by a federal prosecutor who coordinates the activities of the various federal law enforcement agencies. It is focused around specific goals and targets, such as a particular organized crime group or offense. It relies on mutual planning, shared intelligence, and coordinated actions among agencies that traditionally operate independently, such as the FBI and IRS.

The Federal Law Enforcement Training Center was established in 1970 to consolidate the training of law enforcement officials from 50 federal organizations. It conducts a wide variety of courses, ranging from basic training for new agents (instruction in working with informants, conducting surveillance, and working undercover) to specialized and refresher courses for more experienced practitioners (advanced law enforcement, photography, white-collar crime). The number of students enrolled in courses increased from 2,174 in 1975 to 16,414 in 1986.

In 1978 Congress required all federal Cabinet agencies to create the office of Inspector General. This enhanced federal law enforcement capability. One of their major concerns was the discovery of fraud in government programs. Some offices, such as that of the Department of Agriculture, which with hundreds of agents is the third largest federal police force, have used undercover means in ferreting out "fraud, waste, and abuse."

Between the mid-1960s and mid-1970s, the CIA provided a number of local police departments with training, technical assistance, surveillance equipment, and intelligence information. The extent of support cannot be determined from the available documents. Some was provided surreptitiously: for example, CIA agents working with police departments pretended to be "consultants" from the Law Enforcement Assistance Administration.[15]

New revenues for undercover work also became available (whether directly or indirectly) as a result of forfeiture laws, fines, and policies that made it possible to keep or sell property ("ill-gotten gains"— money, vehicles, other equipment) seized in undercover and related operations (e.g., those involving RICO and controlled substance violations). Thus the 1984 Comprehensive Crime Control Act made it easier for the government to do this and gave the U.S. Attorney General authority to transfer seized property to states and local police agencies. Over a 21-month period starting in 1981, hundreds of the planes, boats, and vehicles seized by Customs Service agents in drug raids were sold at auction and brought $57.5 million to the federal treasury. In 1985 the FBI's fleet of undercover cars contained 543 seized vehicles, ranging from motorcycles to Mercedes. In 1986 a "senior Saudi prince" paid $150,000 to the U.S. Fish and Wildlife Service because he unlawfully purchased 17 falcons smuggled from the United States. An undercover informer working for the Fish and Wildlife Service provided the birds. The money will be used to pay for tips on wildlife poaching, potentially leading to new undercover operations.

In some cities, revenue from insurance payments or from the sale of property purchased in local fencing stings has been returned to police departments for use in other undercover operations. In southern Florida, over a two-year period the courts in Fort Lauderdale awarded the city $3.1 million in cash and assets, primarily as a result of seizures in narcotics cases. Thus, a new $1 million jail was financed, if indirectly, by those in the drug business. In a period of financial constraint, the potential of undercover work to be self-sustaining and even to raise revenue for other uses, has obvious, if question-raising, appeal.

The private sector has also made financial and other resources available for public or joint public-private undercover operations. Among the suppliers have been insurance companies, manufacturers, trade associations, and chambers of commerce. Some of their contributions have been locations, personnel, and materials. The record industry, for example, contributed $100,000 for Operation Mod-Sound directed against pirated records and tapes.

As noted, the private sector historically has made extensive use of undercover tactics, but generally not for purposes of prosecution. Rather, covert means have been used to recover stolen property, to deny a claim, to gather intelligence, and to manage and fire employees. In recent years, however, many industry groups have become more prosecution oriented.

The insurance industry is a good example. Increases in insurance crime have led many companies to create their own fraud-investigating units. An umbrella organization, the Insurance Crime Prevention Institute (ICPI), supported by 400 companies, was established in 1971. It has no official powers, but it has provided support to a number of law enforcement agencies for insurance-related undercover operations (it financed the first fencing sting in Connecticut). The ICPI contributed to an initial 221 arrests in 1972, the first year after its founding; arrests increased to 1,229 in 1979–80. The National Auto Theft Bureau (NATB), a private organization also sponsored by insurance companies, has played a similar role.[16] In 1981 its agents contributed to the prosecution of 1,706 persons on larceny, auto theft, and fraud charges.

Changes associated with the increased professionalism of local police and prosecutors also support the expansion of undercover activities. Led by such reformers as O. W. Wilson and William Parker, the police professionalism movement that began in the 1950s sought to introduce modern management techniques and ideas. New emphasis was put on record keeping, research and planning, intelligence and crime data collection, and quantitative measurement of effectiveness through indicators, such as the number of arrests or the amount of stolen property or contraband seized.

In the more professional police departments, agents were no longer satisfied with merely isolating crime areas or responding to after-the-fact complaints. Crime fighting via aggressive tactics and prevention was given greater priority. More sophisticated intelligence and planning systems meant greater police initiative and involvement. Greater weight was given to anticipating crime and encountering it on police terms. Persons thought likely to commit crimes (e.g., those with prior convictions) and places where crimes were thought likely to occur were secretly watched, and stop-and-search tactics were adopted. As part of anticorruption efforts, covert means were used internally on a larger and more systematic scale.[17]

Increasingly, it was possible to document the limited effectiveness of many traditional strategies and tactics, thereby encouraging the search for new and better means. For example, received wisdom regarding traditional reactive means, such as the connection between uniform patrol and crime reduction or the effectiveness of detectives and scientific detection, became subject to systematic empirical study and questioning.[18] The wisdom was found wanting.

Undercover work fits well with the above concerns. It grows easily out of an emphasis on planning, prevention, and productivity. It offers a means of actively pursuing crime through direct involvement and police initiative. It fits with the notion of the modern police officer prevailing via intelligence, skill, and finesse, rather than brute force and coercion. It draws on the principle of jujitsu rather than boxing. The changes in organization and attitude attributed to the police professionalism movement encouraged undercover activities well before the arrival of the new resources discussed above. When they did arrive, they found a receptive environment.

The increasingly bureaucratic and professional orientation of state and local prosecutors' offices is also relevant to the expansion of covert operations. With the decline of the urban political machine and greater professionalization in selection, prosecutors are less bound to those in power or to private interests. The professional rewards for prosecution of white-collar crime and corruption seem to have increased and the risks decreased. Given greater investigative resources and political independence than in the past, some prosecutors have aggressively gone after white-collar crime and corruption. Increased independence and professionalism of judges may also mean that, once presented, such cases are more likely to be treated on their merits rather than on political considerations.

With the increased emphasis on white-collar violations and on anticipating crimes that have not yet occurred, prosecutors have become more important in the initiation and supervision of investigations. Involvement during the investigative stage contrasts with their more traditional and passive role of merely prosecuting cases brought to them after arrest. The number of investigators working out of prosecutors' offices and the number of detective bureaus located within state attorneys' general and district attorneys' offices has increased in many jurisdictions.

The relationship between prosecutors and police is an important and little-studied aspect of the administration of criminal justice.[19] Prosecutors play a more active role setting priorities, establishing targets, and supervising undercover work than is the case for other types of policing.

JUDICIAL AND LEGISLATIVE SUPPORTS

The third degree isn't necessary when you've got the facts.
Special agents get the facts.
                    —*FBI Agent Melvin Purvis, 1936*

Recent judicial and legislative changes have encouraged the spread of undercover tactics in two general ways: indirectly, by creating new restrictions on conventional forms of police investigative behavior; and directly, by broadening their legal foundation.

In the historical review, I noted that police behavior over the past century has come to be more controlled by law. Where once arrests could be made without reasonable grounds and evidence obtained almost at will from searches, wiretaps, coercive interrogations, raids, and arrest sweeps, this is no longer the case. Grounds for suspicion must be shown for stopping persons; warrants are required for wiretaps and most searches. Many of the laws that accounted for a large proportion of arrests, such as vague nineteenth-century disorderly conduct and vagrancy standards, have been declared unconstitutional. The growth of civil liberties and civil rights organizations and the provision of defense counsel for the poor have also made questions of proper evidence and procedure more salient.

In a series of major decisions (Miranda, Mapp), the Supreme Court under Earl Warren strengthened and extended the role of law in controlling police behavior. State and local police were required to adhere to many of the same restrictions on evidence gathering as federal agencies.

The exclusionary rule that denies police the use in court of illegally gathered evidence, the privilege against self-incrimination (the confession has always played an insignificant role in the United States), restrictions on interrogation while in custody, and limitations on search and seizure and arrest have indirectly encouraged undercover work.

This contrasts with many European countries where the standard of suspicion for a search or arrest is lower, persons can be held and interrogated for a longer period of time without charges being brought, self-incriminating statements need not be corroborated, and even evidence obtained through illegal searches and seizures can generally be introduced in court. There is far less undercover work for conventional crime in Europe. It appears that, within democratic societies, the greater the restriction on police in overt investigations, the greater will be their use of covert investigations. (This does not hold for totalitarian societies where the few restrictions on overt police behavior occur with extensive covert activities.)

One response to the higher standards in the United States, and to what many police perceived to be new restrictions under the Warren Court, is for them to simply do less; another is to seek imaginative ways around them. The use of informants and undercover work are all means of getting around them and "getting the facts."[20] Problems with the rules of evidence, the search for a suspect, interrogation, suspect's rights, guilt, and testimony are less likely to occur if an undercover officer has been a direct party to the offense, and it has been electronically recorded.

There is an interesting irony at work here: restrict police use of coercion, and the use of deception increases. Restrict investigative behavior after an offense, and increased attention will be paid to anticipating an offense.

Judicial decisions also have provided *direct* support to undercover means by finding them (and a variety of supportive practices) legal. Challenges to covert practices have usually been rejected by the Supreme Court as well as by lower federal courts. For example, the Hoffa case found that paid informants are not subject to Fourth Amendment restrictions the way a form of "surreptitious eavesdropping," such as wiretapping, is. Citizens are not held to have a "reasonable expectation of privacy" that their associates are not police operatives or informants. The White case found that no privacy right is invaded when an undercover agent records or transmits sound. The Russell case adopts a predispositional, rather than a police methods, view of entrapment.[21] The courts have come to favor a subjective approach to entrapment by focusing on the character and presumed predisposition of the arrested person, rather than on the objective behavior of police. Authorities may legally create, encourage, and participate in crime in addition to passively offering an opportunity to predisposed persons. American courts are now relatively indifferent to police behavior in undercover activities until an arrest actually occurs.[22]

Under Chief Justices Burger and Rehnquist, some of the restrictions of the Warren Court have been eased, e.g., on search and seizure. Supreme Court decisions in the past decade are part of the federal judiciary's general retreat from efforts to regulate police behavior during investigative (as against arrest and trial) stages of police activity. The court has made it clear that it is the job of the legislative and executive branches, rather than the judiciary, to set proper standards for police behavior, unless truly shocking circumstances or recognized constitutional rights are involved.[23] Cases that do not result in arrest are even further beyond the normal judicial reach.

Undercover means lend themselves well to inferences of guilty knowledge. They offer a powerful tool for gaining leverage over a suspect and for obtaining probable cause. They are attractive to prosecutors because they permit introducing into evidence conversations and inferences that would be prohibited were they carried out after an arrest. An experienced prosecutor even goes so far as to suggest that "a suspect who remains silent or lies in conversations with an undercover agent [when a lie can be proven] is as good as offering a confession."

Evidence of culpability is offered as a result of (1) admission by adoption (an undercover agent makes a statement, such as "You were paying the sheriff more than we were to let the drugs through," to which the suspect responds, "Yeah") and (2) admission by silence ("You burned that building in order to collect the insurance," to which the suspect says nothing). In the latter case, the assumption is that a nonguilty person would not remain silent. The failure to object offers competent evidence of agreement. Silence is taken as behavior here; in contrast, silence in response to a question at a trial is not to be taken as an indicator of guilt. As an investigation is drawing to a close, but before arrests, even an interview by an agent who identifies himself can yield "false exculpatory statements" that are of substantial value in cross-examination at trial (e.g., that the subject does not know any of the middlemen or never attended any meetings with an undercover agent). From a prosecutor's standpoint, timing is central, and simultaneous interviews are often carried out before subjects can talk to each other or learn of indictments and the existence of tapes. Wiretap information can be particularly revealing at this time.

When it can be independently shown that another person was part of a conspiracy, statements made by co-conspirators can be introduced as evidence against the suspect, even if they were not a party to the conversation. All parties to a conspiracy are equally responsible for what any other conspirators do.

The Supreme Court has sanctioned surveillance practices that support undercover means. For example, it has ruled that a search warrant is not needed for police to track a moving object by monitoring the signal from an implanted radio transmitter. In this case, a beeper was placed inside a five-gallon container of chloroform, a chemical used in the manufacture of methamphetamines. It was tracked over backroads to a secluded cabin. In writing for the Court, Justice Rehnquist stated, "nothing in the Fourth Amendment prohibited the police from augmenting the sensory faculties bestowed upon them at birth with such enhancement as science and technology afforded them. . . ."[24]

Another judicial practice that appears to support undercover means is the acceptance of secret "guilty" pleas. Between 1980 and 1982, at least seventy-five federal defendants in the Manhattan area were permitted to enter secret guilty pleas. Only the judge, lawyers, and the defendant are present at the proceedings, of which a sealed record is kept. The rationale for the secrecy is to shield the undercover work of witnesses or defendants who become witnesses.

Judicial decisions and practices of the past decade have thus legitimated and supported diverse undercover activities. Covert investigations are not seen as unwarranted invasions of privacy nor as violations of the Fourth and Fifth amendments. There are no clear legal limitations on the intimacy of the relationship that may be under investigation, the degree of trickery and deception present, the length of time an investigation may go on, the seductiveness of the temptation offered, or the number of times a person may be tempted.

Although the relative indifference of the courts has not meant an eternally green light for any undercover practice, it has meant that police may largely decide for themselves what the outer limits of permissible undercover behavior are.

LEGISLATION

Unlike some Western European countries or Japan, legislatures in the United States have indirectly supported undercover practices by their consistent failure to set standards and goals for police performance. Legislatures, like the courts, generally prefer to leave such matters to police, thus enacting a kind of legitimacy by default. The failure to prohibit or regulate potentially problematic tactics represents "legislative acquiescence."[25]

Another indirect support may also, ironically, come from state and federal privacy legislation. This legislation has to a degree inhibited banks, credit bureaus, employers, schools, utilities, and public agencies from routinely giving out information to police. There may be an increase in subterfuge, pretexts, and trickery to obtain information that was previously forthcoming through a simple request.

Some indirect support may also have come from the Freedom of Information Act, although this is debatable. Former FBI Director Webster has referred to informants as an "endangered species," and a supervisor of covert FBI operations writes, "to a certain extent, we have had to turn to the use of undercover agents because of increased fear among potential sources that their identities would be divulged, perhaps through FOIA disclosures. This fear has significantly reduced the number of informants on whom we can rely."[26]

Legislatures have more directly encouraged undercover work by the types of laws recently passed. The nature of criminal law and criminal procedure are crucial factors in shaping police behavior. In essence, the history of undercover practices is largely a history of the type of laws an agency enforces and the latitude permitted police by the criminal justice system. The nature of the evidence required for conviction is a central factor conditioning the use of covert means. Although laws regarding an offense are unlikely to rule out the use of undercover means, they may well do the opposite, namely, make it certain that only these means will be used.

In recent decades, changing laws and changing legal definitions of crime have directly facilitated undercover practices. Many new laws and new interpretations regarding corruption, racketeering, contraband, and tax violations have appeared. A clear example of the link between new laws and increased undercover work can be seen with the passage of the 1968 Gun Control Act.[27] This act significantly expanded federal licensing and record-keeping requirements and created a number of new offenses. It criminalized what can be called "derivative" or secondary offenses, such as the failure to file a particular form. Such violations were easily investigated through undercover means. This is also the case with violations created by new wildlife and environmental legislation. Thus the Endangered Species and Migratory Bird Treaty Acts and various amendments in the 1970s prohibited or limited the trade in a number of species. In the case of peregrine falcons, for example, detailed regulations regarding handling, record-keeping, and reporting were established, and it was made illegal to take, possess, transport, sell, or purchase wild birds. Poaching could be dealt with via traditional patrols, but conspiracy, smuggling, fraud, and procedural violations were seen to require covert means.

Some state laws are also changing in ways that are conducive to undercover work. The Model Penal Code and the legislation it has inspired abolish the "legal impossibility" defense to the crime of attempt. A person's liability depends on their state of mind and not on the actual legal status of possessed goods, for example, whether the "stolen" goods they purchased were in fact stolen.

In some states, it is now a crime to purchase a substance, such as sugar, if it is purchased in the belief that it is heroin or to purchase goods from an undercover agent in the belief that they are stolen, even when they are not. As in a Seattle case, agents may have purchased the goods they sell as "stolen" from a reputable dealer, using a government grant. Here it is the "attempt" to carry out a crime that constitutes the offense. The fact that it is factually (though not legally) impossible to carry out is deemed irrelevant.

This change in the status of "stolen" goods came in response to prior laws that required goods to retain their stolen character throughout the process of redistribution.[28] Thus, when stolen property was recovered by authorities, it immediately lost its "stolen" character. In contrast, drugs do not lose their contraband quality when in possession of authorities.

Where the doctrine of "legal impossibility" is subscribed to, it is difficult to convict fences of attempted receipt of stolen property, even if an apprehended thief could be compelled to go along and sell it to the fence. Instead, authorities need to go through the more cumbersome or less practical technique of trying to track the stolen goods from a distance. Where the "legal impossibility" defense has been abolished, however, "attempt" laws make it possible for officials to intervene immediately and to maintain control as the property is exchanged. This also permits "bait sale" stings where an undercover agent seeks to sell supposedly stolen goods without the arrest of any thief or the recovery of stolen property. Because only an "attempt" is at issue, it is not necessary to prove that the merchandise was actually stolen or to identify it positively as the property of a particular victim of crime.

New legislation and judicial decisions against discrimination on sexual and racial grounds have also encouraged and shaped undercover practices. In the case of race, both public and private groups have used covert means to document infractions. It is difficult to prove an intent to discriminate without systematic tests. This has led to what amounts to controlled inquiries following the logic of the scientific experiment. For example, in test cases equivalent black and white individuals may apply for housing or a job where discrimination is suspected. Use of the tactic has been upheld by the Supreme Court.[29]

The traditional sweep or dragnet where people were rounded up without specific cause has long been used as a tactic ("Round up the usual suspects, Louie"). But in the changed legal climate, this was viewed as unconstitutional. The prohibition on sweeps along with increased awareness of sex discrimination has meant changes in vice enforcement. After an Oakland, California, judge found that it was discriminatory to arrest female prostitutes and not their male customers, the Oakland police shifted tactics. Extensive use was made of female police agents who posed as prostitutes and arrested the men who propositioned them. The magnitude of this law-induced shift is revealed in the fact that in 1974, 663 females were arrested for prostitution, while only 21 of their male customers were arrested. In 1975, after the judge's ruling, 651 females and 461 males were arrested.

In addition to the enactment of new laws, the scope of federal law enforcement has significantly expanded. The Supreme Court has broadened the Hobbs Act's application to anyone who obstructs interstate commerce—including those who offer bribes, as well as local, state, and federal officials.[30] Interstate commerce might be obstructed because of a threat of violence and direct extortion or merely by obtaining government benefits passively "under color of official right." This interpretation eliminates a large burden of proof for the government and opened the way to the vast increase in federal corruption prosecutions noted above. The federalization of local crime has also been aided by the liberal application of the Travel Act of 1961. This act makes it a federal offense to use the facilities of interstate commerce (including the mail or telephone) with the intention of engaging in unlawful activity. It offers federal agents a means of gaining jurisdiction over purely local matters that local agents are unable or unwilling to act upon.

In a 1981 decision, the Supreme Court held that the 1970 RICO (Racketeer Influenced and Corrupt Organizations) Act was not restricted to the prosecution of criminal organizations that infiltrate or take over legitimate businesses.[30] This decision upheld the broad interpretation of the law that the Justice Department had been applying. The 1970 RICO statute creates a new category of crime—racketeering. It is now illegal to conduct the activities of any "enterprise" through "a pattern of racketeering activity," defined as a violation of 2 or more of any of 32 state and federal laws. The 1981 decision justified extension of the law to associations of persons engaged in the theft and fencing of property, loan sharking, and narcotics importing and distributing among others. These changes have given federal agents important new tools against corruption and white-collar and organized crime. Undercover means are often used to gather the relevant evidence.

A clear example of how the law's requirements shape police means can be seen in a 1979 Supreme Court decision regarding legislative behavior and criminal actions.[31] The Court held that the debate clause in the U.S. Constitution prohibits an already performed legislative act from being introduced into evidence, even in bribery prosecution; the separation-of-powers doctrine makes evidence regarding legislative behavior nonadmissible.[32] For example, if a member of Congress takes a bribe and in return introduces a bill, evidence on acceptance of the bribe could be introduced in court, but not evidence regarding the legislation. It thus becomes imperative to collect evidence that a person *intended* to do an illegal favor. One source is, of course, testimony by the person offering the bribe, but, because such persons themselves are usually corrupt, they tend to lack credibility and will cooperate only under duress. Much stronger evidence comes when a recording or videotape of the transaction is possible.

There has been an increase in the number of laws that criminalize actions that emerge only as an artifact of efforts to enforce laws. Certain offenses appear as incidental, for example, prosecutors who initially set out to make cases of corruption, food and drug violations, or fraud may be unable to prove the targeted crime, but still be able to prosecute for perjury or obstruction of justice. Such violations appear only after the investigation has begun.

One aspect of this has been the development of rules requiring that bribe attempts and other improper behavior be reported. Such rules can result in integrity tests being taken to a new extreme: targets may face double testing—first, to see if they will accept a corrupt offer and, second, to see if they will report the offer. A person may become a target of an undercover trap not because he is suspected of corruption, but to see if bribes are reported or other procedural rules are followed. This regulation also offers a possible tool for getting rid of an employee seen as troublesome who cannot otherwise be dismissed.

SURVEILLANCE TECHNOLOGY

In 1928 Justice Brandeis wrote: "The progress of science in furnishing the Government with means of espionage is not likely to stop with wiretapping. Ways may some day be developed by which the Government . . . will be enabled to expose to a jury the most intimate occurrences of the home."[33]

Justice Brandeis was correct. The "progress of science" in such matters has been striking, and the development of highly intrusive, easily hidden surveillance technology has encouraged certain types of undercover work and may condition how it is carried out.

Unlike the legal and resource changes supportive of undercover work, the surveillance technology did not emerge in response to changing crime patterns and pressures. It was developed primarily for military, foreign intelligence, and home entertainment purposes. But it found a ready law enforcement market and a supportive legal environment.

Title III of the federal Omnibus Crime Control and Safe Streets Act of 1968 introduces a warrant requirement and other limits on certain forms of electronic surveillance. However, the act also permits wiretap evidence to be introduced in court, something that was previously forbidden (other than for espionage cases). Wiretapping was illegal under the 1934 Federal Communications Act. Some courts have accepted what prosecutors call "dynamic probable cause" for issuing wiretap approval. Granting wiretap authorization is not restricted to a provable narrow crime, but to a combination of likely criminal circumstances. Between 1980 and 1985 the number of federal wiretaps authorized increased from 79 to 243.

Undercover efforts can offer an alternative to bugs and wiretaps, being used when it is not possible to obtain a warrant for electronic surveillance. The undercover agents' information may then provide grounds for a warrant. But they are often used together. Most of the electronic surveillance associated with covert means is not subject to a warrant restriction because it occurs either in public or in situations where one of the parties consents, e.g., the agent or a victim. The single-party consent laws found in most states permit this (although there is always a risk of these changing to a nonconsensual status, e.g., a recorder concealed in a briefcase or other package will continue to record should the agent leave without it, or the agent may be asked to leave a wired room so the subjects can privately confer).

As a result of miniaturization and other technological developments, surveillance equipment has become smaller, easier to conceal, and more portable. It has also become more reliable, more powerful, and more intrusive. Longer-lasting and stronger batteries have temporally and spatially extended transmission range. Aided by remote-controlled and self-activated devices, it has become relatively easy to observe and/or monitor and record transactions secretly. The development of tiny radio transmitters, subminiature tape recorders, night vision technologies, and hidden video cameras illustrates this.

In the past decade, tiny body bugs that operate as radio transmitters came into widespread use. They significantly increase the range and broaden the conditions under which conversations can be overheard. The body bug may carry sound to agents concealed nearby or to a transmitter hidden in the trunk of a nearby car. The sound can be automatically amplified and retransmitted to agents who are farther away. Supporting agents know when to intervene for purposes of arrest or to protect the agent. The entire transmission can be recorded.

In the mid-1970s, reel-to-reel, subminiature tape recorders began to be used on a wide scale. Originally developed for foreign intelligence purposes, their use spread to the film industry and later to police, as entrepreneurs sought new markets. These tiny (1 7/8" by 15/16"), self-contained units can avoid discovery by antibugging devices and the technical and coordination problems that may be present when the sound must be transmitted back to a recording device. They offer superior fidelity and will record for two hours.[34]

By 1975 police (along with the public) were making increased use of video equipment. Video cameras that used 1/2" rather than 3/4" tape became available. This replaced both the standard motion picture camera and fixed-location filming. Videotaping is less expensive and permits instant playback. Smaller, more portable, concealable, and versatile cameras meant new opportunities for creating a visual record of violations. Before these developments, the main use of cameras in covert operations involved still photography using powerful lenses (300 mm) to identify subjects and where possible to show them in the company of the undercover agent at a particular location. This could be introduced in court to counter defense claims that the defendant had never met the target.

Other new or improved technology, such as light amplifiers, zoom lenses, unobtrusive panic buttons, beepers, various infrared, sensor, and tracking devices, and the availability of higher quality, more reliable, small firearms (derringers and Berrettas in lieu of police .38 Specials), has extended the range of undercover means and/or made them more practical. For example, light amplifiers may be used with a variety of cameras or binoculars. They turn night settings into daylight. Known as "starlight scopes," they work on the same principle as parabolic mikes. These have significantly expanded the security, documentation, and surveillance possibilities of night operations.

Developments in computer-aided video photography that permit the reconfiguration of images can offer useful props for an operation. Thus, in the Aryan Nations' contract murder case, the individual who ordered the murder was shown a doctored photo by the undercover agent. The photo made it appear that the intended victim's head had been severed from his body.[35]

The technology may even condition whether or not an operation is carried out. Indeed, some prosecutors are hesitant to authorize undercover means unless a tape can be made. Some police supervisors prefer not to use undercover means unless they can monitor what happens. Technology may become an unwitting factor affecting investigative discretion.

The requirements of technology may introduce departures from the way criminal activities would ordinarily develop. Greater use may be made of the telephone because conversations can so easily be recorded without fear of detection. There may be pressure to interact with and record principal figures rather than working through intermediaries. Undercover activities may be restricted to settings where bugs can be placed, where transmissions will be clear, and where backup support can be hidden, but quickly available. The use of the video camera encourages fixed-location settings, such as hotel rooms, houses, and businesses (although in several cases airplanes used in drug smuggling have been fitted with hidden cameras that recorded the loading of drugs). The organization and fixed location of most police-run fencing fronts clearly reflect these needs.

The technology supports stage management and scripted scenarios. Targets will be encouraged to locate themselves so that they are in front of the camera; aware of the recording, agents may guide conversations to see if incriminating statements can be made. Where a suspect's statements are ambiguous, the conversation may be subtly redirected so that the criminal intent is made clear. Agents may find it necessary to have conversations that were initially not subject to electronic surveillance repeated so they can be documented. There may be efforts to "get the wire humming" by using the grand jury, planting false stories in newspapers, and using agents and informants to spread rumors about pending arrests and cooperating witnesses, in efforts to stimulate conversation.

Electronic surveillance is supportive of undercover work in at least three ways: to enhance security, as a management tool, and to provide evidence. It may enhance the security of an agent or an operation. Should the agent's true identity become known or other unexpected contingencies occur, backup teams can intervene. If an arrest is to be made, waiting agents can move in at a prearranged signal. Electronic monitoring may also be useful as a supervisory and management tool. It permits documenting reports of agents and informants and may thus increase accountability. It may help demonstrate to the jury and judge the nature of the controls over an operation (although the logistical problems involved in promptly reviewing and transcribing the tapes in a complex, wide-ranging case can be horrendous). The volume of taped material can easily outstrip a local office's resources (it takes about ten hours to transcribe one hour of conversation).

In some cases, electronic surveillance allows for immediate feedback. It enables problems to be anticipated. In the case of Abscam, for example, a U.S. attorney was in the basement of the building where the deal was being discussed, monitoring the conversation. In one instance when it looked like the undercover agent was engaging in entrapment, a phone call was put through and he was told how to redirect the conversation.

Of particular importance is the evidentiary role that electronic surveillance can play. The impact of electronically gathered evidence on obtaining guilty pleas is strong (the extent to which this is warranted is another question). Before recorded evidence the suspect could simply lie and say the conversation never took place. Now they can't deny it and instead must explain it. Such evidence tends to keep defendants off the stand. Cross examination by the prosecutor is too big a risk. If the case actually goes to trial their strategy may be to "try the prosecution witness and hope for lightning to strike."

Video also adds an extra dimension in capturing incriminating nonverbal communication. As one agent put it, "a wink can convict" by indicating agreement with, or direction for, criminal activity. The video may overcome actions taken to thwart audio surveillance; for example, talking in code, saying nothing or the opposite of what one is doing or gesturing, passing a note with the figure requested for a bribe, or the destruction of evidence by flushing drugs down the toilet. The video is especially useful where the victim is in an altered state of consciousness. Take, for example, a case where female patients complained of being sexually exploited by their dentist while under anesthesia. Their testimony would be attacked because they were sedated, but, if the dentist's actions were documented via a hidden video camera, the evidence is likely to be unimpeachable.

Video and audio evidence are also important for cases involving public officials. In police corruption cases without taped evidence, accusations of police misconduct simply involve the word of one police officer against another. It is similarly difficult to think of Abscam and its near-perfect conviction record without the evidence provided by videotapes. Without tapes, the situation would have involved the word of a respected congressman against an informant with an easily impugned reputation. The effort would probably not have been undertaken (or at least been less extensive) without the supporting electronic surveillance.

A tape greatly enhances the credibility of testimony. The contrast between the appearance, language, and behavior caught on the tape and the well-mannered image that the defendant may present in court is often striking. Juries are in a better position to see what the agent actually saw, rather than hear it argued about in the courtroom where persons seek to put forward the best possible image. The tape captures the demeanor and tone of the target in a way that after-the-fact verbal testimony cannot. Jurors attuned to television are highly receptive to video evidence. Of course, it can be a double-edged sword should agents forget that video or audio tapes are present (in one case, agents were overheard discussing the sexual activities and attributes of an attractive female assistant U.S. attorney, and, in another, the agent asked an informer to locate a prostitute).

Developments in electronic surveillance have permitted the use of undercover means in instances where they might not have been used because of concern over supervision, security, or credibility in the courtroom. There is nothing deterministic about the technology per se. The uses to which it is put reflect social and political needs. Advances in surveillance technology coincided with the search for better means of carrying out criminal investigations. In a responsive setting, they enhance undercover capabilities.

FOUR

Types and Dimensions

The chief cannot know too much about the community, and he dare
not know too little.

—Police inspector

We shall provoke you to acts of terror and then crush you.
—C. B. Zubatov, Tsarist police director

Contemporary discussions of undercover work frequently offer either
sweeping praise or categorical condemnation without making any distinctions among the types of operations and activities. This is unfortunate, because differences in type and form must be understood before
undercover work can be explained, evaluated, or managed.

Tolstoy has written of the exquisite complexity of the world. To take
one small corner of it—the variety of police investigations is almost end-
less, and, looked at closely, each operation is unique. The social researcher seeks to document this empirical richness but also to generate
concepts that help us see commonalities among seemingly diverse phenomena and differences among seemingly similar phenomena.

What are the main types of operation and the main sources of variation within and between them? There is no one right way to classify police activities. Classifications are judged by their usefulness, which in
turn depends on one's goal. My goals are to document and explain
undercover operations, draw conclusions about their desirability or un-
desirability, and to suggest areas where policy is most needed. Toward
this end, this chapter defines three types of operation based on goals (intelligence, prevention, facilitation) and ten dimensions by which these
can be further contrasted.

INTELLIGENCE OPERATIONS

Intelligence operations use covert and deceptive tactics to gather information about crimes that have already occurred, are or might be planned, or are in progress. The agent's role tends to be relatively passive, involving observation and questioning, rather than an effort to direct the interaction. The agent is an "informational sponge" and like "the fly on the wall" in order not to alter a suspect's environment, although elements of the environment are deceptively presented in order to elicit information and even the most passive agent is likely to have some influence on the setting by his mere presence. There may be pressures in the role (the need to establish one's credentials, reciprocity, deeper access) that push toward a more active status. Yet the agent's goal is to be like an ambulatory wiretap or bug and to reflect back rather than to shape what occurs.

An important distinction is whether the intelligence investigation seeks to discover information about an offense that has occurred or one that might occur. This distinction permits further classification of undercover efforts as *postliminary* or *anticipatory*. Postliminary contrasts with preliminary in that events are believed to have occurred or to be well underway. The goal of a postliminary intelligence investigation is simply to discover information about things that have happened. An example can be seen in a Connecticut case where an agent befriended a defendant accused of arson and murder in a hotel fire. The goal was to learn more about the fire and to gain a confession. A casual encounter in a bar was set up. The agent offered to help the accused. He drove him by the building where the fire occurred and discussed the incident. A case in Houston was similar—an attractive female private detective contrived to meet a murder suspect and dated him for two months. He proposed marriage to her. However, she told him she first wanted to know what it was that seemed to be troubling him. With Houston police listening through a transmitter in her purse, he confessed to the murder of two people and was subsequently arrested.

A disgruntled employee in Baltimore reported to the FBI that his employer had shortchanged school districts in the delivery of plastic eating utensils. An FBI agent posing as a corrupt government auditor went to see the head of the company and indicated that he was aware of the irregularity but had not reported it. The director feigned ignorance, but the next day his treasurer sought to pay back thousands of dollars to the affected districts.

Many of the tactics used by U.S. marshalls in searching for fugitives are classified here. In Los Angeles two Cuban-born investigators infiltrated a community of refugees who came from Cuba in the 1980 Mariel boatlift. They were able to locate and arrest ten fugitives suspected of murder.[1]

Other examples include police posing as reporters seeking off-the-record briefings from political activists; pretending to be a meter reader to enter a house to look for contraband; the Vidocq trick of planting an informer as the cellmate of a prisoner; a police officer dressed as a priest who visits a suspect in jail; and a rape victim wearing a hidden recorder who returns to talk to her assailant.

Whatever might be said about such investigations with respect to privacy and civil liberties, entrapment is not an issue. To quote an IRS official about gaining access to a taxpayer's records by having an agent pose as a potential buyer of his business: "We're not inducing anybody to break the law. The tax returns have already been filed, and the crime has already been committed long before we've come around."

Postliminary intelligence investigations are standard media fare. Someone infiltrates a suspected organization or befriends a suspect in order to find out about missing persons, money, or goods. The continuity offered by such plots is no doubt a useful literary device, but on a statistical basis such investigations are not common. The majority of intelligence undercover operations are (or become) anticipatory, even when initiated in response to a past crime.

Anticipatory intelligence operations tend to be less focused, at least initially. They are more likely to involve the principle of the fishing net, rather than that of the fishing spear. An infiltrator or a contrived setting is used as a diffuse listening and watching post (the logic is similar for the mole within a foreign intelligence service).

This can involve the creation of fronts such as an antiwar group populated only by police agents.[2] In Tampa, Florida, agents pretending to be criminals ran an after-hours club, which was frequented by organized crime figures. They observed interaction patterns, recorded incriminating conversations, and gained extensive knowledge of the criminal milieu. A practice in some local departments is to have an officer (often a new recruit) simply hang out and observe activities in a neighborhood for several months.

Or it may involve the infiltration of an established organization or setting. For example, a state trooper in Philadelphia worked in an undercover capacity as an aide in a state hospital. As a result of his observations, nine persons were arrested on charges that involved abusing the mentally retarded residents. This was the first case to use federal civil rights laws to protect the mentally handicapped.

In some jurisdictions, undercover officers routinely go into correctional institutions to look for drugs, excessive use of force, smuggling, and theft—unlike Vidocq, they seek information on guards as well as prisoners. Plainclothes police pretending to be customers in a bar may be watching for potential drunk drivers, underage drinkers, or violations by bartenders.[3]

Most domestic intelligence undercover operations are short-lived (particularly if not carried out by a special intelligence unit). They either fail to produce information and are thus considered too costly or wasteful, or, if they are useful, the pressure for law enforcement action is likely to give them away. The undercover operation may yield sufficient information to justify obtaining warrants for electronic surveillance or a search, or it may lead to a shift in goals away from passive intelligence gathering to a more active effort to prevent or facilitate violations.

PREVENTIVE OPERATIONS

Waiting for a crime to occur has been compared to "closing the stable door after the horse has gone." The goal of a preventive operation is either to prevent a crime from occurring or to prevent harm if it does occur. Agents clandestinely seek to limit, inhibit, or block the suspect's capacity to carry out an offense successfully. The emphasis is on suspect weakening or victim strengthening (sometimes called target hardening). Deception may be used to restrict the opportunity for violations.

Some of the elements of prevention are based on traditional counterespionage techniques. J. Edgar Hoover writes:

> Counter-espionage assignments of the FBI require an objective different from the *handling* of criminal cases. In a criminal case, the identification and arrest of a wrongdoer are the ultimate objectives. In an espionage case, the identification of a wrongdoer is only the first step. . . . It is better to know who these people are and what they are doing and to *immobilize their efforts* than it is to expose them publicly.[4]

Disruption, subversion, and persuasion may be used, particularly for political cases. The counterintelligence actions directed against political dissidents in the 1960s and early 1970s sought to restrict their access to resources, encourage internal and external conflict, and thwart planned actions.[5] The focus was less on a specifically planned action than on weakening the general ability to act and on creating the belief that covert surveillance was widespread. The concern was with preventing and identifying "risks." Arrest was often not the major goal. The focus on prevention today is more likely to involve arrest—before the crime can be carried out or completed (for conspiracy, attempt, or on unrelated charges), or after agents have secretly structured the environment so that carrying out the crime does little or no harm.[6] For example, seven persons were indicted in 1985 for conspiring to assassinate the prime minister of India during a visit to the United States. An FBI agent posing as a paramilitary trainer identified the project and gathered sufficient information for a federal judge to issue a complaint.

The owner of a decaying building was approached by a "fire broker" about having it burned down for insurance purposes; he notified the authorities and pretended to go along with the idea. Conversations in which the arson was planned were recorded. A "torch" was videotaped saturating the building with a fire-spreading accelerant. He was arrested before he could light the fire. Police received information from a non-participating informer that the robbery of a jewelry store was planned. The store was staked out, and agents posed as salespersons. They permitted the robbery to occur and then made arrests.

In 1969 a New York City police agent who infiltrated the Black Panther Party discovered 24 sticks of dynamite. He replaced the explosive material in them with an inert substance. When the bombs were later planted at several station houses, the damage was minimal. In Chicago an undercover agent arranged for the sale of a bazooka that had been rendered inoperable to gang members who apparently sought to commit terrorist acts for Libya. A hidden transmitter attached to the weapon led agents to several of the gang's arms caches.

Agents who have infiltrated a criminal group may prevent crime by pointing out difficulties and potential problems in carrying out a planned score (e.g., a sophisticated alarm system). The role of the agent-provocateur in stirring up crowds is well known, but there are also counter-provocateurs who seek to prevent violence. Thus, at a large New Haven demonstration on behalf of the Black Panthers, police, dressed as demonstrators, mixed with the crowd. If a speech seemed to be stirring a crowd toward violence, an undercover agent would try to defuse the situation by yelling such things as "I thought you guys didn't want any trouble" and "What do you want to do, get us all killed?"[7]

Another form of prevention seeks to reduce victim vulnerability, rather than to directly deter or block violators. Crime education programs fit here. In an undercover example, the U.S. Postal Inspection Service, using an alias, has placed enticing ads offering an easy way to earn money or lose weight. Persons who responded received politely worded letters, advising them that they ought to be more careful about offers that sound "too good to be true," stamps for the postage expended, and a booklet on mail fraud schemes.

FACILITATIVE OPERATIONS

The goal of facilitative operations is to encourage (or at least not to prevent) the commission of an offense. They best fit popular notions of what undercover work is. The focus is on victim weakening and suspect strengthening, at least temporarily. If not always strongly encouraged, the suspect is at least given a government-provided opportunity to break the law. The covert facilitation of an offense takes a variety of forms: it may involve the deceptive provision of victims, co-conspirators, resources, ideas, motives, or markets. In contrast to the logic of conventional investigations, deception is used to apparently expand opportunity structures.

Two major subtypes of facilitation can be defined, according to the role played by the undercover agent: the agent can be either victim or co-conspirator. The former involves becoming a "target of opportunity" for victimization. Examples include the decoy cop who invites attack by posing as a drunk with an exposed wallet; FBI agents who pretend to run a house of prostitution or a garbage collection business in the hope of becoming targets of extortion; police who leave packages in an unlocked car to see if they will be taken; or wildlife officers who place a stuffed deer alongside a rural road and then arrest hunters who illegally fire at it.

Facilitation by playing the willing partner who conspires with the subject of the investigation is quite a different form of deception. This may involve jointly committing an offense, delegating its commission, or cooperating in its commission, as with buyers and sellers of stolen property. The agent posing as a hit man, fence, car thief, armed robber, pornographic bookseller, influence peddler, corrupt police officer, or the supplier or client for other vices is an example. Agents may play several roles—thus in the Hampton case a man purchased heroin from a government informant; the latter then put the suspect in contact with two other government agents to whom the heroin was sold.[8]

Complex undercover operations are likely to have multiple and even conflicting goals. Intelligence, preventive, and facilitative operations may coexist or be sequentially linked. In the case of consensual crimes, such as vice, there may be a conflict between the goals of facilitation and prevention that is resolved in favor of the former. Arrests for the offense generally serve organizational and personal career goals better than prevention and deterrence. The latter are usually unseen, undramatic, and difficult to measure. Prevention rarely figures in organizational incentives and reward systems. An experienced cocaine smuggler captures this in describing the belated response of federal agents to easily identifiable "amateurs" in the smuggling business flying to Latin America. He notes: "Rather than walk up to someone obviously headed for trouble—where they might flash a badge and say, 'Get smart, kid, it's not going to work'—they will, as a matter of policy, allow him to risk his life with the local heavies, get a few snorts of pure, and walk into jail at the airport back home. Why prevent smuggling when you can punish it—isn't that what jails are for?"[9]

Prevention and facilitation with arrest may also conflict with intelligence goals. Arrests are likely to give the operation away. Because the future is always uncertain and one can never be sure what an intelligence operation will turn up or where it will lead, termination involves the risk of losing important information. Conflict over this is particularly likely when police agencies separate intelligence and operational functions.

In addition to being in conflict, goals may be unclear. Note the ambiguity in the following courtroom exchange, where an attorney cross-examines an arresting officer about his undercover purposes in a gay bar:

"Now, when you go in there, do you try to discourage solicitation?" [Prevention]
"No, that is not my job."
"Your job is to encourage being solicited?" [Facilitation]
"No, that is not my job, either."
"Your job is not to discourage?"
"My job is to see if I can get solicited."[10]

Consider also the ambiguity in the goals of traffic enforcement in unmarked cars. There is the goal of intelligence—discovering patterns of infraction and those who are responsible. There is the goal of facilitation in lulling people into the belief that they can get away with speeding because no police vehicle is visible. This is particularly clear when unmarked cars are used in conjunction with deceptively offered police advice over CB radios that "all is clear, no smokies." But there is also the goal of the prevention of speeding by creating the impression that any vehicle may contain police radar.

In spite of the mixed nature and complexity of the goals of many undercover operations, the categories of intelligence, prevention, and facilitation are convenient for classification.

CONTEXTUAL AND BEHAVIORAL VARIATIONS

In order to discuss variation within a given type of investigation and similarities across different types, it is necessary to note some further distinctions. I have identified ten dimensions useful for classifying and comparing undercover operations:

1. grounds for initiation
2. specificity in target selection
3. degree of self-selection
4. correspondence to real-world criminal behavior
5. natural and artificial criminal environments
6. intent and autonomy
7. carrying out an offense or not
8. who plays the undercover role
9. deep and light cover
10. use of the results.

GROUNDS FOR INITIATION

The first dimension considers the grounds for beginning the operation. Do police have reason to believe that an infraction has been carried out or is being planned? Has a problem been identified? Are there "hints and allegations" and "incidents and accidents" that suggest fertile grounds for an investigation? Jurisdictions vary in the threshold required to begin an investigation. A broad distinction can be made between instances where police have no prior intelligence grounds for undertaking an investigation and those where they have such grounds, although there are degrees of this. When there is prior intelligence, it can vary from knowing that a given crime has been carried out or is planned, to knowing where and when, to knowing who the victim was/is and who is responsible.

The information's quality can be assessed by whether it is consistent with other sources of information and known facts, whether the source has given reliable information before, whether it seems plausible, and the degree of specificity implied in future plans (varying from loose talk to clearly delineated plans).

The source of the information may be citizens, victims, media accounts, informers, or police. The terms *reactive/proactive* refer to whether legal mobilization is in response to citizen or police initiative.[11] Legal mobilization has two broad components: broad problem area and specific case. In defining a broad area for investigation, e.g., corruption or subversion, police may be responding to citizen concerns, or they may do this on their own initiative. Similarly, in a given case, they may target a person or setting in response to a specific complaint, or on their own initiative. There are advantages and disadvantages found with the four types of mobilization seen when the above are combined (citizens or police as offering the information and broad problem or specific case). From a standpoint of traditional democratic theory, police are thought to be most accountable when they react to citizen concerns about problem areas and respond to particular complaints. We associate totalitarian practices with settings where police have absolute discretion to define areas for investigation and can target at will. But, as noted, a strictly reactive model of policing will leave large areas untouched.

SPECIFICITY IN TARGET SELECTION

A related dimension considers whether the investigation is focused on a particular target or on a category of persons or situations. Where intelligence suggests that a particular person(s) is engaged in a given activity, this can lead to a specific focus, but often authorities merely know that a crime pattern exists, without knowing who is responsible.

This suggests four types of targeting selection. These emerge from combining the grounds for initiation and specificity of target selection dimensions.

In the first case (table 2, cell A), specific intelligence permits initiating a focused investigation around a known offender. This is a classic textbook case and one that most closely fits popular images. Social control agents have reason to believe a person or group has been carrying out or

TABLE 2   PRIOR INTELLIGENCE AND SPECIFICITY IN
TARGET SELECTION

		Based on intelligence?	
		yes	*no*
Directed against a known target?	*yes*	A. focused investigation	C. ulterior motive investigation
	no	B. partially focused investigation	D. random investigation

is planning to carry out illegal actions; an undercover operation is undertaken to see if the expected evidence can be gathered. Complaints and informers are important here. An example is the targeting of a New York dentist after female patients complained they had been assaulted while under anesthesia. A warrant for video surveillance was obtained, and a policewoman posed as a patient, inviting the assault, which then occurred. Police watching nearby quickly intervened. Another example is the contract homicide. A person reports that he has been approached to carry out a murder. He is instructed to play along, and the homicide is faked.[12]

In another case, police received complaints that a butcher shop was selling falsely labeled kosher meat. Investigators secretly marked non-kosher meat and sold it to the suspects, who were arrested after they sold it as kosher.

In table 2 (cell B), there is intelligence regarding a pattern of victimization or infraction, but the specific identity of the offender is unknown. There is intelligence about offenses, though not the identity of the offenders. A broader net necessarily must be cast, but the casting is still conditioned by prior, though less focused, intelligence (e.g., the place, time, or nature of the criminal opportunity and victim).

Anticrime decoys or fencing operations deployed on the basis of crime statistics and complaints illustrate this type. Where victims or suspects have clearly distinguishing attributes, ploys and surveillance are organized based on these characteristics. Thus, policewomen in Miami posed as stranded expressway motorists in response to a pattern of highway robberies. After many complaints that interracial couples were facing police harassment, New York City had an interracial couple from its internal affairs section, with arms entwined, approach numerous police with requests for information, carefully noting their response.

In Boston women jogging around a reservoir complained of assaults by a male runner. The area was staked out, and an undercover policewoman jogged in the same area. She was bothered by a man matching the description given by earlier complainants, who was arrested and charged with indecent assault.

Mass media advertisements are a means of diffuse targeting. For example, a U.S. postal inspector, using an alias, placed the following ad in *Swinger's Life* magazine: "Young, attractive couple, anxious to exchange correspondence, experiences, photos. Love parties, and believe three isn't a crowd." A defendant answered, requested a meeting, and offered to sell movies for $15. The postal inspector said that, because he was leaving on vacation, he could not meet, but he enclosed a $15 money order and requested the "reel of film you feel would be most enjoyable." The defendant sent a film and was then arrested for violating postal regulations. In Los Angeles an ad in the newspaper for "companions" to accompany a gambling junket was used by police as a way of apprehending call girls who otherwise eluded detection.[13]

In the other two cases of target selection in table 2, an investigation is undertaken not because of, but *in search of,* intelligence. The operation answers the question, "Will they or won't they?" The investigation is undertaken entirely at police initiative in the absence of any but the most general grounds (if that) for suspecting that the crime in question is occurring: "trolling" or "fishing" for would-be offenders. The goal is more to see if, and at what point, persons will break the law if given the chance, rather than to apprehend a person thought to be criminally predisposed or to deal with a troubling crime pattern. In table 2 (cell C), in what amounts to an ulterior motive investigation, there is a focused target, but not because of prior intelligence (at least regarding the undercover offense). This usage is likely in conflict situations and where authorities abuse their authority for personal ends. The undercover tactic becomes a resource to damage a person's reputation, to harass or be able to arrest those suspected of other crimes for which evidence to establish guilt is lacking, or to gain coercive leverage.

In contrast, in table 2 (cell D) investigators start with a violation and, in what amounts to random integrity testing, look for violations. For example, "lost" wallets are left in various places where police will find them, the goal being to see if they will be turned in intact. Undercover police pose as thieves and go to bars and appliance stores offering bargains on "stolen" television sets and stereos. Middlemen hoping to earn large commissions cast a wide net in bringing in elected officials they know little about as targets for bribes. This form is commonly used in the private sector, for example, in the secret testing of cashiers.[14] It is consistent with the advice of an officer who said: "You can't miss if you shoot first and call whatever you hit the target."

There is a theory of discovery that justifies use without specific grounds.[15] This can offer protection against charges of political targeting. Clever conspirators who leave no tracks may occasionally be discovered this way. Random investigations may also serve to deter potential offenders in general by encouraging the "myth of surveillance" wherein anyone could be a police agent or any tempting situation contrived. In discussing the creation of uncertainty in a criminal environment, a character in an Elmore Leonard novel observes: "Wonderful things can happen when you plant seeds of distrust in a garden of assholes."

A related factor is the prior behavior and characteristics of the target or subject who is ensnared. Are we dealing with a committed thief who "would take a hot stove and come back for the smoke" or a naive divinity student or persons of limited capacity overcome by a rare temptation? Targets can be categorized as habitual offenders thought likely to commit the offense, regardless of what authorities do; opportunistic offenders who will take advantage of a situation, but who lack the resources to carry it out on their own; reformed offenders; and persons who have not committed the offense before. Such distinctions are relevant to the legal determination of predisposition when the defense of entrapment is raised and to assessing the ethics and social usefulness of the tactic.

DEGREE OF SELF-SELECTION

Regardless of the nature of prior intelligence and targeting, undercover situations can be contrasted with respect to who initiates the illegal action—the target or the undercover agent. The structure of some undercover operations practically requires a high degree of self-selection, while, in others, target selection depends on the behavior of the undercover agent.

The nature of the offense may affect this. For example, where agents are victims, perpetrators are likely to "volunteer" to commit the offense.

The conflict structure of predatory offenses in general precludes verbal initiation of the offense by the agent. Agents don't approach suspects and say, "I've got a thousand dollars in my pocket. I'm physically weak and I will be walking to my car in a dark, deserted parking lot at 3 a.m." They are forced to rely on nonverbal equivalents, such as the drunk decoy with an exposed wallet. Self-selection can be seen in the fact that only some of those who walk by will choose to take the money and run; others will just ignore the decoy; and some people may even try to help.

The structure of consensual violations permits either the suspect or the agent to be the initiator. Examples of initiation by the suspect include a person possessing stolen goods who chooses to come to a police-run fencing operation,[16] a person seeking to hire (or act) as a hit man, or one approaching an undercover agent about buying or selling vice or contraband. The approach also can be overt as with public advertisements for false tax shelters, phony diplomas, and telephone sex conversations.

In Operation Dipscam, the FBI gathered evidence of wire and mail fraud against mail-order colleges that provided degrees for little or no work. By answering ads in a variety of popular newspapers and magazines, one agent earned 17 advanced degrees. In another and simpler variant, fake college degrees from real colleges were simply sold.

Similar in structure is the policing of telephone sex services that advertise ("Dial A Mistress," "Sweet Talk"). A 1983 law authorizes the Federal Communications Commission (FCC) to impose civil fines against persons operating an "obscene or indecent" service available to minors. To gather evidence, the FCC has to place calls to these services and make transcripts.

Police initiative takes at least two forms. The first runs the risk of entrapment: here the officer approaches the target and proposes the illegal action. Alternatively, through appearance and nonverbal communication, the agent may communicate availability for the violation and wait for the subject to initiate it.

However, one must look beyond the question of who makes the initial approach. The suspect's behavior is conditioned by what the environment offers. In deciding how resources are used, which intelligence is acted upon, and where, when, and in what form facilitative opportunities are offered, investigators structure the opportunity for a suspect to initiate a violation. However, even when authorities choose the target, a degree of self-selection remains in the sense that the person approached could always say "No" (as perhaps half of the congressmen who were approached in Abscam did).

NATURAL AND ARTIFICIAL CRIMINAL ENVIRONMENTS

Undercover activities can be contrasted by where they fall on a "natural vs. artificial" criminal environment continuum. This involves the geographical, temporal, organizational, and individual location of the operation. Does the behavior found in the undercover operation appear to go on in the place and time where it was carried out with people like those arrested? To the extent that it does, undercover activities are in a natural, rather than an artificial, environment. Agents do not create the environment; they simply participate in what is already there.

Agents may infiltrate a criminal group or setting, seeking to become co-conspirators, clients, or victims. The infiltration of a criminal band is the classic example. Local police are sometimes able to infiltrate theft and drug rings. Police seeking drug violations may pose as students or workers in schools and factories where drugs are sold.

The FBI has had some dramatic successes in penetrating nontraditional organized crime groups, such as motorcycle gangs, and it has gotten close to some traditional organized crime families. Between 1981 and 1986, more than 800 members and associates of traditional organized crime groups were convicted. Undercover means, along with electronic surveillance and turned witnesses are responsible. In at least one case, the FBI even prevailed on a "made" member to wear a wire for two and one-half years.

The enforcement of consumer and licensing regulations usually occurs in a natural setting. An agent may pretend to be an accident victim in visits to doctors and lawyers suspected of insurance fraud or to be suffering from a common cold in visits to "Medicaid mills" suspected of providing unnecessary treatments.[17] In the latter case, investigators were subjected to electrocardiogram, tuberculosis, allergy, hearing, and glaucoma tests. An agent may pose as a "little old lady" about to be placed in a nursing home by her son, as part of an inquiry into payoffs for such placements (as did an 81-year-old woman, described as New York's "oldest undercover operative").[18] Agents may respond to mail-order offers of illegal goods and services—whether for term papers or endangered species. They may pose as consumers in visits to suspect appliance repair services or to bars and liquor stores. For example, two 15-year-old Boy Scouts who belonged to the Law Enforcement Explorers Post of Huntsville, Texas, took part in a covert beer-purchasing operation. Eight liquor store clerks were arrested for illegally selling beer to the boys.

The rare cases where police are able to turn an ongoing criminal enterprise into a police front operation offer an ideal case of a natural criminal environment. The operation continues, but its goals change as police control it, for example, police may take over what had previously been a real fencing operation. New York City police posed as operators of a working brothel (though the crime they were concerned with was extortion, not prostitution).

Perhaps less "natural," but still on the natural side of this continuum, are actions initiated by police, but done within a diffuse criminal milieu (rather than a suspected criminal organization). For example, police may start their own criminal organization for processing stolen cars, laundering money, or distributing pornography in areas where such activities go on. They may act as purchasers or suppliers in an environment where vice is known to be present, for example, posing as prostitutes[19] or their customers on a street corner or in a bar where, and at times when, prostitutes and their customers are known to do business.

In contrast to the above, which to varying degrees occur in a natural criminal environment, are the undercover operations created in milieus not known to be criminal.

Examples of the use of artificial criminal environments include the agent provocateur who comes to a college campus with no organized student protest (let alone violence) and tries to create it; police posing as thieves who see if randomly selected merchants or bar patrons will buy "stolen" electronic goods; a police fencing operation set up in a low crime area; undercover agents in a frontier town setting up a bar to be a center for gambling and prostitution in the expectation that organized crime would be moving in (though it had not yet); and police agents indicating they want to buy stolen guns in an area where gun theft was not a problem (before their presence sparked a wave of theft).

CORRESPONDENCE TO REAL-WORLD
CRIMINAL BEHAVIOR

The focus here is on what is done, not on where and when it occurs as with the previous dimension. We ask if this is the way the violation is carried out in the real world. Two major parts of this are the reproducibility of real-world criminal behavior and the nature of the temptation.

There are both practical and legal reasons for modeling covert operations on real-world conditions, up to a point. Policy guidelines stress the importance of this. Operations that depart markedly from real-world settings and behavior are likely to engender suspicion on the part of all but the most unsophisticated targets (although greed often overcomes caution). They may preclude effective prosecution by offering evidence of government overreaching and violations of due process.

However, full correspondence between real and undercover transactions is often difficult to achieve and, for certain offenses, impossible and undesirable. The effort to achieve it may conflict with the need to gather evidence and prohibitions against entrapment, illegal search and seizure, participation in violent crimes, and hurting otherwise uninvolved third parties. Undercover agents often cannot or will not literally behave the way "genuine" offenders do.

For court presentation, the investigation needs specifics—who, when, where, why, and how. But those involved in criminal activity are likely to be circumspect, revealing no more than is necessary. An experienced agent advises: "Never ask the guy a question—about anything. . . . If he tells me, 'I can reach a judge if you do what you gotta do,' it would be out of the norm for me to ask what the judge's name is. Once I'd ask, he'd know I'm a cop. . . . If you could do something for me I don't care how you do it. And that's what hurts a lot of investigations. The big bosses say try to get his name."[20]

There are limits to how close a fencing sting can come to the genuine fencing operation. Police must behave opposite to the proverbial "No questions asked" and "See no evil, hear no evil" characterizing many illegal transactions. For purposes of arrest and to be sure the subject is not an unwary innocent, police fences need to know who they are dealing with.[21] Police seek an admission that the goods are stolen and also try to learn where they are from. A real fence may not want to hear that goods are stolen or know where they are from, other than to be sure they are not from his immediate location. Nor can police as fences be as direct as the fence who works on an "order" basis (telling thieves what and how to steal). Police must deflect questions from burglars about what to steal with statements, such as: "We'll look at whatever you bring in." Nor can they literally reproduce the "hijack to order" conditions under which large-scale tractor-trailer thefts often occur.

The real fence may buy from juveniles; police fences seek to avoid this. The real fence will continue to buy from the same person; police in well-run fencing operations will not keep buying stolen goods from the same person once the several buys required for solid evidence have occurred. The genuine fence may wish only to purchase goods *without* identifying marks; for evidentiary and recovery purposes, the police fence may wish to purchase only goods *with* identifying marks.

Prostitution encounters involving a decoy client offer another example of how undercover operations may depart from real-world transactions.[22] In a genuine encounter, there is negotiation, and the man may
proposition the woman. But for an undercover police officer to do this
risks entrapment. He must wait for the offer to come from the woman.
Knowledgeable prostitutes wait for the man to proposition them—in
rare cases, even requiring this in writing or tape recording it. Some prostitutes require the male to disrobe before discussing business, knowing
that, in many police departments, police are prohibited from disrobing
while on duty, prompting one police officer to observe: "It's not our
hands that are tied, it's our belts." There may be a verbal cat-and-mouse
struggle over who initiates the proposal. The undercover agent, in going
to an area where prostitution is present, seeks to be approached by the
target; the prostitute, aware of the legal rules, seeks to maneuver the
agent into making the first move.

Drug purchasers may be required to use the drug in the presence of
the seller before a transaction is completed. There are various means of
faking or avoiding this.

The legal case is stronger when words and deeds are caught on tape
or when an offer made in a bar or other private place is repeated on the
street. Agents may thus attempt to manipulate targets into "instant re-
plays" where what has been said in private is repeated under monitored
conditions or in a public place. This differs from genuine encounters
and can be another clue for sophisticated offenders that they are dealing
with police.

In genuine criminal encounters, one party may coerce or threaten another party into participating. Drugs and sex may be offered as inducements and as part of ritual exchanges expressing solidarity. Or a series
of illegal credibility-building activities of ever-greater magnitude may be
required to gain acceptance into a criminal organization. To take an extreme example, according to a former leader of a Sicilian Mafia group in
the United States, members were expected to commit a murder in order
to prove themselves. Police obviously will find it difficult to act in this
fashion. With respect to these issues, a high premium is placed on *not*
replicating the behavior of real-world criminal situations. This creates
an opportunity for defensive tactics and tests that the knowledgeable
offender can exploit. The undercover agent cannot continually refuse requests without raising suspicions.

In white-collar violations, euphemisms and rationalizations are often
found that put the illegality in the best possible light. Illegal actions may

be interwoven with actions that are presented in the public interest, for example, a bribe is defined as a way to get around red tape in order to speed up a construction project that will provide jobs or to hasten the release of a life-saving drug.[23] However, when agents routinely participate in this way, it may appear to juries that they have gone too far in gilding the lily, even though their behavior may correspond to what is actually done in bribe situations. But their failure to behave in this way may mean restricting some types of investigation to only the most crude and blatant instances.

To both be convincing and stay within legal and departmental bounds requires appreciable skill. The agent must engage in an intricate dance of point and counterpoint that "keeps his or her behavior both sufficiently distant from criminality so as to avoid jeopardizing an investigation, yet at the same time, sufficiently close in order to project a convincingly corrupt image."[24]

An important part of real-world correspondence is the nature of the temptation. Is it realistic or does it offer a greater temptation than is found in real-world settings? In principle, this is easy to reproduce. One simply offers to pay or agrees to accept the going price for whatever it is that is involved or presents a target for victimization equivalent in attractiveness to those that naturally appear. In practice, this may be difficult to do. Organizational pressures to produce may lead to enhanced temptations. Gaining a competitive edge may require a sweeter inducement. For example, a fencing sting may feel compelled to offer higher prices to attract business, particularly initially. When the offer is highly tempting and unrealistic (unlikely to be encountered in an actual situation), the operation becomes an integrity test to see if temptation can be resisted, rather than an investigation designed to apprehend wrongdoers.

Apart from whether it is realistic or not is the question of just how tempting the offer is. Temptation, of course, has a personal and subjective quality, determined by the needs and perceptions of the target. To an addict experiencing withdrawal because of an inability to find drugs, an undercover offer is likely to be more tempting than to someone without this need. Would John DeLorean, in need of money for his car company, have been as likely to get involved with a drug deal if he had been approached years earlier when he was an executive at GM? A hint that a bribe could fix things is likely to be more tempting to a person on parole facing a mandatory sentence than to a person with no arrest record.

There is an intersection between the "need" of the offender to commit the offense (e.g., strong to nonexistent) and the extent to which authorities engage in facilitation. But, in general terms, extremes can be described. A sprawled decoy feigning drunken sleep with a bulging wallet hanging out offers a greater temptation than does a sitting drunk with a wallet barely showing (some departments limit the positions a decoy can assume and the amount of, and how, money can be shown). Offering to sell contraband at noncompetitively low prices or purchase it at high prices is more tempting than offering the going rate. Offering contraband as a gift or token of friendship is likely to be more tempting than outright sale. A scantily clad policewoman posing as a prostitute offers a greater temptation than does a woman with a less seductive presentation. Police in Washington, D.C., in responding to complaints that it was unfair to dress decoys in hot pants and spiked heels, issued a directive requiring decoy prostitutes to dress more modestly. Here the policy seeks to make police behave less like the people they're imitating in the real-world setting.

INTENT AND AUTONOMY

Authorities have great leeway in the setting of traps. The fact that there may initially be good grounds for an undercover operation or that the situation may permit self-selection still requires contrasting variation in: (1) the degree of certainty about whether the target actually *intended* to carry out the offense, and (2) the degree of *autonomy* in the manifestation of intent.

Providing an opportunity structure is one thing; trying to insure that it is taken advantage of is quite another. This is particularly important when our concern is with the causes of the behavior, rather than only with the technical matter of legal guilt. It is also important to keep the letter of the law and its procedures separate from its spirit.

Other factors being equal, fewer questions regarding intent are likely to be raised when the agent plays the role of victim rather than co-conspirator. Among the latter, intent seems clearer where the subject actually possesses contraband to sell, rather than buying what an agent offers, and least clear when accepted as a gift. It is also clearer where the law enforcement involvement appears as part of a process *after* a crime has been committed (e.g., selling already stolen goods to a police fence) and when the offense is carried out multiple times and/or involves the violation of many different laws. Many jurisdictions have a policy of making arrests only after a second buy has taken place in order to avoid entrapment claims. There is likely to be less doubt about intent when the temptation offered is equivalent or even less attractive than that found in the real world and when only the suspect, not the agent, breaks the law.

The nature of the interaction between the target and the agent bears on autonomy to commit the offense. This varies from minimally to highly facilitative of the violation. At one extreme, there is no face-to-face verbal interaction or deceptive tampering with the environment (beyond police not wearing uniforms). Police may discreetly watch suspects, locations, or likely victims as they occur naturally, waiting to intervene if a crime is attempted. For example, suspecting that collectors are stealing from parking meters, they may "salt" the meters with special coins that glow under ultraviolet light and secretly videotape collectors as they make their rounds.

An opportunity structure may be provided, but without verbal encouragement from police to take advantage of it. Thus, a decoy appears to be sleeping, property may be left in an unlocked car, or objects, such as skis, may have hidden electronic monitoring devices attached that give off a silent signal when moved.

Further along the continuum are preventive and facilitative situations where authorities do interact but, in so doing, merely go along with the suggestions or behavior of the target. Investigations involving compliance with laws protecting consumers fit here. Automotive examples are undercover officers who take cars in for minor repairs and are billed for major repairs or undone repairs;[25] who sell vehicles to used car dealers and then track whether or not the odometers are set back; or who check to see if a car dealer will tell them of defects in a car the dealer is selling that a previous undercover "customer" had informed the dealer about in writing.

Tests involving building, electrical, and other inspectors called in to assess conditions in clear violation of codes are another example. In Operation Ampscam more than one-half the employees of the 26-person New York City Bureau of Electrical Control, the agency that inspects electrical installations, were arrested after a 14-month undercover investigation. Two bogus electrical companies were set up. Payoffs were made at some of the abandoned buildings the agents pretended were going to be rehabilitated. The buildings were complete with dangling wires, water deposits, and lack of grounding. In another part of the operation, agents posed as inspectors and arrested contractors who paid bribes. Mail order services offer agents the chance to test an ongoing activity. In testing mail order services, investigators are simply assessing a service available to the public. A California mail-order medical laboratory that advertised that it would test blood for food allergies for $350 was sued by the New York State Attorney General. The state submitted a sample of cow's blood. (Not only did the lab fail to detect that the sample was nonhuman, it reported that the donor was allergic to milk, cottage cheese, and yogurt!)

At the other end of the scale are cases where agents play a much more facilitative role, whether through coercion, persuasion, or the provision of scarce resources. What is at issue here is not only who initiates the idea, but how far covert operatives go in encouraging and supporting the violation. In some cases, the target is "like a hungry trout snapping at a fly" (as a prosecutor put it) and is clearly self-interested. In other cases, participation is hesitant and halfhearted and/or undertaken out of a manipulative appeal to friendship, compassion, manhood, or patriotism; out of fear or ignorance of the illegality; or in response to a dare. In a landmark case, Sherman, a former drug addict, after several refusals, was eventually persuaded to locate drugs for an informer he met in a doctor's office, where Sherman and the informer were being treated for addiction. The informer claimed to be experiencing withdrawal symptoms and that the treatment was not working. He provided funds for the purchase.[26]

Situations where targets have the resources and knowledge to carry out an offense are distinct from those where government agents supply a skill (how to break into a building, build weapons, make a counterfeit plate, manufacture drugs) or a scarce resource (a chemical required to produce drugs). In an example of the latter, in an effort to draw out "potential producers of hallucinogens and other illicit drugs," federal drug agents have operated fake chemical companies selling materials and instructions for manufacturing dangerous drugs. The fronts obtained business by advertising in such magazines as *Popular Science* and *High Times*. They offered free catalogues listing controlled substances, which are difficult to obtain, along with regular chemical supplies.

A person writing for information was told the sale and manufacture of controlled substances was prohibited unless one was registered with the government. "The bottom line is this: We cannot 'legitimately' make or sell this chemical, but we can supply all chemical equipment necessary to produce it without restriction." The letter then describes a "very popular kit" that for $700 provides all that is necessary. Carl Peterson, who had no previous criminal record, responded to the ad. He purchased the kit and was arrested the next day on drug conspiracy charges. He received a two-year prison sentence. A key question, of course, is whether those arrested as a result of such activity would have been capable of obtaining the materials and manufacturing the drugs without the government's instruction and materials.[27]

In chapter 7, I consider the role of trickery in generating participation—a factor with obvious implications for autonomous motivation. The extent to which authorities persist after rebuffs is also important in assessing how autonomous motivation is. A target who immediately responds to a proposal differs from one who hesitates, or says "No," but later responds after numerous requests.

Linguistic analysis can help discern how willing the target is and the extent to which the agent, rather than the target, directs and manipulates the conversation and events. Social psychological research suggests that autonomy will be greater as the ratio of targets to agents increases, in cases where the agent is not appreciably higher in status or older than the target, and where subtle social influence factors are absent (e.g., where the illegal behavior has not been modeled for the violator by an agent).

Another factor in autonomous motivation is whether or not the subject's life situation is secretly manipulated to increase the likelihood of participation. Examples include generating financial need through loss of a job or arrest on contrived charges, making it difficult for an addict to obtain drugs; encouraging rivalries that an undercover scheme then tries to exploit; contriving a situation where a person is made to appear as an informer; and the classic espionage tactic of using sex as bait.

CARRYING OUT AN OFFENSE OR NOT

Does the primary crime actually occur? Does harm result? Do derivative or secondary violations occur (conspiracy, failing to file a report, perjury, or resisting arrest)?

Police and prosecutors have enormous discretion in deciding what crimes to charge people with. There is much room for choice in converting behavior to formal bureaucratic categories.[28] But, in the actual undercover setting, police discretion can be even more basic in affecting what kind of behavior occurs. Undercover operations clearly indicate the interdependence that may exist between rule enforcers and rule breakers in the production or avoidance of violations.

In some settings, police have three broad choices: (1) prevent any crime from occurring; (2) permit or facilitate a different crime from that presumably intended by the target; or (3) permit the intended crime to occur. An important public policy question is what police should do when they have a choice between there being no violation at all or encouraging or permitting a violation.

Beyond intervening to prevent harm, police can sometimes intervene to prevent any offense from occurring. For example, when a 61-year-old Seattle woman with a history of mental illness hints that she would like to see the judge and prosecutor killed who were involved in a rape case against her son, police may have a choice. Her husband notes one choice: "I had a severely disturbed and distraught wife and they could have just informed me that she had gotten this idea and we could have seen that she got help." Another choice (and the one police picked) is to provide her with an undercover agent pretending to be a killer. Production pressures, a desire for general deterrence, and the belief that bad intentions should be punished encourage the latter.

In the following encounter, an undercover agent in a fencing sting at first supports the occurrence of a crime, but then acts to prevent it. The investigator reports: "The guy [sting client] asked me how much babies go for. He knew a woman who wanted to sell hers. I told him $1,500. We figured we'd take it and then throw the mom in jail too, because any mother who'd sell her own child ought to be in jail. But then the guy changed his story and said he'd have to kidnap the kid, and we told him no way, we didn't want any part of anything like that."

Plainclothes police who watch drunken patrons in bars may intervene before the patrons get in their cars, or they can arrest them after they have driven a short distance. Police in a medium-sized city concerned over an outbreak of burglaries at the homes of recently deceased persons during their funerals have a choice. They can follow the obituary columns (or place fake notices) and set up a surveillance operation, or they can park a marked patrol car in front of the house of the deceased.

The occurrence of an offense bears on the intent, artificiality, and correspondence to the real-world factors considered above, but it goes beyond these. It has important implications for strategy and clearly illustrates some trade-offs. There may be a conflict between preventing the harm from being carried out and the greater certainty regarding intent and more severe sentencing when it actually is carried out. The law may offer an incentive for the crime to be carried out where the penalties for commission are more severe than for attempt or solicitation. There may be a failure to prevent it out of a desire to protect intelligence sources.

There are some situations where it is possible to have it both ways—

to make it appear that the crime occurs, or for it actually to occur under altered circumstances, but to avoid the harm that would be present if it were to have occurred under regular circumstances. False homicides, anticrime decoys, stores staked out as a result of a robbery tip, bait sales (which lure prospective buyers by selling legally acquired goods as if they were stolen), and the substitution of a harmless look-alike substance for a drug (substituting a mixture of kitty litter, brown sugar, and talcum powder for 307 pounds of cocaine found on a Panamanian ship and tracking the shipment) are examples. General inspection procedures that enter "ringers" into a system to see how they are treated are another example.

Conspiracy charges are a partial means of resolving conflict between the goals of prevention and facilitation. To a degree they permit having it both ways, for example, an arrest is made before the actual crime is carried out. However, questions may linger about whether the crime would in fact have been committed, and conspiracy charges can easily be misused. Words are not the same as deeds. Some targets only pretend to go along in response to coercion, or a plan to trick the agent, or in order to carry out their own investigation, with no intention of actually carrying out the offense.

A related question is when and how to terminate an operation. Often the intended crime cannot be permitted to actually occur—the harm may be too great, and there may be no way to simulate the offense; the chance of intervening at the last moment may be too uncertain; or the logistics and resource costs of waiting for it to occur may be too great. Nor can the actual crime be faked. For example, such crimes as arson or the use of explosives do not lend themselves to fakery and contrived evidence of destruction the way homicide does. In such cases, there may be no alternative but conspiracy charges or expensive surveillance, hoping to catch the target in the act before any damage is done.

On the other hand, the investigation may drag on longer than is necessary. How persistent should agents be after an initial refusal? In the landmark Sorrells case, a defendant refused three times before agreeing to obtain moonshine for a government agent. In Abscam, some targets who refused the initial offer were dropped, while others were repeatedly approached. When a suspect in a homicide solicitation case expresses reluctance to the covert agent and says, "I think I'll forget the whole thing," authorities can call off the investigation or, as in a Palm Springs, California, case, they can tell the agent to "go back in and talk to him." In this case the agent's persistence led to an indictment.

Those in the criminal justice system are likely to receive greater rewards for finding the guilty than for exonerating the innocent. When an expensive operation does not find evidence of violations, there may be strong pressures to keep looking or to use questionable means to produce results. Agents may have a strongly held ideology or beliefs that tell them that violations have to be there, even if the evidence thus far suggests the contrary.

Conversely, once adequate evidence has been gathered, e.g., two or three purchases or sales of contraband, does the investigation stop (or at least this phase of it)? Are there production pressures on agents and a desire for regularity in the work that lead them to continue to amplify crime, beyond what was required for the initial evidence?

Unfortunately, training and policy do not always encourage a sense of craftsmanship and pride in making "good" arrests that are the hallmark of the professional officer. Too often the emphasis is on merely "making the numbers."[29]

Of course sometimes agents have little control over when the investigation ends. The agent's behavior may give it away. The agent may not be convincing, his story may be confused, he may forget a crucial element or be unable to adequately respond to changed circumstances, or he may encounter a situation in which his inability to actually act like a genuine perpetrator is a sure giveaway. But even when the above are absent there may be nonverbal behavioral clues (facial expressions, breathing, voice) to the deceit. Just as some police have an uncanny ability to sense violators, some criminals have an equivalent ability to sense covert agents.[30] Some may even hire private detectives to make sure a corrupt offer is what it appears to be.

Some operations are stopped even though more cases could be made, when they begin to strain investigative and prosecutorial resources. Ironically the very success of an operation may lead to its cessation. Beyond a certain point the complexity, scope and volume of cases may threaten to overwhelm the system. The natural limits on the capability of control systems to identify and process violations are particularly evident in undercover cases because of the manifest interdependence between rule enforcers and rule breakers in the generation of the violation. Prosecutors may not want to proceed for still other reasons (e.g., unseemly or illegal investigative behavior, danger of giving away a more important case, other priorities). Or the investigation may be stopped by higher level authorities for benign, or not so benign, reasons.

The investigation may stop because of chance events (e.g., an old friend comes up to an agent at a bar when he is with a suspect and, addressing him by his correct name, asks if he is still in law enforcement) or another suspect recognizes him as the guy who arrested him ten years ago in a different city. Investigations are sometimes given away when the agent is arrested along with his targets by police who are unaware of his identity.

Suspects may be tipped off by persons inside, or close to, law enforcement (e.g., informers, clerks, other agents—in one case perhaps even a judge who issued a warrant for electronic surveillance as part of an undercover corruption investigation). Investigative reporters eager for a story, or to beat their competition, may write about an investigation before authorities are ready to bring it down.

Looked at more generally the discovery of undercover as well as other kinds of secrets is likely to involve one or more of the following: accidents, coincidence, errors, and incompetence; tests and surveillance; informers; and forced disclosure.[31]

WHO PLAYS THE UNDERCOVER ROLE?

It is important to consider who plays the undercover role: sworn agents; private police who are temporarily deputized or who otherwise cooperate in an investigation; victims, witnesses, or co-conspirators; minors; "cooperating subjects" in trouble with the law; informers who cooperate for reasons of money, ideology, or other personal goals; or unwitting informers (also known as middlemen, bagmen, intermediaries, and corrupt influence peddlers). Various combinations are possible, and involvement may change as the operation develops. A standard practice is to start with an informer who is dropped after cutting in a sworn agent. Less frequently, a sworn agent is able to gain access without this. This is likely to require more time and greater resources; for many operations, it is impossible.

The question of who plays the role bears on legality, credibility, ease of supervision, and the kinds of behavior likely to be found in the investigation. As we move from sworn agents to informers to unwitting informers, the likelihood of problems increases, but it is often not possible for sworn agents to play the role exclusively.

DEEP AND LIGHT COVER OPERATIONS

There is a major distinction between "deep" and "light" or "shallow" operations. Simple "walk-ons" or "cameos" (where the agent seeks to make a purchase or sale or acts as an anticrime decoy) are dif-

ferent from longer-term, more penetrating operations, such as the creation of a false front organization or the infiltration of a group.

This is most clearly defined by a temporal short/long-term dimension. The FBI, for example, considers any operation that goes over six
months to be a major (Group I) operation. But related to this is the extent of penetration or immersion into a criminal milieu. For example,
can the agent come home each night, once a week, or infrequently?
What degree of deception is involved relative to identity? Does the agent
experience total social death and rebirth and need extensive "backstop-
ping" in the creation of a new identity, or is this not necessary? Does the
role become a life rather than a job?

Deep undercover operations are more characteristic of federal than
local agencies. They have become more prominent since the mid-1970s,
with the FBI being the major user at the federal level. In general, deep
and light operations vary significantly with respect to the cost, skill,
planning, and supervision they require. Deep undercover operations are
likely to raise more complicated ethical and logistical questions and may
have a broader range of unintended consequences.

USE OF THE RESULTS

In the civics textbook model of criminal justice, evidence from an investigation leads to arrest and prosecution. The investigation is distinct
from the determination of guilt and the administration of punishment.
The investigation is a means to some other end arrived at after a formal
judicial process. In actuality, the situation is more complex. A prosecutor may refuse to take a case. Investigators may not bring their evidence to the prosecutor. An undercover operation may serve as an end
in itself and immediately obtain a major goal, apart from any subsequent judicial proceedings, e.g., in the prevention of harm from a terrorist attack, finding a kidnap victim, the recovery of stolen property, or
getting contraband, such as guns and drugs, off the street. Undercover
operations may also be undertaken to serve personal rather than organizational goals.

Civil law may be involved. The results of an undercover investigation
may lead to fines, license restrictions or revocation (as in the case of a
bar that serves minors or an appliance repair firm cheating consumers),
or to restraining orders and agreements, e.g., not to fix prices.

Incriminating results can be used as a negotiating resource wherein
prosecution is held in abeyance, if a person cooperates, such as by giv-

ing information or participating in a subsequent undercover scheme. In a spiraling, or onion-peeling, model, investigators may seek to work their way up a hierarchy by trading leniency for cooperation at each step. The threat of prosecution may also be used to get an individual or organization to move out of a jurisdiction.

In addition to the sentencing of individuals (as both punishment and incapacitation), a new goal is to break up criminal organizations.[32] In commenting on a major organized crime case, Florida's attorney general states, "our purpose in this suit is to drive people out of business, take over their assets and, hopefully, to drive them out of the state."

Sometimes when the results are presented in court the situation is other than it appears to be, in the sense that investigators had the evidence beforehand. The formal investigation may be a laundering operation so that improperly obtained results can be publicly offered; because the initial evidence came from an informant who was promised he would not have to testify or whose credibility as a witness could be easily challenged; or because the information may have been gathered properly but in a way that the authorities do not wish to have revealed.

Intelligence may be used to verify the fact that targets are perceiving messages the way the government intends them to be perceived or to verify accounts coming from different sources.

The tactic may be used as part of a general inspections strategy or "vital test," simply to assess an organization's conformity to rules, preparedness, and vulnerability. For example, undercover environmental protection agents may visit dump sites and see if they can successfully dump what appear to be toxic waste containers; or a fraudulent disability application may be submitted to a pension board to see if it will be accepted. NSA uses "tiger teams" that try to break into secure communications systems; FAA employees test airport security by trying to smuggle in weapons; and nuclear power facilities are subjected to mock take-overs. The tactic may be used to reward good behavior, as well as to identify problems.

In rare cases, staged operations may be undertaken only as a form of public communication on behalf of a general deterrence. An anticrime decoy program in which both the decoys and the "offenders" are police is one example. The goal is to advertise the presence of the decoy through "arrests." In an interesting private sector example, a New York firm called THEFT (the Honest Employers Fooling the Thieves) hires out unemployed actors to businesses concerned with employee theft. The actors pretend to be thieves. After a period of brief employment, the actor begins visibly stealing whatever he or she can. The "thief" is then "caught" and fired in a very public display. The firm's motto is, "Hire someone to fire."[33]

Investigators may take vigilante action apart from any judicial proceeding. Reporting on his work in an elite New York City drug unit, Robert Leuci observes: "We did what no court of law would do. We took away their dope, gave those guys a heavy fine, and deported them."[34] The efforts to disrupt and subvert political organizations are additional examples.

Results may not be fully (or immediately) used as part of an effort by investigators to maintain control over their work. The desire for a predictable and steady flow of arrests or intelligence may mean dragging cases out, rather than taking sweeping action. Secrecy may be the "end of intelligence, not the means."[35] The pot may be kept simmering and never brought to a boil. Agents sometimes joke about the danger of working themselves out of a job. This is hardly a new concern for those in this line of work. In commenting on informants during the French Revolution, Cobb notes that for the agent "to make a clean sweep of a 'faction' in one go would be a form of professional suicide . . . a 'plot' must be made to last as long as possible, in order to bring in certain groups of people, one group after another, over a matter of months or of years."[36]

In large departments that have separate secret intelligence units, investigations may last a long time because there is an organizational stake in continuing them. Intelligence operations may simply lead to more intelligence operations, to the frustration of those in operational units. As one officer put it: "Everything goes in, nothing comes out." Beyond the mystique of secrecy, this reflects the desire to protect sources and to wait for a really important incident before taking action. The intelligence role can be defined in a way that creates an insatiable appetite for information while limiting action taken on the basis of the information collected.

The Complexity of Virtue

Falsehood is in itself mean and culpable, and truth noble and full of virtue.

—Aristotle

For the congregation of hypocrites *shall be* desolate, and fire shall consume the tabernacles of bribery.

—Job 15:34

If you want to catch a rat, you have to go down into the sewer.

—A prosecutor

Among the most important questions in judging any public policy are: Is it legal? Does it work? Is it ethical? These, of course, can be interwoven. Morality may inspire law; from a vulgar pragmatist perspective, if something works, it is ethical. The definition, measurement, and weighing of costs and benefits in determining if a tactic works reflect values. Nonetheless the legal, operational, and ethical dimensions offer distinct perspectives for evaluating policy.

The legality of undercover means has been well established in American history, even though there will always be gray areas and unresolved issues. There is disagreement about the effectiveness and comparative costs of such covert means as stings and anticrime decoys. But, assuming undercover means are both legal and effective, we must also find them ethically acceptable before we can conclude they are good public policy. Consider, for example, an investigation of vice activities at "Tina's Leisure Spa" in New York City. Undercover investigators engaged in (and paid for) sexual relations with employees of the spa, developing clear evidence of illegality. Affidavits were subsequently filed as part of an effort to close the spa, but the district attorney refused to take action. He stated, "It's unseemly. There is a limit on how far you go to make cases. All sorts of evils flow from going too far."

In considering why some "legal" and "effective" tactics are nevertheless "unseemly" and "go too far," or why some clearly illegal actions nevertheless may seem appropriate, we are dealing with the ethical aspects of covert operations.[1] These are significant, if hazy, dimensions and even more subject to disagreement than the legal and criminal justice aspects. What are the ethical justifications for and arguments against undercover tactics? By what criteria should they be judged?

Conflicts over the ethics of undercover means are often resolved by feelings about a particular enforcement goal rather than by consideration of abstract issues. Both liberals and conservatives tend to base the acceptability of covert means on the ends for which they are used, though they differ on which ends create legitimacy. Thus, although some conservatives may support the tactic when used against drugs, prostitution, and radicals, they are less enthusiastic when it is used against corporate executives. Liberals may oppose the tactic when directed against civil rights and peace groups and the sexual activities of adults but welcome its use against racist groups. Many police strongly defend covert tactics, except when used by internal affairs units in their own departments.

Such reactions generate neither consistent positions nor effective policies. It is, therefore, important to consider ethical criteria that go beyond specific ends. For convenience, I refer to the justifications that advocates and opponents put forth as principles. But my approach is not that of the professional philosopher dealing with generic concepts of secrecy, lying, and justice who advocates a philosophical system from which one can deduce ethical principles. It is rather that of the social observer who has listened to a debate, reports the arguments, and then asks if there is some means of reconciliation and some guidelines that might help in determining the ethical status of undercover investigations.

The following list of justifications and objections regarding the ethical aspects of covert means do not carry equal weight, but they reflect the range of ideas heard in current debate. Any decision or resolution about using or not using undercover tactics must come to terms with these arguments:

For

1.   Citizens grant to government the right to use exceptional means.

2.   Undercover work is ethical when used for a good and important end.

3.   Enforce the law equally.

4.   Convict the guilty.

5.   An investigation should be as nonintrusive and noncoercive as possible.

6. When citizens use questionable means, government agents are justified in using equivalent means.

7. Undercover work is ethical when there are reasonable grounds for suspicion.

8. Special risks justify special precautions.

9. Undercover work is ethical when the decision to use it has been publicly announced.

10. Undercover work is ethical when done by persons of upright character in accountable organizations.

11. Undercover work is ethical when it is undertaken with the intention of eventually being made public and judged in court.

Against

1. Truth telling is moral; lying is immoral.

2. The government should neither participate in, nor be a party to, crime nor break the law in order to enforce it.

3. The government should not make deals with criminals.

4. The government should not offer unrealistic temptations or tempt the weak.

5. Do no harm to the innocent.

6. Respect the sanctity of private places.

7. Respect the sanctity of intimate relations.

8. Respect the right to freedom of expression and action.

9. It is wrong to discriminate in target selection.

10. The government should not do by stealth what it is prohibited from doing openly.

ETHICAL DECEPTION

There are some principles that would render undercover tactics categorically or contingently ethical: the broadest justification lies in the "social contract" view of the world, which holds that *undercover work is ethical because citizens grant to government the right to use exceptional means, such as coercion and deception, in order to be protected.*

Consistent with this view is the traditional belief that the end justifies the means, making *undercover work ethical when used for a good and important end—protecting society from crime, apprehending criminals, preventing crime, substituting a police victim for a citizen victim, gathering intelligence and contraband and even protecting the potential offender.*[2] If the intent is noble, then the action is justified, even if it has some bad effects.

According to these arguments, the ethical acceptability of means is contingent on ends. Thus, Thomas Jefferson felt that should "the public preservation" require the leader to go beyond the "strict line of the law . . . his motives will be his justification." Abraham Lincoln suspended habeas corpus during the Civil War, explaining that sometimes one had to amputate a foot to save a body. The granting of "wartime power" to governments, for example, is comparable to the resort to covert means to combat a crisis in crime control. Such a "state of siege" mentality can be seen in former Governor Wallace's suggestion during the 1968 presidential campaign to "let the police run the country, but just for a few years until the mess gets cleaned up." A related argument holds that, even if no crisis exists, exceptional means may be justified on the grounds of prevention, and that the failure to use them may lead to a government's loss of legitimacy, the possibility of a more repressive government, or the rise of vigilante groups using far worse techniques.

This justification may even apply to perpetrators. When undercover means result in the prevention of a serious crime, offenders may be spared paying as full a price as they would if they were successfully to complete the crime. For vice offenses, the belief that enforcement "is for your own good" would also apply here (e.g., saving someone from possible drug addiction). It may be believed that government has the obligation to prevent us from harming ourselves, as well as others. "We may have saved their lives," states a customs official about an undercover operation that led to the arrest of 13 people in Louisiana who planned to invade the country of Surinam.

The principle that there should be *equal enforcement of the law* commonly refers to equal treatment for rich and poor, men and women, minorities and nonminorities. But equity can also be considered with respect to types of offense. The failure to use undercover tactics for white-collar, consensual, or conspirational offenses, while actively carrying out a war on street crime using conventional means, is inequitable. Undercover tactics offer an important means for dealing with the crimes of higher-status offenders who may otherwise be virtually immune from prosecution.

Undercover tactics may be seen as ethical because they are consistent with the principle: *convict the guilty*. Advocates argue that covert means offer greater certainty of guilt and provide evidence that goes beyond the standard of "no reasonable doubt" required to convict. Taking the bait, being in possession of the contraband, or going along with an undercover scheme is thought to offer clear evidence of guilt.

Undercover means permit police to literally catch offenders in the act, avoiding problems of confessions (whether coerced or otherwise), perjury, mistaken identity, and intimidated witnesses. When police themselves play the undercover role, the need to depend on informers or witnesses with questionable reputations is reduced. With other tactics (lie detectors, voice stress, handwriting analysis, or after-the-fact testimony of witnesses), there may be a greater risk of convicting an innocent person. Conversely, because the evidence from an undercover investigation may involve a video and/or aural tape or testimony of a participating officer, there is less likelihood that the guilty will be found innocent.

In addition, undercover work may be seen as ethically preferable to other means because *an investigation should be as nonintrusive and noncoercive as possible*. Covert investigations can be more directly targeted than a wiretap or room bug that is indiscriminate. Undercover means often avoid elaborate dossiers, extensive documentation, and long drawn-out investigations. They permit rapid determination of guilt or innocence, because a person either goes along with or refuses the illegal opportunity. When an investigation involves overt methods, such as searches, subpoenas of records, or the interrogation of witnesses, the reputation of subjects later found innocent is often damaged. The identity of the subject of an undercover investigation is kept secret; when no evidence of guilt is found, the fact that an investigation occurred need not be made public.

Searches, electronic surveillance, grand jury subpoenas, and compelled testimony are usually carried out against the subject's will. Information from informers is often obtained by coercively "twisting" or "leaning" on them. In contrast, undercover operations structured to permit self-selection involve voluntary actions on the part of the subject. Even with targeted subjects, coercion is lacking in the sense that the tempted person is always free to refuse the opportunity. Deception replaces coercion.

Running through the two principles above is a "lesser of evils" or "least drastic alternative" morality, wherein a less than perfect means may be nonetheless ethically preferable to no means, or an even worse means. The assumption is made that, whatever harm may lie in using undercover tactics, even worse harm would appear were other means to be used or were nothing to be done. Tyranny is seen as less of a threat than anarchy.

Another principle espoused by advocates is based on the norm of reciprocity: "Do unto others." Although violence and deception on the part of the state are normally undesirable, proponents of covert means argue that *when citizens use questionable means, control agents are justified in using equivalent means*. It is the idea of "fighting fire with fire," the morality of "An eye for an eye."[3] News headline writers often play on the implicit irony and morality here ("Con Man Conned," "Police Fool Thieves") in stories describing undercover operations. As poetic justice, though offenders are not quite hoist with their own petards, they are at least beaten at their own game. The principle serves to legitimate, or at least soften, the moral bite of many con games.[4] The moral appeal of the movie *The Sting* lies here, as a swindler is swindled. In rare contrast, the film *Absence of Malice* receives its moral power when a suspect uses deception against the government agents who initially misuse deception against him.

Another justification is that *undercover work is ethical when there are reasonable grounds for suspicion*. The grounds may involve persons or situations, and suspicion may be created by victims, witnesses, audits, paper trails, threats, informers, or surveillance. The stronger the grounds, the greater the justification. At a minimum, the nature of the offense must be specified, and some information limiting it to particular locations, categories of suspect, or victims must be provided.

The specific identity of a suspect, however, need not (and often will not) be known in advance. Targeted street decoy operations are a good example. Were undercover operations to be restricted to known suspects, this would work to the advantage of experienced offenders who are skilled at avoiding arrest and suspicion, as well as first-time offenders who are not known to police. Through a catch-22 logic, they would escape arrest via undercover means. However, by targeting an undercover operation toward a given milieu where a pattern of crime occurs and by structuring it to permit self-selection rather than preselection of particular suspects, the operation becomes entirely consistent with Fourth Amendment values that preclude government from intervening in the private affairs of its citizens without grounds for suspicion.

Implicit in the justifications that involve broad social goals is the justification of self-defense. If undercover agents are asked to take risks on society's behalf, society must recognize that *special risks justify special protections.*[5] The well-being of the agent justifies deception in the search for evidence, after an investigation has begun, prior to arrests, and in the creation of new identities in the Witness Protection Program.

Some proponents of undercover operations argue that forewarning equals justification: *undercover work is ethical when the decision to use it has been publicly announced.*[6] People are given notice, and the players then attempt to outwit each other.[7] The basic repertoire of potential moves and consequences is known, and those used by police have been arrived at democratically. This concept of playing by the rules holds even from the perspective of many criminals. When arrested, some are docile and almost philosophical, feeling "this time the breaks went against me and the cops won."

Announcing the rules beforehand may also permit a degree of self-selection, when people choose to participate in activities where they know they may be deceived by control agents. Persons in certain high-risk occupational roles, for example, cashiers in contexts where dishonesty is easily hidden, where undercover practices are likely, may actually consent to their use. Agreement to be tested becomes a condition of employment. Assuming one has the option to refuse, consenting to surveillance is regarded as making it more ethical.

Undercover work is ethical when it is undertaken with the intention of eventually being made public and judged in court. This principle applies the test of publicity after the fact. Lying in undercover operations (assuming the truth will eventually come out) is thus different from lying in perjured testimony.

This justification assumes that the need to make a case for the deception before a judge and in cross-examination from a skeptical defense attorney will hold police accountable for deception. Presentation of the evidence requires disclosing the facts of the undercover investigation. Where these are distorted or withheld, the adversary system offers a means of discovery. The increased use of video and audio tapes in the courtroom is thought to enhance the accuracy of police testimony.

Undercover work is ethical when it is carried out by persons of upright character in accountable organizations. According to this assumption, deeds become ethical through the character of those who carry them out. Undercover work is legitimate when it is done by trained professionals sworn to uphold the law. Proponents argue that state practitioners of the covert arts are not "rogue elephants on a rampage" (a phrase used by Senator Church to describe the CIA),[8] but carefully chosen, monitored, supervised, and subjected to restrictive departmental, judicial, and legislative standards and oversight, not to mention their own consciences.

Most of the justifications for undercover work are not categorical assertions but involve contingencies (the objective, the kind of people involved, proper procedures) that make the operations ethical. Even so, most people experience at least some unease in the face of such tactics. Why should this be the case?

DECEPTIVE ETHICS

Those who justify undercover work argue that it represents *ethical deception,* but, to others, the effort to justify it represents *deceptive ethics* and involves logically irreconcilable elements. One police leader, when asked about the ethics of undercover work, shook his head and said, "that's like trying to invent dry water or fireproof coal."

The central (though not the only) ethical objection to undercover work is its very dependence on deception. A fundamental tenet of our culture is that, other factors being equal, *truth telling is moral, and lying is immoral.* Deception represents a form of lying.[9]

The morally undesirable character of deception can be seen in widely scattered places, such as the Ninth Commandment, Immanuel Kant's absolutist position that truth telling is an unconditional duty, legal judgments against fraud, false representation and perjury, and various aspects of popular culture—for example, George Washington and the cherry tree.[10] A literal application of the Law Enforcement Code of Ethics would even preclude undercover practices because it calls on an officer to be "honest in thought and deed in both my personal and official life."

Lying is wrong because it violates the trust that is central to human relationships and a civil society. It also must be avoided because of its tendency to expand. In Augustine's words, "little by little and bit by bit [it will] grow and by gradual accessions will slowly increase until it becomes such a mass of wicked lies that it will be utterly impossible to find any means of resisting such a plague grown to huge proportions through small additions."[11] Lying has long-range consequences.

Deception is likely to increase because it is required to protect the original deception and because it has a morally numbing, contagious quality.[12] Pinocchio's ever-extending nose symbolizes this. The acceptance of deception at the investigative stage eases the way for its use at the stage of interrogation after arrest and in courtroom testimony (where it is clearly prohibited).[13] To accept questionable means for good ends allows that they are also available for bad ends. Those against whom it is directed may use deception as self-defense or in retaliation.

The government should neither participate in, nor be a party to, crime nor break the law in order to enforce it. The state should not teach bad moral lessons or engage in "conduct that shocks the conscience." Justice Holmes wrote: "For my part I think it less evil that some criminals should escape than that the government should play an ignoble part."[14] For government agents to behave as criminals negates the difference between them. For agents to participate in or facilitate crime tarnishes the government's image. Law enforcement agents must set a moral tone and example. When they fail to do so, citizens may act in equivalent ways, and suspicion, mistrust, and lack of respect for, and cooperation with, government increase.

An August 1984 editorial in *Hawk Chalk* (the journal of the North American Falconry Association) captures the essence of these objections. The editorial was written in response to the U.S. Fish and Wildlife Service's "Operation Falcon":

> Three years of running a sting; three years of instigating illegal activities; three years of non-enforcement of falconry regulations; three years of some part of the falconry community watching someone "get away with" and try to persuade others into illegal activities; three years of watching authorities ignore reports that he was doing so—this is not the way to inspire respect for the USFWS or obedience to falconry regulations.

George Bernard Shaw once remarked that "just because God and the devil are on different sides of the fence doesn't mean they can't be friends." A former commissioner of narcotics, Harry J. Anslinger, stated in praise of a famous undercover agent, "if it meant making a case, he would grow a tail and dance with the devil."[15] These statements highlight an important aspect of much undercover work: the need for cooperation with criminals and persons of questionable character who are uniquely situated to catch other criminals.

Such cooperation is anathema to those who believe that *the government should not make deals with criminals.*[16] As the Law Enforcement Code of Ethics holds, the police officer should act "with no compromise for crime and with relentless prosecution of criminals." Persons who violate laws should be punished, not rewarded. They should be officially shunned, not made allies. It is a mockery to let evildoers profit from their wrongdoing. Dependence on such persons has a negative symbolism: it is unseemly for government to enter into such alliances.

It can also be unwise, given the belief that one cannot make deals with the devil without becoming tainted. A Southern folk saying catches this: "If you lie with dogs, you get fleas." This is the converse of the belief that covert action is ethical when it is carried out by ethical persons. Instead, it is unethical because it involves dealings with unethical persons. Both views presume a spin-off of either contamination or purification by association.

The expression "virtue's greatest ally is a lack of opportunity" suggests a principle involving temptation. *The government should not offer temptations to those who would otherwise be unlikely to encounter them, or offer unrealistically attractive temptations, or tempt the weak.* Religious texts are rich in directives—Lead us not into temptation; Do not offer wine to a Nazarite, or put a stumbling block before the blind. In Proverbs 28 : 10 one reads: "Who so causeth the righteous to go astray in an evil way, he shall fall himself into his own pit." The righteous may be led astray because they are tempted, tricked, cajoled, coaxed, or unaware that a crime is involved.

There are some offenses that certain undercover tactics can turn up a good proportion of the time, on the part of noncriminals as well as criminals. It is wrong to use extremely attractive temptations that go beyond what is found in the real world or temptations that are not normally available. It is also wrong to induce crime on the part of the weak or vulnerable (addicts, alcoholics, juveniles, mentally limited or ill persons).

Some of those interviewed derisively referred to certain forms of undercover activity as "cheap shots," "whore's tricks," "taking candy from a baby," "shooting sitting ducks," "stealing from a blind man," "letting a wolf herd the sheep," or "putting Dracula in charge of the blood bank." Certain arrests were either "too easy" or unrelated to important law enforcement goals. Some covert activities were considered beneath the dignity of, and degrading to, the professional officer, for example, deceiving addicts in search of drugs (or worse, experiencing withdrawal) to engage in some criminal act in return for drugs; the use of scantily clad, attractive policewomen to pose as prostitutes; the use of undercover officers dressed in outlandish costumes at gay bars; and the arrest of juveniles for purchasing small amounts of marijuana from undercover agents.

There is a profound difference between carrying out an investigation against someone when there are grounds for suspicion and carrying it out against someone to see if they can be induced to break the law. It is wrong to carry out an investigation merely to determine if a person can be corrupted. Law enforcement should devote its energies to actual wrongdoers and not to those who may under certain conditions be susceptible to temptation.

It is wrong for government to artificially create criminals and victims. Justice Brandeis wrote in 1928 that "the government may set decoys to entrap criminals. But it may not provoke or create a crime, and then punish the criminal, its creature." [17] The principle of fairness, as well as efficient resource use, underlies this principle.

The ancient medical proverb *Primum non nocere*—"First of all, do no harm"—is the source of the principle: *Do no harm to the innocent.* The Law Enforcement Code of Ethics obligates the officer "to protect the innocent against deception," but undercover operations may victimize the innocent. The secret and open-ended nature of the tactic prevents many of the controls found with conventional means and greatly increases the risk of collateral harm. Innocent "third parties" may be victimized by undercover crimes committed by others; as targets of an investigation, they may reject "the bait" but nevertheless suffer reputational damage and embarrassment.

Opponents of undercover operations further point to the surreptitious and unwarranted intrusiveness of covert tactics with respect to private places, personal relationships, and protected activities. Such operations are seen to violate spatial and social boundaries and values of privacy and liberty, including the right not to be spied on in these special domains. The dangers from intrusion are much greater with undercover means than with electronic surveillance; the actions of a decoy and the creation of a tempting opportunity can affect conversation and behavior in ways that a hidden recording device never can. Human bugs are not only ambulatory, they can ask leading questions and direct or deflect conversations.

Respect the sanctity of private places is best captured in the immortal eighteenth-century words of William Pitt: "The poorest man may in his cottage bid defiance to all the forces of the Crown. It may be frail—its roof may shake—the wind may blow through it—the storm may enter—the rain may enter—but the King of England cannot enter!—all his force dare not cross the threshold of the ruined tenement."

Undercover agents often violate this sanctity when they gain access to a person's home or workplace without a warrant. They may be invited in, but only because of deception—under the guise of friendship, a business partnership, or through the access granted a phony housing inspector or meter reader. It is sophistry to argue that such searches are voluntary. A person may give consent to a meter reader, but only to have the meter read, not to have the house searched. Consent is highly circumscribed; if the target was not duped, access would be denied. When the public-private boundary can be transgressed at will, whether through deception or coercion and force, liberty is impossible. Liberty exists partly because there are private and personal spaces that are beyond official reach.

Respect for the sanctity of intimate relations is another cornerstone of our concept of freedom and dignity.[18] The duplicity and betrayal inherent in covert operations trades in and debases the trust that is essential to, and characterizes, primary relations.[19] Their essence is the openness in communication that is characteristic of relationships where persons can be truly themselves. The common-law privilege precluding spousal testimony reflects a similar concern.

Sometimes both personal trust and professional confidentiality are violated by an undercover operation. For example, the undercover drug agent who enrolled as a student at the University of Texas and took a job as resident assistant in his dorm had, among his duties, drug counseling. But, even in more professional relationships, such as between doctors and patients or lawyers and clients, trust is enhanced and protected by nondisclosure rules. In return for a promise of confidentiality, persons in need of help feel freer to confide. When authorities pose as trusted professionals or surreptitiously use them as agents, this promise is obviously violated.

The right to freedom of action and expression is based on the First Amendment and includes the right to communicate ideas freely, to organize, to demonstrate, and to otherwise enjoy the protections of our political system. Undercover actions in some cases may only seek to create a "myth" of surveillance. The suspiciousness and paranoia generated by the myth may far transcend their actual use, but, by creating uncertainty, they may have a far greater repressive impact (at a much lower cost) than overt forms of surveillance.

Although generalized deterrence as a goal with respect to conventional criminal activities may be appropriate, it chills basic rights when directed against political groups. As a nineteenth-century English observer notes:

> Men may be without restraints upon their liberty: they may pass to and fro at pleasure: but if their steps are tracked by spies and informers, their works noted down for crimination, their associates watched as conspirators—who

shall say they are free? Nothing is more revolting to Englishmen than the espionage which forms part of the administrative system of continental despotism . . . the freedom of a country may be measured by its immunity from this baleful agency.[20]

However, the threat to political action is rarely of such a general nature. Only certain categories of people are likely to be objects of surveillance. This compounds the problem, as the method is then applied unequally. Rather than seeing undercover tactics as a means of *equal* law enforcement, it is seen to offer a dangerous potential for *unequal* law enforcement. As Paul Chevigny observes: "The power to offer a temptation to crime is the power to decide who shall be tempted. It can and often has been used as a way for the government to eliminate its enemies or for one faction in government to get rid of another."[21] This leads to the ethical principle of *not discriminating in target selection.*

Wherever there is discretion in law enforcement, however, there may be discrimination. But what lends the issue particular strength in the application of undercover means is the secrecy and absence of a complainant. Police can take the initiative on whatever grounds they choose. Ideally, the grounds should be universal (based on the seriousness of the offense) rather than personal and political (to get one's enemies). Undercover means permit disguising the latter as the former.

Discrimination in target selection can be seen in two contexts. In the first, a pattern of illegality is widespread (speeding, tax violations). Rather than deciding who to target as a result of citizen complaints, seriousness, or a random process, illegitimate criteria, such as the politics or life-style of the offender, are used. Enforcement of the law is discriminatory, but the person caught is presumably guilty of the offense. In the second, more troubling pattern, politics or life-style are used to determine whose morality will be tested. Although those who succumb to the bait are legally guilty, this guilt is a function of the initial targeting decision. Regardless of whether the context involves an overabundance of violations or a decision about whose morality will be tested, the discrimination permitted by undercover means is troubling.

Twentieth-century technical and social developments have radically altered the nature of law enforcement. The founders of the country could not have foreseen the many imaginative ways that have been devised to alter or evade constitutional protections. Nor have contemporary courts and legislatures usually chosen to get involved in providing concrete regulations for law enforcement.

With respect to undercover work, this suggests that *it is unethical for the government to do by stealth what it is prohibited from doing openly.* This principle recognizes the use/misuse of undercover tactics as a form of displacement or as an alternative to prohibited means. Undercover tactics can be an effective means for getting around restrictions on interrogation (the right to remain silent, to have a lawyer, protection against self-incrimination), testimonial privilege, electronic surveillance, search and seizure, and even entrapment when an unwitting informant is used. Where grounds for judicial warrant are lacking, it is wrong to use undercover methods to accomplish the same end.

IMPLICATIONS

G. K. Chesterton has noted that morality is like art—the line has to be drawn somewhere.

What should we conclude from these opposing arguments? We might conclude that no conclusion is possible because there can be no consensus on how the principles should be weighed or, given the nature of the issue, even what the facts really are. Or we might decide that a conclusion about ethics and undercover work is unimportant. Police will do what they feel they have to do, regardless of what outside observers may say. Concerns over innocence, moral purity, logical consistency, and conceptual distinctions are fine for academic analysts but are unlikely to count for much on the graveyard shift in an impoverished high crime area on Saturday night.

I don't think the situation is quite so hopeless. A degree of reconciliation, integration, and compromise is possible. Logical and empirical analysis can take us far toward reaching conclusions. Policy guidelines and even the law do in fact reflect ethical concerns and help shape work environments, though they are far from the only factors.

Much of the conflict between arguments for and against undercover work is more apparent than real. Many seemingly "conflicting" principles can be reconciled for at least five reasons.

They are contingent rather than categorical, and permissive or restrictive only under given conditions. Unlike the categorical prohibition "thou shalt not lie," many undercover issues deal with different and nonconflicting questions. Only in a few cases are they necessarily opposed. Thus, "respect the sanctity of private places" permits undercover means in public places.

To justify the tactic when there are grounds for suspicion means prohibiting it when such grounds are absent. To permit using it when the agent is the victim, as with anticrime decoys, still precludes making deals with criminals. Concerns about temptation do not preclude operations where the government agent plays a more passive observational role or comes to participate in an ongoing criminal plan. Most principles implicitly call for logical or empirical analysis and contain the qualifying phrase, "if, when, or to the extent that undercover tactics involve [whatever the restriction] they are/are not justified."

They state different aspects of a general principle, for example, "convict the guilty" and "do no harm to the innocent"; "enforce the law equally" and "do not discriminate in the selection of targets"; or "an investigation should be as nonintrusive and noncoercive as possible" and "respect the sanctity of intimate relations."

They can sometimes be weighed with respect to importance. Cultures may differ in how they weigh values, but within a culture there is often a broad-based consensus on the relative importance of competing values. Thus, although most persons would agree that "truth telling is moral and lying is immoral," they would also agree that the end may justify the means, for example, when protection from serious crime comes about as a result of official lying. When values or principles conflict, the less important value may have to be sacrificed.

As court decisions often suggest, *conflicting values can be balanced through compromise,* so that no value is fully realized or fully violated. Thus, a requirement that limits, though still permits, temptation may mean fewer arrests and less deterrence but greater protection of the weak and less entrapment.

Even when principles are logically inconsistent, *empirical research may suggest directives for action.* A considerable amount of disagreement about undercover tactics lies not with principles, but with conflicting beliefs about what the facts are. For example, if research suggests that a large majority of those arrested as a result of street decoy operations show no evidence of previous criminal activity (and turn out to be simply weak or vulnerable persons), many observers would feel that the tactic is inappropriate.[22] The grounds for this would be drawn from the principles stated earlier—Convict the guilty; Don't harm the innocent. Although we may agree that it is immoral to harm the innocent and for the government to increase crime, if research suggests that undercover work (or more properly, particular types under given circumstances) does not do this, then we can simply ignore these principles. Although they remain sound principles, they do not apply here.

Furthermore, some of the arguments between supporters and opponents of the tactic are misplaced because both sides are not responding to the same questions. Failing to differentiate among the following four issues can be a source of confusion. First, can undercover practices be ethical? I think the answer to this is a qualified "Yes." This leads to a second and a third question: under what conditions are they ethical—as a broad strategy or as tactically implemented? If we can resolve these matters, there is still a fourth question: in any given case, to what extent do the conditions for ethical use hold?

Some of the disagreement over Abscam, for example, stems from participants responding to different questions. Supporters often respond to the first and second questions, arguing that undercover practices are ethical, but critics respond to the third and fourth questions, arguing that in some, if not all, of the Abscam cases, the tactic was used in an unethical way.

A COMPASS, NOT A MAP

As suggested earlier, one solution to the problem of conflicting principles is to weigh them. In the criminal justice system, effectiveness often conflicts with humaneness, decency, or fairness. A democratic society gives significant weight to fairness and, thus, formally rejects the notion that the end justifies the means. Ethics attach to means as well as to ends, and some means are just too abhorrent to use. Police are prohibited from torturing people, pumping their stomachs to discover drugs, or harming innocent friends or relatives of the accused. These tactics are seen as so unethical that they are categorically rejected. The moral distinction between crime and criminal justice is maintained only by such restrictions.

However, few persons would argue that undercover means ought to be categorically prohibited or that they should be used indiscriminately without restrictions and guidelines. Given an intermediate position, where and how should the lines be drawn?

It is one thing to suggest why the reconciliation of conflicting ethical arguments is possible, and quite another to reconcile them. What should we answer to the question: is undercover work ethical? We can learn from the response of a wizened old stationmaster who, when asked whether or not the train would be on time, looked down at his watch, hesitated and then said, "That depends." When asked "What does it depend on?" he hesitated again and replied, "That depends too." So it is with undercover work. Whether or not it is ethical "depends." I think much of what it depends on is revealed by answers to the following questions.

Seriousness: is the use of undercover work proposed for crimes of a seriously harmful nature?[23]

Alternatives: are alternative nondeceptive means unavailable for obtaining the same end?

Democratic decision making: has granting police the option to use undercover means been subject to a degree of democratic decision making, however indirect, and has it been publicly announced that such means will be used?

Spirit of the law: is use of the strategy consistent with the spirit, as well as the letter, of the law?

Prosecution: is the goal of the strategy eventually to invoke criminal justice processing and hence make the deception publicly subject to judgment, rather than to gather intelligence indiscriminately, to harass, or to coerce cooperation from an informer?

Clarity of definition: is its use proposed for crimes that are clearly defined, or, if not, can a tactic be devised that insures the target is well aware of the criminal nature of the behavior?

Crime occurrence: are there reasonable grounds for concluding that the crime that occurs as a result of the undercover operation is not an artifact of the method of intervention?

Grounds for suspicion: are there reasonable grounds for concluding that the particular target of an undercover operation has already committed or is likely to commit an equivalent offense, regardless of the government's undercover effort?

Prevention: are there reasonable grounds for concluding that the undercover operation will prevent a serious crime from occurring?

The greater the number and strength of affirmative answers, the more ethically defensible a general undercover strategy is. Questions must also be raised about the ethics of particular activities within the investigation. (It may be ethical as a broad strategy, even when specific aspects are unethical.) The following questions deal with the actual organization and dynamics of the operation.

Autonomy: does the tactic permit a high degree of self-selection and/or autonomy on the part of the suspect in breaking the law?

Degree of deception: does use of the tactic involve minimal or extensive deception, and is the degree of deception involved only that which is necessary to carry out the investigation?

Bad lessons: how far does the tactic go in casting the state in the role of teaching a bad moral lesson?

Privacy and expression: will use of the tactic sufficiently respect the sanctity of private places, intimate and professional relations, and the right to freedom of expression and action?

Collateral harm: how great is the potential for exploitation, corruption, perjury, or abuses and harm to police, informers, and unwitting third parties? Can these be adequately controlled or compensated for?

Equitable target selection: are the criteria for target selection equitable?

Realism: does the undercover scene stay reasonably close to real-world settings and opportunities?

Relevance of charges: are the charges brought against a person directly connected with criminal harm, or do they reflect mere procedural violations?

Actors: does the undercover investigation involve sworn agents playing central roles rather than informers?

Asking such questions is important if one accepts Sissela Bok's position that lying is not neutral and that there should be a presumption against it.[24] To use undercover tactics will require greater justification than is the case for more conventional police methods. The situation is analogous to the greater justification required for, and stricter controls around, the use of force. The greater the extent of the affirmative or "harm-avoiding" answers to the above questions, the more justified an undercover operation is.[25]

The two sets of questions presented above should be seen as navigational aids and not as a flight plan. They are skill-honing devices that can increase the sensitivity of the judgments made by agents, police supervisors, criminal justice officials, and concerned citizens. In noting that some resolution of the disagreements around secret police tactics is possible, our optimism (for both the resolution and the tactic) must remain qualified and guarded.

The title of this chapter is taken from Edward Shils's observation that "civil politics requires an understanding of the complexity of virtue, that no virtue stands alone, that every virtuous act costs something in terms of other virtuous acts, that virtues are intertwined with evil." The contradiction involved in calling something a necessary evil alerts us to the fact that principles do not cease to conflict, even when an operational solution is found. The hallmark of a moral dilemma, of course, is that there is no way out. This is part of the topic's fascination and why persons of good will strenuously disagree. We can not reach a general conclusion about whether undercover tactics should be prohibited or justified on ethical grounds. Paradoxically, no matter what action is taken, there are moral costs. There are clear costs whenever the government uses deceit, and still other costs are at risk. But not to use the tactic can have costs too—whether inaction and inequality in law enforcement in the face of serious crime, or the greater costs that may accompany use of some other tactic.

In dealing with such moral dilemmas, the problem is not only whether we can find an acceptable utilitarian calculus, but that the choice always involves competing wrongs.[26] The danger of automatically applied technical, bureaucratic, or occupational subcultural formulas lies in their potential for generating the self-deluding and morally numbing conclusion that a costfree solution is possible.

SIX

Intended Consequences of Undercover Work

[Fencing stings] are unquestionably the hottest thing in law
enforcement today.
　　　　　　　—A police lieutenant, Washington, D.C.

After the TPF's [tactical patrol unit] first night in front of the Hillbilly
Ranch, all the pimps, prostitutes, pickpockets and parking attendants
in the area knew about the decoy setup and could spot it instantly.
The TPF always claimed it was pulling in major-league criminals, but
I found it hard to believe that any real bad guys could actually fall
for it. It seemed more like a trap for Vermont farmers who had just
dropped the harvest money at neighboring strip joints.
　　　　　　　—L. O'Donnell, 1983

St. Paul said: "All things are lawful unto me, but all things are not expe-
dient." When undercover means are lawful and ethical, is it still necessary to ask if they work? To answer this, a distinction should be made
between operations directed against subjects whose identity is known in
advance and those directed against a more general "market" of suspects. The criteria for judging the former are self-evident; for example,
when an agent pretends to be a hit man and accepts a contract to kill
someone, a homicide may be prevented; when a decoy strategy is used
in response to a particular pattern of assaults (a female decoy seeks to be
a victim by walking at night in a park that has seen a series of rapes), the
offender may be apprehended.[1] These individualized target-specific investigations are judged by their immediate success or failure.

But the evaluation situation for many other undercover operations is
different and more difficult, given unclear or multiple general goals and
a lack of specificity regarding expected outcomes. It may not be clear at
the outset just who the criminals are (or if those who will become a part
of the investigation are in fact criminals), what the crime is, or if one is
even present, or how the operation will develop, change, and terminate.
For example, in Florida what started as an investigation of gambling
and bingo "just grew and grew" to include murder, bank robbery, extortion, bribery, and racketeering in the garbage industry. The complex,

relatively unique, and long-running cases of recent years do not lend themselves well to traditional criminal justice program evaluation. The latter involves before/after quantitative measures and the analysis of a large number of roughly comparable cases.

There is also likely to be disagreement over just what should count as success or failure and how outcomes should be interpreted. In many cases, a crime has not yet occurred and the goal is to test whether or not someone will take the bait. Does the operation "succeed" if someone takes the bait and is found guilty, and does it "fail" if the corrupt offer is refused? If there are strong grounds for predication, then the former is appropriate. But when the grounds for suspicion are muddier, as is often the case, then failure to take the bait may not mean that the operation failed. Indeed, from the abstract standpoint of justice and where the concern is with due process rather than arrest, a fair test in which the corrupt opportunity is rejected is a "success." A lack of arrests may also be taken as a sign of the tactic's effectiveness as a deterrent.

Standing midway between the highly focused and the open-ended diffuse operations are property stings and anticrime decoys. These have general (and sometimes specific) goals, involve a large number of roughly comparable cases (within and between jurisdictions), and before and after measurements are possible. Not surprisingly, it is only in this area that systematic quantitative research on effects has been done.

Proponents of property stings and anticrime decoys argue that they deter crime, result in a large number of arrests, recover much stolen property, and sometimes yield valuable intelligence. They are considered effective and efficient relative to other means of crime prevention. Skeptics dispute these claims, arguing that they have no deterrent effect, that those arrested are often marginal criminals, and that some of the "recovered" property would not have been stolen were it not for the opportunity suddenly provided by agents.

Which perspective is more accurate? It is easier to raise the question than to answer it. There are few in-depth evaluations, and they are subject to criticism, but they do provide some limited answers.

MEASURING IMPACTS

LEAA PROPERTY STINGS

A large-scale evaluation by R. Bowers and J. McCullough examined first-grant Property Crime programs (originally called antifencing programs) funded by LEAA.[2] Between 1974 and 1981, more than sixty programs were funded. Grants typically covering two or three overlapping operations ranged from $200,000 to $450,000 and ran for 18 to 24 months. The undercover sting tactic employed was similar across several jurisdictions: undercover officers posed as fences to purchase from persons they believed to be thieves or fences property they suspected was stolen. Most programs conducted their business from fixed locations (storefronts or warehouses); some used semi-fixed or mobile locations (motel rooms, apartments, vehicles). The major criterion in site selection was the ability to "do good business." Typically, operations were in high-crime areas, often lower-class neighborhoods with predominantly black populations.

Potential suspects were brought into the fencing operation by a process known as "scouting." Posing as thieves, police officers would frequent areas where thieves and fences were believed to congregate and would try to steer them to the storefront. Witting and unwitting informers were often used to add "legitimacy" to the criminal background of the undercover scouts or to the operation as a whole.

The stings resulted in an organized police penetration of criminal milieus on a scale unique in American history. Officials were stunned by the offers they received to sell "virtually anything that could be stolen." In Syracuse, New York, a mobile unit of a television station was offered for sale. In Lakewood, Colorado, it was nerve gas stolen by an employee of the Rocky Mountain Arsenal. In Dallas, Texas, a 250-pound lion named Sam was sold to undercover agents. In New Orleans, a supervisor of munitions for the Louisiana National Guard sold explosives. In San Jose, it was a baby. In Buffalo, New York, a leading businessman offered jewels. In New York, the "management rights" to 11 prostitutes were offered, and on Long Island, a stenographic machine stolen from the court was for sale. A local policeman sold his badge and motorcycle to an Atlantic City sting run by the New Jersey State Police. In some cities, customers offered to carry out homicides on demand.

Some stings specialized in limited areas, for example, endangered species, precious metals, pornography, illegal tapes and records, and autos, but the majority of those funded by LEAA were "all purpose." Among the most common items purchased were cars, electronic goods, office equipment, drugs, firearms, jewelry, silverware, credit cards, government checks, and stocks and securities.

The programs originally targeted fences as well as thieves, but it soon became clear that fences were unlikely to enter undercover storefronts set up to compete with them. Consequently, greater emphasis was put on apprehending thieves and on recovering the stolen property they brought to sell. Another deviation from the original conception was that most buys turned out to be small, rather than large, transactions.

"Buy money" was provided by the LEAA grants. The dollar amount ranged from $4,000 to $10,000 a month. To insure adequate evidence, fencing transactions were videotaped by hidden cameras. A "three-buy" rule (at least three transactions prior to arrest) was suggested by LEAA.[3] In some cases, in a counterintelligence move, police "stole from the thieves." For example, in Jacksonville, Florida, a man came to sell a stolen tractor-trailer with a bulldozer on it, valued at $75,000. While a price was being negotiated, other officers "stole" it. The rationale was to conserve project funds.

Over the life of a sting project, from 10 to 15 sworn officers were typically involved, with about the same number of local and federal agents. Because secrecy was so important, in many jurisdictions police participants were asked to volunteer for a special assignment without benefit of task descriptions. Those assigned to the programs were overwhelmingly white males. Most were experienced officers with 10 to 15 years on the job.

Although the stings were a deadly serious business involving considerable stress and risks, the deception often permitted outlets for imagination and humor; as one officer remarked: "Who said police work isn't fun?" Many of the business names adopted by storefronts were acronyms, such as CTT Inc. ("Catch Thieves and Thugs"), PDQ Moving Company ("Police Don't Quit"), FASCATS Inc. ("Federal and State Catch a Thief Store"), Camp Enterprises ("Crime Always Means Punishment"), and GSH ("Get Stung Here"). In some cities where a series of stings were used, the titles reflected this—YBC Associates ("You've Been Caught Again"), IUA Inc. ("It's Us Again"). Operation Coldwater was directed at a suspect whose last name was Acquafredda. The names taken by agents also sometimes had this playful element—Robert A. Covert, Michael T. Serra (arrest).

There was considerable variation among stings in purchasing property and disposing of it. When possible, it was returned to its original owners; most was turned over to insurance companies that had paid off on stolen property claims. Some was eventually returned to the store to be sold, some was sold at an auction, and some "unclaimed" property, such as cars and weapons, was kept by local police for departmental use.

Bowers and McCullough chose five programs for intensive study—
Detroit, Michigan; Fort Worth, Texas; Jacksonville, Florida; Kansas
City/Overland Park, Kansas; and Los Angeles, California—because detailed records were readily available. An additional three programs—
Memphis; New Jersey State Police; and Oklahoma City—were evaluated
somewhat less intensively. The sample was, unfortunately, not randomly
drawn; some operations were selected as "especially successful" or rep-
resenting the "state of the art."

Open-ended interviews were carried out with police participants,
though not with informers or suspects. Two sets of quantitative data
were generated: the first involved information on "suspects," defined
rather vaguely as "any . . . person who entered a sting storefront or was
encountered during the course of an undercover operation, other than
informants whose presence was expected"; the second involved data on
transactions, defined as "the exchange of money or property."

The number of suspects ranged from 96 in Overland Park to 554 in
Los Angeles; most lived less than six miles from the fences they visited;
about 50 percent of them were actually arrested (Fort Worth was an exception with 91 percent). A majority of those arrested had prior felony
arrests.[4] There were few differentiating characteristics between those the
stings encountered as "suspects" and those actually arrested. All sites
averaged less than ten cents per dollar's worth of recovered property—
the guideline set by LEAA; the median dollars per transaction ranged
from $100 to $400. Transactions involved autos or auto parts more
than any other type of property. A large majority of those arrested
pleaded guilty as charged; there was little plea bargaining; of the fewer
than 10 percent of cases that went to trial, almost all were found guilty
as charged. The video evidence was clearly important here. The rates of
successful prosecution are not as high for persons arrested through conventional means.[5]

Bowers and McCullough use these data, given in table 3, to conclude
that the sting approach was highly effective. They point to the arrest and
conviction of persons with prior arrest records, the large dollar value of
property recovered relative to dollar outlay, and the increased morale
and skill building among officers as support. There is no in-depth comparison of results with more conventional investigative practices, no attempt to apply anything other than a narrow definition of costs and
benefits, and no attempt to assess the program's impact on crime rates.

Westinghouse evaluators using some of the same data applied a time-
series analysis to programs in three jurisdictions. In their words, the re-

TABLE 3   RESULTS OF THE LEAA PROPERTY CRIME
PROGRAM IN SELECTED CITIES

	No. of arrests	Percentage arrests of encounters	Recoveries (in dollars)	No. to court	Percentage dismissed or discontinued	Court Outcome (percentage)				Reduction in incidence of target offense?
						Guilty plea	Guilty at trial	Guilty to reduced charge	Conviction rate	
a. Detroit	176	65	$3,316,650	158	8	92	0	0	92	—
b. Fort Worth	324	91	3,126,330	251	17	73	10	0	83	—
c. Jacksonville	116	48	975,234	99	4	87	9	1	96	—
d. Kansas City	145	50	1,496,356	117	12	82	3	0	85	—
e. Overland Park	45	47	335,898	40	20	70	10	5	80	—
f. Los Angeles	297	54	32,466,612	161	30	57	13	4	70	—
g. Detroit	252	63	10,091,655	212					93	no
h. San Diego										
Antifencing	39	—	413,355	39	—	—	—	—	72	no
Storefront	46	—	220,000	—	—	—	—	—	—	no

SOURCES: (a–f) R. Bowers and J. McCullough, *Assessing the "Sting": An Evaluation of the LEAA Property Crime Program* (Washington, D.C.: University Science Center, 1982); (g) K. Weiner, C. Stephens, and D. Besachuk, "Making Inroads into Property Crime: An Analysis of the Detroit Anti-Fencing Program," *Journal of Police Science and Administration* 11 (Sept. 1983): 311–27; (h) S. Greer, S. Pennell, and B. McCardell, *Sheriff's Department: Crimes Against Property Control (Anti-Fencing Unit)* (San Diego: Criminal Justice Evaluation Unit, 1979).

Notes: In all areas, the suspects were older than their nonproject counterparts. In Detroit (1983), prosecution rates were higher than for similar arrests made with conventional means; this was not true in San Diego. Exhibit 4-37 in Bowers and McCullough has been recalculated. A dash (—) indicates that data were not available.

sults were "cloudy." In only one of the cities was a statistically significant decrease in crime noted, and this was for only one of several simultaneous operations.

DETROIT ANTIFENCING PROGRAM

A more in-depth analysis exists for the Detroit sting program, which
considers the results of five operations over a three-year period before,
during, and after the projects (see table 3, line g).[6] The analysis sought
to determine the impact of sting programs on crime levels; the conclusion was that sting operations appear to have had no effect on crime
rates. The researchers observed that there is no evidence "to support the
conclusion that the presence of a sting operation in an area has encouraged or increased crime . . . or the supposition that crime will decrease
due to attendant publicity that created fear in the thieves following take-
down of an anti-fencing project."

With respect to disposition, sting arrests were more likely to be
prosecuted and less likely to be dismissed once prosecution began than
arrests made through conventional means. On the disposition of property purchased by the sting, the five operations were estimated to have
netted $10 million in property and $9 million in narcotics; 90 percent of
the property was returned to its rightful owners, and the rest destroyed
or sold at auction.

SAN DIEGO SHERIFF'S DEPARTMENT
FENCING UNIT

Under LEAA sponsorship, the San Diego Sheriff's Department received a two-year grant to establish a special antifencing unit to combat
property crimes.[7] During the first year, the unit used informants' information to conduct surveillance and carry out sell-bust and buy-bust
operations. In the second year, officers were deployed in two storefronts
instead, which resulted in the arrest of 46 persons and the recovery of
$220,000 worth of property.

Although it is generally believed that specialized units effect more
"quality" arrests than conventional units, this was not indicated in San
Diego. In fact, during the year the antifencing unit operated as such, the
department complaint (charge) per arrest ratio actually declined (see
table 3). Contrary to findings in the Detroit studies, the San Diego unit
did not show a higher rate of guilty pleas. The evaluation concluded that

the operation did not meet its overall objectives, and additional funding was not recommended. Property crime continued to rise.

BIRMINGHAM ANTIROBBERY UNIT

With a grant from the Police Foundation in 1977, the Birmingham (Alabama) Police Department created a special antirobbery unit (ARU). The ARU operated in cycles, opening for 3 months and shutting down for 3 months over an 18-month period. This schedule provided an "interrupted time series" research design, which is much more accurate for evaluation than after-the-fact studies.

Fifteen officers conducted decoy operations, stationary and roving surveillance, and served warrants. Decoys were deployed in areas with a high incidence of street robberies. Disguised officers would "work" a particular locale by inviting attack through their disheveled appearance and enough exposed money to permit felony charges.

The element of force necessary to classify street crimes as robberies created a dilemma for the decoy operation. If the decoy money was displayed in such a way that it could be obtained with little effort, the unit was open to charges of entrapment. But, using force, for example, by having decoy officers put up some resistance, would subject them to an unacceptably high potential for injury. Consequently, decoy arrests seldom contained the legal elements of robbery, although they were so classified. To reflect more accurately the actual activity, personal larceny was added to the list of targeted offenses.

An evaluation of the ARU examined its effectiveness along several dimensions: apprehension of suspects; quality of arrest and resulting cases; and impact on robbery incidence.[8] It combined the analysis of records and statistics with interviews and direct observation. Because this project was studied in progress, it permitted comparisons between periods when the unit was active and inactive.

The ARU failed as a robbery unit. As a whole, it had little impact on arrest rates for larceny or robbery. In fact, the periods when the ARU was inactive show a higher arrest-to-incident ratio than periods when the unit was operational. On only four occasions were arrests made in the course of surveillance activities; in two of these cases, officers watching stores that were robbed did not know the crimes had occurred until they heard about them on the police radio.[9] The antirobbery unit made 81 decoy arrests over the nine-month period; 6 in 10 of those apprehended had previous arrest records. Decoy arrestees had less serious prior felony records than nondecoy arrests the unit made, or than those arrested for robbery through conventional means (table 4). Decoy arrests were less likely to be rejected by prosecutors, perhaps because they involve police as direct witnesses.

Low morale among the officers emerged as an unexpected problem. This was attributed to the limits on the number of robberies that could be handled by the unit and a sense that some of the decoy arrests involved "persons who were not particularly serious culprits." Boredom may have further reduced productivity: officers sought diversion by "finding a movie or television to watch, or by driving around unassigned areas." The existence of the specialized ARU also contributed to interunit antagonisms.[10] Envy and hostility by noninvolved officers may have affected the degree of cooperation, particularly in the form of information sharing.

NEW YORK CITY POLICE DEPARTMENT'S STREET CRIME UNIT

The New York City Police Department Street Crime Unit (SCU) was organized in 1971. In 1977 it was designated one of LEAA's exemplary projects and thus subject to evaluation.[11] Several hundred specially trained officers were deployed on a monthly basis to precincts in New York City with high levels of street crime. Using plainclothes surveillance and decoy tactics, the units attempted to arrest suspects in the act of committing crimes. The primary objective was to effect quality arrests.

The SCU made 4,413 arrests in 1974; 90 percent of these included a felony charge, two-thirds of them for robbery or grand larceny from a person. Decoys as eyewitnesses rather than as victims accounted for 1 in 3 of the larceny arrests. (In such cases, a de facto blending rather than a decoy strategy is operative.) Of those arrested, 3 out of 4 had previous arrest records, but, unlike Birmingham, their records were as serious as those of persons arrested through conventional means. Conviction rates were higher for SCU arrests than for departmentwide robbery arrests in general.

The level of reported crime in a precinct when the SCU was active compared to the level the following month when the SCU was inactive showed that the unit was "decreasing neither robberies nor larcenies from a person." Unlike Birmingham, this evaluation found extraordinary motivation on the part of SCU personnel.

TABLE 4 RESULTS OF TWO ANTICRIME DECOY PROGRAMS

| | No. of arrests | Suspects more criminally active than those arrested through other means? | Higher prosecution rates than for similar arrests? | Court Outcome (percentage) | | | | | Reduction in incidence of target offense? |
				Dismissed or discontinued	Guilty plea	Guilty at trial	Guilty to reduced charge	Conviction rate	
Birmingham*	81	no	yes	13	70	11	19	81	no
New York City	4,413	no	—	—	—	—	—	90	no

SOURCES: *Birmingham*: M. Wycoff, C. Brown, and R. Peterson, *Birmingham Evaluation Report, Draft Three* (Washington, D.C.: Police Foundation, 1980). *New York City*: A. Halper and R. Ku, *An Exemplary Project: New York City Police Street Crime Unit* (Washington, D.C.: GPO, n.d.). Table IV-16 in Wycoff has been recalculated.
*Larceny and robbery arrests combined.

SUMMARY

Meaningful comparisons are limited by the problems of evaluation design, data quality, program artifacts, and illusive and elusive indicators. The assessment of costs and benefits is inadequate and should go beyond a simple comparison of dollars spent relative to property recovered.[12] Quantitative comparisons should be made between these and more conventional approaches. A broader range of data must be gathered to improve the assessment of costs and benefits. However, taken at face value, certain conclusions can be drawn.

Tables 3 and 4 summarize the major research findings from the five studies. The data generally suggest that stings and decoys result in many arrests, much recovered property, high rates of guilty pleas (with little plea bargaining), and a high likelihood of a finding of guilty for the small proportion of cases that go to trial. The data regarding who gets arrested (hardened criminals vs. easily tempted citizens or many who would escape arrest absent undercover means) are less clear, but the majority of those arrested are not new to the criminal justice system. The data do not suggest deterrent impacts.[13] Several studies even find the opposite. It appears that these tactics in general do not produce more or better arrests than those of the aggregate of officers acting individually.

EMPIRICAL ASSUMPTIONS

The temptation to form premature theories upon insufficient data is the bane of our profession.
—*Sir Arthur Conan Doyle*, The Valley of Fear, *1914*

The justification for the two undercover strategies considered in this chapter rests on ten empirical assumptions:[14]

1.   The fence is the dominant figure in a relatively concentrated and organized system for the distribution of stolen property.

2.   The supply of and demand for illicit goods and services are limited.

3.   The world is clearly divided between criminals and noncriminals.

4.   The existing level of crime is large enough to support stings and anticrime decoys.

5.   Undercover practices can have a major impact in reducing crime, apprehending criminals, and recovering stolen property.

6. Those arrested in stings and decoy operations are repeat offenders who might otherwise avoid arrest.

7. The not guilty (this time) assumption.

8. Undercover operations do not amplify crime.

9. Undercover operations are independent of each other.

10. Undercover operations can control their environment.

To the degree that these assumptions are correct, the more sense it makes to use the strategies, other factors being equal. The empirical evidence considered thus far, as limited as it is, is not reassuring, but much research remains to be done.

These assumptions are not exhaustive and do not form a logical and consistent belief system, of which practitioners are always aware. Some are tacit but no less important as a result. If they turn out to be empirically unjustified, the resulting investigations may be wasteful, ineffective, and even counterproductive. Before a project is undertaken, the empirical evidence for the assumptions should be assessed.

The fence is the dominant figure in a relatively concentrated and organized system for the distribution of stolen property. The antifencing program initiated by LEAA in the early 1970s was developed around a model that assumed stolen property moved through a rationally organized system of theft and resale.[15] The fence was assumed to be the central figure directing the flow of stolen goods. If undercover officers posed as fences, they could infiltrate the system and disrupt the illegal flow of goods. According to the model, fewer property crimes would occur as a result.

Some research questions this assumption. A Miami study found that the stolen property system was far more diffuse than initially assumed. S. Pennell's San Diego study argued that it is not the major fence who receives the greatest proportion of stolen property: "Receivers of stolen property include a myriad of occasional receivers: the bartender at the neighborhood tavern, the gas station operator, the car salesman, the second-hand dealer, and the Sunday shopper at the swapmart."[16]

To the extent that property crime transactions are diffuse and shifting, undercover operators may find it difficult to determine just what kind of network they have penetrated—a marginal effort or a core operation. It may also be difficult to determine if they have penetrated an existing network or created a new one: undercover activities might actually help impose order on a diffuse, loosely coupled system of stealing and receiving. In a self-fulfilling prophecy, undercover agents might create a system out of a loose confederation of thievery. If thieves steal and fence close to home, as research suggests, the establishment of a fencing network may create local opportunities where none existed before. Moreover, they may create a network that can be exploited by real fences when the operation closes down.

The supply of, and demand for, illicit goods and services is limited. The property crime model assumes that these are relatively fixed and inelastic. A corollary is that there is a certain amount of crime that will come out, regardless of what authorities do. All an undercover investigation does is substitute a police for a citizen victim or a police co-conspirator for a genuine criminal.

However, if this assumption is incorrect, that is, if supply and demand are elastic, the strategy may produce the opposite of its intended effect. In the case of the buy-bust and narcotics arrests, for example, if there are few limits on supply, buy-bust strategies may simply create new demand and push up prices. According to a former DEA investigator, "it is very possible that the technique of buy, so called—that is buying evidence from drug traffickers themselves—may be a form of preemptive buying that is counterproductive, since there is no limit on supply, you can keep buying them out." [17] For authorities to sell drugs secretly may similarly increase demand. If the potential supply of stolen goods is not limited, antifencing buy-bust techniques may do little to decrease the property crime rate and may even increase it.

For many vice and petty theft arrests, the supply of violations does seem almost unlimited. A phrase encountered several times in response to prostitution-related arrests was "we had to stop. The jail couldn't hold any more." Boston officers refer to one area of the city as "the well" because at any time and in any weather arrests for theft from a drunken decoy with an exposed wallet can be made.

The world is clearly divided between criminals and noncriminals. Abscam informant Mel Weinberg believes that "a guy's either a crook, or he isn't. If he ain't a crook, he ain't gonna do anything illegal no matter what I offer him or tell him to do." If that is correct, presenting a temptation will not endanger the uprightness of the latter, while the former will commit the offense, no matter what. The following story, inspired by George Bernard Shaw, captures this assumption: "A man encounters a woman in a fancy bar and asks her, 'Would you accompany me to my hotel for $10,000?' She says 'Yes.' Whereupon he asks her whether she would come to his room for $10. She indignantly says, 'No, what kind of a girl do you think I am?' He responds, 'Madam, we have already established that; what we are haggling about is the price.'"

If the major impetus for rule breaking is to be found within the *person* of the rule breaker rather than within the *situation,* then government temptations involve no more than "feeding hungry sharks," "letting a fox loose in the chicken coop." To the question raised in *Measure for Measure,* "Is this her fault or mine? The tempter or the tempted, who sins most?" the answer is clearly only the tempted.[18] If the dichotomy holds, then the righteous have nothing to fear from covert temptations, but criminals will break the law, regardless of this particular government-provided opportunity.

On the other hand, if all or many noncriminals are vulnerable to temptation and if we cannot tell beforehand who's who, then undercover tactics must be used only when there are grounds for suspicion, because to do otherwise runs the risk of creating crimes among the righteous. There is a parallel to the limitations on search and seizure. In order to avoid wrongly invading the privacy of persons who have done nothing wrong, police need grounds to carry out a search.

The situational context is important, even apart from any direct gain for the target. Many "good" persons can be duped into breaking the law when they believe they are doing it on behalf of a government investigation or for some altruistic purpose. Thus, a psychological experiment found that a surprisingly large percentage of unwitting subjects expressed a willingness to participate in a burglary that they believed was to be carried out as part of a government inquiry.[19]

Rule breaking (or conformity) may also be induced by more subtle manipulation of social influence and social learning factors. Setting an example may lead others to behave in the same way. Some behavior involves a nonconscious or only partly conscious mimicry or imitation (coughing, laughing, or smoking in audience settings) and, under some conditions, the expression of aggression. Some social movement activists and undercover agents are adept at affecting crowd behavior. Note also the early research that found that a "plant" who jaywalks or enters a building in spite of a sign saying "Do not enter" served to increase the frequency of such behavior among the unsuspecting.[20]

It is easy to imagine how these principles of behavior might be drawn upon to affect behavior. Thus, if the goal is the apprehension of people who speed, authorities might use a variety of unmarked patrol cars to exceed the speed limit and then use other unmarked cars to arrest the unsuspecting cars who also speed in imitation, or in thinking it is safe to do so. Conversely, they might use the cars to drive within the speed limit. Undercover agents smoking marijuana in public settings might have the effect of encouraging others to do likewise. Agents appearing as street people might steal from one of several drunk decoys on a subway—modeling the behavior for onlookers.

Nonetheless, there are limits. Studies of self-reported involvement in crime find a J-curve pattern, with a large proportion of persons admitting to a few, usually trivial offenses, and only a few admitting to serious crimes.[21] This suggests a gradient effect with respect to secret temptations and/or manipulative efforts. As the crime becomes more serious, the proportion who would be tempted is likely to decrease. On the other hand, we might also predict that the more attractive the temptation and the less the apparent risk of getting caught, the greater the proportion of normally law-abiding persons who would succumb.

Aside from a questionable general deterrence effect, it is unwise to use scarce enforcement resources on marginal, amateur, or first-time violators whose infraction is purely an artifact of the operation. As noted earlier, the design of the undercover program and/or nature of the offense sometimes makes it likely that only serious offenders with a clear predisposition to commit the crime will be drawn in, for example, where careful screening methods are present or where mere possession or sale of contraband is likely to be evidence of illegality.

In cases where the operation is more diffuse and open-ended, where the determination that an offense occurred depends on the interpretation of behavior and motives, and where the temptation and/or pressure from the operative is strong, the assumption is more questionable. Did the person arrested as he bent over the decoy really commit larceny, or was he seeking to help? Did the man arrested for soliciting a policewoman posing as a prostitute intend to violate the law, or was he simply responding to a tempting and ambiguous situation of the kind that occurs daily between the sexes? Was a conspiracy present, or were persons simply trying to impress each other with daring talk? Would the 17-year-old freshmen have tried to burn down an ROTC building without the encouragement and pressure from an older agent provocateur?

There is a likely time dimension to the "who gets caught" question. The "bad person" assumption may hold more for an initial undercover operation than for subsequent ones. If the relation between police and criminals (especially the highly skilled) is viewed as a continuing struggle with one responding to the other's temporary tactical advantage, then there will be diminishing returns with respect to innovative practices. Committed criminals will realize they must be more clever; this will result in the arrest of an increasing proportion of less-skilled offenders.

In the case of storefront operations, as the Westinghouse study suggested, thieves changed their modus operandi in response to a sting. They may steal more cash or focus on property that is difficult to trace. They may visit the fence only once under a disguised identity. In the case of decoys, intended targets may catch on quickly. Members of decoy units report remarks, such as: "Hey cop, better put that wallet in your pants before someone takes it" and "Officer, your purse is open." Sometimes they are even warned: "Be careful; the decoys are out." Over time, the proportion of derelicts, children, and others unable to resist temptation is likely to increase among those arrested.

The existing level of crime is large enough to support stings and anti-crime decoys. Undercover programs that systematically target specific offenses assume that enough incidents occur to justify special operations. In some cities, property stings were closed down after considerable start-up costs because they could not find enough business. The lack of "clients," coupled with the sizable expenditures of time and other resources, can generate undue production pressures, leading police to make questionable arrests.

As noted, the undercover unit in Birmingham suffered a noticeable drop in morale and effort because of the real limits on robberies that were "available" to be processed. The Birmingham evaluation also suggests that even some metropolitan areas do not have sufficient street crime or that the pool of offenders may be too spread out for an effective undercover response.

Undercover practices can have a major impact in reducing crime, apprehending criminals, and recovering stolen property. It is assumed that stings and decoys result in a reduction of their targeted offenses. Well-publicized operations are thought to communicate a threat to would-be offenders. The strategy seeks to create the impression that anyone making an illegal offer or temptation might be part of a covert law enforcement plan, thus dissuading potential offenders. Research thus far has not supported this assumption.

Stings have an obvious public relations value, partly because of the cumulative impact of making many arrests at once. They are welcomed by police who are often hard pressed to show that they are effectively dealing with crime. The press releases issued when a sting is shut down create the impression of a major impact. In 1977 the Criminal Conspiracies Division of LEAA heralded the large number of indictments and arrests attributed to the sting programs—4,600.[22] But this was over a four-year period and involved 62 separate operations. The average number of arrests per program was 65.

Given the small size of sting operations relative to total citywide law enforcement efforts and the small numbers of offenders arrested, it seems unlikely that they have much of an impact. To the extent that most experienced thieves have trusted means of fencing their goods, the idea of deterrence would seem to hold primarily for persons who have found it necessary to deal with strangers.

In Detroit, for example, 176 persons were arrested as a result of three undercover operations over a 24-month period. Assuming an average clearance rate of 4.2 and assuming all crimes were reported, the operations had an impact on 740 reported crimes.[23] But in 1977, the first year of Detroit's undercover operation, a total of 99,677 property crimes were reported. Similarly, in Kansas City, 145 persons were arrested as a result of a sting program that operated for 12 months. It is likely this had an impact on 609 reported crimes—less than 2 percent of the 33,000 property crimes that occurred while the sting was in operation. In areas where the total reported property crime is relatively low, the sting tactic is likely to have a much greater impact on citywide clearance rates. In Overland Park, Kansas, e.g., where there were 3,670 reported property crimes in 1977, the 96 persons arrested in the property sting may have accounted for 11 percent of the total property crime. However, if the crime rate is too low, an operation may not be justified because of a failure to satisfy the previous assumption.

To expect property stings to have a large impact may be as unrealistic as "trying to sweep the sun off the porch with a broom," but there may be reasons to mount sting operations apart from their deterrence value. There is an important difference between what is *statistically significant* according to technical criteria and what is *socially significant*. Impacting 609 crimes and perhaps preventing many more while the perpetrators are incarcerated is not insignificant.

Those arrested in stings and decoy operations are repeat offenders who might otherwise avoid arrest. Even if this assumption is correct and the tactic primarily draws in repeat offenders, the question remains as to whether they would otherwise avoid arrest. The assumption that the tactic garners hard-to-arrest street criminals unlikely to be arrested through conventional tactics is important because it would make little sense to use the tactic if less expensive conventional means were sufficient. A strong belief in this assumption can lead to such responses as that from an officer asked about a sizable number of persons with no prior arrest record who were caught in a decoy operation: "We are cynical enough not to consider them first offenders. It's just the first time they got caught."

The arrest data does indicate that a majority of those caught in stings are not new to the criminal justice system. (On the other hand, approximately 40 percent of American males will be arrested at some point in their lives.) The prior arrests of those caught in stings tended to be through conventional, not undercover, means. The notion that the tactic will flush out those otherwise beyond the law seems questionable in the case of decoys and general property stings. This assumption seems more relevant to white-collar and consensual offenses.

The characteristics of those arrested partly depends on the nature of the offense. Thus, in one large operation, those arrested for purchasing endangered species were a cross section of the population (including a college professor, a policeman, an attorney, and a mortician). This is also the case for those arrested in automobile insurance fraud stings (persons who go along with proposals by middlemen to have their car "stolen" and then seek to collect on their auto theft insurance).

The not guilty (this time) assumption. When the empirical evidence suggests that some of those encountered do not take the bait or otherwise behave illegally, it may still be assumed that they are guilty of other things. A person's mere presence at an undercover site may offer evidence of doubtful moral character. Those found in certain places (storefronts) or out at certain times (late at night) may be presumed to be guilty even if they reject an undercover temptation. Because the access to most storefronts was controlled (you could not just walk in off the street), persons who made it through whatever screening was present were considered suspects. It was assumed they were there to do business. Their actions were electronically recorded, and "all available data regarding that *suspect* were recorded."[24]

Persons who do nothing illegal may nevertheless be viewed as morally flawed, forewarned, or simply clever enough to "make" the police operation. C. Klockars refers to this as "the not guilty (this time)" assumption.[25] The lurking suspicion is present that, if such persons were not either guilty or primed to be, what were they doing out in a high-crime area known for drugs and prostitution at 2 A.M.? They satisfy assumptions about the geographical and temporal location of guilty persons. Anyone out at that time of night, in a place like that, has to be up to no good, even if the police do not actually see them do anything for which an arrest can be made. When starting with such expectations, it is easy to generate a self-fulfilling prophecy where people "fail the attitude test" or where their guilt is helped along by questionable police practices.

Undercover operations do not amplify crime. This point is implicit in the preceding assumption, but it is important to state it separately. There are several independent parts: (1) Would the particular crime in question have occurred without the government's action? (2) Would the targets have been likely to commit an equivalent offense? (3) In an overall sense, does use of the tactic have the longer-range effect of preventing more crime than it creates?

There are at least eight possible answers when these questions are combined. They are not all equally likely to occur, and they have different implications regarding public policy (the tactic is most desirable when the answer to all three questions is Yes and least when it is No).

There are at least nine ways in which covert social control may amplify crime:

1.   It may generate a market for the purchase or sale of illegal goods and services and may indirectly generate capital for other illegality.

2.   It may generate the idea and motive for the crime.

3.   It may entail coercion, intimidation, trickery, or persuasion of a person not otherwise predisposed to commit the offense.

4.   It may offer a seductive temptation to a person who would not otherwise encounter it.

5.   It may provide the contraband or a missing resource or ingredients essential for the commission of the crime.

6.   It may provide the context for false records and framing.

7.   It may generate a covert opportunity structure for illegal actions on the part of the undercover agent or informant.

8. It may lead to retaliatory violence against informers.

9. It may stimulate a variety of crimes on the part of those who are not targets of the undercover operation.

The extent to which and the conditions under which the above may occur call for empirical assessments. But the assumptions that the tactic will reduce crime must be balanced by asking whether it could also increase it.[26]

Undercover operations are independent from each other. There is a tendency to treat undercover operations as if a sting in one area will not be affected by a sting in an adjacent area. For reasons of security, police agencies in a given region may not tell each other about their undercover projects. This can result in competition for clients as well as in undercover agents responding to each other as potential criminals.

There may also be a "contamination" effect, when publicity about a sting in one city negatively affects targets in an adjacent city or targets of another police agency. For example, the well-publicized closing of a sting in a northern California city that had used business cards to draw in clients resulted in the business of an ongoing sting in an adjoining city that used the same means to drop to practically zero. In other cities, sting publicity resulted in suspects in the storefront looking underneath boxes and behind walls for surveillance equipment and posing tests for undercover officers.

A lack of independence in terms of timing is suggested by the fact that stings are likely to be less effective once the secret is out and offenders know what they need to adjust to. As such, the tactic may have something of a self-destruct quality. The lack of temporal independence can be an added cost and sets covert tactics apart from conventional investigative means that can be used repeatedly in the same form.

Undercover operations can control their environment. This assumption subsumes some of the others, specifically, that the systems that undercover operations penetrate are relatively bounded, static, understandable, understood, and subject to rational control. It is believed that elaborate operations can be secretly staged without significantly changing the worlds they enter or the agents who are involved. It is assumed that a bounded little world subject to full (or at least sufficient) police control can be created apart from the broader social and geographical context with a large number of unknowns. The possibility that the secret intervention itself may become a dynamic factor that alters the environment is rarely considered.

This assumption is consistent with the belief that serious offenders will commit the same offense in the same way, regardless of the undercover opportunities that happen to be offered. All the undercover operation does is intervene in a recurring pattern of crime. It is also consistent with the belief that covert police can gain control over, channel, and limit the illegal behavior of those they deal with.

Most police agencies assume that secrecy can be maintained and that the behavior of offenders will not be altered, either strategically to neutralize the operation or toward a new class of victim or offense; that innocent parties will not be dragged in (as victims or offenders); and that agents themselves will not be harmed by the operation. The possibility that offenders may be able to exploit and control the operation for their own ends may not be acknowledged.

In arguing for the importance of examining these assumptions, I do not suggest that all the evidence for them must be present before the tactic is used. There may be judicial, organizational, and symbolic reasons apart from any measurable crime impact for undertaking such operations.[27] Thus, justice may be served in a given case when a particular individual is arrested, regardless of broader impacts. Nor do I argue that all police engaged in covert activities accept them. The statements discussed are background assumptions of varying degrees of relevance that are likely to be drawn on when police publicly justify the use of undercover tactics. In the occasional case where those interviewed doubted a particular assumption or two, this was usually submerged in favor of the trade-offs that seem to be present and a belief that the risks were worth taking.

These ten empirical assumptions raise questions that are difficult to answer, but, in considering the desirability of a broad undercover strategy, they must certainly be asked. The evidence from the quantitative research considered here and from the qualitative examples that follow make it clear that these assumptions are often questionable.

SEVEN

Unintended Consequences: Targets, Third Parties, and Informers

Oh, what a tangled web we weave,
When first we practice to deceive!
—*Sir Walter Scott*

History shows that bad police methods breed disrespect for law,
shake the confidence of law-abiding citizens in the administration of
justice, and weaken the national morale.
—*Police Chief William Parker,*
Los Angeles, 1957

Complex interventions are likely to result in a mixture of intended and unintended consequences. When such interventions involve secrecy and a variety of "unknowns," the unanticipated consequences can be extensive.[1] Some of these consequences are beneficial: undercover operations may discover intelligence that helps prevent planned crimes or helps solve other crimes, including some that authorities were unaware of. Because of their dramatic appeal, such positive results are often made public. But the focus of this and the next chapter—unintended negative consequences—is less likely to become public. In the worst cases, undercover work may spread damage like an invisible virus—contaminating whatever it touches. It can, in the words of a veteran agent, "lead to a deep pile of hurt."

Here I examine the unintended consequences that involve targets, third parties, and informers; the next chapter looks at those that involve police. Both are necessarily more impressionistic than the preceding chapter, because there are almost no quantitative studies. The problems to be considered vary with respect to frequency and severity, but none is trivial. We need to know both how often such problems occur and how their frequency in covert investigations compares to overt investigations.

The absence of systematic studies is certainly not grounds for ignoring these effects. Drawing attention to them can be a necessary first step toward their eventual measurement. Given the subject matter, a skeptical attitude is often in order. Involved parties (whether police or suspects) may have both means and incentives to deceive in their public presentations. However, while any given case may be distorted or simply wrong, when a number of equivalent cases appear it is likely that a more generic pattern has been identified. Here the analytic researcher has an advantage not enjoyed by the historian or journalist. The latter usually focuses on a particular case, and the accuracy and validity of that case are of the utmost importance. However, the situation is different (though in degree) for the researcher who looks across a large number of cases and seeks general patterns and types.

CONSEQUENCES FOR TARGETS

COERCION AND TRICKERY

Undercover operations vary according to the degree of intent and autonomy shown by the target.[2] At the far end are cases that clearly go beyond the spirit of the law because of the degree of coercion or trickery they involve. Investigation becomes instigation. Such cases are unintended and undesirable as formal law enforcement policy, although they may be intentional on the part of aggressive agents anxious to make cases: "Get the numbers up," "Go for the body count," or "Develop a scorecard."

Participation may result from intimidation rather than free choice. A need to project a credible criminal image and a reliance on informers accustomed to using violence (or threats of it) sometimes result in coerced participation. For an assistant U.S. attorney in Washington, D.C., for example, charged with taking money in return for giving information to those he thought were organized crime figures, it involved persistent telephone calls, a threatening call to his wife, and a warning that he might end up missing if he did not cooperate.[3] An informer made threats against the life of John DeLorean and his children if he failed to go along with a drug deal. In Alaska FBI agents and a convicted armed robber ran a bar, where they posed as East Coast Mafia figures with money to invest and protection to sell. An FBI agent posing as "Cosimo Morgante," the group's "heavy muscle," appears to have intimidated some participants into illegal activities.

Trickery is, in some ways, an alternative to coercion, but, in other ways, they are equivalent because both elicit behavior that is nonvoluntary. Trickery is, of course, inherent in the tactic, but some forms seem particularly unfair, as when the offense is benignly presented as incidental to a broad social goal or legitimate personal goal or where its illegal nature is disguised, denied, or made ambiguous.

Rommie Loudd, the first black executive with a professional sports team, organized the Orlando, Florida, franchise in the World Football League. The league failed, and Loudd went broke. He received a phone call from a man who offered to put him in touch with people who would put up $1 million to reorganize the team. However, as an initial condition, Loudd was told he first had to loosen up the financiers with cocaine. He at first refused the offer but eventually introduced the caller (an undercover agent) to two people who sold him cocaine. Loudd, though he had no previous criminal record, was sentenced to a long prison term. The audio tape catches the undercover agent saying to his partner, "I've tricked him worse than I've tricked anybody ever." In another Florida case, a female undercover officer offered sexual favors to a suspect if he would sell her marijuana.

The U.S. Fish and Wildlife's "Operation Falcon" made use of a "free sample" strategy to involve subjects in subsequent illegality. A falconer cooperating in the investigation gave colleagues highly desirable birds that had been illegally taken. Recipients were subsequently arrested for manipulating federal identification bands and falsifying records to conceal the illegal source of the birds.[4] A prosecutor may use a grand jury to unwittingly trap a target into committing perjury, for purposes other than eliciting facts material to a substantive investigation of a crime. For example, Paul Rao, a Chief Judge of the Federal Customs Court in New York, was indicted for perjury as a result of a simulated robbery case. A long-time acquaintance whom he had not seen for many years approached Rao and asked him to help a friend's son who was supposedly in trouble. Rao suggested the agent see "a lawyer [who] knew the judge" and recommended his own son. A year later Rao was called before a grand jury and denied he had made that statement. A special grand jury then indicted him for perjury.

In a Virginia case, an officer arrested a suspect for murder and then offered to drop the charges in return for a bribe. The suspect paid the bribe and was then arrested for both murder and bribery.

A person who purchased a drug kit from disguised drug agents asked them: "Isn't this unlawful?" (The kit was equipped to make methedrine.) He was told: "No, it's public information, and there's no problem with this." Beyond an outright denial of illegality, the ambiguity of some laws, words, and deeds can be exploited to play on the target's wish to be reassured that nothing unlawful will occur.

In perhaps the most questionable of the Abscam cases, two city councilmen were told that an Arab investor wished to build a convention center and possibly redevelop the port area of the financially troubled city of Philadelphia. In accordance with the "Arab mind" and "Arab way of doing business," the councilmen were told that they had to convince the investors that they had friends in high places. In order to do this, money had to be accepted from the investors. The defendants were not asked to offer any commitments or to do anything improper, contingent on accepting the payment. The situation was structured so that acceptance of the money would be seen as payment for consulting services. Neither of the defendants asked for money, and both indicated that no payment was necessary. They were simply told that the project would not come to the city if they did not accept the sheik's "gift."

In several other Abscam cases, defendants were similarly led to believe that they would not have to take any illegal action. The main informant coached New Jersey Senator Harrison Williams in what to say, almost putting words in his mouth: "You gotta tell him how important you are, and you gotta tell him in no uncertain terms without me, there is no deal. I'm the man who's gonna open the doors. I'm the man who's gonna do this and use my influence, and I guarantee this." The senator was then told that nothing wrong was happening: "It goes no further. It's all talk, all bullshit. It's a walk-through. You gotta just play and blow your horn." The crime shifts from bribery to fraud.

Ignorance of the law is no excuse for its violation. However, when a government agent gives a person a chance to break a law that is ambiguous to begin with, encourages that person by claiming that no wrongdoing is involved, and then places the violation within a socially desirable goal, the situation is, at the least, questionable as public policy.

CONTRIVED EVIDENCE AND THE ILLUSION OF CERTAINTY

I knew I was a victim
of someone's evil plan.
The stool pigeon walked in
and said, "There's your man."
I was framed.

> —M. Stoller
> and J. Leiber,
> "Framed"

In the above cases (and whatever the mitigating circumstances), behavior suggesting an offense occurs. But there are cases where the offense does not occur—where the situation is manipulated by the under-cover agent to make it appear that it has occurred. The hidden nature of the "offense" and the fact that there is usually no complainant other than the accusing officer can be conducive to outright framing and false testimony. False accusation is one type of the broad category of wrong-ful conviction.[5]

Some decoy arrests fit into this category. In order to prove criminal intent, officers are instructed to wait before making an arrest. The meaning of a suspect's behavior may become clear after a brief period of time. This contrasts with some verbal exchanges where the ambiguity inheres in the language. The person picking up a wallet, for example, must give some indication that he intends to commit larceny (by walk-ing away with it or putting money from it in his own pocket) and is not simply trying to be helpful.

The desire to make an arrest, however, or to protect the defenseless decoy from potential assault may mean that police take immediate ac-tion once a person bends over or touches the decoy. This may result in the arrest of "good samaritans" who pick up the wallet to identify and return it to its rightful owner, as well as those bent on robbery.

In New York, a minister spent 14 hours in jail after an encounter with a decoy. The minister's claim that he was trying to help the appar-ently unconscious decoy was accepted, and no charges were brought.

In Philadelphia, four members of a decoy squad were indicted on charges that they had framed suspects on robbery charges. Their highly aggressive tactics resulted in praise for the team's productivity, but some of those arrested were simply trying to help the decoy.

Persons may be arrested for trying to help the potential offender and prevent a crime as well. Thus, in a Washington, D.C., case, a religious young man was walking down the street and observed a new blue bicycle parked on the sidewalk, a drunk lying nearby, and a van parked across the street. He also observed another young man eyeing the bicycle. He approached him and said, "Don't do it, man. There are cops all around." The other man then turned and walked away. He was stopped and ques-tioned by police who spilled out of the van. They then arrested the first young man and charged him with "obstruction of justice." The case again points out the conflict between the goals of crime facilitation and crime prevention. From another perspective, police might have wel-comed the young man's actions because they prevented a crime.

Offenses involving contraband items, where mere possession can re-sult in criminal charges, lend themselves well to manipulation by agents.

For example, an informer working for the Los Angeles Police Department's intelligence unit delivered a box containing hand grenades to the house of two antiwar activists. Shortly after, they were arrested for possessing hand grenades. A waitress in Tyler, Texas, was arrested for a drug violation. Her "crime" centered on a pill wrapped in a napkin placed on her tip tray. The pill was an illegal "downer." The waitress unrolled it and asked: "What's this?" An undercover agent said: "Oh, my god. I gotta have it." The waitress reports: "I tossed it down on the bar and walked off." She was indicted for delivery of narcotics, fired from her job, and kicked out of her apartment as a result. The agent later acknowledged: "There were some bad cases made, just so we could get the numbers up."

Paul Lawrence, a Vermont undercover officer, had a reputation as a supercop who carried out a one-person crusade against drugs. He was responsible for 600 drug convictions over a five-year period. Many of his drug purchases never took place. Persons he suspected or was angry with (in at least one case, it involved a woman who refused to go to bed with him) were arrested on Lawrence's claim that they sold him drugs. Lawrence supplied drugs already in his possession as evidence. In what the governor of Vermont called "a very sad day for Vermont law enforcement," complete and unconditional pardons were granted to those convicted as a result of Lawrence's uncorroborated testimony. In poetic justice, his downfall came as a result of an undercover investigation in which he was the subject.[6]

One means of avoiding these kinds of situations is the documentation offered by electronic surveillance. "Doubting" Thomas says, "Except I shall see . . . I will not believe" (St. John 20:25). It is generally believed that the "tapes don't lie." But do they tell the full truth and nothing but the truth? Electronic means are hardly foolproof. In fact, they may cause problems aside from the civil liberties and privacy questions they raise. They create a potentially illusory sense of certainty. They may be manipulated to give a distorted picture and lull observers into uncritical acceptance of the documentary record. The grainy, poor quality of many video recordings (a function of the quality of the equipment used, lack of light, or distortion from a mirror that the sensing chip may be concealed in) can give the impression of watching a sleazy B-grade movie. Seeing (or hearing) should not automatically lead to believing.

An example of how a tape can be misused to make it appear that a target has committed a crime can be seen in the actions of informer Marvin Bray. Bray was part of an FBI investigation into municipal corruption among judges in Cleveland and attempted to set up a veteran judge. With the hidden tape recorder on, he asked the judge to revoke an arrest order for a friend who had skipped a scheduled court appearance. Such requests are fairly routine, and the judge agreed to it. Bray then left the judge's quarters and later said into the tape: "That envelope on the table is for you, judge." He then offered the tape as evidence that the judge had accepted a bribe in return for revoking the order.

In another example, a swindler-turned-informer in Operation Bri-Lab (bribery labor) admitted fabricating a conversation at the New Orleans office of a reputed Mafia leader. He appears to have fabricated other conversations regarding kickbacks and bribery efforts as well.

One major way that tapes distort the truth is through omission and selectivity. The tapes usually record only a small part of the total interaction; they do not present the broader context or conversations and behavior that may have gone on before or concurrently with what was recorded. Unless a complete record is provided, changes in motivation over time will be missed. A person who was entrapped and initially had misgivings may not only be talked into doing the crime but may ultimately become an enthusiastic participant. If only the later stage is recorded, a successful defense of entrapment is unlikely. John DeLorean's attorney suggests that the public and a jury should be told: "Okay, he's shown on the video tapes doing all that stuff. But what was the process that led to his ending up there in front of the camera? How do you feel about what they did to get him to say and do all that in front of the camera?"

Threats, entrapment, inducements, temptations, coaching, extreme trickery, assurances that the action is legal or otherwise part of a government inquiry, misbehavior by the government agent, and other conversations or events that would change the interpretation placed on the electronic record and that might be sufficient to block prosecution may be saved for encounters that are literally off the record.

There is also the possibility of erasing incriminating parts of a tape. Thus, a legal wiretap in New York City recorded evidence of hijacked television sets as well as the ancillary police theft of some of them. The section of the tape containing evidence against the police was erased. An observer noted: "Tomorrow they [detectives] would deny the erasure under oath. This was perjury, but it was irrelevant to the case of the four hijackers."[7] Forms of "editing" can include losing or not reporting a tape; "forgetting" to activate the recording device; claiming it malfunctioned or could not be used for security reasons; speaking inaudibly, over background noise or interfering static, or beyond the range of a recording device.

Even when blatant trickery or technical editing in one form or another is absent, careful linguistic analysis may be required to insure that conversations mean what they appear to. Jurists accustomed to watching TV crime dramas where villains and heroes are clearly willful about their actions may approach staged law enforcement video and audio encounters in the same way. Frequent references to a corrupt practice may lead the unreflective observer to tie the target into the scheme, even when the target may be a passive participant. In a phenomenon linguists refer to as "contamination," one party to a conversation has a secret agenda to which he keeps returning, thus creating the impression that everyone involved in the conversation agrees with the speaker. But the failure to actively reject an offer or to vocally or visibly disagree with a line of conversation may reflect politeness, posturing, intimidation, or disinterest, rather than acquiescence. Even saying "Uh-huh," "Yeah," or "Yes" may mean "I hear you" or "I understand" rather than "I agree."

Linguist Roger Shuy has identified four strategies by which persons may be made to appear guilty on a tape:[8] *scripting*, which involves putting words in a target's mouth (in Senator Williams's case, the informer told him exactly what to say); *criminalizing*, which involves paraphrasing what a subject said to make it sound illegal; *camouflaging*, which involves hiding incriminating suggestions in language that disguises their meaning; and *preventing* the target from making statements that might later help the defense. Another strategy involves *persisting* and the refusal to accept "No" for an answer.

The difference between a normal conversation with its roughly equal exchanges and spontaneous open-ended quality and a conversation where one party is following a script to coax incriminating statements from the target and keeps bringing the subject back to an illicit offer may not be readily apparent. As linguist Mary Gallagher observes, "people merely hearing tapes of artificial conversations . . . apply normal standards of interpretation to those tapes."[9]

The fact that such techniques can be used does not mean that they will be. The law and morality suggest a more neutral role for the agent—giving the target an opportunity, yet not pressuring him. The following excerpt from a transcript used in the training of FBI agents offers a good example of how an agent ensures that the subject has criminal intent:

AGENT: "I'm gonna talk to you like you were my kid brother, or something
           . . . just because I'm available and I could do business, don't, don't
           get sucked in by that just because it's a way to make money. . . . I
           frankly don't need the business, and, ah, if there's some other way
           you can survive without doing it, my advice to you because you
           already had the light shined on you and they probably [are] giving
           you your last chance would be go do something else."

SUBJECT: "Right, I understand where you're coming from."

AGENT: "Yeah, so, I . . . just wanted to lay that on you and if you're still
           bound and determined then it's a new ball game, but at least we've
           talked about it."

SUBJECT: "I'm still bound [and] determined."

A tape may be misleading in its suggestion of innocence, as well as of guilt. Rule breakers may turn such tactics around and use them in a contrived and hidden way against authorities. The situational ambiguity that authorities try to use to create the impression of guilt may be exploited by the clever violator to create the opposite impression.

Police worry that sophisticated violators may "alibi" themselves on the tape. Suspects who believe a conversation is being taped may pretend they are moral and pure, while the undercover agent is pretending to be dishonest. They may act to explain away criminal intent, cast blame elsewhere, offer incriminating statements about innocent persons, and forcefully express disinterest in a corrupt offer or claim ignorance of prior offenses. An officer stated: "I had an informer make an undercover contact even though we knew the crook was suspicious. The crook played dumb, said he didn't know what the informer was talking about. Of course the tape was played in court. Fortunately, we had so much other evidence it looked like an alibi. But it's always a hazard."

After an investigation has begun, offenders may feign contriteness and a change of heart should they come to suspect that they are targets. This appears to be the case with a Massachusetts state representative who accepted a $5,000 bribe from an FBI agent, then gave it back several weeks later. A comparison of the taped conversations at the time he accepted the bribe and when it was returned can be interpreted to suggest that he had been tipped off and in the later encounter used the tape to set the stage for his defense. What appeared to be his carefully orchestrated behavior was successful, as he was acquitted of extortion charges.

In an attempt to neutralize an undercover operation, a target may fail to give a *verbal* answer to a question, such as "How much would it cost to fix the case?" or "What will you pay?" In a "do unto others" situa-tion, the target may himself secretly tape encounters and try to lead agents into making compromising or incriminating statements.

When offenders are secretly taping and authorities exceed legal limits (and perhaps for this reason are not themselves taping the encounter), the results may be not only embarrassing, but fatal to the case at hand. For example, a Jewish Defense League informant secretly taped his ses-sions with police and then used these in a successful court defense. The police officer he had contact with made various promises and threats outside the presence of the informant's attorney. For example, in return for his cooperation he was told, "You're not going to jail on either one of them [charges], and, if you ever say that I said it, I'm gonna run you over with a truck." Unaware that the conversation had been taped, the officer denied in court ever making such statements.[10]

POLITICAL TARGETING

In September 1980, Robert Bauman, a popular leader of the New Right seeking election to a fifth term in the U.S. House of Represen-tatives from Maryland, was charged with solicitation for prostitution and given a six-month suspended sentence. The arrest cost him an elec-tion he had seemed assured of winning. Bauman claims the decision to arrest him was political, disguised to ensure his defeat and prevent his growing popularity from making him an eventual opponent of Mary-land's Democratic U.S. senator. He writes, "obviously, someone within the Carter administration made a calculated decision to finger me for action."[11]

Regardless of the merits of this particular case, it is clear that under-cover means have the potential to be used in an inequitable and dis-criminatory way. Private and particularistic, rather than public and uni-versalistic, criteria may direct target selection and the use of results.

Any government power can be abused, as a 1971 memo to President Nixon from John Dean implies: "We can use the available political ma-chinery to screw our political enemies." But the potential for misuse of undercover means appears to be greater than for overt means. The tactic is well suited for partisan political use.

The routine discretion in the law enforcement role, the breadth of such criminal laws as conspiracy, and the legitimating imperative to fol-low up on suggestions of illegality (which sometimes are secretly con-trived by agents wishing to carry out an inquiry) can mask the political motivation that may lie behind an investigation. Secret investigations carried out at police initiative, particularly those that involve "integrity testing," are a powerful means of discovering or creating discrediting information.

The increased procedural complexity and reporting requirements of government organizations increase the likelihood of getting at least something on a targeted person, even if it is unrelated to the original suspicion.[12] Merely carrying out an investigation may generate secondary or derivative rule breaking that is solely an artifact of the investigation. For example, a New York City policeman who was suspended reports that an internal affairs agent playing an undercover role "came to me with a deal. I told him to get lost. He was wired, and *they charged me with failure to report him.*" In another example, an official of New York City's Department of Buildings was approached by an undercover investigator who offered him a bribe if he would submit falsified architectural plans. The bribe was rejected, but the official was suspended because he failed to report the attempt. Political targets may be approached not because of suspected corruption, but merely to see if they can be tempted or at least tripped up by failing to report a bribe.

Undercover means fit within a general conception of social control through threat. As with other privacy-invading tactics, such as electronic surveillance or access to confidential records, they may be carried out with no intention of formal prosecution. The goal may simply be to exercise control by threatening to reveal incriminating results. The unused investigative data may be filed away as long as those implicated continue to cooperate with the controlling agent. Cooperation may be legal, such as offering information or setting up others, or illegal, such as through payoffs.[13]

J. Edgar Hoover was a master at using the technique in this intimidating way, primarily through his files on important people. Richard Nixon similarly abused this power with his "plumber's unit" and "enemies list." At the municipal level, some police chiefs have made extensive use of intelligence data for partisan ends. Thus, Chicago police sent Mayor Richard Daley regular reports on the activities of persons defined as political "enemies." Mayors in Seattle, Detroit, Houston, and other cities discovered after their elections that their predecessors had made them targets of police intelligence units. Los Angeles's now disbanded Public Disorders Intelligence Division gathered materials about the personal and political activities of Mayor Tom Bradley, members of the Los Angeles City Council, and the Police Commission.[14] Groups seeking police reform, such as the ACLU and other nonviolent organizations, were also targets of surveillance. A top mayoral assistant, unpopular with police because of his role in police department reforms, was arrested for lewd conduct under questionable circumstances and resigned.

During periods of rancorous political conflict, the use of such tactics is likely to increase. The investigation by the Select Committee to Study Governmental Operations with Respect to Intelligence Activities (the Church Committee) of domestic intelligence practices documented many examples of the politically motivated use of undercover means against civil rights, antiwar, student, and feminist activists in the 1960s and 1970s. Activists and counterculture figures who could not be arrested for their political beliefs or life-style sometimes became the targets of undercover drug and other investigations instead. For example, the FBI intensely monitored former Beatle John Lennon's public and private life for nine months before the 1972 Republican convention. There was fear that Lennon would lead an antiwar demonstration that would embarrass President Nixon by disrupting the convention. Police were urged to see if Lennon could be "arrested, if at all possible, on possession of narcotics charges," so he would become more "deportable." [15]

DAMAGED REPUTATIONS

The above discussion assumes that an undercover investigation will find evidence of wrongdoing, but even an investigation that finds no such evidence can otherwise do harm or be politically exploited. Transcripts of conversation may become public during the pretrial discovery period in which the names of innocent persons are mentioned. But even in cases where there is no prosecution because of insufficient evidence, improper official behavior, or rejection of the offer, the subject of the investigation may still be damaged through leaks to the media. A case that cannot be made in court may still be made in the press. Such disclosures may "cruelly wound the truly innocent, damaging their reputations beyond hope of recovery." [16]

For politicians (for whom matters of public reputation are central), the issue is particularly salient. The story is told of the Southern politician who accused his opponent of sleeping with pigs. "But you know that's not true," said an aide. "I know it," said the politician, "but I want to see the sonofabitch deny it." In a similar fashion, to have it known that one was a suspect in a covert government investigation cannot help but cast a shadow on a person's reputation. Many people will assume a presumption of guilt, particularly if the material is taped. The need to perceive a just world supports this. Social psychological research has documented the tendency to blame those who are accidentally injured and to see them as deserving of their fate.[17]

Government efforts publicly to clear a person's record by sending a Justice Department letter (such as the one sent to Senator Larry Pressler after he indicated he was not interested in the Abscam deal) stating that an "intensive investigation revealed no evidence of illegality that warrants our further investigation" are inadequate compensation. In fact, further publicizing an incident may only compound the damage, much as when one tries to clean a paint spot with a paint-spattered rag. The public image of institutions (such as Congress or the courts) may also be damaged in the course of a covert investigation.

Reputational damage may appear unintentionally from benign sources. A conflict may exist between the public's First Amendment right to know, a defendant's right to have access to the prosecution's information, and an individual's right to privacy. When lies told about real persons or organizations to create credibility or gain access surface during a trial, harm may occur. When information on a law enforcement video or audio tape becomes public, innocent persons may suffer. Thus, it was headline news when the names of three important senators were mentioned by an informer as potential Abscam targets, though the senators in fact never became targets.

Because undercover investigations frequently rely on informers who exaggerate their knowledge of others' wrongdoing, tape-recorded conversations are often rich in hearsay, gossip, distortion, outright fabrication, or slander. The tape does not evaluate for quality or discriminate among "more" or "less" plausible statements the way an experienced police agent would. Seasoned officers are likely to take a skeptical attitude toward much of the information provided by informants, an attitude not likely to be matched by the public (for whom a taped record enhances the legitimacy of the information).

Damage also may result when suspects are erroneously identified. The superficial and clandestine nature of light undercover operations and the careful guarding of information may mean problems in identifying suspects. For example, an honor student in a Texas high school was wrongly identified as a drug dealer and was taken from the school in handcuffs. An undercover officer posing as a student at the school said she bought methaqualone pills from a student she knew only as Jeff. She then looked in the school yearbook and identified the arrested student.

The student had been home sick the day the drug sale occurred. Two weeks after the arrest, the student was cleared, but not before he had been suspended from school, barred from running in a student election, given failing grades in his courses as a result of being unable to take final exams, lost a part-time job, and suffered rejection and labeling (students began calling him "Quaalude Covington").

When the focus of covert operations was primarily on known suspects, investigations were relatively bounded, predictable, and controllable. But with the move to the more complex deep-undercover operations of recent years, this is less true. As the focus has broadened to using organizations to fight organizations and as general types of criminal activity, such as corruption or dealing in fraudulent securities, have been targeted (rather than particular suspects whose identity is known), the danger of direct or indirect harm to innocent third parties has increased. This is related to: the need to infiltrate a legitimate organization in order to gain access to an illegitimate one; the need to create organizational fronts that engage in real-world public transactions in order to establish credibility and gather appropriate evidence; and the need to cast a broad net (at least initially) when the focus is not on a known suspect.

THIRD PARTIES

DIRECT CRIMINAL VICTIMIZATION

You can't pose as hunters without having to kill.
> —*Special agent, U.S. Fish and*
> *Wildlife Service, 1983*

The web of interdependence is dense and complicated. Interventions in nature or in human relationships can have far-reaching consequences, often untraceable. In covert operations, the government's role in third-party victimization may never be discovered. Invisibility can mean a lack of recourse that compounds harm.

Persons or institutions who have no connection with criminal activity may be harmed. The most obvious cases involve the victims of government-inspired or government-facilitated crimes. Sometimes, undercover means prevent victimization; sometimes, they create a victim instead. Innocent persons may be caught in the mesh of deceit or victimized by a government-subsidized criminal who is in a position to use the framework of the investigation to enrich himself. Even if those responsible are eventually prosecuted, the government's indirect complicity is not lessened, and those harmed may not receive compensation. For example, persons whose property is stolen for the purpose of sale to a police-run fencing operation may never get it back.

The loss may not be reported, or the property may lack distinctive identification, or the police sting may refuse to purchase it. In some stings, up to one-half of the property purchased was not returned. If the property is returned, there is no compensation for the trauma and otherwise disrupted activities, for example, the problems caused by having a car stolen, that may accompany the initial loss.

It might be argued that such victimization is a necessary, if unfortunate, consequence of covert operations because the loss of property (at least initially) is consistent with the sting's goal of making arrests. But even more troubling—because they are in no way related to formal goals—are the collateral crimes that may accompany undercover efforts. For example, in Lakewood, Colorado, two young men learned that a new fence—in reality, a police front—was buying stolen cars. They stole several cars and sold them to the sting. During one of these transactions, they showed the undercover officers a .45 caliber automatic they had taken in a burglary. They used this gun to steal another car and kill its owner, then sold the car to the sting. The second time they stole a car and killed its owner and tried to sell it to the fence, they were arrested, and the operation was closed.

Agents may find it difficult not to be an accessory to a crime when a group they have infiltrated suddenly suggests a robbery or assault at that instant, e.g., while driving past a liquor store. The same day a Berkeley, California, officer was awarded a certificate of merit for his undercover work, he was named in a negligence suit claiming he had deprived a woman of her constitutional rights by "maliciously and oppressively" facilitating the theft of her purse. The purse snatcher made his getaway in a city car driven by the undercover agent. The agent was given a share of the $300 proceeds, and only after dropping off the purse snatcher and a companion did he telephone police with a report. The officer claimed that to do anything else would have given away his police identity and been dangerous.

Victimization may occur when a surveillance team waits for an offense to occur before taking action. For example, one agent described how five officers watched a suspect commit six burglaries over the course of a week, before finally arresting him. Their rationale was to impress the judge with what a bad actor he was so that he would receive a substantial prison sentence.

Agents may participate in a less serious crime as part of a plan to prevent a more serious one. In Puerto Rico an undercover agent was charged with kidnapping.[18] He had infiltrated a band of reputed terrorists. He and several members of the group commandeered a taxi to take them to a television relay station which they planned to sabotage. In his defense, the agent claimed he was simply part of a government plan that involved the kidnapping of the taxi driver who was to be held hostage. A jury found him not guilty.

Another type of damage to third parties involves crimes committed by informers who exploit their knowledge of, or involvement in, undercover operations. They may misuse the false identification and supporting documents, for example, credit cards. They may seek to sell government property used in the investigation. A substantial number of damage suits have been filed against the government by parties claiming harm from undercover operations. Such was the case with the informer in Operation Frontload, an investigation into organized crime in the construction industry. Under controlled conditions, the informer (Norman Howard) was to sell construction bonds to contractors to offer protection against projects not completed on time. The FBI vouched for him ("a former police officer," "a straight arrow") to the insurance company that certified him as an insurance agent with the authority to issue bonds. The insurance company was not told that a false name was used, that Howard had a criminal record, or that he had become an informer to avoid a nine-year prison sentence and fine.[19] Howard sold bonds on his own, using his new credentials, and peddled at least thirty worthless construction bonds for $300,000 in fees. Insurance officials claimed his actions cost them millions of dollars in business losses. By the end of 1984, the federal government had paid several million dollars in settlement costs in nine lawsuits.

FBI informer Joseph Meltzer used his knowledge of Abscam's false front (Abdul Enterprises Ltd.) to swindle dozens of innocent business persons out of thousands of dollars. He told them he was the representative of a wealthy Arab sheik seeking to make investments in the United States. After receipt of a fee, Meltzer said he would arrange for the investments and listed the Chase Manhattan Bank as a reference. A vice president of the bank confirmed to callers that Abdul had deposits in the bank. Beyond the loss of their investments, swindled businessmen complained of further financial reversals, including the loss of their businesses, in addition to marital and mental health problems (including several suicide attempts) as a result of the operation.[20]

FBI informer Charles Leggett offers another example of the exploitation of resources provided by an undercover operation. Leggett obtained a phony $1.75 million certificate of deposit from the Justice Department. He used this as collateral for a bank loan to purchase southern California real estate, then defaulted. The Continental Bank of Chicago successfully sued the federal government for damages.

INDIRECT HARM

Third parties need not be directly victimized to suffer economic loss. In Operation Re-Coupe (*sic*), innocent car dealers and buyers appear to have been the unwitting victims of an undercover investigation into auto theft. In this operation, the FBI set up a "chop shop," an auto salvage and retagging operation called LeBlanc Motors near Sikeston, Missouri, to sell parts, vehicle identification number plates, and matching vehicle titles to known auto thieves. In a retagging operation, the offender obtains title to a wrecked car and removes the identification number. A matching car is then stolen and retagged with the other number. The front provided the special brads (otherwise available only to car manufacturers) for retagging. The front also purchased and resold stolen cars.[21]

These actions resulted in the direct and indirect sale of about one hundred stolen cars, unbeknownst to the dealers or individuals who purchased them. The operation appears to have breached sales contracts and warranties of title. As a result, used car dealers in St. Louis, Memphis, and Dixon, Illinois, filed damage claims and lawsuits against federal, state, and local officials.

When the operation closed, innocent car buyers had their vehicles confiscated. Innocent businesses that sold the cars suffered damage to their reputations and pocketbooks. For example, word quickly spread that eight cars sold by John Lightner in rural Dixon, Illinois, had been seized by police. His sales dropped by more than two-thirds, and bankers balked at offering loans for cars sold on his lot. Rumors persisted that he was dishonest, though no evidence of this was presented. Similarly, the Mid-South Motor Company in Memphis had to reimburse almost $200,000 to people who bought cars originally obtained through LeBlanc Motors. Mid-South's insurance policy was cancelled, necessitating a new one at an increased premium of $15,000 a year. It also incurred interest and legal expenses and damage to its reputation.[22]

Even citizens who knowingly cooperate with undercover operations may experience losses and find the process of being reimbursed cumbersome. For example, Robert Phelps, a real estate broker, purchased a bar in Colorado in 1978 that was to be used as an FBI front for an investigation of bribery. The bar was renamed Scotland Yard. It was operated for a year solely by undercover agents and was losing $6,000 a month. When he pointed out the mounting losses and asked who would buy the bar once the investigation was over, agents advised him he "need not worry." In March 1979 the agents suggested that he sell the bar. It sold for one-half of its original price and Phelps claimed that he was left "with broken promises, a run-down bar and a bunch of bills." He filed suit against the government to recover what he claims to have lost.

Another form of third-party victimization may be seen in the activities of police impersonators. As undercover work has become more prevalent, it may have subtly encouraged an increase in crime involving impersonators. Undercover police can serve as role models for impersonators, whose tales may have become more credible as a result of the public's knowledge that undercover work is common. Regardless of a person's appearance and the absence of a uniform, a quickly flashed badge or fake identification card, along with a claim to be an undercover officer, may convince the unsuspecting. Where it is known that police make extensive use of unmarked cars, offenders with portable red lights attached to the roof of their cars may find it easy to pull people over.

Classic con games, such as one in which the "mark" is persuaded to withdraw money from a bank in order to help test secretly the honesty of bank employees, may have become more believable because of the public's increased awareness of secret government integrity tests. The extent of police impersonation is probably greatly underestimated by official statistics, because those preyed on are often either embarrassed at having been swindled or are prostitutes, homosexuals, or others seeking to buy or sell narcotics and are thus unlikely to report their victimization.

Another by-product of covert operations may be retaliatory attacks on informers (or those perceived to be informers). Part of the increased homicide rates in the 1970s, particularly among minority youth, has been attributed to the vastly augmented amounts of federal buy money for drugs and information that became available. This increased the opportunity for persons to become informers, some of whom were subsequently attacked or killed as a result. Violence and competition among groups involved in contraband trafficking may also have increased. The self-protective actions of undercover agents (whether police or civilians) to cast suspicion away from themselves and onto others by accusing them of being informers may also lead to criminal assaults as a result of mistaken identity.

When divorced informers are given new identities by the Federal Witness Protection Program, their former spouses and other relatives may suffer as a result. For example, Tom Leonhardt spent eight years trying to find his children after they and his former wife and her new husband, a criminal witness, were relocated by the program.[23]

According to some observers, protected and endangered fish and wildlife have also been "victims" of undercover actions as a result of the stepped-up enforcement efforts of the U.S. Fish and Wildlife Service. The Service's increased use of covert means has often ironically required killing fish and wildlife in order to protect them. For example, as a result of one investigation, about fifty people, mostly Yankton Sioux Indians, were arrested for killing bald eagles, an endangered species. Their leader said: "The government is talking about how the eagle is diminishing, but why did they allow these birds to be slaughtered for *two years* during this operation?" A defense attorney notes that his client "sent them [undercover agents] four or five eagles, and they could have stopped right there. But they contacted him 100 times over two years. They're supposed to be protecting animals, and they're out killing them." A special agent for the service said: "Sometimes you have to sacrifice wildlife . . . it's worth it."

PRIVACY AND PROTECTED RELATIONSHIPS

A red-headed woman took me out to dine.
She said, "Love me, baby, leave your union behind."
     —*Almanac Singers, "Talking Union"*

As the above cases illustrate, the damage to third parties (or targets) from undercover operations may be financial, psychological, physical, or reputational. In addition, privacy and trust may also be victims. Undercover operations share with wiretapping the invasion of privacy, but without the restraint or inherent limitations imposed by judicial warrant. Like a gigantic vacuum cleaner or a tornado, everything may be drawn into the vortex, regardless of whether it is related to the initial investigation.

The most private and delicate of human emotions and personal relationships may be denigrated on behalf of an investigation. "Under-the-covers" undercover operations are a clear example. In a topic that is rarely discussed, sexual encounters may be used for investigative purposes. A familiar example involves jealous or rejected girlfriends who are an important source of police information. But another form (anticipatory rather than after-the-fact) involves the creation of intimate relations for purposes of an investigation. The exploitation and manipulation of such relations raises more troubling moral issues.

Although an undercover agent who induces someone to participate in an illegal scheme or divulge information via coercion is not the same as one who induces someone to participate out of love, there is a parallel, not unlike the similarity between rape and seduction. An experienced undercover agent offered the following practical advice, "never arrest anyone you sleep with." This may harm the agent's objectivity and the quality of the case when it is presented in court. It may also create jealousy or resentment on the part of other targets.

As part of an attempt to infiltrate the Weather Underground, a federal agent developed a relationship with a woman who became pregnant. After considerable indecision and at the urging of the agent, she had an abortion. The agent's work then took him elsewhere, and he ended the relationship. The woman apparently never learned of his secret identity and true motives. The situation would have been more complicated had she decided to keep the child, died in childbirth, or become mentally unstable.[24]

In Los Angeles, an undercover agent who had infiltrated a local Maoist political organization became the boyfriend of one of the women he spied on. Under oath, the agent testified that, after initial consultation with his superiors, he regularly engaged in sexual intercourse with the woman. The relationship was used to help gather information about the woman and her associates and to establish the agent's credibility. He testified that, during the 17 months he was undercover, he never heard anyone in the organization talk about committing crimes nor did he see any weapons. In some agencies, romantic involvement with a target is grounds for dismissal, but in others it is permitted. Los Angeles Police Chief Daryl Gates has defended the policy of permitting undercover officers to be involved in "a romantic way" with a potential target of investigation. He said that to prohibit undercover officers from having sex in the line of duty might "seriously endanger" their lives.[25]

Undercover male officers playing the role of "Johns" seeking to arrest female prostitutes may annoy, embarrass, and even terrify women they wrongly approach who are sitting innocuously at a bar or innocently standing on a street corner. Ironically, such enforcement may be in response to the complaints of other innocent women accosted on the street by men who think they are prostitutes because of the neighbor-hood they are in. An equivalent problem is not likely to be found when female decoys are used. Regardless of the gender of the agent, the use of decoys in this manner can inhibit interaction, damage trust, and in-crease paranoia among persons seeking companionship. Recipients of friendly introductions may wonder whether they are genuine or part of a ploy by police decoys.

Intimate relations have also been exploited for purposes of disrup-tion. Thus, an aspect of the COINTEL program involved the writing of anonymous letters to spouses of activists accusing them of infidelities. A Klan informant testified that he was instructed "to sleep with as many wives as I could" in an attempt to break up marriages and gain information.[26]

Edmund Burke, who wrote about the fear of being spied on "by the very servant who waits behind your chair,"[27] would have been appalled by the case of Arthur Baldwin, the owner of a legal topless bar in Memphis that police wanted to close down. An investigation was car-ried out to see if Baldwin was liable for criminal prosecution on other grounds. Lacking information that would justify a warrant for elec-tronic surveillance or search and seizure and apparently having little or no reason to suspect Baldwin, a generalized undercover investigation was carried out instead. An agent insinuated himself into Baldwin's life. He worked in his bar, served as his chauffeur, looked after his child, and even lived in his house for six months. During this time, the agent took some white powder seen on Baldwin's dresser and had it analyzed. On the basis of this evidence, Baldwin was arrested and convicted on co-caine charges.

Whatever its implications for the invasion of privacy or the effective use of scarce enforcement resources, police behavior in the above case was within the letter of the law. But some covert operations come close to violating or actually do violate constitutionally protected relationships. A number of political cases have involved infiltrators transgressing privi-leged attorney-client communications. For example, a trespassing case against 50 antinuclear protestors was dismissed by the California Su-preme Court in 1979 after it was discovered that one group member was a sheriff's deputy who had interfered with their legal defense. In 1981 charges were dismissed against 15 demonstrators at the Seabrook, New Hampshire, nuclear power plant after it was revealed that one of the defendants was an informer who had been a participant in privi-leged attorney-client discussions. In rare instances, the informer may even be an attorney. Thus, an FBI informer in New Jersey was accused of defrauding clients and associates; in addition, it is alleged that he passed detrimental information to the FBI regarding a client, abusing the lawyer-client relationship.

Lawyers, of course, may also exploit the protections offered by the attorney-client privilege. As a prosecutor put it, they may use "the titles, the knowledge, the privileges of an attorney both as a shield and as a sword" to protect illegality. Issues around the privacy and confidentiality of attorney-client communications are becoming more salient. The President's Commission on Organized Crime has called for active pursuit of "renegade attorneys" involved with organized crime, including increased use of electronic surveillance and undercover means.

The structure of the attorney-client relationship lends itself well to undercover activities directed against attorneys. Attorneys are expected to advise clients about the law. The line between helping clients understand the law so they can stay within it and advising them on how to avoid prosecution can be hazy. An attorney can be indicted on conspiracy charges if he is present at meetings with people he thinks are his clients at which plans for illegal action are discussed, even if he repeatedly indicates he does not want to be involved. That was the case with a prominent Greensboro, North Carolina, defense attorney known for his work with civil-liberties and union groups. The attorney believed that he had been retained by two persons facing federal charges, who were, in fact, FBI informants who were granted immunity from federal charges as a result of their cooperation. One of the informants secretly tape-recorded conversations at which the attorney was present. The two informants discussed their ongoing drug business along with much small talk. The tapes indicate that the attorney was aware of their efforts to set up a drug deal, but he made it clear that he did not want to get involved. He also talked about helping one of the defendants set up a legitimate business. At their final meeting, one of his presumed "clients" showed him a suitcase with phony cocaine and tried to persuade him to deliver it. The attorney refused to touch the suitcase and walked away, at which point he was arrested. A jury found him guilty of conspiring to distribute cocaine.[28]

Although not constitutionally protected in the same way as the lawyer-client relationship, the relationship between reporters and their sources has clear implications for a free society. When the confidentiality of that relationship can be breached at will, whether by holding reporters in contempt of court if they refuse to reveal sources or documents or by police pretending to be reporters, the quality and independence of mass communication must suffer. Respect for the integrity of the news-gathering and reporting process is vital to a free press and open society. To the extent that people wonder whether reporters might be policemen in disguise or informers, the sharing of sensitive or controversial information is less likely, and freedom of expression may be chilled. This also applies to the infiltration of classroom and religious settings. Damage may be done not only to the privacy of the individuals directly involved, but to the institution itself. Freedom of expression requires a climate of trust and openness.

During the protests of the 1960s, the tactic of police posing as members of the media was often used, and it still occasionally is. A 1984 article reports 13 cases of police pretending to be members of the media in the preceding eight years.[29] This is probably only a small fraction of the total number of cases, most of which are not discovered.

Police investigators in Morristown, New Jersey, arrived at a rally to protest the state's marijuana laws in a vehicle labeled "Channel 6— New Jersey's Morning News." They also wore a logo for the nonexistent Channel 6. Posing as reporters, they videotaped "interviews" with demonstrators. A state police officer in Welch, West Virginia, was provided a cover identity as a reporter for the *Welch Daily News* and worked out of the newspaper, as part of a narcotics investigation. To be sure, not all police impersonation of the press involves evidence gathering tied to the role of reporter. Such impersonation also may be used by bodyguards, by summons servers, and to effect an arrest.

The FBI's guidelines do not prohibit the tactic. However, operations involving impersonation of a reporter, doctor, lawyer, or clergyman are among the "sensitive circumstances" that must receive approval at the highest level. IRS agents can impersonate the above categories, but not to gain confidential information associated with the professional role, only to pose as investors. Most local police departments do not prohibit the issuance of press credentials to police. Los Angeles is an exception. Its manual states:

> The use of a news media cover by an officer to obtain intelligence information is not an acceptable form of undercover activity. Once a police officer is discovered in such a role, particularly in a crowd-control situation, legitimate members of the media become suspect and could possibly be exposed to danger. In addition, such undercover activity does damage to the trust which should exist between members of a free society and the news media which serves them.

Apart from impersonation, the use of audio and visual surveillance as part of undercover operations can involve further invasions of privacy. A general problem of electronic surveillance is that it is indiscriminate and hard to confine to just the target. A telephone line or a video lens has an open-ended quality that not only gathers data on targets, but also on those who happen to call them or enter an area being videotaped. Some persons in no way involved in questionable activities are likely to have their words and deeds recorded by agents. Where the investigation involves the legislative or judicial branch, for example, bugging the chambers of a judge as in the Chicago Operation Greylord, the legitimate confidentiality of conversations may be violated.

INFORMERS

There has always been one untidy phase of police work, a distasteful but vitally important ingredient in the chemistry of manhunting . . . informers.

—Melvin Purvis, 1936

The frequency and seriousness of the problems this "untidy phase of police work" may cause make informers the weakest link in undercover systems. A majority of undercover operations must rely to some degree on persons in the criminal milieu for information, technical advice, "clients," contacts, and introductions involving legitimation of the agent's own disreputability. They are most likely to be needed in cases where the investigation involves a co-conspirational role. When police must depend on persons whose professional lives routinely involve deceit and concealment and who have a motive to lie, the price may be heavy. In the understated language of the government document, this "occasionally may require a degree of cooperation with persons whose motivation and conduct are open to question." [30] Problems include (1) going beyond legal, ethical, and departmental restrictions to make cases; (2) collateral crimes and double-dealing; and (3) the informer coming to control the sworn agent rather than the reverse.

Working with informers can be "an excruciatingly difficult and delicate task." They often have strong incentives to see that others break the law. Because of charges they are seeking to avoid, a desire to punish competitors or enemies, or the promise of drugs or money, they may have little concern with equitable and principled law enforcement. For example, Mel Weinberg (described by a judge as an "archetypical, amoral, fast-buck artist") had a three-year prison sentence waived and received $133,150 for his cooperation in the two-year Abscam investigation. A part of the growing "books by crooks" phenomenon, he also received $15,000 to write about his exploits. In a questionable contingent payment policy, according to a Justice Department memorandum, he also "would be paid a lump sum at the end of Abscam, contingent upon the success of the prosecution."[31]

Informers may ignore the standards intended to limit police behavior and make false claims about the misbehavior of targets. Whether out of self-interest or deeper psychological motives, some informers undergo a transformation and become zealous supercops. They may "grow a badge" and create criminals or sniff them out, using prohibited methods. They may then lie with impunity about their tactics.

Counterproblems may also be present when the informer serves as a double agent or is otherwise unreliable as a result of ambivalence, an instinct for self-protection, or incompetence. In the case of the 1960s' social movements, about one in four of the cases that became public involved conversion to the perspective of the infiltrated group. Among some infamous cases of informers turning on the government are Lee Harvey Oswald (who shot President Kennedy) and Sara Jane Moore (who attempted to kill President Ford).

Informers rarely appear in court and hence cannot be effectively challenged. This is because the information they provide is used to obtain a warrant or they are "cut away" after providing an introduction for a sworn agent. Informers must be available when their appearance is essential to the guilt or innocence of the accused or where they participate in a charged transaction. But they generally need not appear when they are "merely" the means to some other legitimate technique, such as a warrant.

"Cleaning up" improperly gathered evidence or evidence that initially comes from a source that must be protected is a fascinating and rarely studied topic. Police can be highly inventive in finding legal ways to obtain information they have already obtained illegally.

The apparent strength of cases made through undercover means also results in a large percentage being plea-bargained, and hence they never reach the stage of an open trial. Occasionally, a case will be dropped rather than force the informer to appear in court. A condition of the agreement between informers and authorities may be that the informers' identities will not be revealed and that they will not have to testify.[32]

Problems of trickery, coercion, and contrived evidence are more pronounced with informers than with sworn agents simply because they are inherently much less accountable and not as constrained by legal or departmental restrictions. As one officer candidly said, "informers, particularly unwitting informers, are desirable precisely because they can do what we can't—legally entrap." Police need not directly tell informers to act illegally, but the structure of the situation makes supervision difficult. As one federal agent put it: "Trying to control informers is an ulcer factory." Informers may believe that they are immune from prosecution. As an informer in a novel by criminal defense attorney Paul Chevigny tells it: "I liked the excitement. Like being a stunt flyer in your dreams—no risk of crashing." [33]

Problems with informers are even more likely when middlemen are drawn into an operation, such as the use of "unwitting informers" who do not even know they are part of a police operation. [34] Witting informers can be told of the legal and administrative limits on their behavior and that, if they fail to honor these, they may face formal charges. But unwitting informers (sometimes referred to as "unguided missiles" by police) are exempt from this. They cannot be wired or expected to tape record phone calls or keep a detailed written record. Their claims about past misbehavior or the predisposition of potential targets are more often suspect.

The use of such duped participants can involve a delegation of law enforcement investigative authority. This may have the unintended consequence of offering them a license to pursue whatever target they choose, as long as they assert that the person selected is predisposed to commit illegal actions. What may turn out to be "baseless inculpatory representations about innocent private citizens or public officials" are not easily verified. [35] Validating their assertions may be difficult, given the circuitous path involved, the illegal and conspiratorial nature of the alleged behavior, and the inability to communicate openly with the unwitting informer.

Abscam middleman Joseph Silvestri illustrates this problem. He was apparently led to believe that he could earn a $6 million broker's fee for helping an Arab sheik invest $60 million in real estate. A condition for his earning the fee was gaining the cooperation of political figures in order to ensure that everything went smoothly. It is not surprising that he cast a wide net in seeking to gain "cooperation" from elected officials. Many of those he approached were not interested, although this did not prevent damage to their reputations when it was revealed that they were targets of an undercover investigation. [36]

A device used by some fencing stings is to employ street people to spread the word that a new fence is paying good prices. The unwitting informer may be paid a commission for each transaction he is responsible for and also collect a fee from the person selling the property.

The price of gaining the cooperation of informers may be to ignore their rule breaking in other settings. In addition to this (somewhat principled) exchange, informers may commit a variety of other crimes that are neither sanctioned nor intended by their control officer. Undercover situations lend themselves well to exploitation by informers for their own criminal ends, apart from their role as agents of law enforcement. Experienced officers often assume that an informer is up to more than meets the eye. As one officer put it: "It comes with the territory. You know the creep is up to something behind your back. You just don't know what it is. They can still make some great cases. Your fear is it will come out in court. It's the 'high rollers' who are hardest to control. You need to literally live with them."

Urban, street-wise and hungry, and playing by different rules, some informers have a competitive advantage over suburban white-collar agents who supervise them. The government sometimes comes in a poor second when it is required to deal with master con artists operating secretively in their natural habitat. The successes as well as the problems of Abscam owe a considerable amount to the cleverness of the principal informer. John Wall, a former prosecutor, observes: "Every time the federal government jumps in bed with a paid informant, it jumps in bed with the devil, and when you're in bed with the devil you better watch out, because the devil's shrewder than you are."

The government may be the direct victim of a scam. Some of Mel Weinberg's compensation appears to have come from his running "a scam within a scam." He helped to recover $2 million worth of supposedly stolen certificates of deposit for which he was paid $15,000. However, it is questionable whether they actually were stolen, rather than being counterfeits created under his tutelage. Weinberg also appears to have received expensive gifts and kickbacks on some of the bribes he helped arrange.

In one of the stranger public dramas to grow out of recent anticorruption efforts, the FBI became ensnarled in its own web during an investigation of alleged municipal judicial corruption in Cleveland.[37] The tale involves questions of competence, secrecy, exploitation by an unwitting and then witting informer, and even a dash of poetic justice. Marvin Bray, a court bailiff, did not know that two men hanging around the court who indicated an interest in bribing judges to fix cases were really FBI agents. Bray said that he had two judges in his pocket and agreed to set up payoff meetings. Over an 8-month period at least twelve tape-recorded meetings were held between two "judges" and the agents. The FBI paid out $85,000. In a wonderful example of pluralistic ignorance, the "judges" did not know that the fixers were really FBI agents, and the FBI agents did not know that the judges were really imposters. Bray had persuaded two acquaintances to pose as judges, using the deceptive ploy that they were part of an official undercover operation to protect the judges and root out corruption.[38] One of the imposters was a man in his thirties, and the judge he pretended to be was 68. Although the investigation lasted four years, the identity of the targets who were elected officials had not been certified.

Once Bray realized that he had been dealing with government agents, he disappeared. The FBI located him. Bray was able to convince them that there really was corruption in the court and that he would help them gather evidence by directly approaching judges. The FBI then helped him get his court job back by having a doctor write and explain that he had been absent from work for medical reasons. After he offered the fraudulent tape of a judge accepting a bribe described earlier, the investigation was closed.

Another form of exploitation involves the informer secretly and selectively "giving up" sworn undercover agents or otherwise using his relationship with police to further his own criminal ends. The informer's knowledge of police can be a resource exchanged within the criminal environment, for example, offering information on who the members of undercover units are, what cars they drive, when they work, and what their strategies, priorities, targets, and operating procedures are. Drug dealers may plant informers as a means of monitoring police behavior and giving up competitors, while continuing to deal themselves.

An informant who has helped arrange a purchase of contraband may in actuality be responsible for an effort to rob the undercover agent of the money brought for the purchase. Or the informer may sell the same information to several law enforcement agencies, concealing the fact that he has done so.

The controller-informer relationship is usually seen to involve the former controlling the latter. There may be a kind of institutionalized blackmail. Prosecution, prison, and/or public denouncement as an informer are held in abeyance as long as cooperation is forthcoming or help in gaining leniency on a pending sentence is offered. Most of those interviewed preferred to have a "hammer" over the informant rather than one cooperating only for money ("He's a man without a country, no way will he expose us"). But the situations can sometimes be reversed. The skilled or fortunately situated informer may be able to manipulate or coerce the control agent as well. This appears to be the case with former FBI agent Dan Mitrione, who was involved in Operation Airlift. Mitrione and an informer posed as electronic debugging experts ready to help pilots smuggling drugs in Florida. Mitrione let his informant close a large cocaine deal, and he kept some of the proceeds. Suspicions in the FBI were raised when Mitrione began speaking affectionately of the informer.

Good supervisors are concerned when they encounter the sounds of moral relativity. As one put it, "I worry when I hear things like 'there are good crooks and bad crooks, and so-and-so is really a pretty good guy.'"

Getting too close to an informant can cause problems. There is a potential conflict that can be difficult to manage. Informers should be treated fairly, and a bond may develop between the agent and the informer. This can be exploited by the latter. The agent may come to take the side of the informant against the agency. A gradual seduction process may occur as the agent is charmed by the informant and/or comes to sympathize with his problems and gets drawn into the web. Rules are bent (a violation that would be cause for terminating the relationship is overlooked; the informant is loaned an extra $200 to make up for the $500 he needs when the agency approves only $300). The tables may slowly turn as the informant gets something on the agent.

In "graymail" cases, informers may be able to coerce or manipulate police into granting them immunity. This may be the case when a trial and related publicity would expose an ongoing investigation, secret sources, operational techniques, classified information, or government dirty tricks and illegality. Or it may be part of the exchange involved in gaining their cooperation. An Abscam informer used his knowledge of the case to have the Chase Manhattan Bank vouch for his phony schemes. Although victims complained, he was able to continue for a year and a half. He was arrested only after the Abscam investigation ended. The Justice Department initially dropped embezzlement and several other charges against Teamsters' Union President Jackie Presser. An agent in Cleveland claimed that Presser had the FBI's authorization for his illegal actions, making it difficult to prove criminal intent. The case was reopened after prosecutors questioned whether Presser's crimes had in fact been authorized. The agent was fired and indicted. His actions appear to have been undertaken in order to protect the informant and the investigations the informant had helped with, and not for personal gain.

A related phenomenon involves crimes committed by persons who have been relocated with new identities as a result of participation in the Federal Witness Protection Program. While the cases on which they cooperated are being prosecuted (and even after that), their criminal activities may be protected. An official of the U.S. Marshall's Service reports: "I probably answer 35 letters a month from either creditors who are left in the danger area or from creditors who are left in the relocation area or from people who have in fact been defrauded as a result of witnesses using our documentations."[39]

The problems created by informers can be lessened by awareness and constant vigilance and by appropriate policies and procedures, which include written guidelines, criteria for selection and evaluation, centralized informant records, and explicit instructions. In some cases, a written "memorandum of understanding," which states what is expected and what is prohibited, is appropriate. The suitability of the informant for the role and the likelihood of effective control must be considered before an operation is authorized. Where possible, replacing informants with agents or unwitting with witting informants is desirable. Sworn agents not only make good witnesses but they are always available to testify. Electronic surveillance and cross-checking other sources of information can increase accountability. When the informer is unlikely to testify in court, the need for supervision is even greater. Emotional involvement with the informer should be minimized. Finally, it is important to create "the sense that the informant is the organization's property, not solely that of the individual agent." The problems created by the use of informers are not insurmountable. However, they are a continuous challenge.

EIGHT

Unintended Consequences: Police

The policeman never rubs off on the street; the street rubs off on the policeman.

—Robert Leuci, 1982

To bust a doper, become a smoker.

—Police station graffito

The FBI's reputation for integrity and its clean-cut, straight arrow image is attributable in part to J. Edgar Hoover's refusal to allow agents to face the temptations and problems confronting undercover police. Similarly, Los Angeles's Chief William Parker felt that the establishment of personal relations between officers and suspects "would invariably fester into a spot of corruption or prove a source of embarrassment even when capably and honestly conducted."[1] As they recognized, the social and psychological consequences for police who play undercover roles can be severe. He who sups with the devil must indeed have a long spoon. What is there about undercover work that is conducive to negative effects on police, and what are these effects?

Undercover situations tend to be more fluid and unpredictable than routine patrol or investigative work. Agents have greater autonomy, and rules and procedures are less clearly defined. The need for secrecy accentuates problems of coordination, increases the potential for error, and lessens the probability that problems will be discovered.

The major organizational problem of any law enforcement agency—how to supervise a dispersed set of employees—is compounded. Undercover agents are removed from the usual controls and supports of a uniform, a badge, a visible supervisor, a fixed time and place for work, radio or beeper calls, and a clearly bounded assignment. These have both a literal and symbolic significance. Their formal and visible nature enhances accountability by advertising to police and the public who the individual is and what is expected of him.

SOCIAL AND PSYCHOLOGICAL
CONSEQUENCES

Unlike conventional police officers, undercover agents tend to be involved primarily with criminals; the deception is continuous, the criminal environment is pervasive. The agent's ability to blend in, to resemble criminals, and to be accepted are necessary conditions for his effectiveness. As an undercover agent with twenty years of experience put it: "A guy who is two degrees off plumb will survive out there, while a choir boy from MIT will be in a lot of trouble."

To the extent that agents develop personal relationships with potential targets, they may experience pressure, ambivalence, and guilt over the betrayal inherent in the deception. Romantic entanglements are an extreme example; more commonly, agents may come to feel sympathy for their targets and develop an understanding of why they behave as they do. A highly productive officer who, before his undercover assignment, saw the world in black-and-white terms reports he became "a different kind of cop." Going undercover, he learned "what it's like to be on the other side of the fence." He started "seeing the criminal element being just regular people, but caught up in their own thing."[2] Another deep-cover agent says: "Boy, it can get gray out there . . . just because a guy's a criminal doesn't mean you can't like him and that he doesn't have the same interest[s] as you do [e.g., baseball or fishing]." Such attitudes can lead to passivity and even the protection of particular targets. Consider, for example, an agent who came to feel close to a target: "He was a 72-year-old guy. The king pin. There was enough evidence. You go to christenings, weddings, Sunday dinner. It's easy to say hey, it's the other guys. He really isn't so bad. I won't testify against him."[3] The agent may falsely report back that the group cannot be penetrated or that no violations are occurring. The fear of being "made" or "burned" (discovered) may also mean the failure to pursue a case vigorously.

Another agent described the feelings of betrayal he had on concluding an operation when his unknowing target "protected" him. In a sell-bust transaction, the agent arranged for contraband to be sold to a suspect he had befriended. The eventual arrest was arranged in such a way as not to cast suspicion upon the agent. When the arrested suspect was interrogated about his source for the contraband, he refused to "give up" the agent.

In contrast, when the agent plays the role of victim and develops a strong identification in this direction, the result may be an overly aggressive crusade. Joseph Wambaugh describes a member of the San Diego decoy squad who played the role of aliens who had been robbed, stabbed, raped, or terrorized: "He began to feel what *they* felt . . . to *feel* the poverty and fear. It made funny pains in the stomach. . . . It made them sigh a lot. Finally it made them mad."[4] In this case, the strong identification meant vigilante actions and personal crusades, as the decoys sought to teach "the crooks that there was a price to pay" for their behavior, regardless of departmental policy and the law.

Covert work is very intense. The agent is always "on." For some agents, the work has an addictive quality as they savor the sense of power, intrigue, excitement, and their protected contact with illegality. They may be both attracted and repelled by the role they play. The strong male bonding and secrecy that are characteristic of police work may take a conspiratorial turn as undercover agents adopt a protective code of silence not unlike that of organized crime.[5]

In his analysis of how patrolmen can avoid becoming corrupted by the use of coercion, William Muir stresses the importance of conversation and interaction with supervisors. The same conditions are likely to reduce the corruption of those licensed to use deception. Yet for the undercover agent these conditions may not be as available. Isolation and secrecy may work against the undercover agent's developing a morality that permits the use of deception in a bounded and principled fashion. Isolation from other contacts and the need to be liked and accepted by members of a criminal subculture can have undesirable consequences. To do well, you must "get your mind inside the bad guy's mind." But "playing the crook" may increase cynicism and ambivalence about the police role and make it easier to rationalize the use of illegal and immoral means, whether for agency or corrupt personal goals. As one agent jokingly put it when asked about his speeding and running stop signs (unrelated to any enforcement effort): "We're here to enforce the law, not to obey it."[6]

When an insensitive supervisor fails to help the agent cope with the moral complexity of the issues or fails to communicate support and questions what the agent does, it may seem to the agent that "everything bad that happens to me comes from the good guys, and everything good comes from the bad guys. You start to wonder." On the other hand, as long as the tactic produces results, some supervisors may not wish to know what agents are doing or what the role is doing to the agent.

The stress the agent experiences can be intense. Some supervisors are more concerned with making cases than with the well-being of their agents. They may not share the priority implicit in the remark of a wise supervisor who said: "Cases will always be there, agents won't." A state police officer who spent two and one-half years undercover reports:

> My nerves are really up. I'm starting to get to where I can't keep a meal down. I would eat with them . . . twenty minutes later, I would be throwing my guts up on the side of the road. I started to feel these chest pains. I really felt like I was having a heart attack. I would have diarrhea on a daily basis.
>
> I go to this doctor . . . I go to my sergeant on the undercover gig the next day and say, "I went to the doc, and he wrote this down for you." I figure this is it. I have a note from the doctor saying I'm under stress, too much stress. They'll have to let me out of this job.
>
> He laughs. I say, "What are you laughing about?"
>
> "We got a million dollars wrapped up in this. You're not physically hurt. You're going through stress. You'll be all right. You can handle it." That's the mentality of cops: You can handle anything. Don't worry about it, kid, you can handle it. I was devastated.[7]

Agents may also experience stress as a result of being away from family members and their normal environment; a lack of clear markers indicating how the investigation is going or when it will end; or working with other agencies that may have different goals and procedures. Another source of strain can be the pressure to succeed because of the large expenditure of resources the case requires and the close observation it is likely to receive. The agent who works with a wire or video is subjected to much more intensive supervision than is normally the case when reviews are restricted to after-the-fact written documents and statistics. However imperfect, video and audio records offer a much fuller form of observation. In big cases at crucial meetings, the contact and case agents, supervisor, undercover coordinator, and senior managers may all be listening in, along with outsiders such as U.S. attorneys and sometimes selected members of the press. Such data also permit repeated reviews by others far removed from the initial situation. Not surprisingly, this is a source of strain for some agents.

The secrecy required for undercover work offers rich opportunities for shortcuts, financial rewards, and self-aggrandizement. Agents may learn the technical skills needed for complicated offenses. Their knowledge of how police operate lessens the likelihood of discovery, as does the usual absence of a complainant. Moral corrosion or a lowering of standards may occur when agents are granted the power to engage in conspiracies on behalf of law enforcement and are immersed in a seamy, morally relative world.

New York City's elite narcotics force, the SIU (Special Investigating Unit), illustrates many of these issues.[8] Its members gave heroin to informants, set illegal wiretaps, committed perjury, and sometimes took bribes. They also engaged in vigilante tactics, such as seizing drugs and cash and summarily ordering foreign dealers out of the country (referred to as "taking the devil's money to do the Lord's work" or "make them bleed, bust their ass, and steal their weed").

This highly select unit (chosen from the "best guys in all the precincts") roamed the city, had no assigned precinct, and were exempt from many of the bureaucratic restrictions faced by others. Belief in the special elite character of the unit resulted in a lessening of supervision ("they supervise themselves"). The unit made major arrests and seized large quantities of drugs. Its spectacular success did not suggest corruption, but effectiveness and opportunities for corruption often go hand in hand.[9] The unit did not fare well: of 70 SIU detectives, 52 were indicted, 2 committed suicide, and 1 had a mental breakdown.

Undercover agents may come to have an exaggerated sense of their own power. The highly committed members of the elite San Diego decoy unit wanted no part of ordinary police duties and came to feel apart from, and superior to, other police:

> They started to come to work looking like something that fell off a boxcar or was pushed off by a railroad bull. They'd work in their yards or wash their cars or haul fertilizer or whatever, and they'd come to work rank. Unshaven. . . .
>
> They'd tell their wives and friends, and fellow cops who worked patrol and detectives, that they *had* to dress and look and smell like that. That out in the canyons they had to *be* aliens. That their performances might make the difference in whether they lived or died. Then they'd look at some ex-partner who had to wear a police uniform every day and follow the rules of conduct suitable to the department and the city and the state and the U.S.A., and they'd say, "Aw, fuck it! How would *you* know?" The implication being that some cop brother who didn't work [in the unit] was, in the final analysis, the same as a lizard-shit civilian.[10]

A number of the interview, news, and nonfiction and fiction accounts in the literature suggest that some deep-cover agents undergo a striking metamorphosis.[11] As lying becomes a way of life, the agent may become confused about his or her true identity. Familiarity can breed affection as well as contempt. This is particularly likely to the extent that the agent is cut off from friends and becomes immersed in a new life. The phenomenon of "going native" is a danger well known to social science field researchers.[12] A few agents "cross over."

The parallel to the informer who comes to identify with police is the officer who comes to identify with criminals. In his novel *Mother Night,* Kurt Vonnegut observes that "we are what we pretend to be, so we must be careful about what we pretend to be." Or, put more prosaically by a vice-squad detective: "You're working with dope fiends and perverts all day, and a guy on the vice squad usually goes down; he deteriorates; he becomes like the people you work with." [13] Most agents, however, do not turn into "weird guys," even though the potential for adverse effects is there.

A Connecticut officer from a conservative family background spent a year posing as a street person and riding with a motorcycle gang. He was overtaken by the role. He reports: "I knew [it] was a role-playing thing, but I became total, 100 percent involved. I became what I was trying to tell people I was, and it confused me. Believe me, it confused me a lot." [14]

Robert Leuci, who served as the model for the book and film *Prince of the City,* noted a gradual change in himself and the officers he worked with:

> I began to wake up in the morning and look at myself in the mirror and see my reflection—and I didn't like what I saw. . . . I didn't like the way I was dressing. . . . We all started wearing pinkie rings. I *hated* them, but I found myself wearing one . . . spending a lot of money on shoes. . . . It seemed like I was becoming like the people I was *after.* I started looking like Mafia guys. You look at those guys—they talk out of the sides of their mouths—they talk like there's a big criminal conspiracy going on, even if they're only talking to their kids. They're never up front. They live a life of whispers. So then I found myself talking to my father in the same way. [15]

An officer in San Jose describes how he changed after being "buried" in a deep-cover operation: "This was really strange. . . . For the first nine months I was really nervous and afraid. . . . You meet a lot of bad people and you've got . . . no cover. But I still remember one day . . . something snapped. I just felt it like a jolt going through . . . and I was no longer afraid or nervous. It was like I had a handle on things . . . a short time after that . . . I didn't believe I was a cop."

Most of the same social and psychological factors involving agents and targets are operating in political settings as in criminal ones. But there is an additional paradox here when an ideological issue involves matters of class, age, ethnicity, race, religion, or gender. The agent must share at least some of these attributes in order to be credible, and this common bond increases the likelihood that the agent will understand and sympathize with the group's goals.

In the logical, though not necessarily ethical, equivalent of under-cover police who become like criminals, some agents who infiltrate po-litical groups become converts. Their political beliefs may change. In the 1960s, more than a few sworn agents concluded that the groups they infiltrated were not serious threats, but committed people with genuine concerns. They came to see government efforts to police the politics of activist, nonviolent groups as illegal and counterproductive.[16]

An officer's personal habits may change as a result of easily accessible vice opportunities. Police may become consumers or purveyors of the very vice they set out to control. In Chicago, an officer was suspended for operating a prostitution ring. He had initially posed as a pimp and infiltrated the ring as part of a police operation. When the investigation ended, he continued in his role as a pimp. A vice detective referred to involvement with prostitutes as an "occupational habit," then corrected himself, saying, "I mean occupational hazard." This kind of involve-ment is sometimes cited as a factor in police divorces. Many of the tales about police and prostitutes are of the same genre as those regarding priests and nuns or doctors and nurses. They say more about the needs of the teller than the actual situation. Whatever the facts, this is hardly a significant social issue.

With drugs the problem is more serious. Little is known about police drug use and addiction. Departments have become increasingly con-cerned as officers raised in a more permissive culture have entered the force. Undercover officers may be even more prone to their use than conventional officers because of greater stress, isolation, and accessi-bility. Drug use is frequently linked to the covert role and life-style that the agent is affecting. Its use is at least informally justified. Most drug officers certainly do not develop drug problems, but there are tragic cases, and the risk is real. The risk is greater for local police involved with street-level users than for federal police who are more likely to play the role of higher-level dealers.

In April 1979, in what was described as the "biggest drug bust in East Texas history," 79 people were arrested as the result of an eight-month operation involving a male-female undercover team. The widely acclaimed investigation brought recognition to the Tyler, Texas, police department; its police chief received the Law Enforcement Leadership Award of the year. The female agent was named "Rookie Cop of the Year," and her male partner became "East Texas Outstanding Peace Officer of the Year." But alas, the glory was short-lived. Most of the con-victions were reversed or set aside. The agents and the chief were all convicted of felonies.

The two young agents planted drugs, wrote fictitious cases, committed perjury, and planted, bought, sold, and used drugs. They became a part of, and helped strengthen, the local drug culture. In what was described as an "eight-month party," they played the role of high-living, drug-using swingers. But it ceased to be a role. In a recycling effort, the agents supplied and sold drugs accumulated through the undercover operation. Both agents developed addictions. The male officer was shooting heroin and had used methamphetamines, Quaaludes, Demerol, Preludins, cocaine, and marijuana. The female agent used cocaine heavily: "If it was an all-night thing, you'd go through a quarter of an ounce very easily, or half an ounce." This could cost $1,200, all subsidized by the taxpayers who were financing the investigation. Eventually, the officers sought help. The male partner reports describing his problem to the chief: "I pulled up my sleeves and showed him the needle marks on my arms." According to the officer, the chief offered him several days rest and told him to continue with the investigation. The chief eventually was indicted on charges of violating the civil rights of some of those arrested.

In another case, a former Illinois police officer who was also an ordained Baptist minister was brought to Louisville to play a deep undercover role in a drug investigation. His highly praised activities led to 107 indictments, including persons identified as dangerous career criminals. But, in almost half of these cases, those arrested "skated" (were let go). A credibility problem emerged that meant that many of the cases had to be dismissed. The undercover officer refused to testify for fear of incriminating himself. He had developed a drug dependence and spent buy money on drugs for himself. He was arrested. Suffering from severe stress, he institutionalized himself.

Relative to most occupational groups, police have high alcoholism rates. Job stress is a likely factor. In Washington, D.C., an undercover narcotics and liquor investigator was forced to retire on a full disability pension at 34 because of job-related alcoholism. His assignment required him to frequent taverns and to drink. Before joining the police, he seldom drank and had excellent physical health.

Some agencies prefer to have unmarried persons play covert roles. They may find it easier to begin a new life in a different environment and will not have strains related to family life. Little public attention has been given to the emotional toll that may be taken on family members of those playing undercover roles. There are no data on divorce rates among undercover agents as against police in general, but interviews and case materials suggest that they are probably higher. Should the agent be so inclined, the role is supportive of affairs. It also can offer a useful cover, as one supervisor in Los Angeles discovered. He received a call from the wife of an agent who complained that her husband's undercover assignment was keeping him away from home too many nights. The wife did not know that the operation had ended months before.

The strains on a marriage or a relationship are considerable: the odd hours, days, or weeks away from home; unpredictability of work schedules; concern over safety; late-night temptations and partying that the role may bring; and personality and life-style changes that the agent may undergo. The need for secrecy and the inability to share work details and problems, as well as limitations on a spouse's talking to others, can be costly. Knowledge of the agent's skill at acting, deception, and lying can increase paranoia and suspiciousness once initial doubts appear. The wife of one agent observes, "When you live under cover, you live a lie. You can't confide in friends about the pressures on your husband; you can't even tell your children what their father really does. You live under constant strain."

Although extreme, consider the case of an officer who was promoted for his outstanding work in infiltrating an international drug ring. He gained access to the ring by having an affair with one of its female leaders. His wife was proud of his heroic efforts and promotion, but, when the full details of the investigation became clear, she sought a divorce. An officer who got divorced in the middle of a three-year operation observed: "Imagine having a relationship with someone where you can't talk about what you do and where you suddenly say 'I'll see you in a week' and just disappear. There is also stress on her because you may not come back." For some agents, the "job becomes the mistress."

Even when there are no significant adverse effects, certain nonvoluntary undercover assignments, such as the enforcement of laws involving the sexual behavior of consenting adults, may engender resistance and low morale. Agents may see such work as undignified, unchallenging, demeaning, and socially unproductive. Assignment to the morals squad is often met with humorous jibes and derision; the language used to describe such assignments ("fruit shakes," "pussy posse") hardly suggests a righteous struggle between the forces of good and evil.

In an interview with Baker (p. 258n.3, below) a vice officer responsible for arresting a nude male dancer observes, "I hate to think that's my job in life, to go around telling guys to cover their buns and girls that they can't get their T-shirts wet." Some vice officers report feeling ridiculous beginning, but not consummating, a sexual act. To do so risks losing a case because they would be seen as willing participants. There may be pressures in the other direction as well. Apart from personal temptation, completion of the act may offer clearer evidence of intent and permit bringing higher charges. It may also reflect no training. One rookie officer in Atlanta chastised for such behavior in a homosexual encounter simply told his supervisor, "I thought you were supposed to go all the way."

Posing as a prostitute is generally not the type of work envisioned by a professional female officer. Ironically, some persons become police to escape the very environment undercover work may put them back into. A Detroit policewoman states, "I went to Michigan State University . . . and I studied hard to be a policewoman, but I don't think all the training was done so I could pose as a prostitute." She was suspended for refusing to pose as a streetwalker, believing that such work was degrading and immoral.

Another decoy in Boston who hated the assignment tried to disassociate herself from the role: "I just blanked out, went dead." She was angered by the political pressures which resulted in charges not being brought against a priest and a politician's son who had propositioned her. In another case she used her discretion to prevent an arrest, but she felt sad and uncomfortable in rejecting a man's offer by telling him, "no it's not because you're physically handicapped, it's because I'm a cop." She also felt her department had a double standard for both female officers and prostitutes because there were no routine assignments in which male officers posed as homosexual prostitutes. She didn't like the station house jokes about "working the street," and some male officers made her feel she was "doing in" innocent guys just out for a little fun. In court she was outraged by the personal attacks and innuendos offered by defense attorneys regarding her role and the seeming indifference of judges to this.

LEAVING THE ROLE

Any fool can tell you the truth, but it requires a man of some sense to know how to lie well.

—*Samuel Butler*

When the investigation ends, the agent may feel relief, but he may be unable simply to return to an ordinary existence. If there is a danger of reprisals, it may be necessary for him to move to a new location and change his appearance and some customary behavior patterns. Apart from this, some agents experience subsequent personality changes and difficulties in readjustment. Ironically, some of the qualities thought to aid in effective undercover work (being outgoing, extroverted, a risk taker, adept at role playing) also may be associated with problems once the role ends.[17]

An experienced officer observed that training a policeman to act like a criminal can be "like training a vicious dog. When you're through with him, you don't know what to do with him." Although this is certainly overstated, problems may appear in the transition from a covert deep-cover agent to a conventional police role. Like an actor caught up in a stage part, the agent may have trouble leaving the role. There are parallels to the re-entry problems sometimes faced by combat soldiers. The agent may initially find it difficult to shed fully the trappings of the caper, whether it be in language, dress, hairstyle, or conspicuous consumption. He may be hesitant to return false identification or jewelry used in the operation. The agent may miss the more free-wheeling expressive life and work style and the excitement and attention associated with the role. After the high of a successful case, some agents have trouble fitting back into normal office routines. They may have discipline problems and show various neurotic responses and in a few cases appear to have a split personality.

Consider, for example, a northern California police officer who rode with the Hell's Angels for a year and a half. He was responsible for a large number of arrests, including previously almost untouchable higher-level drug dealers. He was praised for doing a "magnificent job." But this came at a cost of heavy drug use, alcoholism, brawling, the breakup of his family, and his inability to fit back into routine police work after the investigation was over. The result was resignation from the force, several bank robberies, and a prison term.[18]

FBI agent John Livingston spent two and a half years posing as a distributor of sexually explicit materials in Operation MiPorn (Miami pornography). The operation—the largest federal pornography investigation ever undertaken—was hailed as a great success and received extensive media coverage. Livingston was praised for his excellent work, but he had trouble separating from his role. He continued to use his undercover name in situations unrelated to his FBI work and to frequent bars and places he had been during the investigation. After two brushes with the law, he was eventually arrested for shoplifting and gave his undercover alias. He split up with his wife and lost many friends.

Psychiatric evaluation found that he had difficulty distinguishing his undercover from his real identity. Fourteen indictments that had resulted from his prior covert work were dropped because they were believed to be tainted by the investigator's confusion. Livingston initially demonstrated a "lack of candor" in describing his actions to his superiors. In what another former FBI agent characterized as "shooting our wounded," he was fired from the FBI after 17 years of service. He eventually obtained a disability pension.

Although not experiencing that degree of trouble, a northern California officer reports difficulty in returning to regular police work:

> At first it was really kind of strange and weird and scary and funny. I'd be riding in a patrol car, and I wouldn't be in the frame of mind of a uniformed police officer. I'd see another patrol car, and I'd tense up in knots. I really felt like the crooks. It would take me a second to realize that "hey, he's one of us." People would flag me down and I'd just wave back and keep driving. They want a cop, not me. I'd find myself answering [radio] calls and flipping back to my old [street] vocabulary. It was very embarrassing. I'm still having problems.

The agent may develop a cynical, suspicious, and even paranoid world view and feel constantly on guard. Things that were once taken for granted may be doubted.

There may be interactive effects. If the agent has changed, colleagues may perceive this and act differently toward him, which may further encourage his paranoia and estrangement. Peers and supervisors may add to the problem should they not welcome the agent back with open arms. They may look skeptically on the recently submerged agent, wondering if he or she is (or always was) a bit strange. They may be ambivalent about what the agent has done. Perhaps they respect the agent's skill and courage, but also think that the agent was out having a good time and not doing much with an expense account, a fancy car, and an apartment while they were stuck in the office working regular hours. An agent who described this asked rhetorically: "If they think it's so much fun, why don't they volunteer then?" The FBI's pool of volunteers consists of approximately 500 people out of almost 9,000 agents.

Feelings of anger and bitterness may develop if the agent comes to feel that his sacrifices and the risks he took are not sufficiently appreciated. Or he may feel that the results of the investigation were not worth the effort. He may doubt his ability to fit back into a bureaucratic routine.

If the agent has been in a deep-cover operation and has had little contact with his family, the family situation may change as well. The family has managed on its own and may have developed new ways of coping. Family members may show increased independence. This can be an added source of tension for the agent once the assignment ends.

Most agents in deep undercover roles do not experience severe personality disorders, but the potential is there. All agents are likely to be changed to some degree.[19] In response to the problem, the FBI started a psychological health program in 1983. A central feature of this is to have constant contact with the agent and to remind him that he is part of a group effort. He must be helped to stay "in an agent state of mind." Since the program began, problems have gone down, although the number of agents working undercover has gone up.

To begin with, there is an effort to avoid problems ("we don't just open the phone book to choose our undercover agents") by careful selection. All undercover officers are volunteers. In a personal interview, they are warned of the risks and dangers. They are shown a video from the program "60 Minutes" of the difficulties faced by Livingston (described above). They are disabused of the notion that "they are junior G-men or Rambo or that they will spend their time on a fancy yacht in Florida." They are given an array of psychological tests and taped in a role-playing session. They must want to play the role for the right reason (not because they want to move to a new city or to escape marital difficulties). Their family situation is assessed, and spouses must be agreeable to the assignment. They undergo a two-week training program.

Beyond a small percentage who are told they should not work undercover or that they are not yet ready, a distinction is made between the majority who seem to be best for short-term operations and those who are also suited for the more demanding long-term roles. The latter "are very independent, deeply motivated, very goal oriented. They know who they are and where they want to go." They have strong personalities and pride in themselves. For conventional criminal cases they need to be "street smart," an attribute not obtained in the classroom.

Once a major operation begins, an important concern is to keep the agent aware that he is part of a team and not a lone wolf. He is expected to dictate or write regular administrative reports. He will have a contact agent or handler with whom he deals directly on a daily basis to the extent possible. There is also a case agent and a supervisor who are to stay in contact with him several times a week and weekly, respectively. An undercover coordinator and the special agent in charge of the field office are to have monthly contact. And a team from Washington head-

quarters will visit the site after three months. Aside from offering procedural and tactical support, an important part of their job is to let the
agent know that they care and to "communicate total support." The
match between the agent, handler, and supervisor is crucial.

Handlers, supervisors, special agents in charge, and field coordi-
nators also undergo training. The handler should be someone of equal
rank with knowledge of the undercover situation who acts as a buffer
between the agent and the agency. Because objective assessments are
crucial, it is preferable that the handler and the agent not be close
friends.

Both the undercover agent and those working on the case with him
are trained to recognize signs of stress and indications that the agent
may be headed for difficulty. FBI agents are systematically monitored
for such signs. (Can he come out of the role during meetings and when
not on assignment? Does he keep appointments and meet paperwork
requirements? Does he follow orders? Does he seem too close to the bad
guys? Is he taking undue risks? Is he ready to testify and prepared for
the termination of the operation? Are there changes in his regular habits
and attitudes or signs of stress?) Should a problem be identified, the
agent can be pulled out, reevaluated, and given additional training or
support. As volunteers, agents can "jump out anytime" without this formally counting against them. Agents are required to take time off from
the role. They are given three extra days off per quarter and expenses to
return home (most assignments are not local).

In the FBI there is a presumption against the agent playing another
role for at least three years. Noting how socially and psychologically
draining the work can be, a supervisor states: "It takes a lot out of the
individual. A space is needed before pursuing another investigation. We
don't want to develop career undercover officers. That's O.K. for the
CIA, but for us it's better in and then out." Monitoring continues even
after the assignment ends. In a "delayed stress syndrome," problems
sometimes may appear months after the investigation ends.

THE TANGLED WEB OF
MISTAKEN IDENTITY

If you don't make some mistakes, you're not in business.
                                        —FBI Director Webster, 1983

The size of big-city police departments and the fact that the United
States has many public and private law enforcement agencies with over-

lapping jurisdictions may mean undercover police responding to each other, or being responded to by uniformed police, as law violators. Secrecy can be conducive to failures in coordination, wasted resources, injury, and negative publicity for police.

At the most benign level, this may involve nothing more than a large number of municipal parking tickets written for unmarked police vehicles each year; patrolmen unsuspectingly intervening to "rescue" a decoy just as he or she is about to be robbed; or local police responding to suspicious persons in a car who turn out to be part of a federal stakeout. But there are more dramatic and costly instances.

ENFORCING THE LAW AGAINST EACH OTHER

As a form of control, or because different agencies are involved, agents who have infiltrated criminal or radical groups often may not know who the other police agents in their midst are. They may make appealing targets for each other. Each agent is likely to be immune from prosecution and may, therefore, take both an assertive approach to illegality and a positive response to proposals from their counterparts. The need to establish credibility, as well as to discover or generate wrongdoing, may result in undercover police agents finding each other attractive as potential lawbreakers.

An early twentieth-century case illustrates this. Chicago's police chief was concerned with "mashers" on the public streets. He sent Jack Rohan, "the best looking flatfoot in the department," to walk the streets and "bring in any female that attempted to flirt with him." He then sent out Alice Clements, a "dashing policewoman" new to the force, to "pinch each man who made a pass at her." They ended up arresting each other.[20]

An undercover New York City policeman in a homosexual bar struck up a conversation with an effeminate man wearing mascara. The men decided to go for a walk, and, after several blocks and a series of suggestive comments, the undercover policeman said, "You're under arrest." The other man said, "You can't arrest me. I was about to arrest you."[21] He was also a New York City undercover policeman.

Undercover narcotics agents, unaware of each other's true identities, may sell to, or purchase drugs from, each other. In Florida, drug charges against two men were dropped when it was discovered that they had helped two departments make a drug transaction with each other. Acting as middlemen, the defendants thought they were facilitating the sale of cocaine. Unbeknownst to any of the participants, the seller with 2.2 pounds of cocaine was a Pompano Beach undercover agent, and the buyers were Fort Lauderdale undercover agents.

Unreliable informants may increase the likelihood of interagency conflict. A detective notes that an informant may go to city police and say, "'I've got a great case for you.' The city police say, 'Great, we'll buy it.' He then goes across the street to the sheriff's office and says, 'I've got a great case for you.' It's the same case and they buy it too. We end up with two sets of investigators out in the field working the same case, wasting your time, and they may shoot each other out there because they all look like suspects. You don't know the players without a program."

A more common interagency problem involves an informer, facing charges as a result of one agency's investigation, helping another agency in an unrelated case and receiving considerations as a result. For example, after hard work, one agency arrested a major drug trafficker, who faced a 25-year sentence. He then went to another agency and offered "excellent information" on a pornography ring. Some cases were made and the second agency's support at a sentence reduction hearing was instrumental in a more lenient sentence. Agents who made the original case "went ape" when they learned of the deal. They saw a major violator getting off the hook as a result of help with a minor violation. Increased communication among agencies regarding informants and investigations can minimize such problems, although other costs may appear.

The expanded use of undercover means as a tool against police corruption has resulted in stings within stings, as the original police targets turn the tables and arrest those seeking to arrest them. A case in Bridgeport, Connecticut, for example, has all the makings of a classic Keystone Kops fiasco. As part of an FBI corruption investigation, an informer offered the superintendent of police a $5,000 bribe. The superintendent rejected the bribe and arrested the informant. As the arrest was being made, a bugging device was discovered on the informer. An officer then said into it, "whoever you are, come out and join the party." Among those party to the action were two journalists hoping to publicize a dramatic crime-fighting effort. One journalist was with the FBI and had been tipped off by them, and the other was with local police, having been tipped off by them.

The superintendent later sought to have the FBI agents arrested for bribery. The FBI threatened to arrest him on obstruction-of-justice charges. A public dispute also emerged over what should happen to the bribe money and the FBI's bugging equipment seized by local police. Bridgeport's mayor wanted the $5,000 to be spent to buy Christmas toys for poor children, while the FBI demanded its money and equipment back.

In what the sheriff of Galveston County, Texas, described as "the sting that got stung," a man approached sheriff's deputies with an offer to "buy protection" for a cocaine-smuggling operation. He offered to pay $75,000 in bribes to three county officials. In response, the sheriff's department set up its own undercover operation for what it thought was a major drug-smuggling operation. After several meetings, the bearer of the bribe was arrested and spent the night in jail. Sheriff's deputies monitoring an FBI radio frequency heard a voice say, "they've got our man!" The message was sent from an FBI agent on the ground to agents in an aircraft circling the hotel where the bribe meeting occurred. Sheriff's department officials sought to prosecute the agent, but the district attorney was unwilling. County officials submitted a $7,000 bill to the FBI for expenses incurred in their part of the investigation.

For legal, ethical, and organizational reasons, the predicate justifying these failed operations usually is not made public. In its absence, the agency initiating the operation may receive unwarranted negative publicity. In the short run, cooperation between agencies may be harmed by such incidents. There is also the risk that competing agencies will make illegitimate use of covert means as part of interagency struggles.

Undercover officers working different crimes may also collide. Thus, two undercover "scouts" seeking stolen property to purchase for the Washington, D.C., sting encountered two undercover narcotics detectives who were working the same area. The former "were knocked down in a muddy street and spent tense moments staring up at the muzzle of a pistol until their identity was made clear." [22]

The situations considered thus far involve reciprocal efforts of undercover officers seeking to arrest each other. Perhaps more common are situations where a uniformed officer seeks to arrest the undercover agent or where one agency spots the backup surveillance for an undercover agent. In small agencies, this is not likely to be a problem, but, in large heterogeneous agencies, undercover officers or those acting as cover for them may easily be mistaken for suspects. The likelihood of this is increased if they draw an undercover weapon, such as an automatic or a derringer, rather than the traditional police revolver.

Crowd and arrest situations can be particularly problematic. In crowd situations, undercover agents may suffer along with other demonstrators if police use force indiscriminately.[23] In arrest situations, undercover agents may have difficulty convincing other police that they are not what they seem to be.[24] A federal agent posing as a member of an outlaw motorcycle gang had to spend five hours at a New Jersey state police barracks after a search of his car revealed weapons. In response to his claim of being an FBI agent, the incredulous arresting officer stated, "Sure, and I'm Lana Turner." An undercover policeman recalls chasing a suspect: "It must have been some sight, this wild-looking hippie [the undercover policeman] running through the streets with a gun in his hand. The cops pounce on him and cuff him. He tries to tell them who he is and what's happened, but they don't believe him. Seeing what he looked like, you can't blame them." [25] In a similar incident, a doubting policeman who happened on two "drug-selling" undercover detectives suspiciously suggests that "maybe they stole the shields . . . faked ID. What better front? They're out here pushing shit with the best cover in the world." [26] Misidentification may also occur when off-duty police or police in civilian clothes respond to a street situation.

Although arrests are sometimes staged to add credibility to an operation, unintended arrests may occasionally serve the same function. Thus, the agent in Operation MiPorn was arrested by local police in Florida, along with a real offender, for possessing obscene material. However, charges were dropped because the agent's attorney (in real life and in the undercover operation) convinced the court that the pair had been illegally searched. Unlike some of the other cases, it was not necessary to tell the court the true facts, nor did the incident expose the operation's cover. Indeed, it strengthened it.

Arrest fiascoes can be undone, although sometimes only at a cost of giving an operation away. But, in the case of weapons, the situation is more serious. Undercover police may be shot by other police; black and Hispanic officers are particularly vulnerable in this regard.

In Washington, D.C., a uniformed policeman responding to a robbery-in-progress call killed an undercover policeman who had his gun drawn. In Houston, during a buy-bust drug arrest, an undercover policewoman was killed by a uniformed officer who mistook her for a criminal when she approached with her gun drawn to help with the arrest. Three FBI agents in New Jersey, staked out inside a bank, were wounded by other FBI agents who took them to be robbers during an attempted bank robbery. In extreme cases, undercover police may unknowingly shoot at each other.[27] Thus, in Detroit a policeman was killed in a shoot-out between undercover city and county police. A shoot-out in France between two rival gangs involved undercover police agents who had infiltrated both gangs.[28]

Problems of communication and recognition are compounded when international police efforts are undertaken. In several foreign countries, U.S. drug agents have shot local undercover police during raids. In a decoy squad that operated along the U.S.–Mexican border, there were a number of incidents in which police from Mexico encountered San Diego police pretending to be illegal aliens. During the eight months that the controversial program operated, six persons were unintentionally shot, all of them lawmen (three from each side of the border), by other lawmen.[29]

A related problem involves encounters between public and private police. In Boston, a security guard wearing a Santa Claus costume was arrested by police after a citizen saw a gun sticking out of his costume. In a New York City market, two plainclothes officers fatally shot a plainclothes security guard whom they mistook for a robber. The guard was making an unannounced security check and thought the officers were robbers.

UNDERCOVER AGENTS AS VICTIMS OF CRIME AND ASSAULT

By their very nature, undercover efforts may stimulate crimes other than those that police seek to facilitate. Undercover police operating without the protective identity marker of a uniform often present attractive targets: In Boston, two men received 20-year prison sentences for the armed robbery of a drug agent. They sought to relieve him of the buy money he had brought to purchase drugs. In the shoot-out that followed, an accomplice was killed. In Miami, a drug agent was killed and another wounded in a motel room after a drug buy went sour. In New York, a pioneering sting operation disguised as an industrial cleaning plant had to be unexpectedly shut down. A would-be thief, thinking he was ripping off a rich fence, sought to rob the store and was subsequently shot. (The incident greatly increased awareness of safety issues. It was captured on video and later used as part of LEAA's sting training program.)

The successful infiltration of the Bonanno family in New York by FBI agent Joe Pistone was stopped in part because of concern for Pistone's life. This was not because he was identified as a police agent, but because of his very success. He carried off his part so well that there was fear he would get caught in a deadly struggle between rival organized crime factions.

Police may also be attacked by citizens who mistakenly take them for criminals. A restaurant owner spent the night guarding his property after several burglaries. He left protective gates and the front door unlocked, hoping to entice intruders. At 3 A.M., a deliveryman seeing the open gates called police. Two officers dressed in jackets and blue jeans, though wearing their badges, responded and entered the darkened restaurant. They heard a rustling sound and shouted, "Police! Stop! Don't move!" In the darkness and excitement, the restaurant owner came at them screaming and was shot to death by the officers.

Innocent people who misperceive a situation also can be arrested. They may come upon an undercover operation and take benign action that police misinterpret. For example, two college students in Boston heard a woman scream and intervened in what they thought was a crime in progress. The "crime" actually involved a decoy squad seeking to arrest the woman's male companion. The two students were arrested and charged with assault and battery and helping a prisoner escape.

Police pretending to be drug dealers may be attacked by vigilantes playing an undercover role. This apparently happened in the Los Angeles case of "Los Tres del Barrio" when a narcotics agent was shot while trying to purchase heroin. The altercation involved three members of a Chicano self-help organization that, in addition to offering immigration counseling and English lessons, sought to rid the community of drug dealers by taking direct action against pushers. The three received long prison sentences.

Police may simply encounter persons with a private crusade. A member of Boston's decoy unit, posing as a drunk, had his glasses knocked off and was given a bloody nose by an irate citizen. The assaulted officer reported: "He didn't try to rob me; he just didn't like drunks." In San Diego, a policewoman posing as a prostitute was stabbed by a transvestite in a dispute over turf. The transvestite felt he had proprietary rights over the territory in question and resented what he thought was competition.

RESISTING ARREST

Arrest situations involving undercover and plainclothes officers can escalate when both criminals and bystanders doubt that they are in the presence of real police. Timing is critical. There is a thin line between too visible a uniformed police presence before the arrest actually occurs and an insufficiently visible presence when the arrest is attempted. The former may tip off suspects; the latter may cause citizens to question the authority of undercover agents. Some agencies prohibit undercover officers from participating in arrests. An additional reason for this is the belief that arrested persons will be more cooperative and less angry if the agent who deceived them is not present.

Some of the initial anticrime decoy programs experienced high rates of injury to both police and citizens. Thus, over a three-year period Detroit's now disbanded STRESS ("Stop The Robberies —Enjoy Safe Streets") program resulted in 3 officers killed and 100 injured, while 16 alleged offenders were killed and 58 injured. Doubts over the police identity of officers dressed to blend into the street environment played a role in this.[30]

Citizens may resist arrest when confronted by armed undercover agents whose claims to be police may not be believed or who fail to identify themselves properly. A citizen who seeks to look closely at a plainclothes officer's badge or one who is skeptical may be marked as a troublemaker. This can lead police to take "remedial action" to affirm their authority.[31] For example, in a tragic case of mistaken identity, a New Jersey schoolteacher was shot as he sought to escape from shabbily dressed drug agents in unmarked cars who pulled him over.

NINE

Controlling Undercover Operations

Duplicity in individuals is, of course, the basis of civilization, but the
double life of state agencies, cops as cabdrivers, cops as bag ladies,
cops as tourists—this is schizy, it's tribal theater, it taps into
existential energies, it releases hot mysterious powers. I like my cops
in uniforms with badge numbers I can read. I like police departments
with budgets argued at public hearings. Officers, detectives, should
be neatly dressed and easily identified.

—E. L. Doctorow, Lives of the Poets, *1984*

You can't find useful informants who are boy scouts, who are upright
citizens. So . . . you're either not going to fight crime, because there
are these unsavory characters who . . . may be exaggerating or
fabricating or doing crazy things themselves, or you proceed, but you
try to limit the risks. You try to hedge your bets.

—*Justice Department official, 1981*

This chapter is about limiting risks and hedging bets. If one believes that
covert tactics are inherently unethical or uncontrollable, then prohibiting them is warranted, but such a conclusion is neither realistic nor defensible. As a police supervisor notes: "One is tempted to say, since you
can't control undercover investigations, don't have them. But that's impossible because it means you are immunizing certain kinds of criminal
behavior." Recent social, technical, and legal developments have been
conducive to the expansion of undercover actions, and the kinds of low-
visibility offenses for which the tactic is sometimes uniquely suited are
increasing.

It is also politically unrealistic to think that the tactic could be abolished. Public pressures for action against crime are strong. "Law and
order" issues have ceased to be a code for repression and prejudice. Liberal and conservative viewpoints have come much closer together on the
importance of crime control measures.

The position that advocates the abolition of covert tactics also over-
looks the fact that there are differences in their use, and that there are
conditions that can be affected by policy makers and under which problems can be minimized. Considered at the most abstract level, the con-

cern is with police accountability. The debate over controlling undercover actions is one part of a much larger debate about the control of police in a democratic society.[1] Where should the lines be drawn between internal and external controls? Who should guard the guards? What standards should be applied?

With respect to undercover means, the major internal forms of control are guidelines, review boards, and operational procedures. The major external forms of control are the courts, prosecutors, legislative oversight, and auditors.

CURRENT CONTROLS

INTERNAL CONTROLS

Guidelines. As bureaucratic agents of the state, police need defined parameters within which to operate, but the diversity and uncertainty of their work often preclude the creation of fixed rules. Police administrators face a great challenge in seeking to combine accountability with flexibility; centralized control with decentralized service; and, in the case of undercover work, careful supervision with secrecy. The literature on police discretion has stressed guidelines as one response to these contradictory demands.[2] Guidelines formalize voluntary restraints and seek to mold police behavior without unduly restricting it. They suggest rather than command and are subject to internal creation and change.

Not surprisingly, guidelines are the major policy tool put forth by federal agencies in response to criticism of covert practices. One reason is the desire to forestall more sweeping and binding efforts by courts and legislatures, but there are also organizational reasons for favoring guidelines.

One of the last actions of the Justice Department under President Carter was to issue guidelines to govern the undercover operations of the FBI. These followed the issuance of earlier guidelines dealing with such sensitive law enforcement activities as domestic security investigations, the use of informants and confidential sources, search warrants, and racketeering enterprises. Other federal agencies that use guidelines for undercover activities are the Immigration and Naturalization Service (INS), the Internal Revenue Service (IRS), and the Drug Enforcement Agency (DEA).

The situation at the local level is much more diverse. A few large municipal police departments have fairly comprehensive and detailed guidelines; some have well-developed guidelines primarily for particularly sensitive investigations, such as political intelligence or narcotics. But, in general, undercover guidelines are not well developed at the local level.

Guidelines emerged partly from the realization that many of the intelligence abuses of recent decades, however unethical or ineffective, were technically legal. They also resulted as part of a broad trend that emerged in the 1970s to limit discretionary law enforcement. The criminal law is broad and grants enormous discretion to police to decide whom to investigate. As John Elliff notes in his consideration of FBI intelligence practices, "The criminal law alone does not supply effective standards to guide the exercise of this discretionary authority, to ensure that decisions on priorities are not made for arbitrarily or politically motivated reasons, and to maintain accountability to the public." [3]

FBI Guidelines. The FBI has gone the furthest in developing and using guidelines to limit discretion. Several broad assumptions guided this development. Guidelines "should not be a catalog of do's and don'ts. Rather, they should focus on establishing or formalizing sound procedures to assure that critical judgments are made at appropriate levels of authority and are recorded and, therefore, susceptible to subsequent review within the bureau, by the department, and by the Congress." Guidelines must be "realistic enough so as not to interfere with effective and appropriate investigative activities." [4] And guidelines are merely advisory and do not establish any rights or provide penalties for violation.

The FBI undercover guidelines are based on three major principles. The first suggests a threshold requirement: to begin an investigation there should be "*a reasonable indication that the undercover operation will reveal illegal activities*"; it must presume "a well-founded suspicion of criminal activity" established through appropriate information. [5]

A second principle is *to make "reasonably clear" to all concerned the illegal nature of the proposed action*. This is seen as a protection against unwitting involvement, particularly by persons brought in by intermediaries. A third principle instructs agents *to model undercover operations on the real world as closely as they can*. The opportunities offered should not be more enticing than those in everyday life. Beyond the question of fairness, unrealistically attractive rewards may give away the operation or hurt conviction chances.

The FBI Review Committee. The FBI guidelines create a Criminal Undercover Operations Review Committee that must approve certain operations. Based on such factors as the length of an operation (over six months), its cost (over $20,000), and whether or not it involves sensitive circumstances,[6] the FBI guidelines distinguish between group I and group II investigations. Group I includes the longer, costlier, or more sensitive investigations and must be approved by the local U.S. attorney, by FBI headquarters, by the Criminal Undercover Operations Review Committee, and by the FBI director or a designated assistant director. Group II investigations require the approval of only the local supervisor.

Group I operations require a proposal noting legal, ethical, and operational considerations, goals, cost, potential for entrapment and due process violations, and economic loss to either individuals or the general community.

Although the FBI review committee initially was most concerned with civil liability, its concerns have broadened considerably to include image—the "general propriety" of an approach. Negative factors are balanced against likely benefits, and approval is contingent on a plan to "minimize the incidence of sensitive circumstances" and to "minimize the risks of harm and intrusion that are created."

The guidelines mandate a yearly report summarizing the types of undercover operations approved. In 1982 there were 309 group II and 75 group I operations. The review committee met 19 times and approved 88 of 95 applications (24 were new and the remainder were renewals or changes). The number of proposals reviewed remained roughly constant over the next five years. Among the seven applications rejected, three were new, two involved changes in an existing operation, and two were renewals. All of the operations were expected to take longer than six months and to involve expenditures of over $20,000. About one-half involved "sensitive circumstances." The review committee seeks to combine traditional bureaucratic internal agency expertise and review with some of the features of a warrant requirement.

Reviews limit the discretion of local agents and create a documentary record. A review locates responsibility for the action at a high level of authority and, symbolically and concretely, calls attention to the issues at stake. Although the committee is not broad-based and remains primarily an FBI-based approval system, its members are highly experienced, and four representatives from the Criminal Division of the Justice Department are included.

EVALUATING INTERNAL GUIDELINES AND
REVIEW BOARDS

We are getting an increasingly better handle on the by-product
problems of undercover operations.

> —*FBI Director William Webster*

There is much to be said for internal efforts at control. The publication of voluntary restraints, which go beyond the law in limiting what
police may do, are a unique feature of American law enforcement. One
can hardly imagine the secret police of totalitarian countries (or even
most European countries) publishing guidelines to curtail their actions.
Such voluntary restraints on police power can help protect privacy and
liberty.

Guidelines foster consistency and professionalism and can make police work more predictable, fair, and efficient. Guidelines may be welcomed because "it is certainly much easier to operate when you know
what you may or may not do." They can help create a greater awareness
of the "moral dimension" of an action, and their effectiveness may be
enhanced because they are internally developed and not generated by a
distant body, such as the Supreme Court.[7]

Guidelines also may increase police accountability by offering outsiders criteria by which to judge performance. The knowledge that violations of the guidelines will be used by defense attorneys seeking dismissal or seeking to characterize an investigation as out of control can
have a moderating effect on police behavior. Well-publicized limits on
police authority may enhance public confidence.

However, the strengths of guidelines also can be their weaknesses.
They can be created, changed, or abolished at will without external notice (as in the Federal Register), public hearings or debate, and without
what the head of one agency refers to as "the laborious process of legislative amendment." Officers who violate them cannot be prosecuted,
nor are there statutory penalties for failure to comply. Guidelines are
merely advisory.[8] Unlike statutes for which a legislative history exists,
the interpretation of guidelines is left to the head of the agency.

Finally, there is the dilemma that arises with the effort to regulate any
controversial practice: increased control may discourage or prohibit
certain extreme practices, but it may legitimate the use of more "routine" controversial techniques. There is an implied endorsement. Investigators may be given a clearer mandate to use questionable means and

develop the confidence that their actions will be upheld in court and publicly accepted because they are within the guidelines.

Guidelines and the related review boards ought to be judged by two criteria. First, are the standards they apply fair, reasonable, comprehensive, clear, and consistent? Second, how does their implementation affect agency functioning?

If one were to imagine the best possible guidelines as well as the worst, the FBI guidelines issued in 1981 by Attorney General Civiletti are certainly on the good side, but they could be stronger. They are, in some ways, weaker than earlier guidelines regarding domestic security and the use of informants; there are also omissions, inconsistencies, ambiguities, loopholes, and no categorical prohibitions. They permit the director to approve (under unspecified conditions) inducements to crime to a person not suspected of engaging in, or having engaged in, or likely to engage in the illegal activity in question. And they do not specify conditions under which agents may participate in the commission of serious crimes (including crimes of violence) or interfere with the attorney-client and other privileges. Nor do they address the issue of illegal acts that occur only in response to the opportunities provided by government. However, the FBI guidelines call attention to most of the major ethical and social problems that can emerge, and they seek to minimize socially damaging actions by establishing some important safeguards. Although not mandatory, they do establish the presumption that they will be followed—unless a written case is made for extraordinary circumstances.

The Justice Department and the FBI argue that there is a need for flexibility and openness in any guidelines. Indeed, reality's richness can never be fully anticipated in a listing of formal rules. Fast-breaking developments, extenuating circumstances, and emergencies require room to maneuver. As currently written, the guidelines offer wide latitude. But do they work?

The appropriateness of guidelines involves questions of values and priorities; their effectiveness is an empirical matter. In principle, effectiveness should be easy to determine. We need simply ask, "How does the system work in practice?" Are the guidelines communicated, understood, and honored? Does a review committee work as publicly stated, or is it merely a rubber stamp? Given the secretive environment of law enforcement, its concern with public image, and the (not unrelated) lack of public research, these are not easy to determine.

In the case of the FBI guidelines and review committee, there is marked disagreement over their effectiveness. Consider, for example, the diametrically opposed assessments of Abscam. A deputy assistant attorney general in the Criminal Division observes, "I believe that the FBI had this investigation well in hand, and it was controlled." In contrast, a congressman with ten years experience as a prosecutor who had supervised other undercover operations said that, if Abscam was "not an operation out of control, then there is no such thing as an operation out of control."[9]

The heart of the debate is not so much over the substance of the guidelines or the intentions of a review committee, but over how these are expressed in practice. New bureaucratic standards from headquarters that can easily change and are general across diverse local contexts often meet with a lukewarm reception in field offices. Rules and related paperwork may be seen to inhibit action and to be unrealistic, given the job to be done. As one practitioner observed, "That's [ethics, guidelines] interesting stuff. But frankly I don't know if I give a shit. I have a job to do. How can you be ethical when you deal with unethical people?" The delays in gaining headquarters approval can be very frustrating to agents who often must act quickly or risk losing credibility and unique opportunities. Written policies may be seen as nothing more than busy work for aging headquarters bureaucrats of questionable competence who are far removed from the real world of law enforcement. As one agent put it, "Those guys in Washington are lucky to find a desk, let alone a crook."

Those subject to bureaucratic regulation are often masterful at manipulating it. The advice sometimes given to investigators, "think like a crook," can be misapplied. Apart from high principle and good intentions among the Washington executives who review proposals, the review depends on the quality of the information they are given. In this sense they may be captives of those whom they regulate. When, in their eagerness to make a case, agents exaggerate or lie about the predicate, approval may be forthcoming (e.g., in seeking approval for the DeLorean case an agent who was to play a key role described the automobile executive as a person "involved in large-scale narcotics transactions," although that was false. If he had told the truth it is unlikely the case would have been approved). Questions regarding agents' knowledge and understanding of the guidelines have also been raised.

The relationship between formal structures and actual behavior is a theme that runs throughout the hearings on undercover matters. From the perspective of congressional critics, the issue was well put by former Congressman Harold Washington, who listened to the testimony of FBI Director William Webster regarding the elaborate controls that are in place and then observed:

> Now we have listened to this magnificent superstructure which you described; on paper it looks good . . . you have made distinctions between special agents, informers, bagmen . . . of structuring it in such a way that you get only those who are likely to . . . select themselves. The question remains, How could the name of Senator Pressler . . . Congressman Rodino . . . be brought in this, clearly innocent people, notwithstanding all of this careful structure that you put together?[10]

The Senate Select Committee documented many instances where specific guidelines (and FBI rules generally) were not followed. The Subcommittee on Civil and Constitutional Rights did a case study of an investigation into alleged corruption in the Cleveland Municipal Court (Operation Corkscrew). In order to see how well guidelines and safeguards were working, staff persons were given access to the relevant FBI documents. The report concludes that "virtually every one of the principal safeguards was either directly violated, ignored, or administratively construed in a manner inconsistent with their stated purposes. . . . The FBI's insistence that the guidelines were followed is inaccurate. The analysis shows that the safeguards . . . were little more than rhetoric, offering at best limited constraints upon the investigators, and little or no protection to the public."[11] Some evidence suggested that working agents knew little about the guidelines, confirming the need for widespread and clearly stated dissemination.[12]

Internal evaluations by the FBI, on the other hand, have reached positive conclusions about the appropriateness and effectiveness of guidelines on undercover operations: "control and monitoring of informants . . . is strict and abuses have been held to a minimum"; or "with few minor exceptions, the program was in compliance with both internal FBI regulations and Attorney General Guidelines."[13] While not denying that there occasionally have been problems, the FBI argues that these were most likely during the initial 1977–1979 period of using covert means when it was least experienced and there were no review boards or guidelines. Claims about problems or the failure to follow guidelines since 1979 are disputed or seen as atypical: "minor imperfections," "innocent in nature," or a necessary cost.[14] There are, after all, risks and costs to any investigative technique, as well as to doing nothing, in the face of a serious crime problem. It is possible to learn from mistakes. The key is seen to lie in balance, extensive planning, oversight, and a continuous search for improvement.

The tendency of the media and critics to focus on instances where there have been problems draws attention away from the many highly successful cases. In the absence of a representative sample of cases measured in degrees against the many problems that can occur, precise quantitative assessments cannot be made. At the federal level, the more extreme problems are atypical, but they are so serious when they do occur, and there is such a large gray area, that new external controls (a warrant system or legislation of the guidelines) have been recommended. External controls supplement internal ones.

EXTERNAL CONTROLS

Courts/Entrapment Defense. Compared to traditional police methods, undercover means are relatively unhindered by constitutional or legislative restrictions. Judicial controls are quite limited. The major control—the exclusion of evidence—applies equally to covert and overt methods.

The entrapment defense was created by the Supreme Court in 1932 to protect otherwise innocent persons who are tempted by government agents into committing a crime. Convictions are denied because these people pose no risk to society; the defense offers a formal method for expressing disapproval of overbearing and unreasonable enforcement tactics. However, as currently interpreted, the entrapment doctrine leaves police enormous latitude in generating opportunities for crimes to be committed.

The present entrapment doctrine focuses largely on the defendant's state of mind—specifically, whether or not the person was predisposed to commit a crime. This is known as the subjective standard (in contrast to an objective standard that focuses on the behavior of police). Its purpose is to discourage police misconduct, but it does not focus on police activity. "Predisposition" is difficult to define. In contemporary usage, it refers to a current willingness to commit crime, apart from the nature of the inducement. Any defendant who commits the crime by accepting an inducement can be seen to be predisposed, because he or she has willingly gone along with the opportunity.[15] In practice, the test of predisposition may become whether the person violated the law.

The defense of entrapment is rarely used; to use it the accused must admit that the crime in fact occurred. In addition, because what is at issue is a person's character and past behavior, normally inadmissible evidence may be presented in court. When loose or nonexistent standards result in the targeting of an otherwise innocent person, even if pleading entrapment results in acquittal, that person's reputation may still be damaged.

Many observers do not see any coherent principle behind the doctrine or see it as just plain wrong on other grounds. It gives police little practical guidance. It permits the conviction of persons with prior records, no matter how unrealistic or excessive police behavior is; at the same time, it provides for the acquittal of those thought not to be predisposed, no matter how controlled police behavior is. This may have the subtle effect of directing attention toward known past offenders, but ignoring more skilled offenders who are able to mask their violations.

The entrapment doctrine is also limited by a reporting bias; courts can act only on cases that are brought to their attention as a result of someone being charged with a crime. The doctrine does not protect against abuses associated with failed operations or other nonprosecuted cases. An example of the latter is the use of an undercover operation to gain damaging information in order to coerce someone into becoming an informant or to cooperate otherwise. The situation is the same for the exclusionary rule.[16] Ironically, abuses may be most likely to occur in cases that are not brought to the courts' attention.

Even with cases that do come to court, trial judges who rule on the admissibility of evidence and the dismissal of cases restrict their attention to the case at hand. Because their decisions are not directly communicated to police leaders, a practice that the court has found objectionable may simply continue. One innocent individual may be protected, but there is no broader accountability.

In 1984 six states had legislation providing for an entrapment defense if police conduct was such that a normally law-abiding person would have committed the offense, given the opportunity. In considering current reforms, it would be helpful to know how police and criminal behavior in these states with an objective standard differs from states with the subjective standard.

Another protection that in principle might serve to lessen police overzealousness involves due process. In theory, the doctrine is violated when persons are convicted on the basis of outrageous government conduct.[17] In fact, the Supreme Court has never ruled on an undercover case where a violation has been found. Thus, in practice, "due process" has had little relevance to contemporary police actions, even for cases that are "shocking to the universal sense of justice."

If due process does not compensate for the current weaknesses of the entrapment doctrine, neither do other principles that might guard against improper police actions. The doctrines of equal protection and selective prosecution may serve as a defense against improper targeting; and the traditional principles of excuse or justification may offer protection against persons being induced to commit offenses under duress. In practice, these are difficult to prove and appear to have had almost no impact. Nor do laws prohibiting criminal solicitation, which in some European countries limit police participation in covert schemes, generally have an effect in the United States.[18]

Prosecutors. Prosecutors constitute another form of control over police: the kinds of cases investigators develop, and the means they use, are conditioned by perceptions of what U.S. attorneys or local prosecutors will accept. There is considerable variation among jurisdictions.[19] Criminal law has become much more complicated in recent decades, for example, the law of search and seizure. Police have an increased need for the prosecutor's advice, and prosecutors have become more prominent within the criminal justice system.[20] Some officers still feel, "hey, I'm just putting in my twenty years either way," but putting together a good case that will garner a conviction is a major determinant of police behavior.

In the past decade, the Attorney General and the Criminal Division of the Justice Department have played a more important role in oversight of the FBI. Before a case can be sent to the FBI review committee, it must have the approval of the local U.S. attorney. In particularly important cases, prosecutors may play a direct supervisory role and be involved in specific tactical decisions. Regardless of whether there is any review of the initial or ongoing operation, prosecutors may block questionable cases (even if legal), knowing they will be unlikely to get by a jury.

At the state and local levels, there is usually much less prosecutorial review for undercover operations. When there is interaction, it is usually during the early stages of an investigation where legal advice may be required by nontraditional approaches to complex crime problems or at the end, rather than during the operation.

Prosecutors can help keep police behavior legal, broaden the perspective brought to bear on an investigation, and enhance public accountability. But there is a danger here of unwarranted political interference. Prosecutors in the U.S. (unlike Europe) usually serve for only a short time, using the office as a career stepping-stone. This short-term focus may conflict with the long-range interests of career law enforcement officers. On the other hand, to the extent that prosecutors are actually part of an investigation, they may find it difficult to play an independent supervisory role.[21]

The prosecutor's concern is likely to be with strictly legal issues, rather than with guidelines.[22] Their scrutiny tends to be greatest as an investigation draws to a close and decisions must be made about arrest, charges, and prosecution, rather than at the beginning of, or during, the investigation.

Legislative Oversight. Senator Patrick Leahy of Vermont remarked in 1983:

> Is Congressional oversight really adequate, or is it a case where people like yourself [FBI Director Webster] come up, read a good, thoughtful statement into the record, and then come back two days later and give the same statement to another group of people with no followup, no cross correlations? I mean, when we talk about all of these things eventually coming under the oversight of elected representatives of the people, isn't that really, in many ways, a farce?

Compared to the congressional monitoring that went on under J. Edgar Hoover, what we have today is certainly not a farce. Under Hoover, congressional oversight of the FBI was perfunctory; in fact, many people thought the FBI monitored Congress, rather than the other way around.[23] Hoover made an annual appearance before Congress to request a budget increase and to tell of his agency's achievements. His legendary public relations skills, and fear and trembling over the files he supposedly kept on congressmen, generally resulted in superficial oversight. However, with Hoover's death, the Watergate scandal, and the concerns raised by Abscam, the nature of congressional-FBI relations changed. Congressional groups began to conduct probing inquiries.

With their power, resources, and access to the media, congressional committees can play an important oversight role. They can focus public attention on troubling issues, and their hearings can focus on needed legislation and offer a forum for the review of agency policies and performance. With control over appropriations and legislation, they can subtly (and not so subtly) affect agency behavior.

There are six regular oversight committees concerned with the FBI.

The most congressional attention has come from the House Subcommittee on Civil and Constitutional Rights and the specially created Senate Select Committee to Study Undercover Activities of Components of the Department of Justice.[24] Congress has given its approval to FBI undercover operations through annual budget appropriations and by granting exemptions from standard government requirements (leasing buildings, making contracts, and handling revenues) that would either interfere with or preclude many operations.

The congressional groups have held important hearings, gathered useful data, and issued thoughtful recommendations. However, Congress is limited in its ability to oversee and influence directly the actions of executive agencies. It is debatable whether the significant increase in congressional oversight has resulted in more effective oversight. This is related to the absence of strong central oversight committees, the dispersed nature of oversight responsibility, and the conflicts over turf among committees.[25] Indeed, various law enforcement agencies may play off committees against each other.

An important factor that limits congressional oversight is the dependence of committees on information provided by the agencies being monitored. Congress may be informed after the fact about matters it believes require prior consultation.[26] The committees concerned with monitoring the FBI have commented on the difficulty of obtaining needed materials. In its final 1984 report, the House Subcommittee concludes that "reports received from the Department of Justice regarding undercover operations have been wholly unsatisfactory . . . replete with self-serving, inaccurate, and misleading data." Malcolm Wheeler, deputy counsel of the Senate Select Committee, observes, "it is very difficult for Congress to oversee the FBI and the Department of Justice. We cannot get documents like the Luskin Report [a Justice Department memo analyzing the problems of undercover operations]. . . . We had to struggle mightily to get the documents that we did get and we got them under severe limitations."[27]

Such mechanisms as the Government Accounting Office and the Office of Technology Assessment seek to improve this situation, but they are also often dependent on agency revelations. A senior GAO official notes that "the FBI is the agency that we have the most difficulty [with] in getting the records we need to do our job properly."[28]

Access to information is even more difficult when the agencies have a mandate to operate secretly and where their professional expertise is at least partly based on being masters of deceit. Law enforcement agencies have legal and ethical justifications for withholding information—the need to protect privacy, sensitive techniques, and investigations or court cases in progress. As with the recourse to "national security" to justify unnecessary secrecy, legitimate exemptions can be used to shield information that should not be protected.

Even if cooperation were perfect, congressional oversight would at best be episodic. It can deal only with broad policy questions and symbolic reaffirmations. Implementation of its goals and specific operational and management supervision must rest with the law enforcement agency's bureaucracy. Nonetheless, a statutory requirement to keep oversight committees adequately informed may help them obtain the cooperation and information they need.

In a few local jurisdictions, police intelligence investigations are monitored from time to time, but there is no routine oversight of undercover operations. In response to revelations of extensive police spying on law-abiding groups, the Seattle City Council created an ordinance in 1979 placing restrictions on intelligence gathering and requiring an outside audit of intelligence files.[29] Several court-ordered settlements in other cities mandated similar requirements. Such oversight is clearly superior to the occasional lawsuit or civilian complaint that arises on an ad hoc basis after the fact and probably covers only a fraction of incidents. Legislation like the Seattle ordinance seeks to prevent abuses from occurring and, if they do occur, to provide a means for routine and systematic discovery and redress. It may have symbolic meaning to both police and citizens in calling public attention to the important value society attaches to civil liberties and public accountability. Contrary to initial fears, these ordinances do not appear to inhibit law enforcement and have been accepted and, in some cases, welcomed by police.[30]

SUGGESTED REFORMS

With the present methods known to us . . . the accountability and control of undercover investigations is very problematic.
                                                —A police chief, 1983

WARRANTS

When the problems of covert means are acknowledged, the predominant law enforcement response is to strengthen internal controls. This is politically the easiest course, and there are theoretically sound reasons for it. Critics, however, question whether the guards can adequately guard themselves.[31]

One proposal would require prior judicial authorization for undercover operations, on the principle that those with investigative and prosecutorial duties should not be the sole judges of when to use such constitutionally sensitive means.[32] To protect Fourth Amendment rights, a warrant is now required for police use of wiretaps and bugs. Because undercover operations can be even more intrusive than electronic surveillance, proponents argue that a warrant should be required here also.[33]

The model for the warrant proposed by the House Subcommittee on Civil and Constitutional Rights is the 1968 Federal Wiretap Act (Title III of the Omnibus Crime Control and Safe Streets Act), which requires judicial authorization for disclosure and use of intercepted wire or oral communication. A request for judicial authorization for an undercover investigation would have to include the following information: (1) the nature of the operation; (2) the basis for conducting the operation; (3) objective facts and circumstances that indicate that suspects are engaging or are likely to engage in criminal activities; (4) reasons why less intrusive measures won't suffice; and (5) steps taken to minimize invasion of privacy or other civil liberties abuses.

Most undercover warrants would likely be approved, as is the case with requests for wiretap authorization, but this need not suggest a rubber stamp, because enforcement agents are likely to present cases consistent with the standards needed for approval. This is particularly likely if Congress were to establish a civil damage action against the government for persons targeted by an undercover operation without a court warrant (and if the head of the law enforcement agency in question were required to conduct a disciplinary hearing and make public its findings).[34]

If an effective warrant system were to be developed, the following would have to be determined: (1) the definition of "undercover"; (2) the standard (or standards) for issuing a warrant, which may range from probable cause to demonstrable facts and which might vary depending on the situation subject to the warrant requirement—for example, require probable cause when a temptation is offered, but a lesser standard when the goal is to collect intelligence or the agent plays the role of a passive victim; (3) the situations where the warrant would be required, ranging from every undercover operation to much more limited conditions;[35] (4) timing—should the warrant be required when a general investigation is begun, when specific individuals are targeted, when an organization is infiltrated, or when an inducement is offered? When should renewal be required? and (5) a means of monitoring compliance with the warrant.

Opponents argue that abuses occur too infrequently to justify such an extreme departure from the traditional role of the judiciary, and they feel that existing remedies are adequate.[36] A warrant system would create new problems but fail to solve old ones. By involving judges on the side of the prosecution so early in the investigatory process, their objectivity at subsequent pretrial and trial stages might be limited. There is the danger that the court will become an official arm of the prosecution. Critics warn against a move toward a European inquisitorial system where the judiciary both supervises the investigation and conducts the trial.

Another layer of procedure and uncertainty might lessen investigative initiative and further slow the judicial process. Informants may be less willing to come forward; there may be fewer investigations because of the need to fill out applications and delays due to obtaining authorization; courts could be overwhelmed with litigation questioning compliance.

Critics of the warrant process also argue that the analogy to the intrusiveness of wiretaps is misdirected. A wiretap is indiscriminate, capturing both criminal and noncriminal phone users and conversational content. In contrast, an undercover operation may be focused just on the criminal parts of a person's life. The "probable cause" standard associated with wiretap authorization is seen as inappropriate in undercover contexts. Undercover operations are initiated precisely because offenses or offenders are difficult to detect or identify ahead of time. An important goal of such investigations is to *develop* probable cause—the standard for arrest and indictment. A probable cause standard would greatly reduce the number of undercover investigations, but to use a lesser standard would trivialize judicial involvement.

The feasibility of warrant administration and oversight in undercover cases also has been questioned. It is relatively easy to determine if warrants are executed properly in cases of electronic surveillance. But similar oversight for the more varied and dynamic activities of an undercover investigation would be much more difficult. There is also concern that a warrant requirement would lessen the security that undercover operations require and make them more vulnerable to discovery, particularly at the state and local level.

LEGISLATION

The Court has said repeatedly that it's not [their] job to decide
questions of policy about law enforcement, that's Congress' job . . .

it's Congress' responsibility to make the hard judgment about
what kind of law enforcement techniques are permissible and what
kind are not.

—*Professor Lewis Seidman*

Senator Charles Mathias of Maryland observes that standards for
undercover work "are so important that they ought to be written into
the statute books, rather than relegated to the netherworld of administrative rules that may be changed with the stroke of a pen." [37] The Senate
Select Committee recommends that the FBI, DEA, and INS be given explicit statutory authority for undercover work. [38] Other major recommendations are to legislate threshold standards for the initiation of an
investigation and to legislate an entrapment defense.

The recommendation to establish statutory thresholds addresses a
critical need, specifically the need "to feel secure," as Congressman
Hughes of New Jersey noted, "that the Government will not target us . . .
won't follow us . . . will not wiretap us . . . will not put our reputations
in question unless there is some reasonable basis." [39] These basic protections for innocent persons separate us from a police state. The means we
have to protect the innocent from arrest are generally adequate (although repeated solicitations and providing an otherwise unobtainable
ingredient are permitted). This cannot be said of the means to protect
them from being tempted by a covert inquiry.

To avoid random integrity tests, discriminatory targeting, and the
other problems that unrestrained undercover operations can create, two
types of standard are needed, corresponding to the initiation and specificity dimensions considered in chapter 4. The first involves criteria for
the initiation of a general investigation in a given area, and the second
involves targeting particular persons or organizations.

Attention is most frequently focused on limiting the conditions under
which the tactic can be used. But an opposite approach focuses on *pre-
scribing* conditions when the tactic must be used. One controversial example argues this should be the case for the readily overlooked offenses
of those in high-status positions. [40] This is seen as a way to even up the
scales of justice.

A related issue is the need to specify criteria for when an investigation should continue or stop. Knowing when (in the words of one agent)
"to pull out the plug" as against when "to run out the string" has rarely
been formally approached. The likelihood of prematurely stopping (let
alone starting) an investigation seems greater when high-ranking officials appear to be implicated. [41]

One ambitious response to the enormous discretion that undercover police have would be to codify the meaning of due process. A narrower response is to create legislation that changes the test for entrapment by placing limits on the methods investigators can use in inducing persons to commit crimes. As noted, current entrapment doctrine focuses on the predispositions of the target and places no limits on the actual behavior of police. In declining to set standards for appropriate police behavior, the Supreme Court has encouraged Congress to create legislation to fill the gap.[42]

The Senate Select Committee has recommended legislating an entrapment defense based on an objective standard of police behavior: "A defendant should be acquitted on entrapment grounds when a law enforcement agent—or a private party acting under direction or with the approval of law enforcement authorities—induces the defendant to commit an offense, using methods that would be likely under similar circumstances to cause a normally law-abiding citizen to commit a similar offense."[43]

The Senate committee also recognizes that some undercover practices are so overbearing that defendants subject to these tactics should be acquitted on entrapment grounds per se. These tactics include (1) the use of threats; (2) the manipulation of targets' personal or vocational situations; or (3) the provision of goods or services necessary to the commission of the crime that the defendant could not have obtained without government participation.

Legislation might also be passed to prohibit outright certain morally questionable behavior that seems to run against the spirit, if not necessarily the letter, of the law, for example, intrusion into protected and/or intimate relationships and communications. Thus, it has been proposed that an undercover or cooperating source be prohibited from (1) posing as an attorney, physician, clergyman, or member of the news media for purposes of establishing a professional or confidential relationship with private individuals; (2) adopting a pretext or pose in order to solicit privileged or confidential information from an attorney, physician, clergyman, or other person under the obligation of a legal privilege of confidentiality; and (3) giving testimony in any proceeding in an undercover capacity in a manner that denies due process rights to any person.[44]

New indemnification legislation has been proposed to compensate innocent parties for undercover injuries, because current remedies are not adequate. The existing vehicle for redress is the Federal Tort Claims Act. This was amended in 1974 to provide a means of compensating victims of certain acts by federal law enforcement officials. The kinds of abuses that emerge out of undercover operations—in particular, criminal activities conducted by informants—should be explicitly covered as well. A revision of this legislation might also make clear the government's liability for the misdeeds of criminals relocated with new identities through the Federal Witness Protection Program.

The indemnification legislation recommended by the Senate Select Committee would cover three types of abuse: (1) harms directly resulting from illegal activity undertaken by agents or informants acting legitimately to further undercover operations; (2) harms by the independent illegal activity of an informant or government employee who was able to commit harm because of his/her participation in an undercover operation; and (3) harms caused by negligence on the part of federal agents in the course of supervising or controlling undercover operations. Beyond offering redress, such legislation might have a preventive impact because of the government's interest in avoiding costly lawsuits and claims.[45]

The damage may, of course, go beyond financial and physical harm to the invasion of privacy and damage to reputation. The Privacy Protection Act's provision for claims regarding government invasion of privacy offers one model for dealing with the issue.

Legislation containing broad principles, threshold standards, some general prohibitions, and a changed entrapment standard is desirable. However, day-to-day management issues should be left to guidelines and internal policies, even if enforcement agencies are required to develop guidelines in specified areas. At the federal level, these might be established in cooperation with congressional oversight committees.

A cooperative process for developing guidelines (rather than legislating their substance) would maintain flexibility and enhance their significance and visibility. This could avoid the problem of legislation being either so general as to be meaningless or so specific as unduly to restrict necessary activities. It would also broaden the perspective and kinds of expertise involved in their creation and work against unilateral changes in interpretation.

REDUCED RELIANCE ON UNDERCOVER MEANS

Undercover problems have led to more stringent policy guidelines and management reforms, but not to a broad questioning of the tactic itself or of its long-range implications. Another solution would be to reduce reliance on covert means. The need for the tactic could be reduced through (1) legal changes in the definition of crime; (2) more effective crime prevention; (3) lessening restrictions on overt investigations; and (4) measures to increase the flow of information between citizens and police.

If prostitution, homosexuality, gambling, and narcotics were not treated as crimes, for example, undercover work could be significantly reduced. In 1984, 11 states had decriminalized marijuana use, and many localities had adopted a de facto policy of nonenforcement, absent any strong complaints. Societal tolerance for sexual behavior between consenting adults has increased. In California police must believe that third parties who are confronted with questionable behavior are offended by it before they can make arrests for violations of laws regarding adult sexual behavior.

Although not advocating legalization, the National Commission on Gambling notes the advantages of a less stringent attitude toward gambling.[46] The case for treating heroin and cocaine as health, rather than as criminal, problems is more controversial and complicated, but even here decriminalization is becoming a more prominent part of the debate.[47]

Apprehension of an offender, whether through undercover or other means, indicates a failure of social control—in the sense that the damage has likely already been done. Law enforcement is by definition after-the-fact. More effective crime prevention for the kinds of behavior where covert means are used most often would obviously reduce the need.

The U.S. attorney in Operation Corcom in Oklahoma, perhaps the largest and most successful federal investigation of corruption, observed that "we can win all these cases, but if the system isn't changed, we've lost the war." Factors that appear to lessen the likelihood of corruption include limits on campaign contributions and spending; public financing of election campaigns; disclosure laws; tighter conflict-of-interest laws; restrictions on political party leaders, legislators, and former officials who go into private business; higher salaries; stricter rules for competitive bidding; centralized purchasing; better accounting and audit procedures; a requirement that bribe offers be reported; and independent ethics committees with enforcement powers.

Equivalent crime prevention measures can be identified for other areas, such as improved drug education and rehabilitation programs, identification numbers on auto parts and other frequently stolen property, and enhanced restrictions on foreign financial transactions.

The use of undercover tactics is partly related to restrictions on gathering evidence. Limitations (in the U.S.) on search and seizure and arrest and interrogation make covert means an attractive alternative. This is also true for the protection against self-incrimination. If these restrictions were weakened or other means were available to increase the flow of information to police (greater use of hotlines for crime reporting and neighborhood watch groups; increased protection for whistle blowers; more extensive use of grand juries, compelled testimony, and electronic surveillance; requiring citizens and organizations to report more information about themselves to government; and greater information sharing among government agencies), there might also be less reliance on undercover means.

To reduce the use of undercover tactics at a cost of selecting some of the above options is reminiscent of Edmund Burke's observation that some political decisions involve choices "between the disagreeable and the intolerable." But the possibilities for lessening covert means do exist, even if some of them are far from attractive.

IRON LAWS AND THIN LINES

There is broad agreement over the goals in this debate. We seek a society with both liberty and order. Civil libertarians do not advocate crime, nor do police leaders want police abuse. Disagreement appears with respect to the balance among competing goals and over the likely cost and effectiveness of various means.

Most of the internal and external controls and proposed reforms are supplementary and address different needs. Accepting one usually need not mean rejecting others. Warrants, for example, are intended to raise the internal curtain on covert work so that it can be critically reviewed by outside authorities. The control function is located apart from the activities and people being controlled; the emphasis is primarily on whether or not to begin an investigation and on the control of targeting, rather than on how an investigation is carried out. The warrant implies a two-tier system of control—judicial review (and sanctioning via dismissal of a case or assessed damages) and, as a consequence, self-regulation. Similarly, legislation (whether threshold standards or prohibitions) can set some broad boundaries. An objective standard for entrapment would reduce the likelihood of improper inducements.

However, any complex organization with a diffuse "product" must rely heavily (though not exclusively) on direct self-regulation. Those within an agency are in the best position to carry out day-to-day supervision and to see that broad legislative and judicial mandates are implemented. Guidelines and bureaucratic practices apply here. There is a need for appreciable flexibility and discretion within a context of solid leadership.

But, even with the best laws, policies, supervisors and agents, the use and control of undercover tactics are more difficult than is the case with overt tactics. The problems of control increase the longer the time period, the broader the geographical area, the more varied the criminal activities, and the more intrusive the technique.

Undercover work involves some unavoidable trade-offs and risks. A theme that recurs throughout this book is the paradox of undercover operations: doing good by doing bad (lies, deceit, and trickery); to see police act as criminals and criminal informers act as police; to seek to reduce crime and, in fact, to increase it; to see restrictions on police coercion result in increased police deception.

Other operational paradoxes involved in efforts to manage and control covert investigations are related to conflicts between gathering intelligence and taking action that gives the intelligence away; between bureaucratic control and innovation; between prevention and apprehension; and between secrecy and open communication. The very power of the technique also can be its undoing. These tensions can be stated as the following hypotheses:

1. The goal of equal law enforcement (in the sense that different categories of serious offenses have roughly equivalent chances of being prosecuted) may conflict with our expectation that there be some grounds for suspicion before an investigation can be carried out. Random integrity tests may create equity, but at a cost of violating the latter principle. Conversely, the more stringent the criteria for initiating an operation and the more formalized and routinized the controls, the greater the difficulty of apprehending the highly skilled offender and those involved in offenses where there is no complaint. The solution to this is a less stringent standard for them, but this solves one equity problem at the expense of creating another.

2. Elaborate legislative controls on undercover operations with strong sanctions for violations would reduce abuses but might also unintentionally inhibit legitimate uses.

3. The higher the level of supervision, the poorer the quality of information available for decision making and the greater the time required for a decision.

4. The more extensive the controls, the greater the likelihood of leaks and the greater the cost of the operation.

5. The further the undercover agent is socially and organizationally from the target, the more objective and hard-hitting the inves-

tigation is likely to be, even as there may be less understanding of the subtleties involved and greater difficulty of access. Put another way, it takes one to know one, but with firsthand knowledge there can be added restraints.[48]

6.   Electronic surveillance offers a means of documenting transactions and enhancing safety, but it also increases the risk of discovery. The most crucial meetings may be the initial ones, which are least likely to be recorded for security reasons. Later taped meetings may simply refer to "our understanding" or "our deal."

7.   A sophisticated cover story may be required to gain access, but its very complexity may mean that the agent has trouble remembering it and that he is more vulnerable to discovery via checking.

8.   Multiple agencies/agents playing undercover roles can serve as a check on each other, but this also increases the risk of their becoming unknowingly ensnarled in each other's investigations.

9.   The closer an operation comes to the real-world context in which the violation occurs, the less the concern that the offense is solely an artifact of the investigation or of government overreaching, yet the greater may be the threat to the officer's safety, the difficulty of obtaining documentary evidence, and the harm done from the crime.

10.   A requirement that operations stay close to real-world criminal situations may conflict with other moral or legal requirements to make clear the illegal nature of the transaction, not to mix legitimate objectives and criminal opportunities, and not to use coercion, intimidation, or manipulation to gain compliance.

11.   A policy of avoiding juveniles in property stings and related efforts may help the public image of an operation and keep some weak and immature youths from going astray. But it also means avoiding a group that disproportionately contributes to street crime.

12.   New recruits may be successful in gaining initial entry because they are not known and don't seem like "cops," but their inexperience can mean an increased vulnerability to problems. However, aside from greater difficulty of access, there also may be a point at which too much experience is dysfunctional for the individual agent and the agency.

13.   The more involved in crime an informer is, the more useful he is likely to be, yet the more difficult he may be to control, the weightier the ethical issues, and the greater the potential damage to public image.

14.   Unwitting informers can be a means of penetrating inaccessible criminal milieus and may protect authorities against charges of political

targeting, but, because they are not knowingly a part of the investigation, they cannot be directly controlled.

15. From a prosecutive viewpoint, the less paid the informer the better, and payment must not be tied to the number or identity of subjects, but this runs contrary to the basic expectation that performance and reward will be linked and the need to motivate informers for difficult and dangerous work.

16. For both moral and pragmatic reasons "you need to treat informers like human beings with dignity." The friendship and guidance the agent offers, along with leniency or a degree of protection for minor violations, is likely to mean a more productive and reliable informer. But the line between such friendship/reciprocity and the agent being compromised can be thin.

17. For local police, a significant expansion of undercover activities is likely to mean fewer visible police patrols (which many citizens find reassuring) and fewer police to respond to citizen requests. For example, in 1979 the New York City Transit Police curtailed an expanded and effective anticrime decoy program because citizens felt increased apprehension as a result of seeing fewer uniformed officers.

18. Within police departments and other organizations, internal investigative mechanisms, such as random integrity tests and the use of unidentified "field associates" who secretly report on the misbehavior of their peers, may increase the amount of corruption discovered, but they communicate distrust and may lead to lower morale and have a negative labelling impact—all factors conducive to corruption.

19. Law-enforcement media representatives face a conflict between the need to protect an ongoing investigation and their task of honestly keeping a free press informed. If the representative is uninformed, agency interests will be protected, although journalists will seek out other sources. If the representative is knowledgeable, there is the danger of disclosure or lying to the press.

20. The exemplary straight-arrow image of a law-enforcement agency that inspires citizen respect and cooperation is likely to undergo erosion, the greater the resort to covert and devious methods.

21. Some of the personality characteristics that draw people to undercover work and make for successful presentations are also associated with an increased risk of undesirable personality and behavior changes when they leave undercover roles.

22. Up to some reasonable point, the longer an operation goes on,

the more damage it may do (in the failure to prevent harm or in actually stimulating or contributing to it): logistical problems with witnesses and evidence may be greater, suspects may flee, and the individual's right to a speedy trial may be denied. But in addition, the greater the certainty about the occurrence of the crime, the higher the level of offender likely to be arrested and the better the evidence. The requirements of prevention and facilitation may conflict.[49]

23.   Concluding an operation, even with quality arrests, usually will necessitate divulging the identity of the agents and the tactics used.[50] This is the classic dilemma of acting on the information received from spying. Not to act risks damage to your side, but to act may alert your adversary to your means of collecting information. Like a bee that dies after using its sting, police stings (to a greater extent than other means) have a self-destructive quality. Within the same locale, the very success of the tactic can be its undoing. Agents cannot rest on a proven method but must continue to be inventive.

24.   In principle, a major advantage of anticipatory or preemptive undercover police action is the greater opportunity for planning, deliberation, and control relative to situations in which police behave reactively, for example, calls about crimes in progress, hot pursuits or having to respond to whatever event occurs, when and where it occurs. Yet the rational impulse presupposes adequate information on which to make decisions. When Robert Burns wrote that our best laid plans "gang aft agley," he didn't have the confounding effects of secrecy in mind. In many undercover situations it may not be clear who the players are, or even what the game is. In undercover work, for things to go as anticipated may mean they do not go as planned. The unknowns and the emergent nature of the process often result in unpredictable events that can severely undermine the effort to plan ahead. Some investigations resemble Greek tragedies more than strategic game plans. Circumstances that agents thought they could control may come to control them.

It is easier to describe the above paradoxes than to solve them. But awareness can at least mean better-informed choices. In calling attention to the problems and limits of undercover means, I am not arguing for the fashionable notion that nothing works. It is true that there are no easy answers, but the choice is hardly between perfection and abject failure. As we have noted, there is great variation across undercover situations. Sound policy and planning can make a difference in both protecting liberty and maintaining order.

In chapter 4, I defined three types of operation and a number of dimensions useful in description, classification, and explanation. The distinctions are of more than academic interest; they can also help us in considering the desirability of various types of undercover activity. From my analysis of the ethical and operational aspects, the following conclusions seem warranted.

Postliminary (after-the-fact) intelligence operations raise fewer problems than anticipatory investigations because they are likely to be more bounded. Futhermore, because the crime has already occurred, intent, discriminatory enforcement, and entrapment are less likely to be issues. With respect to anticipatory investigations, those of a preventive nature may forestall harm but sometimes leave doubts over whether the criminal action would actually have been carried out. Among those of a facilitative nature, there is always the danger of entrapment. In general, the providing of a target for victimization is likely to raise fewer problems than co-conspiratorial operations.

Undercover operations organized on the basis of prior intelligence or complaints that stay close to real-world criminal conditions are superior to random integrity testing or to the creation of an artificial criminal environment with unrealistically attractive temptations. Covert investigations should mimic actual criminal settings as much as possible given the constraints, and the emphasis should be on a recognized crime problem. The goal of an investigation should be to determine if there is sufficient evidence to warrant judicial proceedings.

Operations directed against persons who have behaved autonomously, where the opportunity for self-selection is maximized, where the nature of the criminal activity is clear, and where the undercover agent's role is passive or, at least, not highly facilitative are preferable to their opposites. Light undercover operations and those where the major role is played by a sworn agent are likely to raise fewer problems than deep undercover operations and those where the major role is played by a witting, or worse, an unwitting informer.

Because at their worst undercover tactics are so troubling and at their best so filled with ethical and operational dilemmas, they must be used with extreme caution, and only after consideration of alternative means and the cost of taking no action.

TEN

The New Surveillance

Everywhere the State acquires more and more direct control over
the humblest members of the community and a more exclusive power
of governing each of them in his smallest concerns. This gradual
weakening of the individual in relation to society at large may be
traced to a thousand things.

—Alexis de Tocqueville, 1835

Discovery and invention have made it possible for the government,
by means far more effective than stretching upon the rack, to obtain
disclosure in court of what is whispered in the closet.

—Justice Louis Dembitz Brandeis, 1928

When I began this research, I was skeptical about the desirability of
undercover tactics on specific as well as on general grounds. As applied
to the political cases of the 1960s, there was much to be concerned
about. Abuses were widespread. Beyond this, the spread of undercover
means seemed to represent one more example of the extension of state
power feared by Alexis de Tocqueville and later social theorists.

Over the course of the research, my skepticism regarding the tactic
itself softened, even as my concern over the general issues raised by
Tocqueville increased. It became clear that, given the American context,
covert means were sometimes the best means. Furthermore, the recent
overall record of such federal agencies as the FBI, BATF, and IRS suggests that (with appropriate preparation and controls) problems could
be held to an acceptable level. However, I reached this conclusion reluctantly. At best, in a democratic society, it will never be possible to be too
enthusiastic about undercover operations. There is always the risk of becoming overconfident and insensitive to the dangers that literally and
figuratively lurk beneath the surface. Something of the caution and respect for danger that characterize professional explorers and adven-
turers is needed. Once one ceases to doubt the difficulty of the challenge,
becomes complacent, and loses any fear, problems are more likely.

The study of undercover police is ultimately about much more than
cops and robbers: it is one strand of the new surveillance. Powerful new
information-gathering technologies are extending ever deeper into the

social fabric and to more features of the environment. Like the discovery of the atom or the unconscious, new control techniques surface bits of reality that were previously hidden or didn't contain informational clues. People are in a sense turned inside out, and what was previously invisible or meaningless is made visible and meaningful. This may involve space-age detection devices that give meaning to physical emanations based on the analysis of heat, light, pressure, motion, odor, chemicals, or physiological process, as well as the new meaning given to visible individual characteristics and behavior when they are judged relative to a predictive profile based on aggregate data.

RECENT DEVELOPMENTS

HUMAN INFORMERS

Perhaps most clearly related to undercover means, though less costly, is informing. In what amounts to a break with eighteenth- and nineteenth-century American attitudes, informing is now seen as an element of good citizenship, commanding growing institutional and technical support.

Federal cabinet agencies, for example, now provide hotlines for the reporting of instances of "fraud, abuse, and waste." Protection for whistle blowers has increased. The Federal Witness Protection Program provides relocation and a new identity to informers.

Programs, such as TIP (Turn In a Pusher), are found in hundreds of communities. Connecticut has a "turn in a poacher" program, and Seattle encourages motorists to dial 734-HERO to report persons wrongfully driving in expressway lanes reserved for carpools and buses. WeTIP Inc., a private organization that counts large corporations among its clients, offers a nationwide hotline for reporting suspicious activities that employees are hesitant to report locally.

A Texas police sergeant who coordinates a successful crime-reporting program was quoted as saying that "we get husbands turning in wives, wives turning in husbands—we've even had mothers turn in their sons." In 1986 the presidential-led war on drugs not only saw parents turning in their children, but children turning in their parents (a drug hotline in Boston averaged twelve such calls a day).[1] There are also more generalized forms of informing: one sheriff's department gives out leaflets that ask, "Do you know something the sheriff should know?"

COMPUTERS AS INFORMERS

The scale of human informing is, however, dwarfed by electronic informers and blacklists. The gigantic data banks made possible by computers raise important surveillance questions. Many basic facts are well known. Credit card companies, airlines, hotels, and car rental agencies record what we spend, where we went and how long we stayed. Health records are increasingly computerized, and more than nine out of ten working Americans have individual or group health insurance policies; pharmacies have begun to keep computerized records of patient's drug use and health characteristics; individual financial transactions increasingly involve electronic tellers and electronic check and credit card authorization; electronic funds transfer has become central to banking. Cashless transactions (electronic funds transfer at point of sale) are an increasing percentage of all sales. The size and reach of criminal justice data bases, such as the FBI's National Criminal Justice Information Center, continue to grow.[2] Marketing firms collect demographic, consumption, and life-style data on practically the entire population.

Computers qualitatively alter the nature of surveillance—routinizing, broadening, and deepening it. Organizational memories are extended over time and across space. Rather than focusing on an isolated individual at one point in time and on static demographic data, such as date of birth, surveillance increasingly involves complex transactional analysis, interrelating persons and events (for instance, the timing of phone calls, travel, and bank deposits).[3]

A thriving new computer-based, data-scavenging industry now sells information gleaned from such sources as drivers' licenses, vehicle- and voter-registration lists, birth, marriage, and death certificates, land deeds, telephone and organizational directories, court records, and census-tract records. Bits of scattered information that in the past did not threaten the individual's privacy and anonymity now can be joined.

There is a proliferation of generally unregulated data base services that landlords, doctors, employers, and others can consult (for a fee, of course) to check on prospective renters, patients, and employees, usually without their knowledge. Prospective employers, for example, can check on everything from an individual's political activism to the filing of worker-compensation claims. Such data bases often contain errors, outdated information, and information that is open to different interpretations. However, our lives are increasingly shaped by them. The chance to obtain basic needs and services such as medical care, insurance, housing, jobs, bank loans, and credit is conditioned by our "data image" in remote computer files.[4]

It is possible to purchase address lists on a vast array of people presorted into categories such as "bank credit card holders," "gay businesses and organizations," "conch soup buyers," "antinuclear power contributors/activists," and "subscribers to the Sex Over Forty Newsletter."

The government's use of computer matching and profiling has come into increased prominence in the past decade.[5] Matching involves the comparison of information from two or more distinct data sources. In the U.S., hundreds of computer matching programs are routinely carried out by government at state and federal levels. The matching done by private interests is far more extensive. Profiling involves an indirect and inductive logic. Often, clues are sought that will increase the probability of discovering violations. A number of distinct data items are correlated in order to assess how close a person or event comes to a predetermined model of known violations or violators, or desirable or undesirable applicants. Predictive profiles for letting people into, or out of, systems are increasingly used and rarely subject to public validation or criticism. Decisions are made about persons not as unique individuals or on the basis of their current behavior, but as a result of their membership in a statistical category with a given probability of behaving a certain way in the future.

A common form of matching involves randomly or categorically checking persons and property (such as cars) against various official or unofficial watch and wanted lists, or against more general profiles, such as those believed to be characteristic of drug couriers. An example of such matching is practiced by the large Treasury Enforcement Communication System (TECS), encountered by people leaving or entering the country when their passport information is entered into the computer at the immigration checkpoint. Another example involves the various data bases that make up the National Crime Information Center, most notably its extensive collection of arrest records.

Matching may involve comparing data bases, for example, bank records with welfare records to see if recipients have hidden income. The Selective Service, in addition to making use of driver's license records in each state, purchased an ice-cream chain's "birthday club" list and compared this to its list of draft registrants to search for young men who had not registered. In one match that yielded little, boat ownership records in Hawaii were compared against lists of those receiving food stamps.

The IRS generated public controversy when it sought to buy commercially compiled lists that direct-marketing companies use to target customers. The goal was to identify tax violators by correlating their tax returns with income estimates based on such factors as car model owned and census tract characteristics.

Both political and technical developments have encouraged the spread of computer matching. The 1974 Privacy Act passed under the guidance of the late Senator Sam Ervin included a "routine use" provision for data collected by the federal government. This was intended to prohibit the government from collecting information for one purpose and using it for an unrelated reason. But since 1980 the executive branch has claimed that there is a generalized government interest in any information that happens to be in the federal domain, that is, data collected for a certain purpose may be used for any purpose. The meaning of "routine use" has been severely stretched.

In addition, the 1984 Budget Deficit Reduction Act now requires states to correlate tax, medical, and social security records in order to receive federal funds for social welfare programs. This is likely to be extended to any recipient of government benefits, for example, student loans and veteran's benefits. The 1986 tax law requires all children over the age of 5 to obtain a social security number if they are to be claimed as dependents.[6]

Matching also has been facilitated by computer networking. The spread of microcomputers and computer-based communication devices makes record linkage easy to do, but difficult to control. The files to be compared need no longer be on the same computer, and the distinction between physically separate data bases has been blurred. Distributed data processing is making the notion of the single, isolated data bank obsolete.

From the mid-1960s to the early 1970s, Congress—expressing historic American concerns—rejected plans for the creation of a mammoth national data bank. Instead, agencies were to create separate, unrelated files. But recent technical developments have facilitated an end run around the political process. Unique identifiers, such as one's social security number, are not needed to forge links among distinct personal data bases because available software easily permits linking records based on a configuration of common elements, such as the same name, address, and date of birth. There is de facto integration of many data bases.

With the low-visibility integration of previously distinct bodies of information, computer matching can centralize authority and eliminate organizational boundaries and checkpoints.

In the near future individuals may become carriers of all their records. A computer chip could be embedded in the skin or, as is currently done in the military, in a tag worn around the neck. A wallet-sized "smart card" embedded with a chip that can contain up to 800 pages of personal information is now being tested.

VISUAL AND AUDIO SURVEILLANCE

The sensing chip for a video camera (unlike the traditional glass lens) requires an opening no bigger than a pinhole. Video cameras can be concealed in walls and other objects, such as picture frames, mannequins, books, and attache cases. An advertisement promises that, "When you carry this ordinary-looking briefcase, you're really videotaping everything that occurs. . . . The pinhole lens is virtually invisible, and there's still plenty of room inside the case for papers, etc." A tiny handheld video camera the size of a deck of cards is available. The cameras that monitor the interior of many stores are often inside ceiling globes that are capable of complete 360-degree movement. Amber or mirrored surfaces hide where the camera is aimed. A video-scanning device can be placed at roads or bridges to check license plates automatically against those in a data base; at the same time, a picture of a vehicle's occupants can be taken. A video camera exists that can distinguish guards from intruders, and there are efforts to develop one that can identify particular people in a crowd.

"Mini-awacs" that can spot a car or a person from 30,000 feet up have been used for surveillance of drug traffickers. Conversely, a hidden lens can be installed in aircraft as a security device that makes it possible for monitors on the ground to see and hear activity in the plane up to 200 miles away. Satellite photography from 180 miles up (a telescope is aimed back at the earth) has been used for "domestic coverage" to determine the size and activities of antiwar demonstrations and civil disorders. Computer-enhanced satellite photography can identify vehicles moving in the dark and detect camouflage.

The "starlight scope" light amplifier developed for the Vietnam War can be used with a variety of film and video cameras or binoculars. It needs only starlight, a partial moon, or a street lamp 500 yards away. When it amplifies light 85,000 times, night turns into day. Unlike earlier infrared devices, it gives off no telltale glow. The light amplifier can be mounted on a tripod or worn as goggles. Attached to a telescopic device, its range is over a mile.

There have been equivalent advances in the detection of sound: lasers and parabolic microphones that, when aimed at a window, permit eavesdropping without the necessity of entering the physical premises; low-level microwaves aimed from outside a building at small cone-shaped metal cavities or steel reinforcing rods hidden in a wall also use sound-wave vibrations for remote eavesdropping; a voice-activated, refrigerator-sized tape machine that can record up to 40 phone conversations at once; and subminiature tape recorders the size of a matchbox. Tiny transmitters can be hidden in clocks, hooks, picture frames, table legs, electric toothbrushes, and umbrellas.

New forms of communication are technically easy to intercept absent special, expensive precautions. The transmission of phone communications in digital form via microwave relays and satellites, cellular automobile and cordless telephones using radio waves for transmissions, and communication between computers offer new possibilities for eavesdropping.[7] Even most conventional telephones are potentially "hot on the hook." They can be easily wired so that the microphone in the telephone sends voice signals to a terminal, even when the phone is not in use. Using relatively inexpensive technology the image seen on most unprotected computer screens can be reproduced a mile away without ever gaining access to the premises where the computer is. Even electronic typewriters can be bugged so that a unique electrical signal for each letter typed is transmitted and reproduced elsewhere.

Surveillance of workers on assembly lines, in offices, and in stores has become much more comprehensive with computerized electronic measures.[8] Factory outputs and mistakes can be counted more easily and work pace, to a degree, controlled. Much has been written of the electronic office, where the data-processing machine serves both as a work tool and monitoring device. A bank vice president responsible for workers who code credit card data states, "I measure everything that moves."

Software developments permit management to document the activities of anyone using the company computer system—without the user's knowledge. With a program called CNTRL, managers can observe on their own screen all input entered by the employee and all output from the computer to the user's terminal as it occurs. Subliminal messages can also be sent. One such program called "The Messenger" can be called up by the VDT operator. Images of mountains and streams are displayed along with subliminal messages, such as "My world is calm." More ominous are subliminal programs that the worker may have no knowledge of or control over.[9]

Automatic telephone switching technology can record when, where, to whom, and for how long a call is made, regardless of whether it is long distance or to another extension within the same organization.[10] Phone systems designed as intercoms or paging devices allow managers to listen to conversations in other offices without being detected. Phone and computer monitoring is a condition of work in an increasing number of telecommunications, word processing, programming, and customer service occupations.

The National Security Agency uses 2,000 staffed interception posts throughout the world, satellites, aircraft, and ships to monitor electronic communication from and to the United States.[11] Its computer system permits simultaneous monitoring of 54,000 telephone calls and cables. Given the secrecy that surrounds this agency, little is known about its efforts involving computer speech recognition. But, to the extent that a machine can instantly pick out particular conversations or voices from thousands that are being monitored, surveillance has taken a quantum step forward.

Video, audio, and other forms of surveillance are often combined. They can be activated by sound, motion, heat, air currents, vibrations, odor, or pressure. Integrated "management systems" are available that offer visual, audio, and digital information about the behavior of employees and customers. For example, at many convenience stores information may be recorded from cash register entries, voices, motion, standing on a mat with a sensor, or taking an electronically tagged item beyond a given perimeter. Audio and/or visual recordings and alarms may be programmed to respond to a large number of "triggering devices." In one system, the camera and voice recorders operate randomly for 15 seconds of every two minutes. They also start running whenever the cash register is open or closed for longer than a specified time, when particular keys on the cash register are hit "too often" (clear or no sale keys), when more than 50 dollars is in the cash register, or when the last bill is removed (suggesting a robbery). In another system backroom monitors can see on their computer what a cashier rings up, while closed-circuit television shows them what items are actually taken out by the customer. Participants in Behavior Scan, a marketing research endeavor, automatically have their television viewing correlated with records of their consumer purchases.

ELECTRONIC LEASHES

There are a number of devices that can be attached to a person or an object that permit remote monitoring of location and/or physiological condition. The telemetric devices first used to study the movement of animals are increasingly being applied to humans.

Consider, for example, the electronic "leashes" marketed for children and convicts. One device consists of a tiny transmitter (complete with animal and balloon decals) that fastens to a child. A monitor gives off an alarm if the child goes beyond a specific distance. An electronic anklet, bracelet, or necklace that signals a central computer via telephone if the device is removed or if the wearer goes more than a short distance from home is being used on probationers. Given prison overcrowding, such devices are likely to be used more extensively.[12] They can be combined with a breathalyzer and video cameras.

The technology, of course, can be used for punishment as well as monitoring. An electrode could be implanted in the body of an offender with "an automatic shock schedule [that] could be triggered if the offender moved away from the approved probation/parole area."[13] The severity of the shock could increase as the person moved farther away.

In other systems, where subjects are not restricted to their residence, their whereabouts are continuously known. The radio signal is fed into a modified missile-tracking device that graphs the wearer's location and displays it on a screen. Thus, some police departments have initiated automatic vehicle monitoring (AVM) to help supervisors track patrol cars at all times. Some companies are using satellite technology to pinpoint the location of their trucks on a video screen.

In another system tested in Hong Kong, a small radio receiver in a vehicle picks up low-frequency signals from wire loops set into streets and transmits an identification number, indicating where, when, and how fast a car is driven. Self-contained monitoring devices also can be attached to a vehicle to gather data on the driver's behavior. For example, a computer the size of a paperback book (aptly called the "Tripmaster") can be attached to a truck or car, keeping track of speed, shifting, idling, and when and how long the vehicle is driven.

There also are various hidden beepers that can be attached to vehicles and other objects to trace their movements. A homing device welded to the body of a car has been developed as part of an antitheft system. When a car is reported stolen, a police radio tower broadcasts a signal that causes the transmitting device in the car to emit its own silent pulse, which can be picked up by a police car several miles away. A signal flashes the car's identification number, and a light on a compass-like dial points in the direction of the car.

The use of electronic article surveillance (EAS) systems is constantly being extended, including department and record stores, libraries, hospitals, and even supermarkets. In some supermarkets, a buzzer sounds and lights flash if a customer goes through checkout with a concealed item.

Location also can be tracked through card-security systems. In some work settings, employees are required to carry an ID card with a magnetic stripe and check in and out as they go to various "stations" (parking lot, main door, a specific office or computer terminal, the bathroom). The computer controls access to each area, making continuous monitoring possible.

There also are nonelectronic leashes, such as chemical tracking agents visible only through ultraviolet light or chemical tests. The Soviet Union's use of an invisible chemical dust to monitor the whereabouts of Americans is an example.

Much more than location can be electronically monitored. A "nonintrusive appliance load monitor" has been developed at M.I.T. that can generate an "exact usage history" of all appliances in a home. This can be legally and inexpensively installed on a utility pole, far from the site being monitored and without the consumer's knowledge. As the technology evolves, the seemingly benign, unseen electronic umbilical cords that link us to the outside world will increasingly be drawn on for information about behavior.[14]

PERSONAL TRUTH TECHNOLOGIES

The past decade has seen the increased use of supposedly scientific "inference" or "personal truth technology," based on body clues, such as pulse, eye movements, voice, blood, urine, and saliva. The effort to measure physiological responses as indicators of guilt or innocence is part of an unhappy history involving the cruel methods of trial by ordeal, but current efforts seek the mantle of scientific legitimacy. Biological surveillance can be more intrusive than electronic surveillance.

Drug testing has spread as a result of advances in biotechnology with an inexpensive scanning test and confirmatory tests involving gas chromatography and mass spectrometry. An even newer machine scans eye movements and claims to be able to detect the amount and kind of drugs a person has taken. Another technique claims to be able to identify drug use through the analysis of a strand of hair.[15] Another development eliminates the consent required by the traditional breath analyzer. A "passive electronic sensor" concealed in a flashlight automatically measures alcohol levels in the breath when merely pointed at a person.

The traditional polygraph is increasingly being supplemented by new developments involving the application of laser technology to eye movements and the measurement of stomach flutters and voice tremors. Covert voice stress analysis, for example, electronically analyzes a person's voice for subaudible microtremors, which, it is claimed, occur with stress and deception.[16] Brain waves can be "read" as clues to certain internal states, such as surprise, concentration, confusion, and fatigue.[17]

A related use of biological indicators is for means of personal identification that go beyond the rather easily faked signature or photo ID. A variety of biometric identification products are available. These are based on the sensing of individual characteristics, such as fingerprints, veins, handwriting, voice, typing rhythms, hand geometry, and retinal patterns. In the last, for example, a person's eyes are photographed through a set of binoculars, and an enlarged print is compared to a previous print on file. Retinal patterns are said to be more individual than even thumbprints. The automated matching of fingerprints and new laser and other techniques for picking up latent prints have significantly increased the precision and usefulness of that technique. More reliable still, although expensive and time consuming, is the DNA matching of blood samples.[18] A computer chip that is read with a scanner has been implanted in cattle for identification and record keeping purposes. Equivalent human applications are likely—perhaps at first for children and those with memory problems.

Different measures can, of course, be combined, for example, a "hybrid multisensor system" that uses voice, fingerprints, and handwriting. The availability of almost foolproof means of identity fits well with the interests of those who advocate a mandatory national ID system.

CHARACTERISTICS OF THE NEW
TECHNOLOGIES

The surveillance devices discussed above differ, of course, from each other, but they are related by being used jointly. Video and audio surveillance often coexist and rely on computer processing. Hotlines generate investigative leads. These, along with night vision devices, beepers, lie detectors, and computer files, are an integral part of many sophisticated covert operations. They are also related because they are strands of a broader social trend. The new forms of surveillance tend to share, to varying degrees, ten characteristics that set them apart from most traditional forms of social control.

The new surveillance transcends distance, darkness, and physical barriers. As many observers have noted, the historic barriers to the old Leviathan state lay in the sheer physical impossibility of extending the rulers' ideas and control to the outer regions of vast empires; through closed doors; or into the intellectual, emotional, and physical regions of the individual. Technology, however, has gradually made these barriers penetrable. Physical limitations and, to some extent, human inefficiency have lost their usefulness as unplanned protectors of liberty. Sound and video can be transmitted over vast distances; infrared and light-amplifying technology pierce the dark; intrusive technologies can "see" through doors, suitcases, and fog. Truth-seeking technologies claim to uncover deep, subterranean truths.

It transcends time; its records can be stored, retrieved, combined, analyzed, and communicated. Surveillance information can be "freeze-dried," [19] available many years after the fact in totally different contexts. Abstract and frequently outdated, these records come to have a reality of their own apart from the person or events they purport to describe. Computer records, video and audio tapes and discs, photos, and various other technological "signatures" have become increasingly standardized and interchangeable. Information can be converted into a form that makes it portable and easily reproduceable and transferable through telecommunications. Data can migrate to faraway places; they can be collected in one place and time and be joined with data collected elsewhere. Data sharing becomes possible on an immense scale.

It has low visibility or is invisible. It becomes ever more difficult to ascertain when and whether we are being watched and who is doing the watching. There is a distancing (both socially and geographically) between watchers and watched; miniaturization and remote control increase the difficulty of discovery. Surveillance devices can either be made to appear as something else (one-way mirrors, cameras hidden in a fire extinguisher, undercover agents) or can be virtually invisible (electronic snooping into microwave transmissions or computer files). This contrasts with traditional wiretapping, in which changes in electrical current are clues to the presence of a tap, but, even when wires are used, they may be unrecognizable. There is a special paint that, in conducting electricity, serves the function of a wire from a mike. There is even a bug that literally looks like a bug.[20] Audit trails are even more difficult to establish.

It is often involuntary. Information can be gathered without the participation or even awareness of the target.

Prevention is a major concern. Anticipatory surveillance strategies seek to reduce risk and uncertainty. Modern management attempts to make control more predictable, reliable, effective, and relatively all-inclusive. As little as possible is left to chance.

It is capital- rather than labor-intensive, therefore increasingly economical. Technical developments have dramatically altered the economics of surveillance; it has become much less expensive per unit watched. It becomes economical to monitor persons and situations that were previously ignored. Information is easily sent back to a central source from different places. A few individuals can monitor a great many, concurrently or retroactively.

The characteristics that follow are related to the economic changes that facilitate expanded surveillance.

It involves decentralized self-policing. As Foucault observes, control is not exercised from afar, as with monarchical power, but is expressed directly from within the social relations and settings to be controlled.[21] Economy is enhanced because persons increasingly participate in their own monitoring. Control, like a pacemaker, is implanted in the very context to be managed. Those watched become (willingly and knowingly or not) active partners in their own monitoring, which is often self-activated and automatic. Beyond hotline reporting, an important aspect of this process is that persons may be motivated to report themselves to government agencies and large organizations or corporations in return for some benefit or to avoid a penalty or to carry a wallet-sized "smart card" containing vast amounts of personal information; another is the direct triggering of surveillance systems by its subjects when, for instance, a person walks, talks on the telephone, turns on a TV set, checks a book out of the library, and enters or leaves controlled areas; another is the instant feedback on their productivity that pink-collar workers may see on their video display terminals.

It triggers a shift from targeting a specific suspect to categorical suspicion of everyone (or at least everyone within a particular category). Between the camera, the tape recorder, the identity card, the metal detector, the tax form, and the computer, everyone becomes a reasonable target. The new forms of control are helping to create a society where everyone is guilty until proven innocent; technologies that permit continuous, rather than intermittent, monitoring encourage this.

It is more intensive—probing beneath surfaces, discovering previously inaccessible information. Like drilling technology that can bore ever deeper into the earth, today's surveillance is able to probe ever deeper into physical, social, and psychological areas. It hears whispers, penetrates clouds, and sees through walls and windows. With blood and urine analysis and stomach pumps, it "sees" into the body, and, with voice stress and polygraph analysis, it attempts to "see" into the psyche, claiming to go beneath ostensible meanings and appearances to real meanings.

It is more extensive—covering not only deeper, but larger, areas. While multiple indicators collect ever more data, unconnected surveillance threads are being woven into gigantic tapestries of information. In sociologist Stan Cohen's imagery, the mesh of the fishing net has not only become finer and more pliable, the net itself is now wider.[22] As the pool of persons watched expands, so does the pool of watchers. The uncertainty over whether or not surveillance is present is an important strategic element. Mass monitoring has become a reality.

TOWARD A MAXIMUM-SECURITY SOCIETY?

The awesome power of the new surveillance lies partly in the paradoxical, never-before-possible combination of decentralized and centralized forms. Surveillance is capable of being laserlike in its focus, as well as absorbent.[23]

The state's traditional monopoly over the means of violence is supplemented by new means of gathering and analyzing information that may even make the former obsolete. Control is better symbolized by manipulation than coercion, by computer chips than prison bars, and by remote and invisible tethers than by handcuffs or straitjackets.

The new surveillance has generally been welcomed by those in business, government, and law enforcement. Examples of its effectiveness are readily available: apprehending criminals, detecting corruption, and preventing crime. It can help verify compliance with arms control and test ban treaties and can monitor health. Americans seem increasingly willing, even eager, to live with intrusive technologies because of their benefits: the ease of obtaining consumer goods with a credit card, the saving of taxpayer dollars because of computer-matching programs, and the comfort of security systems based on video surveillance. Of course, some compliance is voluntary in only the most superficial sense. Advertising may play a role in convincing people they need things that are harmful or destructive. Cooperation with requests for data, or to undergo a lie detector or other tests, is "voluntary" only at the risk of not obtaining a needed benefit or job.[24]

The new surveillance is justified by positive social goals—the need to combat crime and terrorism, to protect health, or to improve productivity. Extensions occur gradually; it is easy to miss the magnitude of the change and the broader issues it raises. Our notions of privacy, liberty, and the rights of the individual are quietly shifting, with little public awareness or legislative attention.

Observers of the criminal justice system, in focusing on prisoners, have noted how reforms involving diversion, electronic monitoring, halfway houses, and community treatment centers seek to diffuse the surveillance of the prison into the community at large. But what is equally striking is how techniques and an ethos once applied only to suspects or prisoners are applied to the most benign settings.[25]

In a 1791 book, *Panopticon or the Inspection House,* Jeremy Bentham offered a plan for the perfect prison. There was to be constant inspection of both prisoners and keepers; cells were to be constructed with bars (rather than opaque doors) around a central inspection tower. His ideas helped give rise to the maximum-security prison, which today is characterized by perimeter security, thick walls with guard towers, spotlights, and a high degree of electronic surveillance. Many of the kinds of controls found in prison are diffusing into the society at large. It is important to ask if recent developments in technology, culture, and social organization are not pushing us toward becoming a maximum-security society.

The maximum-security society is composed of five interrelated sub-societies:

1. a *dossier society,* in which computerized records play a major role

2. an *actuarial or predictive society,* in which decisions are increasingly made on the basis of predictions about our future behavior as a result of our membership in aggregate categories

3. an *engineered society,* in which our choices are increasingly limited and determined by the physical and social environment

4. a *transparent or porous society,* in which the boundaries that traditionally protected privacy are weakened

5. a *self-monitored society,* in which auto-surveillance plays a prominent role.

In such a society, the line between the public and the private is obliterated; we are under constant observation, everything goes on a permanent record, and much of what we say, do, and even feel may be known and recorded by others we do not know. Data from widely separated geographical areas, organizations, and time periods can be merged and analyzed easily. Control is embedded and preventive; informers, dossiers, and classification are prominent. The society becomes, in Erving Goffman's words, a "total institution," and there is no longer a backstage.[26]

As the prison ethos diffuses ever more into the society at large, the need for actual prisons may decline. Society becomes the functional alternative to the prison. This, of course, is what the community corrections reform movement has long sought, but it did not envision that the broad population could in a sense become the prisoners, not just those who have been found guilty through a process of adjudication.

The trend in North America and perhaps in other industrial democracies is toward, rather than away from, a maximum-security society. What Ericson and Shearing refer to as the "scientification of police work" offers not only new ways of doing things, but a new means of legitimizing police power. It is both instrument and ideology.[27]

SOME NEGATIVE FEATURES

We must learn to subvert, sabotage and destroy our enemies by more
clever, more sophisticated and more effective methods than those
used against us. . . . It may become necessary that the American
people will be made acquainted with, understand and support this
fundamentally repugnant philosophy.

—*The Hoover Commission, 1954*

Experience should teach us to be most on our guard when the
government's purposes are beneficent. Men born to freedom are
naturally alert to repel invasion of their liberty by evil-minded rulers.
The greatest dangers to liberty lurk in insidious encroachment by
men of zeal, well-meaning, but without understanding.

—*Justice Louis Dembitz Brandeis, 1928*

Apprehension over the new surveillance certainly does not mean indifference to pressing issues of national security, crime, drug abuse, productivity, or health. When the goal is important and the proposed
means are highly intrusive and/or of questionable reliability, we must
consider alternatives. We must be careful not to adopt a cure that is
worse than the disease. The morality of the means is as important as
that of the ends.

Benjamin Franklin's observation, "They that can give up essential liberty to obtain a little temporary safety deserve neither liberty nor
safety," [28] is too strong for many citizens in today's world. But, where
only questionable means are available, it is necessary to think carefully
about imposing them. One of the truisms of the last quarter of the twentieth century is that government cannot solve all problems that ideally
should be solved. There are some problems it may be better to live with
than to solve. With fewer intrusions by government and large organizations, we would no doubt have a less efficient and more disorderly society, but one with increased liberty and privacy. [29]

Without seeking to deny either the positive aspects or complexity of
the moral issues, it is worth considering some of the negative features of
the new surveillance that generally receive insufficient attention.

There are increasingly fewer places to run or to hide. A citizen's ability to evade surveillance is diminishing. There is no exit from the prying
eyes and ears and whirring data-processing machines of government and
business. To participate in the consumer society and the welfare state,
we must provide personal information. To venture into a shopping mall,
a bank, a subway, sometimes even a bathroom, is to perform before an

unknown audience. To apply for a job may mean having to face lie-detector questioning or urine analysis. Birth, marriage, and death certificates, driver's licenses, vehicle registrations, voter registration lists, phone directory information, occupational permits, educational and special-interest directories—all present an invitation to more finely attuned manipulative efforts by a new breed of government agents, market researchers, and political campaign planners who use the enormous quantities of data available through computerization.

The new surveillance goes beyond merely invading privacy, as this term has conventionally been understood, to making irrelevant many of the constraints that protected privacy. Beyond the boundaries protected by custom and law, privacy has depended on certain (technically or socially) inviolate physical, spatial, or temporal barriers—varying from distance to darkness to doors to the right to remain silent. An invasion of privacy required crossing these barriers. With much of the new technology, many of them cease to be barriers.

Important American values are increasingly threatened by the permanence and accessibility of computerized records. The idea of "starting over" or moving to a new frontier is a powerful concept in American culture. The beliefs that once a debt has been paid to society it is forgotten and that people can change are important American traditions. Americans pride themselves on looking at what a person is today rather than what he may have been in the past. Devices, such as sealed or destroyed records, prohibitions on certain kinds of record keeping, and consent requirements for the release of information, reflect these concerns.

However, with the mass of easily accessible files, one's past is always present, for erroneous or sabotaged data, as well as for debts that have been paid. This can create a class of permanently stigmatized persons. In the words of sociologist Ken Laudon, computers offer the possibility for "an automated blacklisting capability thousands of times more powerful, yet considerably more silent than the blacklists of the McCarthy era." Starting over may be much more difficult. When the search of dossiers is combined with other forms of screening, for example, carriers of AIDS antibodies, and predictive profiles regarding the characteristics of a good worker, it is easy to imagine a work force divided between people thought to be good risks and others. This would create an enormous waste of human resources as people were locked out of jobs for which they were otherwise qualified. Increased crime and demands on the welfare system would be the likely results.

As computerized record-keeping becomes ever more routine, there may be increasing reluctance to seek needed services (as for mental health), to take controversial action (filing a grievance against a landlord), or to take risks for fear of what it will look like "on the record." Conformity and uniformity may increase—at the price of diversity, innovation, and vitality.

A related factor is the changing nature and location of the things we wish to keep private. Fifty years ago, our "private" papers could be kept in a desk drawer or a safe deposit box. Increasingly, personal information is held by such large organizations as banks, credit card and insurance companies, and hospitals. Information as a form of "private property" is less tangible. It can be seen or sent without a trace, and often without consent. Because the Fourth Amendment was designed for more tangible forms of property and at a time when individuals had much greater physical control over the things they wished to keep private, it does not cover recent incursions. The intrusive nature of the new surveillance is inconsistent with the spirit, if not the letter, of the Bill of Rights. In the face of these developments, it is important to rethink the nature of privacy and to create new protection for it.

Some safeguards, ironically, rely on such technologies as encrypted or scrambled communications and debugging devices. Legislation and heightened public awareness are also important. In the mid-1980s, less than one state in five had laws requiring written standards for the collection, maintenance, and dissemination of personal information.

The new surveillance is relatively one-sided: it is likely to increase the power of large organizations, but not that of small ones or individuals. There is hardly equal access to these means, even if most of them are theoretically available to all and do not remain the exclusive property of the state (as in totalitarian countries).

By offering accessibility (whether legitimately or illegitimately) to data bases, a means of creating alternative communication networks via electronic mail and bulletin boards with links to international telecommunications and a private printing press, the personal computer can break the state's monopoly of information. This is nicely illustrated by the U.S.S.R.'s unwillingness to make personal computers easily available to its citizens. The seeming paradox of computers perceived in the U.S. as a symbol of Big Brother and in the U.S.S.R. as a symbol of liberation is partly resolved by separating large, institutionally controlled mainframe computers from small, privately controlled microcomputers.

For those with the resources to employ them, countermeasures may reduce the impact of surveillance, or private citizens or public interest groups may use technology to monitor government and corporate activity. However, the scale is still overwhelmingly tipped toward surveillance by government and large organizations. In spite of the spread of home computers and mail-order snooping (and snooping detection devices), individual consumers, renters, political dissenters, loan applicants, and public interest groups clearly do not have the capabilities of credit card companies, market research firms, landlord associations, police intelligence units, the NSA, banks, or large corporations. As a result, the new surveillance technologies are an important factor in lessening the power of the individual relative to large organizations and government. Privacy and autonomy can be the victims.

Anonymity, involving the right to be left alone and unnoticed, is also diminished. The easy combining and mining of publicly available data bases to generate precise lists, such as for sales pitches and solicitations, can be unsettling. The targeted appeals that become possible through linkage with automatic telephone dialers or word processors can create a sense of invasion and vulnerability that far exceeds one's reaction to junk mail addressed to "Occupant." Aside from the annoyance factor, the "personalized" solicitations make one wonder: "How do they know this about me? How did they find this out? What else do they know? Who are they?" One need not be a Franz Kafka character to feel uneasy.

The fragmentation and isolation characteristic of totalitarian societies occur at least partly because individuals mistrust each other as much as organizations. To a certain degree, skepticism has always been vital to democracy as well: thus, the system of checks and balances.[30] To question and to not take the world at first appearances are also important ingredients of wisdom and scientific advancement. However, the new surveillance may be helping to create a degree of suspiciousness that goes too far. Community, liberty and openness can hardly thrive in a society of informers or where everyone is treated as a suspect.

Anonymous informing can be conducive to false and malicious accusations; it encourages distrust.[31] Similarly, trust can be damaged when authorities seek to create a "myth of surveillance" by encouraging the perception that any transaction might be monitored and involve a hidden integrity test, informer, bug, or camera. A memo entitled "Responsibilities of Sales Personnel" given to employees in the large retail firms serviced by a leading private detective agency perfectly captures this: "Systematic checkings are made of every employee; you never know what day or hour you are being checked."

Deceptive efforts to make people think that surveillance devices are more powerful than they really are may be undertaken. Many people stand in fear and trembling of supposedly scientific investigative techniques. Former President Nixon's remarks on the Watergate tapes are instructive in this regard, "Listen, I don't know anything about polygraphs, but I do know that they'll scare the hell out of people."[32]

Advocates argue that creating the perception of surveillance is a deterrent to criminal behavior. It may be. But it may also deter legitimate behavior, such as the expression of political positions or obtaining benefits to which persons are entitled.[33]

When deception is "sanctioned" through government example, it becomes both more acceptable to the public and easier to rationalize. Cultural standards about deception seem to be softening, as the behavior of some investigative journalists, social scientists, and public relations and marketing specialists suggests. It does not seem far-fetched to anticipate that husbands or wives or those considering marriage might someday soon hire attractive members of the opposite sex to test their partner's fidelity. Beyond commonplace industrial espionage, businesses might hire undercover agents to involve their competitors in illegal actions or have saboteurs infiltrate and disrupt their activities. Some evidence suggests an increased use of undercover means in the private sector.[34]

The proliferation of new techniques may create a lowest-common-denominator morality. Ironically, in order to protect privacy and autonomy, the very tactics of those seeking to lessen them may be adopted in self-defense, as the quotation at the beginning of this section argues. For example, the office of special prosecutor set up to investigate Watergate had vibration detectors, closed-circuit television, alarm tapes on windows, venetian blinds closed at all times, heavy drapes on windows that were drawn whenever sensitive conversations took place, periodic checks for bugs and wiretaps on phones, and 24-hour security guards.

The technique also may be used offensively, of course. Gathering information about competitors by using intelligence agency techniques is becoming a part of strategic business planning. It is likely that private citizens will increasingly be using new electronic forms of surveillance against each other. Through advertisements in major national periodicals (not simply esoteric security publications) and mail-order catalogues, a vast array of surveillance and countersurveillance devices have been brought to mass audiences. In the best free-market tradition, some firms sell the devices as well as the countermeasures needed to thwart them. One large company offers a "secret connection briefcase" that in-

cludes a "pocket-sized tape recorder detector that lets you know if someone is secretly recording your conversation," a "micro-miniature hidden
bug detection system which lets you know if you're being bugged," a
"miniature voice stress analyzer which lets you know when someone is
lying," a "built-in scrambler for total telephone privacy," and an "in-
credible six-hour tape recorder—so small it fits in a cigarette pack."

There is a commercially available at-home urinalysis kit with the
lovely double-think name of "U-Care," making it possible for parents to
mail a child's (or other suspect's) urine sample for analysis. There is a
company that will analyze secretly recorded voice tapes for stress and by
return mail offer an assessment of truthfulness. The widely sold small
unobtrusive transmitters that permit listening at a distance (to a child
sleeping or for intruders) can easily be turned to other uses. The secret
taping of phone and face-to-face conversations seems to be increasingly
common.

Surveillance practices in work settings are also increasing and may
produce alienation on the part of employees. Secret testing or monitoring
of employees communicates mistrust and may be cynically responded to
in kind.

Some other negative aspects can be briefly mentioned. Surveillance
may involve "fishing expeditions" and generalized "searches" rather
than proof of any specific wrongdoing. The spirit of the Fourth Amendment is violated because the burden of proof is shifted from the state to
the target of surveillance. These ideas turn the traditional American belief that you are presumed innocent until proven guilty upside down. As
one baseball player said, "I don't take drugs and I don't believe I have to
prove I don't." There is also the danger of presumption of guilt by association or by statistical artifact. Because of the technical and often distant nature of the surveillance, the accused may (at least initially) be unable to face the accuser. It may even be presented as if it were in the
individual's self-interest: "It can offer proof of innocence"; or "If you
have done nothing wrong, you have nothing to hide." But more than
results must be considered. Such arguments ignore the moral component of the means and the fact that the innocent may nonetheless suffer
harm from an intrusive investigation. We value envelopes around letters
and the confidentiality of spousal communication not to protect illegality, but because liberty is destroyed when such boundaries can be
crossed at will.

The focus on prevention can entail the risk of wasting resources on preventing things that would not have occurred or, as is sometimes the case with undercover activities, of actually creating violations through self-fulfilling effects.

Powerful new discovery mechanisms may overload the system. Authorities may discover far more violations than they can act on. There is a certain wisdom to the ignorance of the three "no evil" monkeys.[35] Having information on an overabundance of violations can lead to the misuse of prosecutorial discretion or demoralization on the part of control agents. Charges of favoritism and corruption may appear when only some offenses can be acted on.

In many science fiction accounts, control is both highly repressive and efficient; there is virtually perfect control over information (whether in the discovery of infractions or in the management of beliefs). As many poignant examples suggest, the new surveillance clearly is less than perfect, and it is subject to manipulation and error.

Computer matching may find valid correlations but can be no better than the original data it deals with, which may be dated or wrong. The data it uses are often rather blunt and acontextual and their meaning unclear. The validity and completeness of criminal record files varies significantly across jurisdictions.[36] Chemical analyses that may correctly identify drugs in a person's system cannot reveal how they got there (thus, THC may appear in the bloodstream because a person smoked marijuana or simply because he was around people who were smoking it). Nor do they reveal current levels of intoxication, because what is measured are the levels of chemical by-products created as the body metabolizes the drug. Evidence of drug use appears some time after the drug has been taken. An intoxicated person can thus score negative, and a person who has not used drugs for several weeks can score positive. Nor does such analysis determine whether a drug was used on or off the job.

There also may be false positives, as a result of the effect of prescription drugs, cold remedies, herbal teas, or the amount of melanin in the skin, or false negatives as a result of switched urine. The electronic transmissions from locational monitors can be blocked by water in a bathtub or waterbed, and the metal in mylar wallpaper, construction beams, and trailers—making it erroneously appear that a person has violated the "house arrest" requirement of probation. The inquisitor in 1984 tells the frail Winston, "I am always able to detect a lie." Such certainty cannot be claimed for the polygraph, a tactic labeled unsatisfactory by the American Psychological Association because it turns up "an unacceptable number of false positives."[37]

Machines are not infallible, nor are the humans who administer and interpret the various tests. Fairness and due process require that careful attention be given to issues of reliability and validity. They also require that one be able to confront his or her accuser and know what the evidence is.

Although deterring or discovering some offenders, the routinization of surveillance, ironically, may grant an almost guaranteed means for successful violations and theft to those who gain knowledge of the system and take action to neutralize and exploit it. (The polygraph, for example, can be confounded by biting one's tongue or stepping on a tack in one's shoe, tightening the sphincter muscles, meditation, or drugs.) Over time, many of these systems will disproportionately net the marginal, amateur, occasional, or opportunistic violator rather than the more sophisticated. The systematization of surveillance may grant the latter a license to steal, even while headlines hail the effectiveness of the new techniques.

CONCERNS FOR THE FUTURE

In focusing on the power of recent surveillance methods, I do not suggest that we are hapless victims of technological determinism who can do little more than bemoan the loss of liberty. The fact that the technology can be misused does not necessarily mean that it will be. To a greater extent than in most countries, the United States has laws and policies restricting its use.

Even in the unlikely event that no problems occur (or could all be solved), there are still ample grounds for concern. A problem of a different order is seen in the *apocalypse someday* argument. This calls attention to future disasters, rather than current problems.[38] The potential for harm may be so great, should social conditions change, that the creation of certain surveillance systems may not be justified in the first place. Because there has not yet been a catastrophe, this argument is usually not given much credence, but it is essentially the same argument that informs the nuclear debate.

Once the new surveillance systems become institutionalized and taken for granted in a democratic society, they can be used for harmful ends. With a more repressive government and a more intolerant public—perhaps upset over severe economic downturns, large waves of immigration, social dislocations, or foreign policy setbacks—these same devices easily could be used against those with the "wrong" political beliefs, against racial, ethnic, or religious minorities, and against those with life-styles that offend the majority. A concern with the prevention of disorder could mean a vastly expanded pool of "suspects."

In the *Merchant of Venice*, Shakespeare counsels us that "to do a great right, do a little wrong." But when intrusive and secret tactics are at hand, more is at stake than the immediate goal. Apart from the principle, there is no guarantee that the ratio would not quickly be reversed—to great wrong yielding little right. At times, the extension of secret police practices may be necessary. They may be exercised with restraint and sensitivity by leaders and agents of high moral character. But, unfortunately, once established, there is no guarantee that, in less demanding times, the practices will be rescinded or that future leaders and agents will be scrupulous, absent the legislative controls called for in the previous chapter.

Chief Justice Harlan F. Stone argued that, in a free society, the abuses of power associated with secret police "are not always quickly apprehended or understood."[39] Each small extension of surveillance can shift the balance between the liberties and rights of individuals and the state and relations among the three branches of government. The impact of such shifts may be incremental, but cumulatively they can change relationships and principles central to our form of government.

If totalitarianism ever came to the United States, it would be more likely to come by accretion than by cataclysmic event. As Sinclair Lewis argued in *It Can't Happen Here,* it would come in traditional American guise, with the gradual erosion of liberties. Voluntary participation, beneficent rationales, and changes in cultural definition and language may hide the onerous and potentially destructive aspects of the new surveillance.[40] Writing about this topic in the mid-1980s, I am forced to recall George Orwell. In a great many areas of domestic affairs, we are far from the distressing society he described, and much current-trend data actually suggest increasing movement in the opposite direction.[41]

The traditional social supports against totalitarianism are strong in the United States: an educated citizenry committed to democratic ideals, a variety of independent channels of mass communication, a plethora of voluntary organizations, and constitutional protections for civil liberties. But to judge the state of freedom and liberty only by traditional standards results in a vision that is too narrow and an optimism that may be unwarranted. There is reason for concern about the state of privacy, liberty, and autonomy in the Western democracies. Here is a paradox: if the traditional social supports for democracy have become stronger and domestic state violence has declined, what is there to be concerned about?

Orwell's state had both violent and nonviolent forms of social control ("a boot stamping on a human face" and Big Brother watching). In linking these two, Orwell offered only one of several models of totalitarian control. It was a model based on his experiences during the Spanish Civil War and his observations of the U.S.S.R., Germany, and Italy. In contemporary society, violent and nonviolent forms of social control have become uncoupled, and the latter is in the ascendance. Over the past four decades, subtle, seemingly less coercive forms of control have emerged.[42]

Culture as conveyed through the mass media is an important element of nonviolent control. The manipulation of language and symbols may subtly shape behavior. Culture is invisible and usually taken for granted; we are generally unaware that we are accepting its myriad dictates or that a choice has been (implicitly) made for us. In the past, to a much greater extent than today, culture tended to develop more haphazardly from thousands of diverse sources. Today, we are moving closer to the deliberate manufacture and control of culture found in Orwell's society, though private interests are involved to a much greater extent than is the state.

Mass communication is, in some ways, an alternative to the mass surveillance devices considered here.[43] Rather than having the state watch everyone all the time, it is far more efficient to have all eyes riveted on a common mass media stimulus that offers direct and indirect messages of how to behave and morality tales about what happens to those who stray. Mass media persuasion is far more subtle and indirect than a truncheon over the head. In the United States and in democratic industrial societies in general, there has been a relative deemphasis on physical forms of domestic social control. Our psyches are more invaded by the consumer mentality than by any repressive political needs of the state. Psychological theories of management, market research, advertising, and public relations contribute to this. Specialists invent needs, package products (entertainers, politicians, public issues, or breakfast food), and seek to sell them to the public. Their skills are continually improving, though much art and guesswork remain.[44]

An economy and state oriented toward mass consumption has a

more benign view of workers and the public than did the nineteenth-century laissez-faire capitalist state. The modern state seeks control partly through the prospect of economic redistribution. The masses are motivated not so much by an ever-increasing scarcity or fear of punishment as by the promise of ever-increasing abundance. For the affluent, this involves a dazzling array of consumer goods. For the poor, it involves the various direct and indirect supports offered by the welfare state.

Force and direct coercion are increasingly seen as being brutish and anachronistic, as well as less effective. The ideals of universal citizenship and the welfare state are more compatible with other means, but the absence of physical oppression does not guarantee liberty. The existence of new, softer forms of surveillance and control within democratic states certainly does not call for a lessening of vigilance.[45]

I am not suggesting that the pain and suffering caused by the threat or actuality of violence as against deception and manipulation are equivalent, though both involve coercion and seek to counter informed consent and free choice. The end control result may be the same. However, violence may offer a possibility of choice—go along or suffer—which is absent when deception is the means. Forced to choose, the newer forms of control are less unattractive, although to some observers, such as Paul Goodman, the choice between "the lesser of two evils" is not a choice between half a loaf and a whole one, "but between a more or less virulent form of rat poison."

We are far from being a maximum-security society, but the trend is toward—rather than away—from this. What Orwell did not anticipate or develop was the possibility that one could have a society where significant inroads were made on privacy, liberty, and autonomy, even in a relatively nonviolent environment with democratic forms and the presumed bulwarks against totalitarianism in place. The velvet glove is replacing (or at least hiding) the iron fist. Huxley may be a far better guide to the future than Orwell.[46]

My concern in this book has been with domestic law enforcement. Considering matters more broadly, government is hardly the only player. Domestic intrusions by the state pale relative to what may be done internationally by intelligence agencies or by the private sector.[47] With respect to intrusive technologies, there is far less legal accountability in the private sector than in the public sector. The Bill of Rights, for example, applies primarily to the actions of government, not the private sector. Restrictions on government are not a sufficient guarantee of freedom. Taken too far, they may guarantee its opposite, as private interests reign unchecked. For Orwell, the state and the economy were synonymous, and the threat to liberty was only from big government. But, in our age of large and powerful nongovernment organizations, a broader view and new legal and policy protections are required. Ironically, we need protection not only by government, but also from it.[48] The undercover tactic is compelling and controversial partly because it can be a means for both protecting and undermining our most cherished values.

The first task of a society that would have liberty and privacy is to guard against the misuse of physical coercion on the part of the state and private parties. The second task is to guard against "softer" forms of secret and manipulative control. Because these are often subtle, indirect, invisible, diffuse, deceptive, and shrouded in benign justifications, this is clearly the more difficult task.

In a democratic society, covert police tactics, along with many of the other surveillance techniques, offer us a queasy ethical and moral paradox. The choice between anarchy and repression is not a happy one, wherever the balance is struck. We are caught on the horns of a moral dilemma. In Machiavelli's words: "[Never] let any state ever believe that it can always adopt safe policies . . . we never try to escape one difficulty without running into another; but prudence consists in knowing how to recognize the nature of the difficulties and how to choose the least bad as good." Sometimes undercover tactics will be the least bad. Used with great care, they may be a necessary evil. The challenge is to prevent them from becoming an intolerable one.

Notes

CHAPTER 1

1. M. Purvis, *American Agent* (New York: Garden City Publishing, 1936) However, Purvis, like J. Edgar Hoover, did not oppose such actions when done by local police or informers. He observes that "the informer system periodically arouses certain of the tender-minded citizenry. . . . I have no interest in these sentimental plaints; my business has been to catch criminals, and *so long as the treachery is not mine, I feel no pangs of conscience*" (p. 116; my italics).

2. W. Riley, "Confessions of a Harvard Trained G-Man," *Harvard Business School Bulletin* (Oct. 1982).

3. The actual cost is greater because these figures do not include employees' salaries, related expenses and equipment, or funds spent on confidential informants apart from these investigations. The number of operations is also greater because these figures refer only to operations managed and funded solely by the FBI. Joint operations and "pretext interviews" are excluded.

4. The tactic is certainly not new to the IRS. One of its most celebrated uses was against Al Capone. The agency came under criticism in the early 1970s as a result of Operation Leprechaun, an investigation of offshore bank accounts. As a result, a centralized undercover unit was disbanded. Undercover operations are now carried out in the 52 regions in a decentralized fashion, although there is a headquarters support unit.

5. President's Commission on Law Enforcement and Administration of Justice, *The Challenge of Crime in a Free Society* (Washington D.C.: GPO, 1967), p. 204; President's National Advisory Commission on Civil Disorders, *Report of the National Advisory Commission on Civil Disorders* (Washington D.C.: GPO, 1968), p. 209.

6. This authorization is contained in Executive Order 12333 issued by President Reagan in 1981.

235

7. E.g., prosecutors in Los Angeles and San Diego counties were able to collect $100,000 in civil penalties and an agreement from Sanyo Electric, Inc. that it would not use threats or coercion to force retail dealers to sell its products at the "suggested retail price." This followed from a civil investigation in which a dealer recorded conversations with Sanyo representatives. The dealer was told he would lose the Sanyo line because of his low pricing. According to court documents, the sales representative said, "Listen, I know everything we're doing is illegal. I wouldn't have this conversation if there was somebody in the room."

8. Here the sell-bust has an additional unintended meaning.

9. Operation Snakescam has been called the "largest and most successful fish and wildlife law enforcement investigation ever conducted." Undercover agents ran a wholesale "Wildlife Exchange" and actively sought to purchase protected species. Over an 18-month period, they filled their cages with 10,000 illegally traded animals, experiencing snakebites and animal births in the process.

10. The goal of prevention is clear in IRS Commissioner Eggers' statement that increased enforcement is needed to show those "who insist on playing variations of 'stick the IRS' that the law now creates much greater downside risks. We believe this will lead to a higher level of compliance. . ." (*National Law Journal*, Nov. 15, 1982).

11. Select Committee to Study Law Enforcement Undercover Activities of Components of the Department of Justice, *Hearings, Law Enforcement Undercover Activities* (Washington, D.C.: GPO, 1983).

12. S. Grosso and P. Rosenberg, *Point Blank* (New York: Avon, 1979).

13. Operation Corcom (corrupt commissioners), one of the largest investigations of public corruption ever undertaken, illustrates the traditional case. Under police supervision, using videotaping, an Oklahoma building materials salesman offered kickbacks to county commissioners after having previously made more than 8,000 payoffs worth one million dollars. A U.S. attorney observes, "We simply had Moore do business like he had for 20 years." Several hundred persons were charged, and almost all of Oklahoma's 77 counties were involved.

14. The FBI defines an undercover operation as one that involves a person whose relationship with the FBI is concealed from third parties by the maintenance of a cover or alias identity. However, this excludes operations where persons who are known to be in law enforcement pretend to be corrupt and collapses the vital passive/active dimension.

15. For example, in a New York study after the Mapp decision, which extended the exclusionary rule in search-and-seizure cases to the states, the proportion of cases in which (according to police testimony) defendants dropped or threw evidence to the ground, rather than its being discovered by a search, significantly increased. Comment, "Effect of *Mapp v. Ohio* on Police Search and Seizure Practices in Narcotics Cases," *Columbia Journal of Law and Social Problems* 4 (1968); C. Klockars, "Blue Lies and Police Placebos: The Moralities of Police Lying," *American Behavioral Scientist* 27, no. 4 (March/April 1984): 529–44; S. Bok, *Secrets: On the Ethics of Concealment and Revelation* (New York: Pantheon, 1982); P. Manning, "Police Lying," *Urban Life and Culture* 3 (Oct. 1974): 283–306; J. Skolnick, "Deception by Police," in *Moral Issues in*

Police Work, ed. F. Elliston and M. Feldberg (Totowa, N.J.: Rowman and Allanheld, 1985).

16. These cities are the complete universe for which data were available for both 1971 and 1981 as reported in *Survey of Municipal Police Departments*, Kansas City, Mo., 1971 and *Survey of Police Operational and Administrative Practices*, Police Foundation, 1981. The cities are Cleveland, Columbus, Dallas, Kansas City, Phoenix, Portland, and St. Louis.

17. More precise documentation of the nature of this general increase would be desirable. For example, is the increase relative, as well as absolute? Have undercover means expanded at the expense of conventional tactics, or is any increase part of a more general increase in social control activity? Thus, in its tougher enforcement response, the IRS appears to have increased its use of a variety of information-gathering strategies beyond undercover means and informants. Similarly, looking just at undercover means, have the newer forms increased at the expense of the old, or has there been a general increase? E.g., the increase in covert tactics used against conventional crimes was at least partly related to resources that became available as a result of the decreased use of undercover means and informants in political cases in the mid-1970s.

18. In 1985 DEA, e.g., had over 200 agents and several dozen intelligence analysts in 42 countries. The FBI had 13 offices and 56 personnel abroad (including 29 special agents). House Committee on Appropriations, *Department of Commerce, Justice and State, the Judiciary, and Related Agencies Appropria tions for 1986* (Washington, D.C.: GPO); U.S. Department of Justice, Federal Bureau of Investigation, *1986 Appropriation Request* (Washington, D.C.). The American role in international law enforcement (of which the spread of undercover means is one aspect) is treated in E. Nadelmann, *Cops Across Borders: Transnational Crime and International Law Enforcement* (New York: Free Press, forthcoming).

19. Illustrative of this more specific literature are, on particular agencies and enforcement goals: M. Moore, *Buy and Bust* (Lexington, Mass.: Lexington Books, 1977); J. Q. Wilson, *The Investigators* (New York: Basic Books, 1978); F. Donner, *The Age of Surveillance* (New York: Knopf, 1980); P. Manning, *The Narc's Game* (Cambridge: M.I.T. Press, 1980); V. Navasky, *Naming Names* (New York: Penguin, 1981). On legal issues: R. C. Donnelly, "Judicial Control of Informants, Spies, Stool Pigeons, and Agents Provocateurs," *Yale Law Journal* 61 (1951); J. Lundy, "Police Undercover Agents," *George Washington Law Review* 37 (March 1969): 634–68; G. Dix, "Undercover Investigations," *Texas Law Review* 53 (1975): 203–94; R. C. Park, "The Entrapment Controversy," *Minnesota Law Review* 60 (1976): 163–274; G. Stone, "The Scope of the Fourth Amendment: Privacy and the Public Use of Spies, Secret Agents, and Informers," *American Bar Association Foundation Research Journal* 1 (1976), 1193–1271; L. H. Seidman, "The Supreme Court Entrapment and Our Criminal Justice System," *Supreme Court Review* 22 (1981): 111–55.

On philosophical considerations: S. Bok, *Lying: Moral Choice in Public and Private Life* (New York: Pantheon, 1978); S. Bok, *Secrets: On the Ethics of Concealment and Revelation* (New York: Pantheon, 1982); G. Dworkin, "The

Serpent Beguiled Me and I Did Eat: Entrapment and the Creation of Crime,"
Law and Philosophy 4 (1985): 17–39; F. Schoeman, "Privacy and Police Undercover Work," in *Police Ethics: Hard Choices in Law Enforcement,* ed. W. Heffernan and T. Stroup (New York: The John Jay Press, 1985); G. Stitt and
G. James, "Entrapment: An Ethical Analysis," in *Moral Issues in Police Work,*
ed. F. Elliston and M. Feldberg (Totowa, N.J.: Rowman and Allanheld, 1985).
F. Elliston, *Police Ethics: Source Materials,* Washington DC: Police Foundation,
n.d. On practitioners: M. Harney and J. Cross, *The Informer in Law Enforcement* (Springfield, Ill.: C. Thomas, 1960); R. Hicks, *Undercover Operations
and Persuasion* (Springfield, Ill.: C. Thomas, 1973); J. K. Barefoot, *Undercover
Investigation* (Springfield, Ill.: C. Thomas, 1975); T. Bouza, *Police Intelligence*
(New York: AMS Press, 1976). On first-person, journalistic, or novelistic ac-
counts: D. Agnew, *Undercover Agent—Narcotics* (New York: Macfadden-
Bartell, 1964); A. Schiano and A. Burton, *Solo* (New York: Warner, 1974);
C. Whited, *Chiodo* (Chicago: Playboy Press, 1974); R. Elder, *Chiodo 2: The
Decoy Man* (Chicago: Playboy Press, 1975); C. Payne, *Deep Cover* (New York:
Newsweek, 1979); R. Daley, *Prince of the City* (Boston: Houghton-Mifflin,
1978); J. Wambaugh, *Lines and Shadows* (New York: W. Morrow and Co.,
1984); T. Mills, *The Underground Empire* (New York: Doubleday, 1986);
P. Rosenberg, *The Spivey Assignment* (New York: Holt, Rinehart, and Win-
ston, 1979). On secrecy and deception: E. Shils, *The Torment of Secrecy* (Glen-
coe, Ill.: Free Press, 1956); S. Tefft, ed., *Secrecy: A Cross-Cultural Perspective*
(New York: Human Sciences Press, 1980); R. Mitchell and N. Thompson, eds.,
Deception: Perspectives on Human and Nonhuman Deceit (Albany, N.Y.:
SUNY Press, 1986).

See also the material inspired by Abscam: *Select Committee to Study Law
Enforcement Undercover Activities of Components of the Department of Jus-
tice, Hearings, Law Enforcement Undercover Activities* (Washington, D.C.:
GPO, 1983); U.S. Congress, House of Representatives, 98th Cong., 2d sess.,
Subcommittee on Civil and Constitutional Rights of the Committee on the Judi-
ciary, Report: *FBI Undercover Operations* (Washington, D.C.: GPO, 1984);
R. Greene, *The Sting Man* (New York: Dutton, 1981); G. Caplan, ed., *Abscam
Ethics* (Cambridge, Mass.: Ballinger, 1983); R. I. Blecker, "Beyond 1984: Undercover in America—Serpico to Abscam," *New York Law School Law Review*
28 (1984): 823–1024.

CHAPTER 2

1. On Vidocq, see P. Stead, *Vidocq: Picaron of Crime* (London: Staples,
1953); N. Gerson, *The Vidocq Dossier* (Boston: Houghton Mifflin, 1977).

2. France had a well-established tradition of covert policing, but this was for
the protection of the state. The priorities of the French police were political
threats and public order, rather than crime.

3. One aspect of the concern over public image is its bearing on successful
convictions. Echoing the behavior of current defense lawyers in undercover
cases, P. Stead, *The Police of Paris* (London: Staples, 1957), p. 94, notes that, in

the nineteenth century, "Defense counsel were only too often able to ridicule the Crown case by exposing the character of police witnesses."

4. Vidocq went on to establish one of the first private detective agencies and reporting bureaus. He was the inspiration for characters created by Balzac, Gaboriau, and Poe. See I. Ousby, *Bloodhounds of Heaven* (Cambridge: Harvard Univ. Press, 1976).

5. However, unlike in the contemporary sting, the relationship between controllers and criminals was more cooperative. Thieves knew when they were dealing with police. Secrecy and deception were tools used jointly by police and thieves relative to victims. In the current version of the property sting, these become tools used by police against the thief. In contrast, in principle the thief taker was to operate in response to citizen complaints and only after the crime had occurred. The contemporary sting is anticipatory and preventive. It seeks to deter thieves and make arrests. The recovery of property is a less important goal, and the detective's compensation is not affected by it.

6. On Wild, see G. Howson, *The Thief-Taker General: The Rise and Fall of Jonathan Wild* (London: Hutchinson, 1970); C. Klockars, "Jonathan Wild and the Modern Sting," in *History and Crime: Implications for Criminal Justice Policy,* ed. J. Inciardi and C. Taupel (Beverly Hills, Calif.: Sage, 1980). He is the hero of Henry Fielding's novel *Jonathan Wild* and the character Peachum in John Gay's *The Beggar's Opera.* The material on the history of the British police that follows draws from P. Colqhoun, *A Treatise on Police in the Metropolis,* 7th ed. (Montclair, N.J.: Patterson Smith, 1969); W L. Melville-Lee, *A History of Police in England* (London: Methuen, 1901); S. R. L. Radzinowicz, *History of English Criminal Law,* 4 vols. (London: Stevens, 1948–68); J. Thorwald, *The Century of the Detective* (New York: Harcourt, Brace, and World, 1964); A. Silver, "The Demand for Order in Civil Society: A Review of Some Themes in the History of Urban Crime, Police, and Riots," in *The Police,* ed. D. Bordua (New York: Wiley, 1967). T. A. Critchley, *A History of Police in England and Wales,* 2d ed. (Montclair, N.J.: Patterson Smith, 1972); W. R. Miller, *Cops and Bobbies: Police Authority in New York and London* (Chicago: Univ. of Chicago Press, 1975); T. Reppetto, *The Blue Parade* (New York: Macmillan, 1978); and P. Rock, "Law, Order and Power in Late Seventeenth and Early Eighteenth Century England," *International Annals of Criminology* 16, nos. 1 & 2 (1977): 233–65.

7. Thorwald (1964) observes that "thief-takers lured young people into crime, dragged them into court for the price upon their head. They publicly offered to get back stolen goods in return for a reward commensurate with the value of the goods. The reward, of course, was divided with the thieves, unless the thief-taker himself had committed the theft, which was frequently the case."

8. On Oliver, see E. P. Thompson, *The Making of The English Working Class* (London: Gollancz, 1965), chaps. 14 and 15.

9. Colqhoun wrote that "the French System had arrived at the greatest degree of perfection; and though not necessary, nor even proper, to be copied as a *pattern,* might, nevertheless, furnish many useful hints, calculated to improve the Police of this Metropolis, consistent with the existing Laws; and even to ex-

tend and increase the Liberty of the Subject without taking one privilege away; or interfering in the pursuits of any one class of individual; except those employed in purposes of *mischief, fraud,* and *'criminality"* (1969, p. 529). He sought a metropolitan police, separated from political authority. He wanted the English to copy the French system of providing funds for crime prevention and their system for gathering and dispersing intelligence.

10. The uniform was designed by color (blue), design, and hat to be clearly distinct from the red coats and high leather hats of the military. The military type system, believed to guard against abuses of liberty on the part of the guards, might of course also be used to thwart the liberty of citizens. In the United States in the earliest years, even the uniform was resisted because it was too reminiscent of the recent military experience. See R. Lane, *Policing the City* (Cambridge: Harvard Univ. Press, 1967), pp. 103–5; J. Richardson, *The New York Police: Colonial Times to 1901* (New York: Oxford Univ. Press, 1970), pp. 64–65.

11. According to an 1830 account, the public showed "repugnance" at responding to "the request of a man who has no outward mark of his quality" (Stead 1957, p. 98).

12. Secret police tactics continued to be clandestinely used by the political police and private detective organizations. E.g., the Bow Street Runners, a private detective and patrol organization, which received some state funding, used thief-taker methods in recovering stolen property. As an observer at the time noted, "the qualifications most needed by them were those social gifts which command the largest acquaintance among the most lawless of mankind. One day they would be drinking and roaring out an obscene ditty amidst the applause of their boon companions in a flashhouse; the next day they would return in their official capacity to carry those very companions off to a gaol." (L. Pike, *A History of Crime in England,* 2 vols. [Montclair, N.J.: Patterson Smith, 1962], cited in Reppetto (1978), p. 28. A year after the English police was founded, a sergeant Popay infiltrated a legal political organization—the National Worker's Movement, which caused a scandal.

13. J. Greenwood, *The Seven Curses of London* (London: Stanley Rivers, 1869), cited in Reppetto (1978), p. 28.

14. A. Babington, *A House in Bow Street: Crime and the Magistracy in London 1740–1881* (London: McDonald, 1969), cited in Reppetto (1978), p. 30.

15. Cited in D. Johnson, *Policing the Urban Underworld* (Philadelphia: Temple Univ. Press, 1979), p. 16.

16. Cited in R. Fogelson, *Big City Police* (Cambridge: Harvard Univ. Press, 1977).

17. Cited in Johnson (1979), p. 63.

18. On the loose and questionable alliances between police and criminals in the nineteenth and early twentieth centuries, see the accounts in M. Haller, "Historical Roots of Police Behavior: Chicago, 1890–1925," *Law and Society Review* 10, no. 2 (1976): 302–23; Fogelson (1977); Johnson (1979); and Reppetto (1978).

19. *Atlanta Constitution,* Jan. 22, 1895. There were relatively few detectives, and they had considerable discretion. Swamp Fox Jones, an agent, explains that they might have "to do a lot of things that did not look right to

church-going people." In other testimony, Jones states, "I have been in all predicaments to get on to criminals. I have worked in the Dade coal mines. I have held up trains with robbers, and I have done a little of everything to catch men" and "It's 1,100 I've caught counting this month during the 22 years of my service" (*Atlanta Constitution*, Feb. 9, 1895).

20. Cited in Johnson (1979), p. 49.

21. T. Bingham, "Foreign Criminals in New York," *North American Review* 188 (1908): 383–94.

22. For related reasons, the Bureau of Narcotics was one of the first federal agencies with a significant number of black agents (Reppetto 1978). Pinkerton hired women as detectives long before public police did, but his reasons appear to be different from the above. Rather than hiring females because only they could infiltrate certain groups (e.g., radical feminists, as would be the case later), he hired females because they offered a means of exploiting relationships with males and because women, like children, were usually perceived as background figures not to be taken seriously or suspected of being agents.

23. As municipal departments took on the form familiar to us today, other specialized units were also created, e.g., for traffic, record keeping, personnel, homicide, stolen autos, juveniles, and crime prevention. See Fogelson (1977); S. Walker, *A Critical History of Police Reform* (Lexington, Mass.: Lexington Books, 1977).

24. See Peter Manning, *Police Work: The Social Organization of Policing* (Cambridge: M.I.T. Press, 1977).

25. See, e.g., the discussion in Johnson (1979).

26. Some Western peace officers drawn from the ranks of outlaws never fully broke with their pasts. Thus, a member of the "Billy the Kid" gang became marshall of Caldwell; he was lynched when his effort to rob a bank failed. Henry Plumer was elected sheriff of Banrack, Montana, in spite of a murder conviction; he was lynched for leading a notorious band of road agents.

27. F. Prassel, *The Western Peace Officer* (Norman, Okla.: Univ. of Oklahoma Press, 1972).

28. Reppetto (1978), p. 256.

29. Cited in F. Moran, "Allan Pinkerton: Private Police Influence on Police Development" in *Pioneers in Policing*, ed. P. Stead (Montclair, N.J.: Patterson Smith, 1978), p. 100. The material on Pinkerton draws from Moran and Reppetto.

30. See, e.g., W. Broehl, *The Molly Maguires* (Cambridge: Harvard Univ. Press, 1964). The case also inspired Sir Arthur Conan Doyle's only Sherlock Holmes undercover story, *The Valley of Fear* (New York: The Review of Reviews, 1914), in which the agent tells his prey, once arrests have been made: "So I joined your infernal lodge, and I took my share in your councils. Maybe they will say that I was as bad as you. They can say what they like, so long as I get you."

31. W. R. Miller, "Reconstruction and the Political Context of Political Policing," Dept. of History, State Univ. of New York, Stony Brook, 1983.

32. *Grimm v. United States*, 156 U.S. 604 (1895).

33. *Sorrells v. United States*, 287 U.S. 435, 441 (1932).

34. See, e.g., the historical accounts in H. Cummings and C. McFarland, *Federal Justice* (New York: Macmillan, 1937); D. Whitehead, *The FBI Story* (New York: Random House, 1956); S. Ungar, *The FBI* (Boston: Little, Brown, 1975), from which this section draws. An impetus to the creation of the FBI was congressional anger over a Justice Department investigation of corruption in Congress. Subsequent congressional efforts to prohibit the Justice Department from borrowing agents led the department to create its own detective force. The congressional calls for restricting the FBI that followed Abscam have historical precedent.

35. M. Purvis, *American Agent* (New York: Garden City Publishing, 1936), p. 217.

36. See, e.g., F. Donner, *The Age of Surveillance* (New York: Knopf, 1980).

37. In its examination of the scandal-ridden agency that Hoover was to soon head, a committee, which included Roscoe Pound and Felix Frankfurter, wrote: "We do not question the right of the Department of Justice to use its agents in the Bureau of Investigation to ascertain when the law is being violated. But the American people have never tolerated the use of undercover provocative agents or 'agents provocateurs' such as have been familiar in old Russia or Spain" (cited in U.S. Congress, Senate, *Final Report of the Senate Select Committee to Study Governmental Operations with Respect to Governmental Activities*, 94th Cong., 2d sess., 1976, S. Doc. 383, p. 385).

38. *Final Report* 1976, p. 391. In response to a question in 1931 as to whether the FBI would resort to wiretapping, Hoover responded: "No sir. We have a very definite rule in the bureau that any employee engaging in wiretapping will be dismissed. . . . While it may not be illegal, I think it is unethical, and it is not permitted under the regulations by the Attorney General" (U.S. Congress [1931], quoted in D. Seipp, *The Right to Privacy in American History* [Cambridge: Harvard Univ. Program on Information Resources Policy, 1978], p. 108).

39. *Final Report* 1976.

40. A more comprehensive consideration of covert tactics in the United States would include such topics as the "divorce detectives" who appeared toward the end of the nineteenth century and are now being put out of business by changing standards and no-fault divorce laws; the internal use of undercover agents ("shoo-flys") by police themselves as part of monitoring efforts; the related use of undercover means by reform commissions studying police corruption in cities, such as New York, Baltimore, Chicago, and Philadelphia; and the emergence of traffic enforcement with unmarked patrol cars.

41. See, e.g., J. P. Brodeur, "High Policing and Low Policing: Remarks about the Policing of Political Activities," *Social Problems* 30, no. 5 (1983) and T. Mathiesen, *Law, Society, and Political Action* (London: Academic Press, 1981).

42. Moran 1978, p. 108, fn. 51.

43. See Haller (1976). The requirement that judges be lawyers and that even the lowest criminal courts be courts of written record are related aspects.

CHAPTER 3

1. H. Becker (*The Outsiders: Studies in the Sociology of Deviance* [Glencoe, Ill.: Free Press, 1966]) applies this concept to those who lobby to criminalize

behavior, e.g., temperance advocates. However, there are entrepreneurs of means as well as ends.

2. This perceived restriction on the flow of information into the criminal justice system is equivalent in impact to court restrictions on the ability of police to gather information.

3. There is nothing automatic about increased crime being translated into greater police power. We certainly cannot always assume that enhanced social control follows a crime increase. Historically, persons seeking to extend police power have often justified it by reference to a crisis. The perception that there is a crisis with respect to crime control sometimes owes more to the public relations actions of those seeking to enhance police power than to objective conditions. However, that is not the case for the time period considered here.

4. See J. Katz, "The Social Movement Against White-Collar Crime," in *Criminology Review Yearbook* vol. 2, ed. E. Bittner and S. L. Messinger (Beverly Hills, Calif.: Sage, 1980), pp. 161–84; J. Short and L. Schrager, "How Serious a Crime? Perceptions of Organizational and Common Crimes," in G. Geis and E. Stotland, eds., *White-Collar Crime: Theory and Research* (Beverly Hills, Calif.: Sage, 1980), pp. 14–31; and David R. Simon and Stanley L. Svart, "The Justice Department Focuses on White-Collar Crime: Promises and Pitfalls," *Crime and Delinquency* 30 (1984): 107–20. The generality of the term "white-collar crime" and definitional and measurement problems make precise overall comparisons difficult, but there is considerable evidence for the increase in certain kinds of white-collar crime. E.g., according to the American Insurance Association, 15 to 20 percent of the claims filed in 1982 were fraudulent; a decade before this figure was estimated at 5 percent. According to an IRS report, the nonpayment of taxes by individuals and corporations has gradually increased in the last decade: in 1981 it was estimated to be $3 billion, up from $1 billion in 1973 (*New York Times*, Aug. 29, 1983).

5. H. Finney and H. Lesieur, "A Contingency Theory of Organized Crime," *Research in the Sociology of Organizations* 1 (1982): 255–99; J. Braithwaite and G. Geis, "On Theory and Action for Corporate Crime Control," *Crime and Delinquency* 1982 (April): 292–314.

6. S. Shapiro, *Wayward Capitalists* (New Haven: Yale Univ. Press, 1984).

7. N. Reichman, "Ferreting Out Fraud: The Manufacture and Control of Fraudulent Insurance Claims," Ph.D. diss., M.I.T., 1983.

8. J. Rule, D. McAdam, L. Stearns, and D. Uglow, "Documentary Identification and Mass Surveillance in the United States," *Social Problems* 31 (1983).

9. D. Vaughan, *On the Social Control of Organizations* (Chicago: Univ. of Chicago Press, 1983).

10. S. M. Lipset and W. Schneider, *The Confidence Gap* (New York: Macmillan, 1983).

11. The proportion of the public holding a highly favorable opinion of the FBI dropped to 37 percent from a high of 84 percent in 1965, according to Gallup polls.

12. See the accounts in *Law Enforcement: The Federal Role*, Report of the Twentieth Century Fund Task Force on the Law Enforcement Assistance Administration (New York: McGraw-Hill, 1976); M. Feeley and A. Sarat, *The Policy Dilemma* (Minneapolis: Univ. of Minnesota Press, 1980); John K. Hudyik, *Fed-*

eral Aid to Criminal Justice (Washington, D.C.: National Criminal Justice Association, 1984).

13. Public Integrity Section, Criminal Division, U.S. Dept. of Justice, *Report to Congress on the Activities and Operations of the Public Integrity Section for 1985,* June 1986.

14. Fiscal Year 1988 Budget Request Report; F. Montanino, "Protecting the Federal Witness," *American Behavioral Scientist* 27, no. 4 (1984).

15. See the account based on documents released under the Freedom of Information Act in P. H. Melanson, "The CIA's Secret Ties to Local Police," *The Nation,* March 26, 1983.

16. See Reichman (1983); and G. Marx, "The Interdependence of Private and Public Police as Illustrated by Undercover Investigations," *Crime and Justice System Annuals* 21 (1987).

17. The tactic played an important role in Parker's reform and consolidation of control in Los Angeles; O. W. Wilson used it early in his tenure in Chicago.

18. See, e.g., G. Kelling, T. Pate, D. Kieckman, and C. E. Brown, *The Kansas City Preventive Patrol Experiment: Executive Summary* (Washington, D.C.: Police Foundation, 1974); P. Greenwood, J. Petersilia, and J. Chaiken, *The Criminal Investigation Process* (Lexington, Mass.: D. C. Heath, 1977).

19. See the discussions in J. Hagen and I. Bernstein, "The Sentence Bargaining of Upperworld and Underworld Crime in Ten Federal District Courts," *Law and Society Review* 13, no. 467 (Winter 1979); J. Katz, "Legality and Equality: Plea Bargaining in the Prosecution of White-Collar and Common Crimes," *Law and Society Review* 13, no. 431 (Winter 1979); G. Magarity, "Rico Investigations: A Case Study," *American Criminal Law Review* 13, no. 367 (1980). On the role of prosecutors and police in the construction of charges, see W. B. Littrell, *Bureaucratic Justice, Police, Prosecutors and Plea Bargaining* (Beverly Hills: Sage, 1979).

20. A related factor is the increased reliance on physical evidence made possible by advances in forensic science.

21. *Hoffa v. United States,* 385 U.S. 293 (1966); *United States v. Russell,* 411 U.S. 423 (1973); *United States v. White,* 401 U.S. 745 (1971). These decisions are consistent with the majority views in the earlier Sorrells and Sherman decisions, although, in these cases, the court reversed convictions. *Sorrells v. United States,* 287 U.S. 435, 441 (1932); *Sherman v. United States,* 356 U.S. 369 (1958).

22. However the tolerance does not extend to actions taken once a person has been arrested. The court has broadened the Sixth Amendment's right to counsel to include unsolicited information, e.g., that offered by an arrested person to a cellmate or co-defendant who is an informer. Authorities may not intentionally create a situation likely to induce an admission of guilt in the absence of legal advice. However, undercover means can be used to gather evidence for crimes other than those charged in the current indictment. *Maine v. Moulton,* 106 S. CT. 477 (1985), *U.S. v. Henry,* 477 U.S. 264 (1980).

23. Justice Rehnquist's opinion in *Russell* illustrates this view. Frank Schubert offers a useful account of these developments ("Controlling Undercover Investigations: Due Process and Police Propriety," paper delivered at annual meeting of American Society of Criminology, 1981).

24. *United States v. Knotts,* 103 S. CT. 1081 (1983).

25. K. C. Davis, *Police Discretion* (St. Paul, Minn.: West Publishing Co., 1975).

26. W. Riley, "Confessions of a Harvard Trained G-Man," *Harvard Business School Bulletin,* Oct. 1982: 72. A 1980 FBI study covering a 19-month period found 19 instances of informants and 42 instances of the general public refusing to provide information because they were concerned their identities might be disclosed. More common was difficulty in obtaining information from banks, schools, and public agencies, attributed to state and federal privacy regulations (C. Stern, "FBI Informants," *New York Times,* Feb. 2, 1982).

27. The BATF and its predecessors had, of course, used covert means extensively for liquor enforcement, but this act expanded the opportunity to use them for gun control.

28. For a description, see R. Blakey and N. Goldsmith, "Criminal Redistribution of Stolen Property: The Need for Law Reform," *Michigan Law Review* 74 (Aug. 1976): 1512–1626.

29. The Supreme Court, in unanimous decision, has supported the tactic as a private enforcement tool. It held that individuals have standing to a claim for damages from landlords who have violated the Fair Housing Act. The case was brought by a black fair housing "tester" told by a landlord that there were no vacancies in an apartment house, while a white "tester" was told that there were vacancies. *Havens Realty Corporation v. Coleman,* 455 U.S. 363 (1982). For use of the tactic to document discrimination at a nightclub and later license revocation, see C. Wexler and G. Marx, "When Law and Order Works," *Crime and Delinquency* 32 (1986): 205–23.

30. *United States v. Turkette,* 101 S. CT. 2524 (1981).

31. *United States v. Helstoski,* 442 U.S. 477 (1979).

32. This interpretation requires equivalent legal treatment of Abscam and Koreagate. Abscam, e.g., would have been much more compelling if the congressmen had actually gone ahead and done what they had promised to do, as appears to have been the case with Koreagate. In the latter, the Korean CIA was alleged to have bribed congresspersons who, in return, voted appropriations for Korea. In Abscam no favors were, nor could have been, delivered. Yet, from a standpoint of legal processing, the cases are the same, given the inadmissibility of the actual legislative behavior in Koreagate.

33. *Olmstead v. United States,* 277 U.S. 438 (1928).

34. There are also disadvantages relative to simple radio transmitters. They are bulkier and not as easily concealed, cannot be overheard by supporting agents, must be turned on, and the tapes and batteries run out and must be changed. The technology, of course, continues to evolve—in the several years between writing this chapter and its publication, small close-range handheld detectors that respond to the bias oscillator of the tape recorder became available as a countermeasure, though, if the recorder is inside a metal case, these are not likely to work.

Neither tapes nor transmitters are infallible. Machines malfunction and batteries run down, and competing sounds—television, air-conditioning, traffic— may drown out the conversation. Atmospheric conditions and steel structures can block transmissions. Several agents commented on what seemed to be the uncanny ability of sound equipment to fail at precisely those times when it was most needed.

35. This is probably more believable than the traditional reliance on ketchup to make it appear that a target has in fact been murdered. Such photographs (or other evidence, such as a fake story planted in a cooperating newspaper about a homicide "victim") are often needed to prove a conspiracy when the crime of murder does not actually occur. The loop must be closed by having the "killer" meet with the person who hired him for payment after the job is completed.

CHAPTER 4

1. A related use is the stakeout, where police in unobtrusive street clothes or various disguises (cab driver, delivery person, phone or utility repair person) await a wanted suspect. The intelligence sought is simply whether the person will appear or not. The old Western Union deliveryman ruses to get a wanted person to open the door are similar. Process servers are another group who make imaginative use of deception to gain information and access. Persons may be secretly watched for new violations as well. Washington, D.C., for example, tried a special anti-fraud unit that watched former police and firefighters under fifty years of age who retired on disability.

2. C. Payne, *Deep Cover* (New York: Newsweek Books, 1979).

3. Covertly watching employees and customers is a prominent feature of private security. A private detective catches the essence of this use of the tactic in retail sales and the food and beverage business: "We don't set anyone up, we don't entrap anyone, we don't create situations, we just sit back and observe."

4. Cited in A. Barth, *The Loyalty of Free Men* (New York: Viking, 1951), p. 151 (my italics).

5. E.g., see D. Wise, *The American Police State* (New York: Random House, 1976); R. J. Goldstein, *Political Repression in Modern America: 1870 to the Present* (Cambridge, Mass.: Schenckman, 1978). F. Donner, *The Age of Surveillance* (New York: Knopf, 1980); G. Marx, "External Efforts to Damage or Facilitate Social Movements: Some Patterns, Explanations, Outcomes and Complications" in *The Dynamics of Social Movements,* ed. M. Zald and J. McCarthy (Cambridge, Mass.: Winthrop, 1979), 94–125; R. Morgan, *Domestic Intelligence: Monitoring Dissent in America* (Austin: Univ. of Texas, 1980); D. Garrow, *The FBI and Martin Luther King* (New York: Norton, 1981). On general political criminality, see A. Turk, *Political Criminality* (Beverly Hills: Sage, 1982); J. Thomas, "Class, State, and Political Surveillance: Liberal Democracy and Structural Conditions," *Insurgent Sociologist* 11-12 (Summer-Fall 1981): 47–58.

6. The Attorney General's guidelines for the FBI, issued in response to the previous abuses, now prohibit diffuse targeting and extralegal forms of harassment and prevention.

7. J. Ahern, *Police in Trouble* (New York: Hawthorn, 1972). S. Chakotin, *The Rape of the Masses* (London: London Book Service, 1939) offers a Russian example where "agitators" came to play the opposite role after the revolution in preventing crowd violence.

8. *Hampton v. United States,* 425 U.S. 484 (1976). Justice Brennan ob-

served that in this case "the government is doing nothing else than buying contraband from itself through an intermediary and jailing the intermediary."

9. R. Sabbag, *Snow Blind* (New York: Avon, 1977), p. 120.

10. E. Baskett, *Entrapped* (Westport, Conn.: Lawrence Hill and Co., 1976), p. 68.

11. A. Reiss, *The Police and the Public* (New Haven: Yale Univ. Press, 1971); D. Black, "The Mobilization of Law," *Journal of Legal Studies* 2 (1973): 125–49. The proactive/reactive distinction is commonly drawn to separate undercover from other investigations, but it is not useful for this. The tactics of uniformed police may be proactive, as when aggressive stop-and-search tactics are used. On the other hand, undercover means may be reactive, as when decoy squads are deployed on the basis of citizen complaints.

12. Well-known examples are described in J. Olsen, *"Son": A Psychopath and His Victim* (New York: Atheneum, 1983); G. Cartwright, *Blood Will Tell* (New York: Pocket Books, 1980).

13. The ad said, "Sexy hostesses needed for gambling junket. Entails foreign travel. Expenses paid." Interviews were held, and some applicants were invited to a plush party to meet some of the gamblers. The women were told that the party was "a run-through for the forthcoming trip" and "it's to your advantage to be liked by the men at the party." Fifty-four of the women apparently went too far in their efforts to be liked by the men at the party and were arrested for solicitation for prostitution.

14. E.g., a letter to the editor, *Providence Journal*, Jan. 2, 1981: "On Sept. 25, I was fired from my job as a cashier . . . the management takes it upon itself to test its employees for their 'honesty.' . . . I was at my register when a man rushed up with a package of underwear costing $4.19. I was waiting on another customer when he handed me the price tag and a $5 bill. He said, 'Keep the change' and then rushed for the exit. I tried to stop him and give him his change and receipt, but he paid no attention. Once back at my register, I rang up the sale, but kept the change. I was then told to go on a break. Upon returning, I discovered that my register was closed and a security guard was waiting for me. I was summoned before the head security agent and the store manager, who demanded the return of the 81 cents. The store manager told me I no longer had a job."

Signs prominently displayed in FTD flower shops, meant to reassure customers and motivate shopkeepers, proudly announce that quality and fair pricing are maintained by the use of secret shoppers. "Spy riders" who take flights to grade airline employees are another example.

15. E.g., L. Sherman, "From Whodunit to Who Does It: Fairness and Target Selection in Deceptive Investigations," in G. Caplan, ed., *Abscam Ethics: Moral Issues and Deception in Law Enforcement* (Cambridge, Mass.: Ballinger, 1983).

16. The argument for self-selection in such cases applies best after the operation has become known, and not as clearly to those drawn in initially as a result of the "roping" actions needed to spread the word that the fence is in business.

17. U.S. Congress, Senate, 94th Cong., 1st sess. Special Committee on Aging, Subcommittee on Long-Term Care, *Fraud and Abuse Among Practitioners Participating in the Medicaid Program* (Washington, D.C.: GPO, 1976).

18. As a result of this nine-month investigation, two nursing homes were indicted for illegally accepting cash and pledges. They pleaded guilty to lesser charges and agreed to stop soliciting contributions from the families of residents.

19. They may even receive a degree of cooperation from the real streetwalkers. In Boston, e.g., instances were encountered where genuine prostitutes sent prospective clients who didn't want to pay the full price over to the decoys.

20. B. Edelman, "Eight Years Undercover," *Police Magazine* 3 (1980).

21. Unobtrusive means for discovering this include taking fingerprints left on a glass counter or on glasses from freely provided drinks, collecting names and addresses on the pretext of a raffle, and asking about birthdates because of an interest in astrology.

22. In contrast, situations that involve a decoy prostitute and a client can more closely approximate the genuine encounters. A greater degree of client self-selection is maintained.

23. E.g., see the discussion in J. Braithwaite, *Corporate Crime in the Pharmaceutical Industry* (London: Routledge and Kegan Paul, 1984).

24. J. Wachtel, "The Sale of Bait: A Unique Anti-Fencing Strategy," Master's thesis, Arizona State University, 1980.

25. For a classic journalistic use of this see R. Sikorsky, "Highway Robbery: The Scandal of Auto Repair in America," *Reader's Digest,* May 1987. Sikorsky visited 225 randomly selected garages in 33 states with a car in perfect working order, except for a loose spark plug wire. This simple "problem" was correctly diagnosed only 44% of the time.

26. *Sherman v. United States,* 356 U.S. 369 (1958).

27. Peterson appears to have been an amateur who might not have run afoul of this law without the government's actions. This appears not to be the situation in the case of *United States v. Russell,* 411 U.S. 423 (1973). A narcotics agent supplied Russell with a similarly hard-to-find ingredient used for manufacturing methamphetamine. The agent promised Russell the ingredient if he would first show him a sample and the lab where the drug was to be made. Russell complied and indicated that he had been making the drug for some time.

28. W. B. Littrel, *Bureaucratic Justice, Police, Prosecutors, and Plea Bargaining* (Beverly Hills: Sage, 1979).

29. See J. Wachtel, "Production and Craftsmanship in Police Narcotics Enforcement," *Journal of Police Science and Administration* 13, no. 4 (1985). The emphasis should be on quality, not quantity. Good arrests have both a procedural and a substantive component.

Organizational production pressures may also lead to the *failure* to make any cases. One source of this is too rapid a move to action following the sloppy collection and analysis of raw intelligence. See H. Wilensky, *Organizational Intelligence* (New York: Basic Books, 1967). A variety of other organizational pathologies may appear with secrecy and related information control processes. See, for example, R. Lowry, "Toward a Sociology of Secrecy and Security Systems," *Social Problems* 19 (1972), and R. Wilsnack, "Information Control: A Conceptual Framework for Sociological Analysis," *Journal of Urban Life and Culture* 8, no. 4 (1980).

30. More generally, psychological research has documented the fact that persons vary significantly in their ability to detect deception, e.g., B. M. De-

paulo, M. Zuckerman, and R. Rosenthal, "Humans as Lie Detectors," *Journal of Communication,* Spring 1980; P. Eckman, *Telling Lies: Clues to Deceit in the Marketplace, Politics, and Marriage* (New York: Norton, 1985). Eckman writes of the difficulty in controlling behavioral "leakage" that exists with efforts to deceive.

On the other hand and apart from this ability, as a result of selective perception and greed, suspects may simply not *see* or *believe* evidence indicating that a police operation is present. Agents are sometimes amazed at how gullible suspects can be. Many want to believe that things are as they appear. This failure to identify deception when clues are present seems to be a more general phenomenon found among humans and nonhumans.

31. These generic-discovery means are considered in G. Marx, "Notes on the Discovery, Collection, and Assessment of Hidden and Dirty Data," in J. Schneider and J. Kitsuse, *Studies in the Sociology of Social Problems* (Norwood, N.J.: Ablex, 1984).

Persons engaged in consensual violations face the same issues in trying to maintain secrecy in the face of much that can give them away. Yet unlike agents, they must also reveal their true identity if they are to do business. See P. and P. Adler, "The Irony of Secrecy in the Drug World," *Journal of Urban Life and Culture* 8, no. 4 (1980).

32. As I noted in chapter 3, recent legislation tries to take account of the organizational aspects of crime. E.g., Florida has a tough antitrust law that permits fines of up to $100,000 and the forfeiture of corporate assets.

33. For some employees, this may have an opposite effect—serving as a model for theft and unintentionally providing clues about how to avoid discovery.

34. "Penthouse Interview Robert Leuci," *Penthouse,* Jan. 1982, p. 80.

35. In D. Wise, *The Children's Game* (New York: St. Martins, 1983) a central character states, "Espionage is like the games we play as children. With secret hideaways, or a secret club. The club was not necessarily better than anywhere else, but it excluded the other kids. That's what defined it, made it important. . . . And all of us in the agency revel in our secret world. We are like humanoids, moving unrecognized among the rest of the population. We look just like our neighbors, like anyone else, but each morning we get up and disappear into a secret world. That's our reward, isn't it?" Another character answers, "And our burden" (pp. 192–93).

36. R. C. Cobb, *The Police and the People* (Oxford: Clarendon Press, 1978).

CHAPTER 5

1. For many persons, Clint Eastwood's behavior as a detective in the *Dirty Harry* films is ethical, if illegal.

2. In criminal justice this is often conceptualized in terms of H. Packer's discussion of a crime-control model with an instrumentalist-utilitarian emphasis in contrast to a due-process model with an emphasis on correct procedure (*The Limits of the Criminal Sanction* [Stanford: Stanford Univ. Press, 1968]).

3. E.g., in the case involving Jimmy Hoffa and an informer, the Supreme Court held that, when wrongdoing is involved, the Fourth Amendment offers no

protection against "misplaced confidence" in associates (*Hoffa v. United States,* 385 U.S. 293 [1966]).

4. These often involve deceiving a person who thought he or she was part of an operation to cheat others. Just as criminals when doing wrong have no right not to be deceived by police, so potential criminals have no right not to be deceived by each other, the axiom about "honor among thieves" notwithstanding.

5. J. Reiman, "The Social Contract and Police Use of Deadly Force" in *Moral Issues in Police Work,* ed. F. Elliston and M. Feldberg (Totowa, N.J.: Rowman and Allanheld, 1985) advances this justification for the police use of firearms.

6. On publicity as a criteria, see J. Rawls, *A Theory of Justice* (Cambridge: Harvard Univ. Press, 1971). Publicity may also have some deterrent impact because it may inhibit amateur or minimally committed violators. Ironically, public announcements may work to the advantage of skilled, committed rule breakers who thus gain strategic information that they can use to thwart enforcement efforts. The more general and vague the publicity, the less this will happen. Publicity may also lessen respect for the law or encourage citizens to be more deceptive.

7. A game metaphor cannot be pushed too far, however. In cops and robbers, the legitimation of deception is one-sided; in a card or football game, it is reciprocal. In the latter a distinction is made between legitimate versus illegitimate deception (bluffing against playing with a marked deck); police do not usually make such a distinction in their use of deception.

8. Whether or not it is intended to do so, such a label concentrates attention on characteristics of the agents, rather than on the executive branch leaders who approve or ignore their behavior.

9. Some observers do not define undercover work as lying. A prominent prosecutor who played an influential role in many controversial cases observes: "Undercover work is not the moral equivalent of lying. It's just playing a role like Richard Burton playing Hamlet." This conveniently ignores the fact that although both actors and undercover agents play roles, the audience for the latter is unaware of this.

10. Consider also children's rhymes ("liar, liar, your pants are on fire, the flames grow higher") and negative epithets such as "snitch," "cheat," "sneak," "rat," and "imposter."

11. Cited in S. Bok, *Lying: Moral Choice in Public and Private Life* (New York: Pantheon, 1978).

12. E. Goffman, *Frame Analysis: An Essay on the Organization of Experience* (New York: Harper and Row, 1974) offers a useful consideration of the need to elaborate on the original deception.

13. Deception at the interrogation stage may seem ethically more acceptable than in an undercover investigation because a person at least knows he is dealing with police, but police face stringent restrictions for the former and few for the latter.

14. In *Olmstead v. United States,* 277 U.S. 438 (1928). E. Sagarin and D. MacNamara, "The Problem of Entrapment," *Crime and Delinquency* 16 (1970): 363–78, similarly argue that "law enforcement agencies should employ ethically impeccable standards. Encouragement of crime sullies the banner

of law enforcement and degrades the policeman by making him a party to the crime."

15. S. Vizzini, with O. Fraley and M. Smith, *Vizzini: The Secret Lives of America's Most Successful Undercover Agent* (New York: Arbor House, 1972), p. 9.

16. Of course, this and many of the subsequent ethical objections considered may also appear with conventional means; however, they are particularly likely to be present when covert means are used. The reciprocity may have a moral component involving fair and voluntary exchange—"it's simply a matter of one hand washing the other," as a detective said. In actuality, because the parties rarely meet on equal terms, it may be one hand wringing the other. The coercive power of the state that permits it to offer deals that can hardly be refused can be seen as an additional undesirable element, because it counters the principle of free and voluntary exchange. When participation is coerced rather than willing, accountability and reliability are also more questionable—a point not lost on defense attorneys.

17. A related distinction is between creating a crime that *would not* have occurred except for government intervention and one that *could not* have occurred even with the intervention. In the case of Abscam, no political favors were actually exchanged, although political figures took payment. Because in reality there was no Arab sheik who needed help, the supposed sale of political favors could not actually have been carried out. N. Levin, "The Trouble with Abscam," *New Republic*, Feb. 23, 1980, pp. 18–20, discusses this. It is interesting to contrast Abscam with the scandal known as "Koreagate," which involved alleged payments by the Korean CIA to congressmen. In the case of Abscam, no concrete damage was done, but its targets were prosecuted. In Koreagate, services appear to have been performed and considerable damage done, but no one was prosecuted.

18. F. Schoeman, "Privacy and Police Undercover Work" in *Police Ethics: Hard Choices in Law Enforcement*, ed. W. Heffernan and T. Stroup (New York: John Jay Press, 1985) offers a detailed explication of this principle.

19. As Erving Goffman has argued, a degree of deception remains a part of intimate relations. Indeed, if we could always know what others were really thinking, such relations would be difficult to sustain.

20. E. May, *Constitutional History of England* (1863), p. 275, as cited in J. R. Lundy, "Police Undercover Agents: New Threats to First Amendment Freedoms," *George Washington Law Review* 37 (1969): 634, ed. note.

21. P. Chevigny, "A Rejoinder," *Nation*, Feb. 23, 1980, pp. 201–2.

22. The really interesting question emerges when the research suggests a more varied pattern. What if the figure was 1 in 2, or 1 in 10? What is in conflict here is not so much abstract principles or what the researched facts are, but where to draw the line. How much is enough or too much? How large (or small) must the proportion of unwary innocents, lambs, or falsely accused persons be in order for us to conclude that the tactic is or is not justified? The structure of the argument is similar to that between environmentalists and fishermen regarding the ratio of dolphins to tuna caught in tuna nets.

23. Such cases as that of the notorious "Largo 8" in Florida would obviously be excluded. After a successful investigation, eight retired men were ar-

rested for violating Florida's gambling law. The men were playing poker at their mobile-home village. In a daring investigation, undercover officers seized $24, along with a deck of cards and poker chips. Prosecutors claimed the defendants were playing for money. Perhaps seeking leniency, the defendants did not deny that they had been playing nickel-and-dime poker. By the second day of the trial, the culprits' ranks had thinned to six. One defendant had to be hospitalized for a heart problem, and another for cataract surgery.

24. Bok (1978).

25. Although developed with government in mind, many of these questions can be applied to private-sector uses as well. Cultural values, such as fairness, dignity of the individual, and openness, ought to apply regardless of the setting. Many of the same social dynamics and issues are present. However, less stringent criteria may apply because of the doctrine of employment at will and because the consequences in the workplace are rarely as dire as the loss of liberty that can follow from state uses.

26. C. Klockars, "The Dirty Harry Problem," *Annals of the American Association of Political and Social Science* 452 (Nov. 1980): 33–47, refers to this as the "Dirty Harry" problem. Of course, these may be of a different order, e.g., the moral significance of always causing harm, as opposed to failing to prevent harm. See, e.g., the discussion in "A Critique of Utilitarianism," in *Utilitarianism: For and Against*, ed. B. Williams and J. J. Smart (London: Cambridge Univ. Press, 1973), pp. 93ff.

CHAPTER 6

1. E.g., see some of the harrowing cases described by a courageous New York City policewoman nicknamed "Muggable Mary" in M. Glatzle and E. Fior, *Muggable Mary* (Englewood Cliffs, N.J.: Prentice Hall, 1980).

2. R. Bowers and J. McCullough, *Assessing the "Sting": An Evaluation of the LEAA Property Crime Program* (Washington, D.C.: University Science Center, 1982).

3. Unfortunately, in some jurisdictions the number of buys from the same person went far beyond this, e.g., an El Paso, Texas sting that received favorable publicity because it purchased almost $2 million worth of property in a year, purchased $575,909 from one man and his girlfriend. Over a five-month period, they sold the sting 17 stolen automobiles, four trucking rigs with five semi-trailers, and two trailer loads of merchandise. Another man sold the sting 16 cars in a month. His crime spree was stopped only when an attempted robbery and shoot-out gave away the sting's cover. These cases are reported in C. Cotter and J. Burrows, *Property Crime Program and Project Summaries* (Washington, D.C.: Justice Department, 1981). This report is apparently intended to cast the stings in a favorable light. Bowers and McCullough (1982), p. 79, observe that "all cities indicated their willingness, as well as their experience, to make many transactions beyond the limit." This relates to my discussion of crime amplification.

4. Earlier analysis of some of the same data by Westinghouse, "What Happened? An Examination of Recently Terminated Anti-Fencing Reports" (prepared for U.S. Dept. of Justice, Washington, D.C., 1979, photocopy) found that 84 percent of the 1,620 subjects encountered in 19 operations had at least one

prior arrest. In the first large Washington, D.C., sting, about two in three persons had prior records (R. Shaffer and K. Klose, *Surprise! Surprise! How the Lawmen Conned the Thieves* [New York: Viking, 1977]).

5. E.g., a New York City study found that, in 87 percent of cases, guilty pleas were accompanied by reduced charges (I. Bernstein, E. Kick, J. Leung, and B. Schultz, "Charge Reduction: An Intermediary Stage in the Process of Labeling Criminal Defendants," *Social Forces* 56 [Dec. 1977]: 362–84).

6. K. Weiner, C. Stephens, and D. Besachuk, "Making Inroads into Property Crime: An Analysis of the Detriot Anti-Fencing Program," *Journal of Police Science and Administration* 11 (Sept. 1983): 311–27.

7. S. Green, S. Pennell, and B. McCardell, *Sheriff's Department: Crimes Against Property Control (Anti-Fencing Unit)* (San Diego: Criminal Justice Evaluation Unit, 1979).

8. M. Wycoff, C. Brown, and R. Peterson, *Birmingham Evaluation Report, Draft Three* (Washington, D.C.: Police Foundation, 1980).

9. Washington D.C.'s ROP (Repeat Offender Project) also found that constant surveillance of suspects failed to produce arrests and led to police frustration. The project then gave increased attention to locating persons already wanted on warrants, rather than hoping to catch suspects in the act. S. Martin and L. Sherman, *Catching Career Criminals,* Police Foundation Reports 3, July 1986.

10. Specialized undercover units must confront this problem of boredom. E.g., S. Schack, T. Schell, and W. Gay, *Improving Patrol Productivity,* vol. 2, *Specialized Patrol* (Washington, D.C.: Office of Technology Transfer, National Institute of Law Enforcement and Criminal Justice, 1977), observe that beat officers may slack off in the presence of special units, "officers may come to believe that, if a specialized unit is working on commercial robberies in their beats, they need not be diligent in conducting security checks and field interviews in commercial areas." In describing the decoy unit that operated along the U.S.–Mexican border, J. Wambaugh, *Lines and Shadows* (New York: W. Morrow and Co., 1984) similarly suggests that their isolation and elitism subjected them to resentment and jealousy on the part of those in uniform.

11. A. Halper and R. Ku, *New York City Police Department Street Crime Unit* (Washington, D.C.: GPO, 1976).

12. A detailed critique of the research and suggestions for the kinds of costs and benefits that should be assessed are available in G. Marx and N. Reichman, "Recent Research on 'The New Police Undercover Work': Review and Critique," Law and Society Meetings, Boston, 1984.

13. Two additional studies supporting the finding of no deterrent effect are R. Raub, "Sting Operations: Crime Deterrence or Crime Encouragement," paper delivered at the annual meeting of the Academy of Criminal Justice Sciences, Orlando, Florida, 1986; and R. Langworthy, "Do Stings Control Crime? An Evaluation of a Police Fencing Operation," paper on an auto fencing sting, delivered to the annual meeting of the American Society of Criminology, Atlanta, 1986. Langworthy even finds a slight increase in auto theft during the sting period. Earlier work by Raub did not find an aggregate amplification effect (R. Raub, "Effects of Antifencing Operations on Encouraging Crime," *Criminal Justice Review* 9 [1984]).

The Justice Department's evaluations of its own projects generally reach positive conclusions regarding effectiveness. The observations of those directly involved are often less positive, e.g., M. Walsh, *Strategies for Combatting the Criminal Receiver of Stolen Goods* (Washington, D.C.: LEAA, 1976), p. 114, notes that police involved in antifencing operations had "serious questions as to what had really been accomplished." The idealized image of the New York street crime unit presented in Halper and Ku contrasts with the image presented by participants (C. Whited, *Chiodo* [Chicago: Playboy Press, 1974]; R. Elder, *Chiodo II, The Decoy Man* [Chicago: Playboy Press, 1975]). One experienced decoy officer believes that the decoy with the exposed wallet is entrapment and "an effort to deceive the press and the public with inflated arrest statistics."

14. Although the emphasis here is on undercover projects directed at a broad class of offender or offense, such as street criminals or theft and receiving, some of the assumptions apply to other uses as well.

15. T. Roselius and D. Benton, *Marketing Theory and the Fencing of Stolen Goods* (Washington, D.C.: National Institute of Law Enforcement and Criminal Justice, 1971); and M. Walsh, *The Fence—A New Look at the World of Property Theft* (Westport, Conn.: Greenwood Press, 1977) describe this model.

16. E.g., R. Kennan and L. Peterson, "On Fencing," Miami Police Department, unpublished report, 1973; and S. Pennell, "Fencing Activity and Police Strategy," *Police Chief*, Sept. 1979, pp. 71–75.

17. R. Manuel in *Federal Drug Enforcement, Hearings before the Permanent Subcommittee on Investigations of the Committee on Government Operations,* U.S. Senate, June 1975, p. 30.

18. W. Shakespeare, *Measure for Measure*, Act II, Scene ii. This attitude seems more consistent with a Protestant than a Catholic view of human nature. Undercover tests are more congruent with a puritanical culture expecting perfectability than with a Latin culture stressing man's susceptibility to temptation.

19. S. G. West, S. P. Gunn, and P. Chernicky, "Ubiquitous Watergate: An Attributional Analysis," *Journal of Personality and Social Psychology* 32 (1975): 55–65.

20. A. Bandura, *Aggression: A Social Learning Analysis* (Englewood Cliffs, N.J.: Prentice-Hall, 1973); M. Lefkowitz et al., "Status Factors in Pedestrian Violation of Traffic Signals," *The Journal of Abnormal and Social Psychology* 50 (1955); and A. M. Freed et al., "Stimulus and Background Factors in Sign Violations, *Journal of Personality* 23 (1955).

21. See the discussion in J. Conklin, *Criminology* (New York: Macmillan, 1981).

22. *Some Benefits Realized from Twelve Sting-Type Anti-Fencing Operations* (Washington, D.C.: LEAA, 1977).

23. This is based on the clearance rate reported in the Westinghouse (1979) study.

24. Bowers and McCullough 1982, p. 37.

25. C. Klockars, "Jonathan Wild and the Modern Sting," in *History and Crime: Implications for Criminal Justice Policy,* ed. J. Inciardi and C. Taupel (Beverly Hills, Calif.: Sage, 1980).

26. A more general discussion of this question is in G. Marx, "Ironies of

Social Control: Authorities as Contributors to Deviance through Escalation, Nonenforcement and Covert Facilitation," *Social Problems* 28, no. 3 (Feb. 1981):221–46.

27. P. Manning, *Police Work* (Cambridge: M.I.T. Press, 1977), argues for the importance of the symbolic aspects of policing. Focusing exclusively on the facts and figures regarding costs and benefits can lead one to miss the important role that police play in communicating a moral order. As the French sociologist Emile Durkheim observed, formal social control has a ritualistic quality that can reaffirm shared values (*On the Division of Labor in Society* [Glencoe, Ill.: Free Press, 1959]).

CHAPTER 7

1. On unintended consequences, see R. Merton's pioneering article in *Social Theory and Social Structure* (Glencoe, Ill.: Free Press, 1968) and, as more recently applied to public policy, A. Wildavsky, *Speaking Truth to Power* (New York: Little, 1979); S. Seiber, *Fatal Remedies: The Ironies of Intervention* (New York: Plenum, 1981); and M. Levin, "The Department of Unintended Consequences," *Taxing and Spending,* April 1979.

2. In the formal bureaucratic language of enforcement agencies, the term "subject" rather than "target" is favored. The distinction is noble. However, given the actual language used and the degree of predication usually required to launch a full-fledged federal investigation, "target" is more realistic.

3. A jury found him not guilty, although he subsequently left his job, and his reputation was severely damaged. See J. Lardner, "How Prosecutors Are Nabbed," *New Republic,* Jan. 29, 1977, pp. 22–25; R. Shaffer and K. Klose, *Surprise! Surprise! How the Lawmen Conned the Thieves* (New York: Viking, 1977).

4. Hearings, House Merchant Marine and Fisheries Committee, Subcommittee on Fisheries and Wildlife, Conservation and the Environment, March 14 and July 10, 1985, and Hearings, Senate Committee on Environment and Public Works, Subcommittee on Environmental Pollution, April 18, 1985.

5. One study conservatively estimates that there may be nearly 6,000 erroneous convictions annually for index crimes. Police overzealousness follows errors in eyewitness identifications as the major causes. See C. R. Huff, A. Rattner, E. Sagarin, "Guilty Until Proved Innocent: Wrongful Conviction and Public Policy" *Crime and Delinquency* 22, no. 4 (Oct. 1986):518–44.

6. H. E. Davis, *Mocking Justice* (New York: Crown, 1978).

7. R. Daley, *Prince of the City* (Boston: Houghton Mifflin, 1978), p. 73.

8. K. McKeon, "Did Abscam Manipulate Its Targets?" *Discover,* July 1982.

9. M. Gallagher, "Linguists Could Provide Insights into Abscam Tapes," *Legal Times of Washington,* Aug. 31, 1981.

10. A. Dershowitz, J. Silvergate, and J. Baker, "The J.D.L. Murder Case: The Informer Was Our Own Client," *Civil Liberties Review* 4 (1976).

11. R. Bauman, *The Gentleman from Maryland: The Conscience of a Gay Conservative* (New York: Arbor House, 1986).

12. In commenting on this rule complexity and the discretion it offers supervisors, one policeman observes, "It was like being in a game where the umpires had two rulebooks and wouldn't tell you which one you were playing under" (S. Grosso and P. Rosenberg, *Point Blank* [New York: Dutton, 1979], p. 189). He refers to the official rules and the informal practices perceived as necessary to get the job done; though often contrary, they exist side by side. Reporting requirements are intended to reduce bribes to officers by increasing the risk of discovery, but they may also increase perjury on the part of otherwise honest agents. Thus, should an agent who rejects a bribe but fails to report it later be accused of taking a bribe by a suspect, the tormented agent (whose offense is one of omission rather than commission) is likely to perjure himself in denying that the bribe was ever offered. This also offers another means for clever informers to manipulate their controls.

13. Wiretap material may be similarly used. In a disturbing example, a Southwestern Bell Company executive reports how the company used wiretap information in an effort to coerce local officials into agreeing to rate increases (G. O'Toole, *The Private Sector: Rent-a-Cops, Private Spies and the Police-Industrial Complex* [New York: W. W. Norton, 1978]).

14. There is considerable historical precedent for this in Los Angeles. William Parker is believed to have made important use of secret means in his effort to reform and control the Los Angeles Police Department and its political environment. J. Woods, "The Progressives and the Police: Urban Reform and the Professionalization of the Los Angeles Police Department," Ph.D. diss., Univ. of California at Los Angeles, 1973, p. 420, notes, "newspaper reports implied that Parker knew dreadful things about one or another public figure, and that his secret files made him and the Department invulnerable to political interference." Prior to this, as chief "headhunter" of internal affairs, Parker was widely feared within the department because it was believed that he gathered private information on the "shortcomings and peccadilloes" of his fellow officers, which he kept until it would offer some advantage in departmental politics.

15. J. Weiner, "John Lennon Versus the FBI," *New Republic,* May 2, 1983.

16. U.S. Dept. of Justice, *Unauthorized Disclosure Regarding Abscam, Pendorf and Brilab* (Washington, D.C.: U.S. Dept. of Justice, 1981).

17. M. Lerner, *The Belief in a Just World: A Fundamental Delusion* (New York: Plenum, 1980).

18. Prosecution for crimes committed in the line of duty is unusual. Charges here were brought by an independent special prosecutor investigating the killing of the two suspects.

19. Changes in FBI policy make it unlikely that information would be withheld to this extent again.

20. E.g., see the testimony in House Subcommittee on Civil and Constitutional Rights, *Hearings on FBI Undercover Operations* (Washington, D.C.: GPO, 1983).

21. An account can be found in ibid.

22. The question may also be posed whether any legitimate businesses have been hurt by competition from proprietary fronts run by police. The question is even more appropriate for the CIA, which makes extensive use of long-lasting proprietary fronts.

23. See the account in Leslin Walker's book *Hide in Plain Sight* (New York: Dell, 1980), subsequently made into a film.

24. This is described in C. Payne, *Deep Cover* (New York: Newsweek Books, 1979).

25. It is not clear whether this policy extends to females as well. One law enforcement manual advises: "*Don't take a woman on an undercover assignment:* The subject may become interested in the woman. If this happens, the subject's attention is diverted from those things in which the agent is interested. The woman may be placed in an embarrassing or impossible situation from which extrication might disclose the identity of the undercover agents" (W. Dienstein, *Technics for the Crime Investigator,* 6th ed. [Springfield, Ill.: C. Thomas, 1968]; my italics).

26. U.S. Congress, Senate, Select Committee to Study Governmental Operations with Respect to Intelligence Activities, *Supplementary Detailed Staff Report on Intelligence Activities and the Rights of Americans,* Book 6: 118 (Washington, D.C.: GPO, 1976).

27. Cited in I. Ousby, *Bloodhounds of Heaven* [Cambridge: Harvard University Press, 1976]. Concern over the state's intruding into the privacy of the home remained an issue in eighteenth- and nineteenth-century Great Britain as the modern police system struggled to emerge. An 1850 article took pride in the fact that, unlike people on the Continent, an Englishman could "converse familiarly with his guests at his own table without suspecting that the interior of his own liveries consists of a spy" (p. 181). With the practical disappearance of servants, the wiretap and bug have become the functional equivalent.

28. *The National Law Journal,* Aug. 20, 1984. Lawyers and organized crime are discussed in the final report of the President's Commission on Organized Crime, Report to the President and the Attorney General, *The Impact: Organized Crime Today* (Washington, D.C.: U.S.G.P.O, 1986).

29. M. Genovese, "Impersonation," *Presstime,* Oct. 1984, offers a useful discussion of the issue. See also the testimony of John Seigenthaler, *Hearings, Criminal Law Subcommittee of the Senate Judiciary Committee,* May 16, 1984.

30. "Attorney General's Guidelines on FBI Undercover Operations," Office of the Attorney General, Washington, D.C., 1981.

31. J. Fullam, "Memorandum and Order," U.S. District Court for the Eastern District of Pennsylvania, *U.S. v. Harry P. Jannotte, George Schwartz,* no. 80-166 (Nov. 1980); I. Nathan, "Abscam—Production of Supplemental Information to Defense Counsel," Justice Department memo, Washington, D.C., Jan. 6, 1981; S. Kaufman and D. Rezneck, "Post-Hearing Memorandum in Support of Defendant Frank Thompson, Jr.'s Motion to Dismiss the Indictment on Due Process Grounds," *U.S. v. Frank Thompson, Jr. et al.,* no. CR-80-00291 (March 1980, Pratt, J.); *Boston Globe,* July 18, 1980.

32. DEA, in contrast to the FBI, is more likely to have its informers appear in court. J. Q. Wilson, *The Investigators* (New York: Basic Books, 1978) contrasts the organizational consequences of this; also see J. Skolnick's important discussion in *Justice Without Trial* (New York: Wiley, 1966).

33. P. Chevigny, *Criminal Mischief* (New York: Pantheon, 1977).

34. This is an example of what E. Goffman, *Frame Analysis* (New York: Harper and Row, 1974) refers to as "mediated deception."

35. The phrase is from Select Committee, 1983, p. 47.

36. On Silvestri, see N. Klotz, "ABSCAM's Loose Cannons," *New Republic,* March 29, 1980, citing the account of *Newsday* reporter Anthony Marro.

37. A detailed account is given in U.S. Congress, House, *FBI Undercover Operations, Report of Subcommittee on Civil and Constitutional Rights* (Washington, D.C.: GPO, 1984).

38. This at least was their criminal defense to impersonating a judge. The fact that one person received no compensation and the other a small amount for expenses is consistent with the claim that they were acting out of benign motives, after being asked to help by an agent of the court.

39. *Witness Security Program, Hearings Before the Permanent Subcommittee on Investigations of the Committee on Governmental Affairs,* 1980, p. 269. See also the accounts in F. Graham, *The Alias Program* (Boston: Little, Brown and Co., 1977) and N. Pileggi, *Wiseguy: Life in a Mafia Family* (New York: Simon and Schuster, 1985).

CHAPTER 8

1. O. W. Wilson, ed., *Parker on Police* (Springfield, Ill.: C. Thomas, 1957), p. 198.

2. D. Ward, "Ideology and Generations," Ph.D. diss., Yale Univ., 1981.

3. This and the preceding quotation are from M. Baker, *Cops: Their Lives in Their Own Words* (New York: Simon and Schuster, 1985).

4. J. Wambaugh, *Lines and Shadows* (New York: W. Morrow and Co., 1984).

5. See W. Westley, *Violence and the Police* (Cambridge: M.I.T. Press, 1970).

6. W. Muir, *Police Street Corner Politicians* (Chicago: Univ. of Chicago Press, 1977). Muir's analysis is guided by Lord Acton's observation that "the tendency of coercive power to corrupt its wielder seems nearly unavoidable." This may also be the case for the wielders of deceptive power.

The agent is quoted in J. R. Williams and L. L. Guess, "The Informant: A Narcotics Enforcement Dilemma," *Journal of Psychoactive Drugs* 13, no. 3 (Summer 1981).

7. Baker 1985.

8. R. Daley, *Prince of the City* (Boston: Houghton-Mifflin, 1978).

9. See. P. Manning and L. Redlinger, "Invitational Edges of Corruption: Some Consequences of Narcotics Law Enforcement," in *Politics and Drugs,* ed. P. Rock (New York: E. P. Dutton/Society Books, 1977).

10. Wambaugh 1984.

11. This characterizes cinematic treatments as well (e.g., the films *Cruising* and *Partners,* which involve undercover efforts in response to the murder of homosexuals). Equally interesting, though perhaps rarer, are the changes that may come from playing the role of victim. In one case, a decoy policeman who liked to play the part of the passive victim had been robbed more than 100 times.

12. An anthropologist notes, "the truth I have tried to tell concerns the sea change in oneself that comes from immersion in another and savage culture" (E. S. Bowen, *Return to Laughter* [New York: Harper, 1954]).

13. W. Muir, *Police Streetcorner Politicians* (Chicago: Univ. of Chicago Press, 1977).

14. Ward 1981.

15. "Penthouse Interview Robert Leuci," *Penthouse,* January 1982, p. 80.

16. See, e.g., the accounts in R. Wall, "Special Agent for the FBI," *New York Review of Books,* Jan. 27, 1972; G. Marx, "Thoughts on a Neglected Category of Social Movement Participant: Agents Provocateurs and Informants," *American Journal of Sociology* 80 (1975):402–42; and C. Payne, *Deep Cover* (New York: Newsweek, 1979). There are many historical examples. Father Gapon, a police agent and key figure in the 1905 uprising in Russia, became radicalized in the process, and Roman Malinovsky was an agent who apparently became converted to Bolshevism (B. Wolfe, *Three Who Made a Revolution* [Boston: Beacon, 1961]). An equivalent principled public renunciation of the tactic by those using it against conventional crime is much rarer, e.g., a former Tyler, Texas, policewoman reports feeling guilty about her actions and now believes that undercover actions are wrong and conventional methods should be used instead.

17. E.g., see the discussion in M. Giordo, "Health and Legal Issues in Undercover Narcotics Investigations: Misrepresented Evidence," *Behavioral Science and the Law* 3, no. 3 (1985):299–308.

18. See L. Linderman, "Undercover Angel," *Playboy,* July 1981.

19. In one study of 155 drug agents (Giordo 1985), 26 percent of operational undercover drug agents were found to be "psychologically distressed," using a standard measure (the "psychologically at risk" category of the Health Opinion Survey); this compared to 9 percent of agents prior to their first assignment. For postoperational agents, the figure was 17 percent, and for the general population, 12 percent. I encountered five recent cases of undercover agents apprehended for shoplifting. The actual number of cases is likely larger. This may represent a call for help, a desire to take risks, or a sense of invincibility and being above the law.

20. Z. Lait and J. Mortimer, *Chicago Confidential* (New York: Crown, 1950).

21. C. Whited, *Chiodo* (Chicago: Playboy Press, 1974).

22. R. Shaffer and K. Klose, *Surprise! Surprise! How the Lawmen Conned the Thieves* (New York: Viking, 1977).

23. A former FBI agent who posed as a radical during the 1968 Miami conventions observes, "Any FBI agent who had ever attended a major demonstration as an undercover participant, knew only too well that the greatest threat to his personal safety came not from the protest groups he had infiltrated, but from the angry, frustrated police rampaging and uncontrolled" (Payne 1979, p. 91).

24. Because of the highly secretive nature of their assignment, the need to build and maintain a cover, or because other officials cannot be trusted or are themselves targets of an investigation, some undercover police may be instructed not to disclose their identity, even if they are arrested. This may be at a severe cost, e.g., the case of an FBI undercover agent instructed not to disclose his cover under any circumstances, who was arrested as a radical by Miami police during the Republican National Convention. The undercover agent suffered se-

rious internal injuries and had to be hospitalized as a result of having a police night stick shoved up his rectum while he was in custody (Payne 1979).

25. A. Schiano and A. Burton, *Solo* (New York: Warner, 1974).

26. Whited 1974.

27. Sometimes, of course, police shooting at each other is no accident. There are cases of off-duty police using weapons against each other in bars, traffic, and other situations. The more general problem of off-duty police weapons is treated by J. Fyfe, "Always Prepared: Police Off-Duty Guns," *Annals of the American Academy of Political and Social Science* 452 (1980).

28. J. Mills, *Report to the Commissioner* (New York: Simon and Schuster, 1973) offers a fictional account of a female undercover narcotics agent unintentionally killed by a detective. Even when the identity of the undercover officer is known, playacting can accidentally result in tragedy. In Michigan a state trooper working undercover was killed by local Flint police. As part of an effort to add to his credibility, they had stopped his car in a high-crime area. One of the police who stopped him with a drawn gun accidentally misfired.

29. The decoys were sometimes taken by the Mexican police to be smugglers or aliens. They sought to arrest or deter them and, in some cases, apparently to rob them. In one publicized incident, a Mexican policeman fell into the decoy's web. The officer sprang from ambush with a .45-caliber revolver pointed at the decoys, who were wearing broad-brimmed straw hats and workclothes. He tried to rob them, and a shooting incident followed.

30. See U.S. Congress, Select Committee on Crime, *Street Crime* (Washington, D.C.: GPO, 1973).

31. See, e.g., J. Van Maanen's article "The Asshole," in *Policing: A View from the Street,* ed. P. K. Manning and J. Van Maanen (Santa Monica, Calif.: Goodyear Publishing Co., 1978).

CHAPTER 9

1. The specific controls for undercover means are nestled within more general judicial, legislative, and organizational controls. No matter what the tactic, police are in principle bound by federal and state constitutions, statutes, and common law enforceable in court. The courts may also impose special standards. The violation of court requirements may result in the dismissal of criminal charges and be the subject of injunctions. Prosecutors, whether elected or appointed, may play a role in police supervision. Legislative bodies through the passage of statutes, oversight hearings, control over appropriations, and the ratification of appointments also exercise some control. Executive branch authorities, such as governors, mayors and city managers, agency heads, and police commissions (through appointments, resource allocation, and policy directives), are also a factor. Internally, control is exercised by police supervisors. Policing occurs in a bureaucratic setting with formal policies and procedures designed to serve organizational goals.

2. See, e.g., the discussions in H. Goldstein, *Policing a Free Society* (Cambridge, Mass.: Ballinger, 1977); E. Bittner, *The Functions of Police in Modern Society* (Washington, D.C.: GPO, 1971); K. C. Davis, *Police Discretion* (St. Paul, Minn.: West Publishing Co., 1975).

3. J. Elliff, *The Reform of FBI Intelligence Operations* (Princeton, N.J.: Princeton Univ. Press, 1979).

4. P. Michel, in *Oversight Hearings on FBI Undercover Guidelines*, House Subcommittee on Civil and Constitutional Rights (Washington, D.C.: GPO, 1981), serial 18, p. 82.

5. P. Heymann, in *Hearings for the FBI*, Subcommittee on Civil and Constitutional Rights (Washington, D.C.: GPO, 1980), serial 46.

6. The "sensitive circumstances" that trigger the multilevel authorization process are a catalogue of the major forms of damage that can result from covert operations. Sensitive circumstances include making untrue representations concerning innocent persons; targeting politicians, foreign governments, news media, or groups under domestic security investigation; attending a meeting in an undercover capacity between a subject under investigation and his or her lawyer; posing as an attorney, physician, clergyman, or journalist in seeking otherwise privileged information; giving sworn testimony while undercover; and engaging in most felonies or being involved in situations where there is a significant risk of violence, physical injury, or financial loss to an innocent individual. Such actions are not prohibited, but, if an operation is likely to involve any of them, it must be approved by the review committee and the director or a designated assistant director.

7. E.g., see the discussion in Davis (1975) contrasting court decisions with internal rule making.

8. The Justice Department's guidelines end with a paragraph entitled "Reservations," which states: "These guidelines on the use of undercover operations are set forth solely for the purpose of internal Department of Justice guidance. They are not intended to, do not, and may not be relied upon to create any rights, substantive or procedural, enforceable at law by any party in any matter, civil or criminal, nor do they place any limitations on otherwise lawful investigative prerogatives of the Department of Justice."

9. U.S. Congress, Judiciary Committee, Subcommittee on Civil and Constitutional Rights, *Hearings on FBI Undercover Operations* (Washington, D.C.: GPO, 1983), serial 76, pp. 636, 639.

10. *Hearings on FBI Undercover Operations*, serial 76.

11. House Subcommittee on Civil and Constitutional Rights, *FBI Undercover Operations: Report of the Subcommittee on Civil and Constitutional Rights* (Washington, D.C.: GPO, 1984). In response, see testimony of Floyd I. Clarke, "Hearings," Nov. 17, 1983, in *Oversight Hearings on FBI Undercover Activities, Authorization, and H.R. 3232*, Subcommittee on Civil and Constitutional Rights (Washington, D.C.: GPO, 1984), serial 28, and the FBI's analysis of the *Report of the House Subcommittee on Civil and Constitutional Rights on FBI Undercover Operations* (1984), unpublished memo.

12. Undercover guidelines were drafted after Abscam began. However, Justice Department officials claim that the guidelines simply formalized existing informal policies. Thus, the attorney for an Abscam defendant asked FBI agents "if there were any guidelines or supervisory rules in place that they thought they had to follow, and to a person they testified that there were no such guidelines" (Testimony of Samuel J. Buffone, April 22, 1982, *Hearings on FBI Undercover Operations*, serial 76, pp. 348–49). See also the testimony of Anthony Amo-

roso, who supervised Weinberg, that there were no guidelines at all as to what was expected of him in the undercover investigation (ibid., p. 410). An internal FBI audit found that 23 agents who were operating informants at nine field offices did not have an adequate understanding of the guidelines on the use of informants. Unfortunately, because the report has not been made public, it is not possible to know what percentage this is of agents interviewed (Comptroller General, *FBI Audit Conclusions on the Criminal Informant Program Should Have Been Qualified* [Washington, D.C.: U.S. General Accounting Office, 1980]).

13. Office of Program Evaluations and Audits, Inspection Division, "FBI Undercover Operations in Criminal Matters" in *Oversight Hearings*, serial 28, p. 487. The report does recommend refinements in training, selecting, and debriefing undercover agents. A subsequent analysis of the audit by the GAO argued that the audit's scope and methodology were limited and that the conclusions drawn were unwarranted. Because the GAO itself had only limited access to the FBI file material, it could not fully verify the information contained in the report (Report by the U.S. General Accounting Office, *Costs of FBI Undercover Operations* [Washington, D.C.: U.S. GAO, 1983]).

14. E.g., see the testimony of W. Webster, March 4, 1980, in *Hearings for the FBI*, serial 46, on April 29, 1982, in *Hearings on FBI Undercover Operations*, serial 76, and on April 6, 1983, Select Committee Hearings; P. Heymann, April 29, 1982, in *Hearings for the FBI*, serial 46, and on June 3, 1982, in *Hearings on FBI Undercover Operations*, serial 76; F. Clarke, Nov. 17, 1983, in *Oversight Hearings*, serial 28; and "Dissenting Views of Messrs. Sensenbrenner, Gekas, and DeWine" in *FBI Undercover Operations, Report of the Subcommittee* (1984).

15. E.g., see the discussion in L. Seidman, "The Supreme Court, Entrapment, and Our Criminal Justice Dilemma," *Supreme Court Review* 22 (1981).

16. In *Terry v. Ohio*, 392 U.S. 1, 14 (1968), Chief Justice Earl Warren recognized that "the rule . . . is powerless to determine invasions of constitutionally guaranteed rights where the police either have no interest in prosecuting or are willing to forego successful prosecution in the interest of securing some other goal." See also A. T. Quick, "Attitudinal Aspects of Police Compliance with Procedural Due Process," *American Journal of Criminal Law* 6 (Jan. 1978):1–25.

17. In 1973, in *United States v. Russell*, 411 U.S. 423 (1973), Justice Rehnquist wrote "we may some day be presented with a situation in which the conduct of law enforcement agents is so outrageous that due process principles would absolutely bar the government from invoking judicial processes to obtain a conviction." A nonundercover example of this is *Rochin v. California*, 342 U.S. 165 (1952). In this case, a conviction was overturned as a result of evidence obtained from pumping the defendant's stomach against his will. In concluding that the arresting officer's conduct violated the Fourteenth Amendment guaranteeing due process of law, it stated, "this is conduct that shocks the conscience." However, several years later in the Hampton case, a plurality held that neither due process principles nor the court's supervisory power would bar conviction if the government could prove predisposition (*Hampton v. U.S.*, 425 U.S. 484 [1976]).

18. E.g., an officer who solicits the purchase of drugs, in intending that the target perform a criminal act, may be committing the crime of solicitation. The potential criminal liability may also extend to supervisors, but prosecutors use their discretion to ignore such violations by police (R. Wennerhold, "Criminal Solicitation—Danger for the Unwary Undercover Investigator," *The Police Chief,* Aug. 1977). Even giving contraband away may be legally viewed as a sale.

19. J. Vorenberg, "Decent Restraint of Prosecutorial Power," *Harvard Law Review* 94, no. 7 (May 1981).

20. W. McDonald, "The Prosecutor's Domain" in *The Prosecutor,* vol. 11, Sage Criminal Justice Annals, ed. W. McDonald (Beverly Hills, Calif.: Sage, 1979). A parallel development has been the in-house police legal advisor.

21. E.g., the prosecution's role in Abscam was not without controversy. U.S. attorneys in New Jersey wrote an unusual memo detailing what they perceived as the failings of the U.S. Attorney in Brooklyn to effectively supervise and control the operation. See the testimony of R. Del Tufo, E. Plaza, and R. Weir in *Hearings on FBI Undercover Operations,* serial 76; and E. Plaza and T. Puccio in *Hearings Before the Select Committee to Study Law Enforcement Undercover Activities of Components of the Department of Justice,* U.S. Congress. Senate. 98th Cong., 1st sess., 1983.

22. Former U.S. Attorney Thomas Puccio, who played a major role in Abscam, testified that he was not aware of the FBI's guidelines for dealing with undercover operations and that such guidelines were of little consequence as far as his responsibility was concerned. His responsibility was to prosecute the cases and see that the evidence was gathered in such a way that it could be used in court (*Hearings Before the Select Committee to Study Law Enforcement,* 1983).

23. Hoover kept the system of checks and balances off balance. On the rare occasions when critical scrutiny was shown, he sought to neutralize it by veiled threats or bureaucratic end-runs involving "retroactive classification" or "no file memos." Thus, when Senator Edward Long asked Hoover to turn over records regarding some questionable FBI uses of electronic surveillance, Hoover agreed and even went beyond this, volunteering to make public transcripts of all FBI surveillances. He further indicated that the records "would be of particular interest to the distinguished senator . . . because his name was mentioned on several of them." Long hastily cancelled his request. See N. Welch and D. W. Marston, *Inside Hoover's FBI* (Garden City, N.Y.: Doubleday, 1984), p. 232.

24. Other hearings touching undercover means have been held by the Ethics, Commerce, Appropriations, and Judiciary committees. Ironically, the covert practices that Congress came to investigate emerged partly in response to its earlier pressure on the FBI to shift priorities and methods. Congress was in a delicate position with respect to Abscam. It sought to avoid the impression that its sudden interest in the dynamics and control of federal undercover operations was self-protective or vindictive. The fact that abuses and fundamental principles (not the least of which concerned the separation of powers) were at stake could easily be overlooked. Welch and Marston (1984, p. 278) report that FBI agents sensed "that the congressional probes which followed Abscam were aimed more at the investigators than at the corrupt officials under investigation, and the guidelines which resulted really amount to an implicit OFF button." However, the prosecution of public corruption cases has certainly not lessened since Abscam.

25. E.g., see the discussion in L. Dodd and R. Schott, *Congress and the Administrative State* (New York: Macmillan, 1979).

26. In contrast to the earlier Justice Department guidelines developed jointly with the Subcommittee on Civil and Constitutional Rights, guidelines dealing with undercover activities were presented to Congress only after they had been promulgated. Nor was Congress consulted, or informed, about the revision of the guidelines and some unusual interpretations given them. Without agreement as to what guidelines mean or notification that they have been changed, oversight has little meaning.

27. *FBI Undercover Operations: Report of the Subcommittee*, p. 86; Wheeler in *Hearings Before the Select Committee to Study Law Enforcement* 1983, p. 1013.

28. W. Anderson, March 16, 1983, in *Oversight Hearings*, serial 28, p. 64.

29. The Seattle ordinance provides that a non-police employee review the department's intelligence practices twice a year and file a report. The auditor is appointed by the city council for a three-year term. Persons about whom restricted information has been collected in violation of the ordinance are to be notified by certified mail and are entitled to modest compensation. There are no criminal penalties for violations of the ordinance. See the accounts of Sept. 12, 1979, in *Hearings for the FBI*, serial 46, pp. 31–151; S. Walker, "The Seattle Police Auditor and the Problem of Police Accountability," in *The Politics of Crime and Criminal Justice*, ed. E. Fairchild and V. J. Webb (Beverly Hills: Sage, 1985).

30. As Walker (1985) observes, the principle of the external auditor need not be restricted to intelligence activities. It appears to offer a meaningful mechanism for increasing police accountability. It could help move local police away from a crisis-management orientation, in which police organizations are largely defensive, responding to specific instances of alleged misconduct that have become public issues, to greater concern with the prevention of problems and a focus on the broad quality of police service. At the federal level, the inspectors general, although not outsiders to the same degree, are intended to serve this purpose.

31. Chevigny, Marx, Seidman, Stone, in *Oversight Hearings on FBI Undercover Guidelines*, serial 18; *FBI Undercover Operations, Report of the Subcommittee* (1984); J. Berman in *Hearings Before the Select Committee to Study Law Enforcement* (1983).

32. In *Keith* the Supreme Court states, "[T]hose charged with [the] investigative and prosecutorial duty should not be the sole judges of when to utilize constitutionally sensitive means in pursuing these tasks. The historical judgment, which the Fourth Amendment accepts, is that unreviewed executive discretion may yield too readily to pressures to obtain incriminating evidence and overlook potential invasions of privacy and protected speech" (*U.S. v. U.S. District Court*, 407 U.S. 297, 317 [1972]).

33. Geoffrey Stone observes that undercover intrusions may extend beyond those of wiretapping, electronic bugging, or eavesdropping: "spies and informers see as well as hear . . . the undercover operative may in the course of the investigation be 'invited' to enter the target's home or office or to examine his private papers or effects. The undercover operation, if not carefully controlled, would

thus have the anomalous effect of enabling government to invade the individual's privacy through deceit and strategem when it could not otherwise lawfully do so" (*Oversight Hearings on FBI Undercover Guidelines*, serial 18, p. 4). In addition, electronic surveillance is passive; a covert agent not only reports back what happened but can help make something happen.

34. E.g., see the American Civil Liberties Union recommendation (*Hearings Before the Select Committee to Study Law Enforcement* 1983, p. 999).

35. Limiting conditions could include when members of the executive or legislative branch are involved and when political and religious actions otherwise protected by the First, Fourth, and Fifth amendments are involved. The domestic security guidelines of the Justice Department require something close to probable cause for the use of an undercover investigation of political organizations. No comparable standard now exists in the undercover guidelines for nonpolitical investigation. Stone (1981, p. 6) suggests exempting contacts among strangers from a warrant requirement but imposing it on "trust relationships." The more intimate the relationship, the greater the intrusion on expectations of privacy. Other conditions that might require a warrant: when a fictitious, rather than a real-world, ongoing criminal setting is used; when a verbal temptation is offered (excluding those instances where the agent plays the role of passive victim); when agents sell (rather than purchase) contraband; when a third-party victim is involved; for criminal rather than civil law violations; or when a long-term, rather than a short-term, operation is involved.

36. For a sampling of opposition to the warrant, see U.S. Congress, Senate, Select Committee to Study Law Enforcement Undercover Activities of Components of the Department of Justice, *Final Report, Law Enforcement Undercover Activities*, 98th Cong., 1st sess., 1983; "Dissenting Views of Messrs. Sensenbrenner, Gekas, and DeWine" in *FBI Undercover Operations, Report of the Subcommittee* (1984).

37. May 15, 1984. U.S. Congress, Senate, *Hearings, Criminal Law Subcommittee of the Senate Judiciary Committee*, 98th Cong., 2d sess.

38. This is part of a broad debate about granting the FBI a formal charter. A major factor here is the desire to avoid reliance on "inherent authority" that contributed to abuses, such as COINTEL. See the discussion in Elliff (1979); and U.S. Congress, Senate, *Hearings on S. 1612 Before the Senate Committee on the Judiciary*, 96th Cong., 2d sess., 1980.

39. April 29, 1982. *Hearings On FBI Undercover Operations*, serial 76, p. 430. Hughes speaks from experience as both a prosecutor and a target of Abscam. The latter was based on the unsubstantiated claims of a highly unreliable middleman. He mentioned the names of a number of other innocent congressmen. Sensing that something was amiss, Hughes declined to attend the Abscam meeting. Even more troubling is the case of Congressman Pressler who, contrary to the guidelines, was not told the purpose of the Abscam meeting and, on discovering what it was, made it clear that he was not interested. Absent any valid grounds for suspicion, he was nevertheless subjected to deception, temptation, the invasion of privacy, audio and video recording of conversations, and the risk of damage to his reputation for merely being part of an investigation.

40. J. Braithwaite, B. Fisse, and G. Geis, "Covert Facilitation and Crime:

Restoring Balance to the Entrapment Debate," *Journal of Social Issues* 43, no. 3 (1987); see also the various rejoinders in this issue.

41. This poses the issue of who guards the guards in poignant form and may involve unstated understandings about solidarity and reciprocity among elites, as well as issues of sheer power. Among factors that contribute to the premature stopping of investigations of elites are fear of reprisals, the richness of the reward or favor that may be forthcoming as a result of cessation or a subtle warning, the resources targets can draw on to thwart the investigation, and concern over damaging legitimacy. Targets are likely to be well insulated and the sensitive circumstances of public corruption cases requires a stronger predicate than for nonsensitive cases. The complexity of many such investigations and the fact that they may be of lengthy duration also increase the chance of leaks or accidental discovery.

The damage from letting an investigation continue once evidence against a corrupt official has been gathered may not be balanced by the lure of getting higher-ups. For example, in a controversial action that led to the cutting short of an undercover operation, New York's Mayor Ed Koch refused to reappoint a corrupt city official as a way of continuing the investigation. Koch called the reappointment of a known corrupt official "extremely damaging to the workings of government".

42. See, e.g., the argument in *U.S. v. Russell*, 411 U.S. 423 (1973).

43. *Final Report, Law Enforcement Undercover Activities* 1983, p. 373. Some version of an objective standard has also been endorsed by most legal commentators, e.g., American Law Institute, Model Penal Code 2.13 (Official Draft 1962); U.S. National Commission on Reform of Federal Criminal Laws, "A Proposed New Federal Criminal Code 702(2)" (1971). See the discussion in R. C. Park, "The Entrapment Controversy," *Minnesota Law Review* 60, no. 13 (1976):163, 167; H. Goldstein, "For Harold Lasswell: Some Reflections on Human Dignity, Entrapment, Informed Consent, and the Plea Bargain," *Yale Law Journal* 84 (1975):683; F. Williams, "The Defense of Entrapment and Related Problems in Criminal Prosecution," *Fordham Law Review* 28 (1959):399.

44. E.g., see the recommendations in J. Berman (*Hearings Before the Select Committee to Study Law Enforcement* 1983); the testimony of publisher John Seigenthaler who argues against other proposed legislation that "would establish the disastrous precedent of allowing government agents to infiltrate and co-opt the fundamental independence of the news media" and lawyer Monroe Freedman who notes the chilling effect sham clients have had on the right to effective counsel guaranteed by the Sixth Amendment. He argues that undercover infiltration of a law office should be expressly forbidden and a special prosecutor apart from the Justice Department should be appointed to supervise covert operations directed against judges or lawyers (May 16, 1984, *Hearings, Criminal Law Subcommittee of the Senate Judiciary Committee*).

45. According to this logic, were big settlements to be granted to plaintiffs, police administrators (in order to save money) could be expected to discipline offenders and "to effect organizational changes, formulate needed rules, upgrade training, utilize in-house counsel more extensively, and select officers more carefully" (F. Gilligan, "Federal Tort Claims Act—An Alternative to the Exclusionary Rule," *Journal of Criminal Law and Criminology* 66 [March

1975]: 1–22. See also E. Littlejohn, "Civil Liability and the Police Officer: The Need for New Deterrents to Police Misconduct," *Journal of Urban Law* 58 (Spring 1981): 365–431. Of course, those committing the harm are not likely to be those directly paying for it.

46. United States. Commission on the Review of the National Policy Toward Gambling. *Gambling in America* (Washington: The Commission, 1976).

47. E. Schur, *Crimes Without Victims* (Englewood Cliffs, N.J.: Prentice Hall, 1965); A. Trebach, *The Heroin Solution* (New Haven: Yale Univ. Press, 1982); J. Kaplan, *The Hardest Drug* (Chicago: University of Chicago Press, 1985).

48. Corruption investigations are a good example. Local agencies in general cannot be as effective and decisive as can state and federal agencies. Awareness of this is implied in our emphasis on pluralism and checks and balances. Federal agents may also be in a better position to carry out such investigations because they may have greater resources, more highly trained and skilled agents, and stronger statutes. Of course, in theory this is a two-way street, although we rarely see local or state officials investigating those in the federal government. At the federal level, the role of the outsider, to the extent that it is present, is played by rival agencies.

49. Termination versus continuation can be a source of conflict in cross-jurisdictional cases. The locality (or agency) initially involved will favor termination once it has the required evidence, while others will want it to continue until they have met their goals. As more and more joint investigations are carried out, this problem will increase.

50. The investigation need not end, only its covert phase. The initial information may be used by an investigative grand jury and by agents interviewing suspects and witnesses and following paper trails. Of course even with arrest, if the suspect agrees to cooperate, news of the operation may not become public.

CHAPTER 10

1. E.g., a 13-year-old girl in Tustin, California, turned in her parents for possession of marijuana and cocaine. They were arrested, and she was placed (against her wishes) in a foster home. This well-publicized incident was followed by many other cases—the youngest, a 6-year-old in New Jersey. See G. Marx, "Yes Sir, That's My Daddy: When Children Turn in Parents," *Student Lawyer* 15, no. 6 (1986): 8–10.

2. This is the case for absolute numbers, as well as the kinds of information included. In 1981 there were 1.8 million records in the interstate identification index system (arrest data supplied by the state); in 1985, there were 9.5 million. In 1987 a federal advisory committee endorsed a major expansion that would permit federal, state, and local law enforcement agencies to exchange information on "suspicious persons" who had not been formally charged or tried. A proposal to link the National Crime Information Center with private sector data files was, however, rejected (this time).

3. D. Burnham, *The Rise of the Computer State* (New York: Random House, 1983) offers a useful discussion of this and related themes.

4. K. Laudon, *Dossier Society: Value Choices in the Design of National*

Information Systems (New York: Columbia Univ. Press, 1986) develops this concept.

5. For a discussion of computer matching, see G. Marx and N. Reichman, "Routinizing the Discovery of Secrets: Computers as Informants," *American Behavioral Scientist* 2 (March 1984); N. Reichman and G. Marx, "Generating Organizational Disputes: The Impact of Computerization." Paper presented at meetings of Law and Society Association, San Diego, 1985; J. Shattuck, "In the Shadow of 1984: National Identification Systems, Computer-Matching, and Privacy in the United States," *Hastings Law Journal,* July 1984:991–1005; *Computer Matching: Assessing Its Costs and Benefits* (Washington, D.C.: Government Accounting Office, Nov. 1986).

6. In Sweden, which is often cited as the prototype for such matters, children are given a number at birth that can never be changed. The average adult is in more than 100 data bases.

7. This is discussed in Office of Technology Assessment, *Federal Government Information Technology: Electronic Surveillance and Civil Liberties* (Washington, D.C.: GPO, 1985). The Electronic Communications Privacy Act of 1986 extends legal protection to these forms of communication, but enforcement is another matter.

8. See, e.g., H. Shaiken, *Work Transformed* (New York: Holt, Rinehart & Winston, 1984); R. Howard, *Brave New Workplace* (New York: Viking, 1985); G. Marx and S. Sherizen, "How to Protect Property Without Destroying Privacy," *Technology Review,* Nov./Dec. 1986; and U.S. Congress, Office of Technology Assessment, *The Electronic Supervisor: New Technology, New Tensions* (Washington, D.C.: GPO, 1987).

9. One such program entitled "Subliminal Suggestions and Self-Hypnosis" permits management to send any kind of message—"Relax," "Concentrate," or "Work faster"—unbeknownst to the worker. The messages pass so quickly in front of the watchers' eyes they cannot be consciously detected. See Nine to Five, "Computer Monitoring and Other Dirty Tricks" (Cleveland, 1986, photocopy). Most office computers do not yet receive information at the speeds such programs require. Messages that can be read, such as, "You are not working as fast as the person sitting next to you," also can be sent. A different use is found in some department stores, where messages such as "Honesty pays" are mixed in with music.

10. In a related development, a person whose phone rings now may see a digital display indicating where the call comes from before the phone is picked up. According to some observers, video-telephone communication is likely to be widespread in private homes by the year 2000.

11. J. Bramford, *The Puzzle Palace* (New York: Penguin, 1983).

12. See R. Ball, R. Huff, and R. Lilly, *House Arrest and Correctional Policy: Doing Time at Home* (Beverly Hills, Calif.: Sage, forthcoming); R. Corbett, Jr., and G. Marx, "When a Man's Castle Is His Prison: The Perils of Home Confinement," Paper delivered at annual meeting of American Society of Criminology, Montreal, 1987; and articles in *Intermediate Punishments: Intensive Supervision, Home Confinement and Electronic Surveillance,* ed. B. R. McCarthy (Monsey, N.Y.: Criminal Justice Press, 1987). A key question is whether it will be used for persons who would otherwise have been sent to prison or be ex-

tended to a new class of minor offenders. The expansive experience with other reforms, e.g., deinstitutionalization and diversion, put forth as ways of reducing demands on the criminal justice system suggests it will be the latter.

13. G. Stephens and W. Tafoya, "Crime and Justice: Taking a Futuristic Approach," *The Futurist,* February 1985. The device has obvious health uses, e.g., for victims of Alzheimer's disease. It also can be used to keep persons away from certain persons or locations. Thus, a former spouse under an injunction to stay away from his former wife could wear a device (as could the wife). If the man came to within a given distance of her, an alarm could be triggered, and a message sent to the judge. One can also imagine various chastity devices.

14. G. Hart, "Computerized Surveillance via Utility Power Flows," unpublished paper, MIT, 1985.

15. The radio immunoassay method extracts drug residue from the hair. Like rings in a tree, the distance from the root also gives temporal evidence. As one eager advocate put it, the "beauty of the technique is that it can't be diluted or switched, there are many samples, and it does not demean the suspect, unlike urine testing." The Yul Brynner look may become very fashionable.

16. One firm offers an "ultra-miniaturized" hand-held system that "in business or personal meetings" helps "determine if your employees are stealing . . . if your associates are cheating . . . if your friends really are your friends." The person need not know that they are being tested and "even your telephone conversations can be analyzed for truth."

17. F. Donchin, *Psychophysiological Monitoring: Possibilities and Prospects,* report prepared for the Office of Technology Assessment, Washington, D.C., Sept. 1986.

18. Previously, it was only possible to exclude a suspect by showing that blood types did not match; now with DNA analysis there is positive identification. More effective means of identification may reduce the chance of erroneous convictions and increase convictions of the guilty, but it may also lead to broad population screens.

The use of genetic markers as criteria in hiring is likely to be much more controversial (e.g., excluding persons from certain jobs because DNA analysis suggests a greater likelihood of developing a particular illness).

19. See the discussion in G. Goodwin and L. Humphreys, "Freeze-Dried Stigma: Cybernetics and Social Control," *Humanity and Society* 6 (Nov. 1982).

20. It is fired like a pellet at a window, where it sticks like a squashed fly, picking up sound in the room (*Observer,* Feb. 2, 1986). Another form is embedded in a tiny blob of epoxy that may be hidden in a book binding or stuck under a chair.

21. M. Foucault, *Discipline and Punish* (New York: Pantheon, 1977).

22. S. Cohen, *Visions of Social Control* (Cambridge: Policy Press, 1985). The new surveillance illustrates Foucault's (1977) principle of "indefinite discipline" (p. 357), where "never-ending judgments, examinations and observation" emerge as a new mode of control.

23. For a discussion of parallel developments in Norway, see T. Mathiesen, "The Future of Control Systems" in *The Power to Punish,* ed. D. Garland and P. Young (Atlantic Highlands, N.J.: Humanities Press, 1983). J. P. Brodeur, "High Policing and Low Policing: Remarks About the Policing of Political Ac-

tivities," *Social Problems* 30, no. 5 (1983) notes a parallel to the historical French tradition of "high" policing. See also Cohen (1985) for a discussion of master patterns of social control.

24. E.g., an IBM spokesman reports on a policy of testing job applicants for drugs: "It's any applicant's decision to make—they're not forced to take the test . . . but it is required if an applicant wishes to be considered for employment." When testing is widespread, in an economy where jobs are difficult to find, this is disingenuous. Secretary of State George P. Shultz, who threatened to resign if required to take a polygraph, has career mobility not available to most people. When Exxon subjected 1,000 white-collar workers in Houston to a surprise search by drug-sniffing dogs, employees were expected to sign waivers the day of the search. If they refused to sign, they faced the possibility of discipline.

25. For a nice illustration applied to Disneyworld, see C. Shearing and P. Stenning, "From the Panopticon to Disney World: The Development of Discipline," *Perspectives in Criminal Law*, 1984.

26. E. Goffman, *Asylums: Essays on the Social Situation of Mental Patients and Other Inmates* (New York: Doubleday, 1964). A related image is the monitoring associated with a hospital intensive care unit.

27. R. Ericson and C. Shearing, "The Scientification of Police Work," in G. Bohme and N. Stehr, *The Impact of Scientific Knowledge on Social Structure, Sociology of Science Yearbook,* vol. 10 (Dordrecht: Reidel, 1984).

28. A. H. Smyth, *The Writings of Benjamin Franklin,* 10 vols. (New York, 1905).

29. See the discussions in R. Sennett, *The Uses of Disorder* (New York: Knopf, 1970); J. Rule, "1984—The Ingredients of Totalitarianism" in *1984: Totalitarianism in Our Century,* ed. I. Howe (New York: Harper and Row, 1984).

30. See the discussion in B. Barber, *The Logic and Limits of Trust* (New Brunswick: Rutgers University Press, 1983). Three centuries before the birth of Christ, Demosthenes wrote, "There is one safeguard known generally to the wise, which is an advantage and security to all, but especially to democracies as against despots." "What is it?" "Distrust."

31. In a useful discussion, J. Gross, "Social Control under Totalitarianism" in *Toward a General Theory of Social Control,* vol. 2, ed. D. Black (New York: Academic Press, 1984) stresses informing as the principal mechanism by which totalitarian states penetrate the private domain: "The real power of a totalitarian state results . . . from its being at the disposal, available for hire at a moment's notice, to every inhabitant." Informing in such societies differs (in degree) from democratic societies in that the focus is more on political beliefs and loyalty; anonymous informing is strongly encouraged; there are few procedural safeguards; and one's first obligation is to the state rather than to family or friends.

32. Lie detectors (polygraphs) are most effective when persons being tested believe that they work and thus tell the truth. This gives rise to a variety of ruses. In what operators call a "stim," a trick sometimes used before an interrogation begins is to show the subject a monitor with a dial. The subject is then asked to

tell a lie and sees the dial go up, supposedly indicating that the lie has been detected. What the subject doesn't know is that the operator causes the dial to
move, independent of what the subject has said. With the subject appropriately
impressed, the examination begins. Another device is to ask the subject to pick a
card from a marked deck or a deck where all the cards are the same. After a
series of questions, the examiner then identifies the card.

33. Some persons eligible for benefits may be hurt as well. Thus, many persons withdrew from a food stamp program after publicity about a computer-
matching program. Whether all those who withdrew were in fact ineligible and
others who were eligible did not apply are important questions. The perception
that benefits are difficult to receive and that persons are constantly being checked
may mean the underuse of welfare programs. With their focus on fraud or abuse
(rather than equity or justice), government computer-matching programs have
rarely looked to see if persons are *not* receiving benefits they are entitled to.

34. G. Marx, "The Interdependence of Private and Public Police as Illustrated by Undercover Investigations," *Crime and Justice System Annuals* 21
(1987).

35. On the discovery of violations, see D. Michael, "Too Much of a Good
Thing? Dilemmas of an Information Society," *Technological Forecasting and
Social Change* 25, no. 4 (July 1984). W. Moore and M. Tumin, "Some Social
Functions of Ignorance," *American Sociological Review* 14 (1949):787–95,
offer a more general consideration of the functions of ignorance.

36. Laudon (1986).

37. The bad news here is not that the tactic is far from perfect (after all what
would it be like to live in a society where it was always possible to tell what a
person was thinking or when he was telling the truth?). Rather the problem is
misplaced confidence in its results. On the polygraph's limitations, see, e.g.,
D. Lykken, "Detecting Deception in 1984," *American Behavioral Scientist* 2
(March/April 1984); L. Saxe, D. Dougherty, and T. Cross, "The Validity of
Polygraph Testing," *American Psychologist* 40 (March 1985):355–66.

38. See the discussion in J. Rule, D. McAdam, L. Stearns, and D. Uglow,
The Politics of Privacy (New York: New American Library, 1980).

39. As cited in A. Mason, *Harlan Fiske Stone: Pillar of the Law* (New York:
Viking, 1956), p. 153. Similarly in a 1976 letter Justice William O. Douglas
wrote, "As nightfall does not come at once, neither does oppression. In both
instances, there is a twilight when everything remains seemingly unchanged,
and it is in such twilight that we all must be most aware of change in the air—
however slight—lest we become unwitting victims of darkness." M. Vrofsky,
ed., *The Douglas Letters* (Bethesda, Md.: Adler and Adler, 1987).

40. Recall Justice Brandeis's warning that "experience should teach us to be
most on our guard when the government's purposes are beneficent. Men born to
freedom are naturally alert to repel invasion of their liberty by evil-minded
rulers. The greatest dangers to liberty lurk in insidious encroachment by men of
zeal, well-meaning, but without understanding" (*Olmstead v. U.S.*, 277 U.S.
438 [1928]).

41. This conclusion is based on other work that reviews a large amount of
empirical data that compare American society to the society Orwell described

(G. Marx, *Fragmentation and Cohesion in American Society* [Washington, D.C.: Trend Analysis Program, American Council on Life Insurance, 1983]; Marx, "The Iron Fist and the Velvet Glove," in *The Social Fabric: Dimensions and Issues,* ed. J. F. Short, Jr. (Beverly Hills: Sage, 1986). In Orwell's Oceania: (1) the state is all powerful and the citizen has no rights nor input into government; (2) there is no law; (3) mass communication is rigidly controlled by, and restricted to, the state; (4) there are no groups, lodges, clubs, associations, or organizations apart from those directly sponsored and controlled by the state; (5) the society is hierarchically organized, but beyond this there is little differentiation, diversity, or variety—everything possible is standardized and regimented; (6) the political and economic systems are merged; (7) there is little social mobility and a low and declining standard of living where all surplus goes into war preparations rather than consumption; (8) individuals are isolated from and do not trust each other; (9) private communication is discouraged, and writing instruments such as the pen are prohibited; (10) learning a foreign language and contact with foreigners are prohibited; (11) individuals are increasingly bored, indifferent, and intolerant, and memory of past liberties fades with each year; (12) proper attitudes and feelings are as important as proper behavior or more so.

42. These are found along with increased concern over capital punishment, police use of force, corporal punishment in schools, and family and sexual violence.

43. As Rule (1984) observes, both mass communications and mass surveillance are part of a broader mobilization of the population, wherein the direct ties between central institutions and citizens are intensified. In contrast to the trend of the last century, information about elites now can flow more freely from the center of society to the periphery as well as the reverse. See also E. Shils's important early statement, *Center and Periphery: Essays in Macro-Sociology* (Chicago: Univ. of Chicago Press, 1975).

44. See, e.g., R. Fox and T. Lears, *The Culture of Consumption* (New York: Pantheon, 1983); and M. Schudson, *Advertising, The Uneasy Persuasion* (New York: Basic Books, 1984).

45. R. Nisbet (*Twilight of Authority* [New York: Oxford Univ. Press, 1975]) writes of the "softening of power."

46. In a different context, Al Capone correctly observed that you can accomplish more with a kind word and a gun than with a gun alone.

47. Of course, these may be linked with what is first developed for military and intelligence uses later being applied domestically. Public and private police may also be intertwined. Five major forms of interdependence are (1) joint public/private investigations, (2) public agents hiring or delegating authority to private police, (3) private interests hiring public police, (4) new organizational forms in which the distinction between public and private is blurred, and (5) the circulation of personnel between the public and private sectors.

48. James Madison's advice in *The Federalist* (Paper 51) should be updated to read, "You must first enable the government to control the governed [and large organizations] and in the next place, oblige it to control itself."

Index

Abscam (Abdul scam), 9–10, 57, 72, 83, 242 n.34, 245 n.32, 263 n.24; evaluation of, 58, 104, 155, 186, 191, 251 n.17; problems with, 131–32, 144, 153, 154, 157, 261 n.12, 263 nn. 21, 22, 265 n.39
Accountability: of informers, 154, 158; of police, xviii, 57, 68, 95–96, 159, 181, 184, 193
Adversary system, 26, 95
Advertisements, 70, 72, 80, 220
Agents provocateurs, 29, 31, 60, 64, 74
Alaska, 130
Alcoholism: of police, 166
Alcohol violations, 30, 63, 73
Anslinger, Harry J., 97
Anticipatory investigations, 23, 39, 45, 46, 61, 62–63, 204, 205, 218, 227–28, 230
Anticrime decoys. See Decoys (police)
Anticrime programs, 179, 207. See also Hotlines; Property Crime Program
Antifencing operations. See Fencing stings
Antilabor activities, xix, 25, 29, 135
Arrest, 43, 47, 48, 57, 75, 118, 123, 176, 178–79, 199, 209; as goal, 24, 25, 64, 66 (see also Prosecution); patterns, 14, 52, 112, 115–16, 120; rate, 44, 124–25
Arson, 61, 64, 83
Aryan Nations' contract murder case, 56
Assassinations, 37, 64, 153
Atlanta (Ga.), 168

"Attempt" laws, 51–52
Attitudes, 36, 39, 199, 207, 235 n.1. See also Public opinion
Attorney-client relationship, 149–50, 176
Attorney General, 43, 186, 187, 190. See also U.S. Department of Justice
Attorney General's Committee on White Collar Crime, 39
Audio surveillance, 58, 131, 212–13, 217
Authorization: for covert operations, 7, 193–95, 261 n.6
Autonomy of actions, 78–81, 105, 130, 205

Bait sales stings, 7–8, 52
Baldwin, Arthur, 149
Baltimore (Md.), 61–62
BATF. See U.S. Bureau of Alcohol, Tobacco, and Firearms
Bauman, Robert, 138
Behavior, 81, 87, 121–22, 209, 226; of informers, 153, 154; of legislators, 53, 58, 137; of police, xviii, xxv, 46–48, 58, 74–78, 140, 188, 189, 197, 204; of suspects, 48–49, 74, 84, 128, 133, 137; of undercover agents, 50, 71, 84, 135, 149. See also Abscam (Abdul scam); Intent of actions; Targets, self-selection of
Bentham, Jeremy, 220
Birmingham (N.Y.): operations in, 115–16, 123

Black Panthers (organization), 64
"Blood money," 19
Bok, Sissela, 106
Bolton, Charles (Black Bart), 27
Bonaparte, Charles, 31
Boston (Mass.): operations in, 70, 120, 248 n.19; police, 23, 168, 177, 178, 207
Bowers, R., 109, 112
Bradley, Tom, 139
Braitwaite, J., 39
Brandeis, Louis Dembitz, 54, 99, 206, 222, 271 n.40
Bray, Marvin, 134–35, 155–56
Brennan, William, 246 n.8
Bribery, 10, 71, 77, 174–75; legal aspects, 52, 53, 54, 139, 265 n.12; of public officials, 53, 71, 135, 137, 155–56, 236 n.13
Budgets, 4, 5, 14, 23. See also Funding; Revenues
Burden of proof, 53–54, 227
Bureaucracy, 25, 35, 37, 40, 45–46, 163, 181, 186, 201. See also Record-keeping; Supervision
Burger, Warren, 48
Burglary, 7, 82, 121, 143. See also Robbery
Burke, Edmund, 149, 200
Burns (agency), 27, 29
Buy-bust operations, 22, 114, 120

Caldwell, Oscar, 29
California: operations in, 6, 52, 80, 83, 127, 149; police, 143, 164, 169, 170, 199. See also Los Angeles (Calif.); San Diego (Calif.)
Capone, Al, 272 n.46
Carter administration, 138, 181
Casey, William, 7
Central Intelligence Agency (CIA), xviii, 7, 42, 43, 95, 172; undercover operations, 245 n.32, 251 n.17, 256 n.22
Centralization of police. See Federal police
Chevigny, Paul, 101, 154
Chicago (Ill.): operations in, 152, 173; police, 64, 139, 165
Chicago Tribune, 23
Church, Frank, xviii, 95, 140
CIA. See Central Intelligence Agency
Civil disorders, 37, 211. See also Protest movements
Civiletti, Benjamin, 185
Civil offenses, 39, 79, 86, 236 n.7
Civil rights, xix, 47, 62, 63, 69–70, 100–102, 166, 193, 194, 220

Civil rights movement, xix, 39; undercover agents in, xvii, 30, 32, 64, 90
Cleveland (Ohio): operations in, 135, 155–56, 187; police, 13, 237 n.16
Cobb, R. C., 88
Coercion, 76, 153, 232, 233, 256 n.13, 263 n.23; by police, xix, 93, 130, 139, 176, 189
COINTEL, 32, 149
Collateral harm, 99, 106, 128, 141, 227
Colorado: operations in, 6, 143
Colqhoun, Patrick, 20
Common law, 100
Communist activities: investigation of, 31–32, 148
Community-police relations, 24, 37
Complainants, 26, 37, 38, 58, 68, 69, 78, 148–49, 205, 207. See also Hotlines; Informers
Comprehensive Crime Control Act, 43
Compromises (system), 24–26
Computers: as informers, 208–11, 217, 218–19, 223–25, 228
Confession, 47, 93
Con games, 94, 146
Connecticut, 94, 207; operations in, 44, 61, 174–75; police, 164
Consensual crimes, 7, 23, 38, 66, 72, 92, 125, 249 n.31
Conspiracy, 49, 51, 83, 92, 150, 152, 154, 246 n.35
Contraband operations, 51, 72, 78, 92, 126, 133–34, 146, 156. See also Narcotics crimes; Poaching
Controls on police, 26, 95–96, 182, 184–88. See also Law, relationship to police; Police, restrictions on
Controls on undercover agents, 193, 201–5; external, 181, 188–93, 195–98, 200; internal, 181–88, 193–95, 200, 203
Cooperation: by citizens, 37, 145–46, 220, 245 n.26; by informers, 155, 245 n.26; by suspects, 8, 10–11, 86–87, 239. See also Complainants; Crime control, and citizens; Informers
CORE (Congress of Racial Equality), xvii
Correctional institutions, 63
Corruption, 11, 30, 33, 46, 54, 142, 228; of judges, 131, 134–35, 152, 155–56, 187; operations against, 28–29, 42, 45, 53, 61–62, 85, 174–75, 199, 267 n.48; of police, 18–19, 24, 25, 242 n.40; of targets, 70–71, 99, 130–32; of undercover agents, 134,

135, 157–58, 161–66. *See also* Political corruption
Cost-benefit analysis, 89, 107, 112, 118, 123, 127, 183
Counter-provocateurs, 64
Covert operations. *See* Undercover operations
Credibility, 58, 59, 165, 166, 173. *See also* Informers, credibility; Witnesses, credibility
Crime control, 3, 32, 126–27, 249 n.2; and citizens, 1, 19–20, 33, 37, 133, 180, 199, 230
Crime dramas, 11, 34, 94, 136, 164, 249 n.1, 258 n.11
Crime patterns, 36, 37–40, 94. *See also* Arrest, patterns
Crime prevention, 9, 21–22, 39, 45, 66, 81, 82, 133, 198–99, 250 n.6; by undercover operations, xix, 63–65, 66–67, 79, 87–88, 92, 105, 109, 118, 122, 124, 129. *See also* Anticipatory investigations
Crime reduction, xix, 45, 112, 114, 116, 119, 123–24
Criminal Division. *See* U.S. Department of Justice, Criminal Division
Criminal investigation, 25, 47, 267 n.50
Criminal justice system, 33, 35, 37, 46, 83–84, 95. *See also* Arrest; Prosecution
Criminal offenses, 39, 51, 53–54, 121, 123, 126–27, 199. *See also specific offenses, e.g.,* White-collar crime
Criminal procedure, 141, 195, 204. *See also* Judicial process
Criminals, 19–20, 37; acting as police, xix, 18, 24, 26–27, 146; relationship with police, 24, 25–26, 74–85, 97–98, 122–23, 159, 160, 164, 239 n.5. *See also* Habitual offenders; Informers; Organized crime; Professionalism, of criminals
Crowds: and police, xviii, 175–76
Culpability: evidence of, 48–49

Daley, Richard, 139
Damage, 144–46, 198, 204, 261 n.6, 266 n.41; to reputations, 99, 140–42, 189, 196, 255 n.3. *See also* Harm; Liability
DEA. *See* U.S. Drug Enforcement Agency
Dean, John, 138
Deceptive tactics, xx, 34, 61–63, 111, 130–32, 153–54; ethics of, 91–102, 106, 136, 161, 163; implications of, 81, 102–4, 225–26

Decoys (police), 7, 41, 85, 94, 133, 161, 163, 178; examples, 65, 69–70, 78, 79, 122, 177, 203; evaluation of, 72, 103, 108, 109, 115–16, 118, 120, 124–25, 179
Deep cover operations, 85–86, 164, 169–72, 205
DeLorean, John, 10, 77, 130, 135, 186
Democracy, 225, 231
Detectives: police, 22, 23–25, 46; private, 242 n.40
Deterrence. *See* Crime prevention
Detroit (Mich.), 179; operations in, 112, 114, 124, 168, 176; police, 139, 176
Dillinger, John, 31
DiMaio, Frank, 29
Discrimination. *See* Law enforcement, equality in; Race discrimination; Sex discrimination
Doctorow, E. L., 180
Douglas, William O., 271 n.39
Doyle, Sir Arthur Conan, 118
Drug crimes. *See* Narcotics crimes
Drug testing, 216, 227, 228, 270 n.24
Drug use, 37; by police, 165, 166
Drunk drivers, 63, 82
Due process, 75, 189–90, 197, 229, 249 n.2
Durkheim, Emile, 255 n.27

Edwards, Don, 39
Egger, Roscoe, 236 n.10
Eighteenth Amendment, 30
Electronic Communications Privacy Act, 268 n.7
Electronic surveillance, 37, 54–57, 59, 73, 102, 162, 214–15, 218; as evidence, 47, 53, 57–58, 76, 95, 112, 141, 150; falsification of, 56, 134–38; problems in use of, 99, 141, 152, 174–75, 202; warrants for use, 49, 54–55, 63, 85, 194. *See also* Wiretapping
Elliff, John, 182
Employees, 44, 87–88, 220, 252 n.25; surveillance of, 29, 212–14, 225, 227, 246 n.3. *See also* Testing, of employees
Endangered Species and Migratory Bird Treaty Acts, 51
England. *See* Great Britain
Entrapment, 15, 30, 33, 48, 62, 135, 154, 198, 200; risk of, 57, 71, 72, 76, 78, 102, 115, 188–90, 197
Environment: of operations, 64, 73–78, 106, 119, 127–28, 182, 202, 205
Environmental violations, 38, 39, 87

Equal protection doctrine, 190. *See also* Law enforcement, equality in
Ericson, R., 221
Ervin, Sam, 210
Espionage, 20, 21, 40, 54, 63, 87, 88, 92. *See also* Industrial espionage
Ethics of tactics, 41, 89–90, 104–7, 185, 197, 201, 202, 227, 233. *See also* Deceptive tactics, ethics of
Ethnic groups: and undercover agents, 25, 29, 42, 110
Europe, 27, 47, 190, 195
European model, 33
"Every Breath You Take" (song), 3
Evidence, 48–49, 50, 84, 86; falsification of, 126, 132–38, 153–54, 166; restrictions on, 47, 53, 199–200. *See also* Electronic surveillance, as evidence; Testimony
Exclusionary rule, 47, 189, 236n.15
Executive Order 12333 (1981), 235n.6
Export law violations. *See* Trade law violations
Extortion, 52, 74

FAA. *See* Federal Aviation Administration
Facilitative operations, 65–67, 77–78, 79, 80–82, 133
False accusation, 133. *See also* Perjury
Family relationships: of undercover agents, 165, 166–67, 169, 170–71
FBI. *See* Federal Bureau of Investigation
FBI–IBM operation. *See* Silicon Valley operation
Fear: of crime, 1, 33; of police, 33
Federal Aviation Administration (FAA), 87
Federal Bureau of Investigation (FBI), xxi, 4–5, 14, 30–32, 39–40, 196, 206, 257n.32; agents, 30, 136–37, 159, 169–70, 171–72, 176, 237n.18, 259nn. 23, 24; Criminal Undercover Operations Review Committee, 183, 186, 190; guidelines, 86, 151, 181, 182–83, 185–86, 187–88, 246n.6, 264n.26, 265n.35; public opinion of, 33, 159, 243n.11; undercover operations, 41–42, 50, 61–62, 65, 73, 130, 134–35, 144–45, 156–58, 174–75, 177–78. *See also specific operations, e.g.,* Operation Corkscrew
Federal Communications Act, 54
Federal Communications Commission (FCC), 72

Federal Law Enforcement Training Center, 42, 43
Federal police, 13, 34–35, 86; formation of, 18, 20–21, 27, 29–32. *See also specific agencies, e.g.,* U.S. Post Office
Federal Tort Claims Act, 197–98
Federal Wiretap Act, 194
Federal Witness Protection Program, 42, 95, 147, 158, 198, 207
Fences, 41, 42, 51–52, 53, 75, 110–11, 118, 119–200
Fencing stings, 7–8, 44, 69, 78, 82, 108, 154–55; evaluation of, 41–42, 72, 109–15, 118, 123–25; history, 19, 24; problems with, 57, 74, 75, 77, 119, 143, 177, 202. *See also* Buy-bust operations; Sell-bust operations
Fielding, Henry, 20
Fifth Amendment, 30, 49
Financial crimes, 5, 34, 61–62, 73. *See also* Fraud
First Amendment, 100, 141, 151
Florida, 87; operations in, 5–6, 44, 62, 108, 131, 173–74, 176, 251n.23. *See also* Jacksonville (Fla.); Miami (Fla.)
Foucault, Michel, 218
Fourteenth Amendment, 262n.17. *See also* Due process
Fourth Amendment, 30, 48, 49, 94, 194, 224, 227, 249n.3, 264n.32
"Framed" (song), 132
Framing: of targets, 132–33
France, 17–19, 21, 176–77
Frankfurter, Felix, 97, 242n.37
Franklin, Benjamin, 222
Fraud, 14, 34, 43, 51, 73, 79, 87
Freedman, Monroe, 266n.44
Freedom of Information Act (FOIA), 50
Fugitive Investigative Strike Team (FIST), 5–6, 42–43
Fugitives: operations against, 5–6, 62
Funding: of undercover operations, 2, 14, 40–41, 110, 111, 114, 183. *See also* Budgets; Revenues

Gallagher, Mary, 136
Gambling, 14, 74, 108, 199, 251n.23
GAO. *See* U.S. General Accounting Office
Gates, Daryl, 148
Geis, G., 39
Geographical mobility, 18, 38
Goals, 200–201, 222; of police, 8–10, 25, 133; of undercover operations, 60, 63, 66–67, 74, 86, 87, 109, 139, 205

Goffman, Erving, 221, 251 n.19
Goodman, Paul, 232
Great Britain, 19–22, 257 n.27
Greensboro (N.C.), 150
Guilt, 78, 93, 137, 255 nn. 3, 5; presumption of, 10, 101, 119, 125–26, 140–41, 227
Guilty knowledge, 48–49
Guilty pleas, 49, 112, 114, 118, 244 n.22, 253 n.5
Gun Control Act, 51

Habitual offenders, 71, 112, 115–16, 119, 124–25, 253 n.9
Hampton v. U.S., 65, 262 n.17
Harm, 93–94, 183, 198, 229; prevention of, 25, 63, 64, 82–83, 86, 92, 205. *See also* Collateral harm; Damage; Indirect harm; Victimization
Harrison Act, 30
Hawaii, 210
Hawk Chalk (journal), 97
Henderson, Sir Edward, 22
Hitchen, Charles, 19
Hobbs Act, 52–53
Hoffa case, 48, 249 n.3
Homicide, 61, 69, 72, 83, 110, 146
Homosexuals: operations against, 98, 168, 173
Hoover, J. Edgar, 4, 5, 31, 33, 63, 139, 159, 191, 235 n.1
Hoover Commission, 222
Horn, Tom, 27
Hotlines, 200, 207, 217, 218
Howard, Norman, 144
Hughes, William J., 196

Identification, 216; of criminals, 75, 118, 120–23, 269 n.18
Illegal tactics, 75, 89, 101, 246 n.6. *See also* Deceptive tactics; Entrapment; Evidence, falsification of
Impersonation, 261 n.6; of judges, 156; of police, 146, 176; of reporters, 62, 151
Indirect harm, 145–47
Individual and state, 2, 4, 206
Individual rights. *See* Civil rights
Industrial espionage, 6, 8, 9, 226
Industrialization, 17, 20, 34, 35
Infiltration: by undercover agents, 1, 7, 25, 27, 64, 142, 177–78
Information access, 116, 186, 192–93, 199, 208–11, 222–25, 231
Information gathering, 37, 67–68, 129, 206–7, 217–19, 226; as goal, 9, 11,

34–35, 45, 67, 201. *See also* Surveillance
Informer-controller relationship, 138, 153–54, 156–58, 203, 262 n.12
Informers, 37, 62, 64, 69, 85, 112, 141, 180, 207–11, 249 n.3; credibility, 20, 87; crimes by, 144–45, 155, 157–58; history, 18, 19; problems with, 19–20, 130, 152–58, 174, 195, 202–3, 225; in undercover operations, 80, 93, 114, 137, 149–50, 157–58, 181, 185; violence against, 127, 146–47. *See also* Paid informers; Unwitting informers
Innocence. *See* Collateral harm; Guilt; Targets, innocence of
Inspector General offices, 42, 43
Insurance Crime Prevention Institute (ICPI), 44
Insurance industry, 44–45, 111, 144, 145
INS. *See* U.S. Immigration and Naturalization Service
Integrity testing, 28, 54, 70–71, 77, 139, 146, 196, 201, 203, 205
Intelligence operations, 20, 32, 61–63, 66, 70, 75, 87, 182
Intent of actions, 51–52, 78–81, 82, 83, 130, 133, 136–37, 157, 168, 188–89, 197
Interagency cooperation, 6, 40, 42–43, 53, 109–11, 202; lack of, 119, 127, 172–77
International cooperation, 15, 177
Interrogation: of suspects, 47, 96, 102, 199
Interstate commerce, 52–53
Intimate relationships: in undercover operations, 49–50, 61, 99–100, 131, 147–48, 167–68
IRS. *See* U.S. Internal Revenue Service
Isolation: of undercover agents, 86, 161, 165

Jacksonville (Fla.), 111, 112
Jefferson, Thomas, 92
Jewish Defense League, 138
Judges, 46, 85, 195. *See also* Corruption, of judges
Judicial decisions, 30, 47–50, 52, 103, 149, 195. *See also* Supreme Court, decisions
Judicial process, 86–87, 168, 189, 205
Judicial review, 165–66, 200, 262 n.17
Juries, 58, 77, 136
Juvenile criminals, 75, 202

Kansas: operations in, 112, 124
Keith case, 264 n.32
Kerner Commission. *See* National Advisory Commission on Civil Disorders
Klockars, C., 126
Koch, Ed, 266 n.41
Koreagate, 245 n.32, 251 n.17
Ku Klux Klan, 32, 149

Laudon, Ken, 223
Law, 50–54, 63, 100, 129, 132, 188; relationship to police, 27, 33, 35, 46–50, 75–78, 89, 105, 193, 196–98, 200–202. *See also* Local laws; State laws; *and specific laws, e.g.,* Federal Communications Act
Law enforcement, xx, 2, 20, 23, 27, 63, 200; discretion in, 81–82, 182, 183, 194–95; equality in, 92, 101, 106, 152, 182, 190, 196, 201, 228, 229; priorities, 25, 34–35, 36, 37–40, 46, 98; supports for, 40–46
Law Enforcement Assistance Administration (LEAA), 40–41, 109–15, 116, 119, 124, 177
Law Enforcement Code of Ethics, 96, 97, 99
Lawrence, Paul, 134
Lawyer-client relationship. *See* Attorney-client relationship
LEAA. *See* Law Enforcement Assistance Administration
Leahy, Patrick, 191
"Legal impossibility" doctrine, 51–52
Leggett, Charles, 144–45
Legislation. *See* Law
Legislative oversight, xxi, 39–40, 43, 191–93, 195–98, 201
Lennon, John, 140
Leonhardt, Tom, 147
Leuci, Robert, 88, 159, 164
Lewis, Sinclair, 230
Liability, 183, 193, 194, 197–98, 263 n.18
Liberty, 33, 100, 200, 222, 230–31, 232–33, 271 n.40. *See also* Civil rights
Lie detectors. *See* Polygraphs
Light cover operations, 85–86, 171, 205
Lightner, John, 145
Lincoln, Abraham, 92
Linguistic analysis, 81, 136, 255 n.2
Livingston, Edward, 17
Livingston, John, 169–70
Local laws, 51, 189, 193
Local police. *See* Police
Long, Edward, 263 n.23
Los Angeles (Calif.): operations in, 62,

70, 112, 178, 236 n.7; police, 134, 139, 151, 167
"Los Tres del Barrio" case, 178
Loudd, Rommie, 131
Louisiana, 92. *See also* New Orleans (La.)
Louisville (Ky.), 166
Luskin Report, 192

Mapp case, 236 n.15
McCullough, J., 109, 112
Machiavelli, Niccolò, 233
McParland, James, 29
Mafia. *See* Organized crime
Mail crimes, 28, 30, 72, 73, 79–80
Massachusetts, 137. *See also* Boston (Mass.)
Mass media, 23, 97, 140, 231, 266 n.44. *See also* Publicity
Mathias, Charles, 196
Meltzer, Joseph, 144
Melville-Lee, W. L., 36
Memphis (Tenn.), 112, 149
Miami (Fla.): operations in, 69, 119, 169, 177; police, 259 n.24
Michigan, 260 n.28
Minorities. *See* Ethnic groups
Misinformation phenomenon. *See* Scarecrow phenomenon
Missouri, 145, 237 n.16
Mistaken identity, 93, 147, 172–79
Mitrione, Dan, 157
Model Penal Code, 51
Molly Maguires (organization), 29
Mondale, Walter, xxii
Moore, Sara Jane, 153
Moral aspects. *See* Ethics of tactics
Morale, 129; of police, 112, 116, 123, 167, 170, 203
Muir, William, 161
Murder. *See* Homicide

Narcotics crime operations, 57, 151, 159, 182; ethical aspects, 80–81, 98, 100, 122, 131, 134, 141–42, 165–66; problems with, 66, 76, 156, 157, 173–74, 175, 176, 178; success of, 44, 65, 88, 131, 167
Narcotics crimes, 5, 14, 34, 51, 120, 150, 199, 207
National Advisory Commission on Civil Disorders (Kerner Commission), xviii, 6
National Auto Theft Bureau (NATB), 44–45
National Commission on Gambling, 199

National Crime Information Center, 208, 209
National police. *See* Federal police
National security, 40, 185, 193
National Security Agency (NSA), 87, 213
New Jersey, 110, 150, 151, 179
New Jersey State Police, 110, 112, 176
New Orleans (La.), 29, 110, 135
New York (city), 49, 80, 87–88, 133, 253 n.5; operations in, 6, 64, 74, 79, 89, 110, 266 n.41; police, 24–26, 69–70, 73, 116, 135, 139, 163, 173, 177, 254 n.13
New York (state), 110. *See also* Birmingham (N.Y.); New York (city)
New York City Transit Police, 203
1984 (Orwell), 228, 231
Nixon, Richard, 139, 140
Nonconsensual status, 55
NSA. *See* National Security Agency
Nursing homes, 73

Obstruction of justice, 54, 133, 174
Occupational safety violations, 39
O'Donnell, L., 108
Offenses. *See* Civil offenses; Criminal offenses
Oklahoma, 112, 199, 236 n.13
Omnibus Crime and Safe Streets Act, 40, 54, 194
Operation Airlift, 157
Operation Ampscam, 79
Operation BriLab (bribery labor), 135
Operation Corcom (corrupt commissioners), 10, 199, 236 n.13
Operation Corkscrew, 135, 155–56, 187
Operation Dipscam, 72
Operation Falcon, 97, 131
Operation FIST (Fugitive Investigative Strike Team), 5–6, 42–43
Operation Frontload, 144
Operation Greylord, 152
Operation Leprechaun, 235 n.4
Operation MiPorn (Miami pornography), 169, 176
Operation Mod-Sound, 44
Operation Re-Coupe, 145–46
Operation Snakescam, 8, 236 n.9
Opportunistic offenders, 71
Oregon, 41, 237 n.16
Organizations, 25, 38, 39, 139–40. *See also* Bureaucracy; *and specific organizations, e.g.,* Federal Bureau of Investigation
Organized crime, 5, 37, 42; operations against, 1, 43, 53, 62, 73, 74, 76, 87, 130, 135, 164, 177–78. *See also* Racketeering
Organized Crime Control Act, 42
Orwell, George, 14, 228, 230, 231, 232, 233
Oswald, Lee Harvey, 153
Overt operations, 11–12, 47, 199–200, 201

Packer, H., 249 n.2
Paid informers, 26, 48, 203
Palmer Raids, 31
Pardons, 19
Parker, William, 45, 129, 159, 256 n.14
Passive surveillance, 31, 61, 63, 79, 205
Peel, Sir Robert, 20
Penalties, 39, 82. *See also* Sentencing
Pennell, S., 119
Perjury, 20, 54, 95, 131, 133, 135
Peterson, Carl, 80–81
Phelps, Robert, 146
Philadelphia (Pa.): operations in, 63; police, 23, 24, 133
Pinkerton (agency), 27–29, 241 n.22
Pinkerton, Allan, 28, 33
Pistone, Joe, 1, 177–78
Pitt, William, 99
Plainclothes police, 23, 25, 29, 116, 176, 177, 178. *See also* Uniformed police
Plant, 31, 62, 121, 157
Plea bargaining, 112, 118, 153. *See also* Guilty pleas
Poaching, 44, 51, 207; operations against, 8, 65, 97, 131, 147
Police, 20–26; image of, xvii, 18, 23, 97, 185, 202, 203; restrictions on, 75. *See also* Controls on police; Detectives, police; Law, relationship to police; Plainclothes police; Unarmed police; Undercover agents; Uniformed police
Policewomen, 176, 259 n.16; in undercover work, 7, 52, 69–70, 78, 98, 168
Police work, 11–13, 255 n.27. *See also* Overt operations; Undercover operations
Political corruption, 5, 42, 53, 130, 137, 263 n.24, 266 n.41. *See also* Abscam (Abdul scam); Corruption, of judges
Political targeting, xvii–xix, 9, 62, 63–64, 71, 88, 138–40, 148, 149, 165, 202–3; history, 22, 25, 31–32, 100–101
Polygraphs, 220, 226, 228–29
Pornography, 30, 74, 169, 174, 176

Postliminary investigations, 61–62,
    78–79, 205
Pound, Roscoe, 242 n.37
Power, 258 n.6, 266 n.41; of police, 33,
    35, 162, 221, 230, 243 n.3; of the
    state, 3–4, 206, 219–21, 229–30,
    251 n.16
Predatory offenses, 72
President's Commission on CIA Activities
    Within the U.S. (Rockefeller Commis-
    sion), xviii
President's Commission on Law Enforce-
    ment and Administration of Justice, 6
President's Commission on Organized
    Crime, 150
Presser, Jackie, 157–58
Pressler, Larry, 141, 187, 265 n.39
Preventive policing. See Crime prevention
Privacy, 3, 63, 106, 224, 225, 233,
    257 n.27; invasion of, 12, 28, 33, 49,
    139, 147–52, 183, 194, 223, 264 n.33;
    right to, 48, 99, 121, 141
Privacy Protection Act, 198, 210
Private eye (term), 28
Private police, 10–11, 27–29, 177, 225,
    242 n.40, 246 n.3
Privileged communications, 100, 149–
    52, 197, 261 n.6. See also Imperson-
    ation
Proactive model, 68
Probable cause, 195. See also Undercover
    operations, justification for
Professionalism: of criminals, 23, 34; of
    judges, 46; of police, 6, 45–46, 84,
    95–96, 98, 111, 168; of prosecutors,
    45–46
Property, 38; recovery of, 24, 45, 51–52,
    111, 112, 114, 118, 143
Property Crime Program, 41, 109. See
    also Fencing stings
Property crimes, 14, 25, 44–45, 53, 74,
    119–20, 135. See also specific crimes,
    e.g., Arson
Property rights, 34
Prosecution, xix, 45, 53–54, 86–87,
    105, 114, 195, 263 n.24
Prosecutorial discretion, 86–87, 89, 190,
    228
Prosecutors, 45–46, 48–49, 84, 89,
    190–91; relationship with police, 40,
    46, 190
Prostitution, 74, 138, 178; operations
    against, 52, 70, 76, 78, 90, 120,
    148–49, 165, 168, 248 n.19
Protest movements, 211; investigation of,
    32, 33, 62, 90, 140, 149–50, 151
Public corruption. See Political corruption

Publicity: about operations, 41, 94, 95,
    97, 127, 128, 140, 188, 252 n.3
Public opinion, 33, 159, 243 n.11. See
    also Attitudes
Public relations, 123–24, 191, 203. See
    also Police, image of
Public support. See Crime control, and
    citizens
Puccio, Thomas, 263 n.22
Puerto Rico, 144
Purvis, Melvin, 4, 46, 152

Race discrimination, xvii, 52, 90
Racketeer Influenced and Corrupt Orga-
    nization Act (RICO), 43, 53
Racketeering, 8, 53, 108, 181
Rao, Paul, 131
Rape, 62, 108
Reactive model, 68
Reagan, Ronald, 5, 235 n.6
Record industry, 44
Record-keeping, 13, 45, 51, 208–11,
    221, 223–25
Recruitment: of police, 24, 25; of under-
    cover agents, 171, 202
Reformed offenders, 71
Reforms: in police departments, xviii, 25,
    26, 139–40
Rehnquist, William, 48, 49
Repeat offenders. See Habitual offenders
Reporters, 62, 85, 151, 174
Reporter-source relationship, 151–52
Reporting requirements, 139, 143
Reppetto, Tom, 28
Resisting arrest, 178–79
Revenues: from undercover operations,
    43–44, 111, 114
Review boards, 9–10, 183, 184–88,
    193
RICO Act. See Racketeer Influenced and
    Corrupt Organizations Act
Robbery, 133, 176, 177; operations
    against, 64, 69, 110, 115–16, 145,
    179. See also Decoys (police)
Rockefeller Commission, xviii
Rodino, Peter, 187
Roosevelt, Franklin, 31–32
Roosevelt, Theodore, 30

Salaries: of police, 27
San Diego (Calif.): operations in, 114,
    115, 119, 177, 178, 236 n.7; police,
    161, 163
Scarecrow phenomenon, 11–12. See also
    Surveillance, myth of
Scotland Yard, 22
Seabrook (N.H.), 149–50

Search and seizure, 47, 99–100, 102, 121, 199, 236n.15
Seattle (Wash.), 51, 82, 192, 193, 207
Secrecy, 85; in operations, 88, 111, 127, 128, 161, 162, 173–77, 185
Secret police, xviii, xxv, 21, 22, 25, 26, 230. *See also* Political targeting
Secret testing. *See* Testing
Seidman, Lewis, 195–96
Seigenthaler, John, 266n.44
Selective Service, 209–10
Self-incrimination, 57, 58, 199. *See also* Confession; Fifth Amendment
Self-selection. *See* Targets, self-selection of
Sell-bust operations, 7, 114, 160
Sentencing, 86, 87
Separation of powers, 53
Sex discrimination, 52, 168. *See also* Women
Sexual intimacy. *See* Intimate relationships
Shearing, C., 221
Sherman case, 80
Shils, Edward, 106–7
Shultz, George P., 270n.24
Shuy, Roger, 136
Silorsky, R., 248n.25
Silicon Valley operation, 6, 9
Silvestri, Joseph, 154
Single-party consent laws, 55
Siringo, Charles, 27
Sixth Amendment, 244n.22, 266n.44
Social contract, 91
Social control, xviii–xx, 1–3, 18, 32–34, 68–69, 126–28, 139, 199, 231–33, 255n.27. *See also* Crime control; Technology, and social control
Social influence, 81, 121, 199. *See also* Behavior
Social organization, xviii, 33, 35, 230–31
Social problems, 40, 185, 271n.33
Social psychological research, 81, 121, 141, 159, 231. *See also* Undercover agents, social-psychological aspects
Sorrells case, 30
Spiraling model, 87
Sports fans, 8
Spying. *See* Espionage
State, the, xviii, 32, 35, 51, 231–33, 257n.27. *See also* Individual and state; Power, of the state
State laws, 51, 189, 249n.32, 251n.23
Stimson, Henry, 2
Stone, Geoffrey, 246n.33

Stone, Harlan Fiske, 31, 230
Stool pigeons. *See* Paid informers
Stop-and-search tactics, 45, 46–47, 247n.11
Street crime, 7, 37, 92, 116
Stress: in undercover work, 161–62, 165, 167, 172
STRESS ("Stop The Robberies—Enjoy Safe Streets") program, 179
Strike forces, 42–43
Supervision: of undercover agents, 46, 57, 59, 95–96, 159, 161, 162, 163, 171–72, 201. *See also* Controls on undercover agents
Supreme Court, 36, 188, 189–90; decisions, 30, 47–48, 49, 52, 53, 249n.3, 262n.16, 264n.32
Surveillance, 2, 3, 14, 114, 115, 116, 143, 229–33; myth of, 11–12, 71, 100, 225–26; restrictions on, 49, 54–55. *See also* Electronic surveillance; Passive surveillance; Testing
Suspects, 63–64, 65, 94, 108, 110, 112. *See also* Behavior, of suspects; Targets
Suspicion: grounds for, 94, 98, 102, 105, 109, 121, 182

Targets, 5, 7–8, 46, 194, 227, 246n.6; consequences for, 131–42; innocence of, 93, 125–26, 137, 141–42, 196; selection of, 8–10, 14, 68–71, 101, 142, 219; self-selection of, 71–72, 76, 80, 93, 95, 205. *See also* Collateral harm; Criminals; Political targeting; Suspects
Task forces, 6
Tax violations, 5, 8, 51, 62, 210
Technology, 36, 56–57, 59, 226–27, 228–29; and social control, 3, 206–7, 208–16, 217–21, 223–25. *See also* Electronic surveillance
Temptation, nature of, xx, 50, 74, 77, 98–99, 101, 103, 120–23, 126, 194, 205. *See also* Corruption; Deceptive tactics
Terrorism, 64, 144
Terry v. Ohio, 262n.16
Testimony, 58, 96–97, 134, 197, 200. *See also* Perjury
Testing, 254n.18; and biotechnology, 215–16, 227; of employees, 10–11, 28–29, 87, 95, 227, 270n.24; of police, 70, 139, 203; of targets, 11, 54, 70–71, 205. *See also* Corruption; Drug testing; Integrity testing

Texas, 207, 237 n.16; operations in, 61, 73, 110, 112, 141–42, 175, 176, 152 n.3. *See also* Tyler (Tex.)

THEFT (The Honest Employers Fooling the Thieves), 87–88

Thief takers, 19–20, 27. *See also* Robbery, operations against

Third parties. *See* Collateral harm; Victimization

Thompson, Ben, 27

TIP (Turn in a Pusher), 207

Tocqueville, Alexis de, 206

Totalitarianism, 224, 225, 228, 230–31, 270 n.31

Trade law, 51, 249 n.32; violations, 8, 9

Traffic enforcement, 63, 66–67, 82, 121–22, 207

Travel Act, 53

Treasury Enforcement Communication System (TECS), 209

Trickery, 34, 130–31. *See also* Deceptive tactics

Trust, xx, 99–100, 265 n.35; violation of, 12, 26, 96, 147, 149, 151. *See also* Intimate relationships; Privileged communications

Tyler, Harold R., 39

Tyler (Tex.): police, 134, 165

Unarmed police, 20–21, 23

Undercover agents, 1, 37, 111; effects of role leaving, 168–72; image of, 6, 34, 159; posing as victims, 7, 69–70, 71–72, 73, 78, 103, 160–61, 177–78, 258 n.11; social-psychological aspects, 84, 160–68, 169–72; role, 61, 65, 75–78, 85, 106

Undercover operations, xxiv–xxv, 11–13, 47, 67; assumptions about, 118–28; evaluation of, 16, 45, 109–18, 119–20, 124; guidelines for, 74–75, 111, 112, 151, 181–82, 190, 193, 198; increase in, 13–15; initiation of, 67–68, 109, 114, 115, 116; justification for, 90–92, 94, 96, 118–28, 194; problems with, 32–33, 160–68; reduction of, 198–200; termination of, 41, 83, 84–85, 115, 196, 204. *See also specific operations, e.g.,* Prostitution, operations against

Uniformed police, 20–22, 23, 24–25, 45, 180, 203, 247 n.11. *See also* Plainclothes police

U.S. Bill of Rights, 224, 232–33, 262 n.16, 265 n.35. *See also* Civil rights; *and specific amendments, e.g.,* Fourth Amendment

U.S. Bureau of Alcohol, Tobacco, and Firearms (BATF), xxi, 5, 206, 245 n.27

U.S. Congress, 43, 210–11. *See also* Legislative oversight; U.S. House of Representatives; U.S. Senate

U.S. Constitution, 53

U.S. Customs Service, 7, 43–44, 92, 131

U.S. Department of Agriculture, 6, 43

U.S. Department of Justice, xxi, 13, 30–31, 39, 53, 181, 185, 192, 254 n.13; Criminal Division, 42, 183, 186, 190. *See also* Federal Bureau of Investigation; Law Enforcement Assistance Administration

U.S. Department of the Treasury, 28, 30, 31. *See also* U.S. Internal Revenue Service

U.S. Drug Enforcement Agency (DEA), 5, 8, 120, 181, 196, 237 n.18, 257 n.32

U.S. Fish and Wildlife Service, 44, 97, 131, 142, 147

U.S. Forest Service, 7

U.S. General Accounting Office (GAO), 192, 262 n.13

U.S. House of Representatives: Subcommittee on Civil and Constitutional Rights, 39–40, 187, 192, 194, 264 n.26

U.S. Immigration and Naturalization Service (INS), 181, 196

U.S. Internal Revenue Service (IRS), xxi, 5, 8, 30, 62, 181, 206, 210, 236 n.10

U.S. Marshall's Service, 5–6, 43–43, 63, 158

U.S. Post Office, 28, 65, 70

U.S. Secret Service, 30

U.S. Senate: Select Committee to Study Governmental Operations with Respect to Intelligence Activities (Church Committee), xviii, 140; Select Committee to Study Undercover Activities of Components of the Department of Justice, 187, 192, 196, 197, 198

United States v. Russell, 48, 248 n.27, 262 n.17

Unwitting informers, 10–11, 85, 102, 154–55, 202–3

Urbanization, 17, 20, 34

Vermont, 134

Vice, 32, 66, 92, 164, 199; operations against, 7, 13, 14, 26, 74, 89, 108, 167–68

Victimization, 20, 38, 58, 69, 99, 142–45, 146. *See also* Harm; Undercover agents, posing as victims

Victims, 7, 37, 63, 65
Video equipment, in surveillance, 55–57,
    58, 162, 177, 211–14, 217
Vidocq, François, 18–19, 24, 62
Vigilante tactics, 88, 161, 163, 178
Vincent, Howard, 22
Virginia, 131

Wall, John, 155
Wallace, George, 92
Wambaugh, Joseph, 161
Warrants, 47, 102, 115, 181, 188, 193–
    95, 200, 205. See also Electronic sur-
    veillance, warrants for use; Wiretap-
    ping, warrants for use
Warren, Earl, 36, 47, 262 n.16
Washington, Harold, 187
Washington (D.C.): operations in, 78,
    133, 252 n.4, 253 n.9; police, 166,
    175, 176
Watergate, 139, 191
Weapons: used in crimes, 37, 176–77
Weather Underground, 148
Webster, William, 1, 50, 172, 184, 187,
    191
Weinberg, Mel, 120, 152–53, 155,
    262 n.12
Wells Fargo, 27

Western frontier: crime in, 26–27
Westinghouse study, 112, 114, 123
West Virginia, 151
Wheeler, Malcolm, 192
Whistle blowers, 200, 207
White case, 48
White-collar crime, 37, 38–40, 53,
    76–77, 125; operations against, 8–9,
    41, 46, 87–88, 90
Wild, Jonathan, 19
Williams, Harrison, 132, 136
Wilson, O. W., 45
Wiretapping, 13, 48, 49, 135–36, 196,
    218, 242 n.38, 256 n.13; warrants for
    use, 47, 54–55, 194, 195
Witnesses, 37, 42, 49, 93, 116, 153;
    credibility, 53, 87. See also Federal
    Witness Protection Program; Testi-
    mony
Women: in undercover work, 42, 61, 73,
    108, 131, 149, 165, 241 n.22. See
    also Policewomen, in undercover
    work

Yankton Sioux Indians, 147

Zubatov, C. B., 60

Compositor: G&S Typesetters, Inc.
Text: 10/13 Sabon
Display: Sabon
Printer: Maple-Vail Book Mfg. Group
Binder: Maple-Vail Book Mfg. Group